STELLA ADLER

ON AMERICA'S MASTER PLAYWRIGHTS

STELLA ADLER

ON AMERICA'S
MASTER PLAYWRIGHTS

EUGENE O'NEILL

THORNTON WILDER

CLIFFORD ODETS

WILLIAM SAROYAN

TENNESSEE WILLIAMS

WILLIAM INGE

ARTHUR MILLER

EDWARD ALBEE

EDITED AND WITH COMMENTARY BY
BARRY PARIS

ALFRED A. KNOPF NEW YORK · 2012

THIS IS A BORZOI BOOK
PUBLISHED BY ALFRED A. KNOPF

www.aaknopf.com

Library of Congress Cataloging-in-Publication Data
Adler, Stella.
Stella Adler on America's master playwrights :
Eugene O'Neill, Thornton Wilder, Clifford Odets,
William Saroyan, Tennessee Williams, William Inge,
Arthur Miller, Edward Albee. / Stella Adler ; edited and
with commentary by Barry Paris.—1st ed.
p. cm.
1. Drama—Explication.   2. American drama—
20th century—History and criticism.
I. Paris, Barry.   II. Title.
PN1707.A335 2012
812'.509—DC23   2012018983

Jacket design by Linda Huang

Manufactured in the United States of America

FIRST EDITION

Contents

WILLIAM SAROYAN (1908–1981)

TENNESSEE WILLIAMS (1911–1983)

WILLIAM INGE (1913–1973)

ARTHUR MILLER (1915–2005)

EDWARD ALBEE (b. 1928)

ILLUSTRATIONS

Apologia and Acknowledgments

SPEECH IS NOT PROSE—no matter how eloquent—especially when spoken by a great actress whose repertoire of inflections, tone shifts, accents, emotional tics, volume, speed tunings, and myriad other vocal nuances defy rendering in print. Conversely, reading is not hearing. Listening to Stella Adler's words is a more powerful experience than examining transcripts of them.

One can do either or both at the University of Texas's great Harry Ransom Center, which houses an enormous cache of hundreds of Adler's audio and videotape lectures, along with thousands of pages of selected transcriptions. They are indexed as well as the center's resources allow, and people who wish to dip into them or search a general topic may do so. But it's an embarrassment of riches. The problem is too much, not too little. How to distill it? Turning such massive raw material into a unified text is easier said than done.

Repetitio est mater studiorum—"repetition is the mother of learning"—the Jesuits of my youth decreed, and Adler, like other legendary pedagogues, employed a great deal of it in the course of a course. Yet repetition is the mother of boredom (and critical brickbats) in print. Nobody is, or could be, Stella Adler's ghostwriter. But someone had to be her editor—to collate, condense, and integrate her lectures as seamlessly and unintrusively as possible. The editing challenge was to remove much of her intra- and inter-lecture redundancy while retaining her most essential, recurring mantras. Sifting through three thousand pages, it was fascinating to see how many different ways she could find to say, "Don't go to the goddamn words!" or "In your choice lies your talent."

That latter dictum haunted me in agonizing over which plays to include and exclude in the volume at hand. Stella Adler and I had discussed and quickly agreed on the Europeans—Ibsen, Strindberg, and Chekhov—for Volume I. But sadly, her death just five weeks later meant we never had time to settle on which American playwrights to incorporate in Volume II.

In the end, I let her determine that by way of a simple quantitative measure: Tennessee Williams, Arthur Miller, and Eugene O'Neill were the shoo-ins, along with Clifford Odets, Adler's closest playwright-friend during their heyday in the Group Theater. Her lectures on those four writers (individually) were more numerous than on all the others combined. But which of their plays to include, the better- or lesser-known ones? There's no debating the relative importance of *A Streetcar Named Desire* vs. *The Lady of Larkspur Lotion,* or *Death of a Salesman* vs. *After the Fall* in theatrical history. But theater, like music, gets dull when restricted to the Top 40. Vicky Wilson and I sought a balance between her revelatory take on the popular staples and her unique unveiling of some obscure ones.

Thornton Wilder and William Saroyan were personally, as well as professionally, beloved by Adler. They demanded inclusion. Her esteem for the plays of William Inge and Edward Albee meant they would round out the second quartet of writers.

Stella and I intended from the outset that her two books should appeal to general readers, not solely (or even mainly) to theater people and scholars. The latter will, I hope, forgive her frequent paraphrasings of dialogue and my conflations of certain lectures. I've tried, in this volume, to accommodate critics of the first volume who wanted more footnote explications, without condescending to the cognoscenti who didn't, and don't. If not satisfied with the results here, those critics can go directly to—other sources.

One can find less opinionated, cantankerous sources—and greater individual authorities on O'Neill, Odets, Williams, et al.—than Stella Adler, but no better font of insight into *all* of them. It is The Big Picture she gives us. She was a Buckminster Fuller type, a universalist among the specialists, not college-taught but theater-taught—a tougher matriculation. The case can be made that she was the most compelling acting teacher of twentieth-century theater, as well as its greatest voice.

Literally. Her unpredictable bursts of trenchant, dagger-sharp,

Yiddish-based humor reached withering heights when directed at students. ("One of us is going to win," she told actress Kyra Sedgwick during a classroom argument. "Which one do you think it'll be?") She was like her voice itself: grand, commanding, intimidating, pontifical, and majestic—in service to the redemptive glory of theater.

Now and always, it is a mesmerizing voice to hear.

* * *

In the beginning . . . the genesis of the Stella Adler books emanated from my brilliant friend and editor Victoria Wilson, followed by a lengthy exodus of my wandering through the analytical desert. She and her patient assistant, Carmen Johnson, are most responsible for leading me out.

Helen Baer, of the fabulous Harry Ransom Center, was invaluable. There is no better, more state of the art, user-friendly archive in captivity. Copy editor Patrick Dillon made countless invaluable contributions. I am very grateful as well to Ellen Adler, Tom Oppenheim, and the late Irene Gilbert.

Maria "Selma" Ciaccia was and is, simply, the greatest researcher, supporter, and technical assistant anyone could ever have. But I could not have done the job without the crucial ongoing help of Ben Paris, Myrna Paris, Ron Wisniski, and Randy Eugene. Additional thanks to Leland Scruby, Allison Drash, the great Brothers Mandelbaum at Photofest, long-suffering Dan Strone of Trident, Merica and Brian Frost, Pamela and Todd Loyle, Attila Li, Tim and Kay Menees, Sean Connolly, Cathy Henkel, Daniel Schwartz, John Barba, and Austin Sillman.

This book is dedicated, on Stella Adler's behalf, to all actors and artists: "Life is boring. The weather is boring. Actors must not be boring," she said. "Life beats down and crushes the soul, and art reminds you that you have one."

BARRY PARIS
Pittsburgh, Pennsylvania
February 20, 2012

STELLA ADLER

on America's Master Playwrights

ONE

ACTOR VS. INTERPRETER

THERE AREN'T two actors in the entire Western world who can really play King Lear. I'll tell you something, there weren't two actors in America they could find to play Willy in *Death of a Salesman,* because of the size of the character. There aren't many who can play these parts. It's a big stretch for an actor to live up to the playwright. But you can't do less.

If you say "I'm an actor," people think you're an idiot. You come from an American tradition where the actor is buried by the government— or worse, where he is invited to *partake* in the government.* The term "script interpretation" is a profession; it's *your* profession. From now on, instead of saying "I'm an actor," it would be a better idea for you to say "My profession is to interpret a script."

Let's start with this: I don't care what you think about me—good, bad, indifferent—and I don't care what I think about you. It's a fair exchange. You have a lot to learn, starting with an understanding that your concept of the theater is the least responsible of any country in the world. I want to make you responsible for being an actor.

You have to come from a tradition where the actor has a better reputation and rightly deserves it. We don't, because our theater has changed so that it's not really much of a theater anymore. We're a film-and-television leftover. That's going to be pretty permanent, but it doesn't have to be fatal. After all, the Greek theater is still around; it's pretty old. The word theater itself comes from the Greeks—it means

* Adler is speaking in 1983, during the Ronald Reagan administration.

"the seeing place." It's the place where people come to see a spiritual and social X-ray of their time. The theater was created to tell people the truth about life and the social situation.

Your job is not to "act." Your job is to interpret. You can't go on the stage as you are. There are no criteria now, good or bad. Everything is in transition. That is not unusual in history. The French Revolution was a transition. The Great Depression was a transition. During that collapse of our economy, we changed from being a middle-class audience into a lower-middle-class audience with money. We are in transition again now, and if you understand that, you will start to understand something about American theater, which is also in transition.

In the nineteenth and early twentieth centuries, American theater was just fooling around. I don't know what we were doing. Nobody does. But I know there were authors called Tolstoy, Chekhov, Andreyev, and Evreinov in Russia; in Germany there was Goethe; in Czechoslovakia there was Čapek; in France, Claudel.*

From Goethe on, all these very, very good plays existed in Europe. We didn't have that. But we played *their* plays. We saw them and acted in them. I acted in one called *Bloody Laughter*† and didn't understand one word of it. I acted in a lot of plays that were so grown-up, while I was an un-grown-up American who didn't know it was my responsibility to understand what I was doing.

Once the playwright has written the play and the play is here, he's done his job. It's closed. It lies there. Then it hangs around for people to see or read or study or act in. It is an extremely difficult literary form, that little play—so few pages. That's a difficult form and one that's not understood. He has done his job; then you come along. You

---

* Leonid Andreyev (1871–1919): prolific Russian playwright and novelist, who combined elements of naturalism and symbolism in such works as *He Who Gets Slapped* (1922). Nikolai Evreinov (1879–1953): Russian symbolist playwright and director. Karel Čapek (1890–1938): the most influential Czech social- and science-fiction writer of the twentieth century, who wrote such plays as *R.U.R.* (1921). Paul Claudel (1868–1955): French poet and dramatist most famous for verse dramas conveying his devout Catholicism.

† Ernst Toller's 1931 Sturm und Drang play in which a German soldier returns from World War I a wrecked man, astonishing sideshow crowds by biting the heads off guinea pigs. ("They want blood? They get it.")

say, "What's my job?" You don't know your job. You don't even know the name of your job. All you know is, "There's a play—I'll act!"

A play has two aspects/essences: it is divided into the literary side (the playwright's) and the histrionic side (the actor's). The histrionic side belongs to the actor and to what he puts into it, how he thinks, what he says and understands through it in his mind, his soul, his background, his culture, his personality, his whole being.

That histrionic side of the actor is what he is and what he adds to the play. The play is dead. It lies there. The other side is the side that people fool around with. That's what makes a man say "I want to be an actor." He's no *shmegegge;** he wants to play King Lear. He wants to play Hamlet.

I remember a man coming to my father once and saying, "I've been working on *Hamlet* for five years." His name was Jack Barrymore. He was working on *The Living Corpse*[†] and he played it well. He worked hard at it and then he worked himself into becoming a drunk, a bum, because the transition happened: the transition from a place called the theater (and Broadway was part of that) into a place called the movies. He was called out to do the movies, and he was not a man who understood the movies, even though he beautifully understood words.

So when the playwright's job is done, you come along and say, "I'll take it from here and just say his words."

But you *can't* just take his words, because the words, by themselves, won't help you. You have to take his soul. You have to take his life, his experience of life, his ethic, what he has said to the world. I'm talking about *real* playwrights. I'm talking about plays that have in them enough to change the thinking of the world. The thinking of the whole world was changed by Ibsen. Nothing was ever the same after Ibsen, because he was a man who, through his craft, through his talent, was able to say the truth. He was able to say it to a certain kind of audience.

His audience was not the king—not royalty or aristocracy. It was *you.* You were a new audience, something that was happening, and he was telling you the truth.

Are you mature enough to take on the Greek classics? I don't know.

---

* Yiddish show-biz term for "fool" or "second-rater."
[†] John Barrymore played Fyodor Vasilyevich Protasov in *Redemption* (1918), an English-language version of Tolstoy's *Living Corpse.*

You would have to study Greek art and architecture and movement. You would have to learn that the temples of religion were connected with the gods, the temple of art had to do with the mind, and the temple of the body had to do with what it was to be a man in Greece. You'd have to understand how the discus thrower and the masks were part of that. To be a Greek actor, you'd have to do a lot. First of all, you'd have to look at the statues and architecture. That's the least you'd have to do—something to understand Greek philosophy.

You are involved with a movement that's two thousand years old, the first movement of a theater that had a text and a value that are still handed down to us. A major part of Greek culture is in our culture, although we don't use it; it's still there. If you go back and study it, you would have a much more serious attitude toward your background. You don't have enough of a serious attitude toward your theatrical background. It's not really your fault—it isn't offered to you.

Understand your profession: "Interpretation" means that I'm going to find the play and the playwright in me. I'm not going to do Ibsen if it's Chekhov. I'm not going to do Chekhov if it's Strindberg. I'm not going to do Strindberg if it's Shaw. These are different playwrights with different minds, and they say different things. The things they say will stay in literature forever. They want something. They have the mind to say something. They find the form to say it.

An actor has to be big, enormous—a giant. His mind, his feeling, his ability to interpret must be that of a giant.

You have to find the character and the place that he is working in. You have to be able to wear the costume. You have to use the words. You have to have the ideas. You have to have the back of the ideas. You have to experience the ideas. You have to have the soul of the ideas.

Shaw didn't act. Chekhov didn't act. Strindberg acted. It led him to the insane asylum. He was there for a long time . . . These men were connected with different kinds of theaters. They were the great Europeans.

We're going to do Odets, Miller, Wilder, O'Neill, Tennessee Williams. They are the great Americans. The American problem of interpretation is very different from the European. I told you that Mr. Barrymore said, "I worked five years on a play." He certainly didn't work on the words, did he? Everybody knows the words: "To be or not to be, that is the question." It's not the words. It's a specific author in a specific moment in history and a specific style that he worked on.

I'll say it again: every playwright writes in a specific moment in history. He does not write *your* history. He's not writing about Reagan. That's not his president. It may be Wilson or Roosevelt or Jefferson. There's a difference between Reagan and Jefferson that comes out of the time. You can't put Jefferson in Reagan's time or Reagan in Jefferson's. Every play comes out of the author in a special moment in history, and there's a special style that goes with that moment. Mr. Jefferson was very close to the French government. He understood and was educated, had a great deal to do with foreign countries. I don't think Mr. Reagan went abroad unless he was paid for it. Every writer writes in his style. The style comes out of his moment in history.

The Greeks wrote in their moment of history. Shakespeare wrote in his. Chekhov wrote in his moment. Odets wrote in his. If you agree that the moment in history determines a great deal of what the playwright wants to say, then you will not say "I think I'll play in Shaw" without knowing the moment in history that created Shaw. Shaw influenced the whole British government! He was influential enough to make a big impression on English society through his dynamic work.

When you do an author, you must know him. If you don't know the author, you're crazy. You must understand him and his time, not *your* time. Your time is quite easily understood. You live in a very industrial moment. There are cars. There's electricity. There's manufacturing. There is science. It's your time. It's not Shakespeare's time. There's no electricity in Shakespeare's time. The time element is the most important thing: the moment in which your playwright is writing; the ethic of that time—the fact that women are sitting here in pants—is very different from the ethic at the moment when Mr. Shaw wrote his plays. There were no [women in] pants. The fact that you wear pants means that a lot has changed. The fact that your hair is cut long or short represents a tremendous change in world circumstances. Walking around in the streets with long hair down to your waist was a sign of insanity not too long ago.

If you went out on the stage in *Samson and Delilah,* you would be considered insane just because you had long hair. It belonged in the bedroom or in the hospital. It did not belong in the drawing room.

Your profession is to interpret, and you have to interpret your time. Your time is different than any other. It is an industrial and scientific time. If you understand that, you will understand also that with it goes a certain kind of ethic. In a previous time, most people went to church. Then Mr. Darwin came along and said, "Never mind the church. You came from a monkey, so shut up about it—you don't need a God." But a lot of people said, "I don't care if I came from a monkey—I still feel like I came from God." Then Freud came along and said that people's confusion came from their psychological inability to solve what was going on in their inner self. He saved a great many people from the insane asylum. Then another kind of a man came along, Mr. Einstein, who changed the world by making the physics of the universe clearer. His scientific mind changed the world.

The world gets changed by certain people. They can be scientists or writers. Listen to them. You don't listen well enough. I want you to gain an understanding of how to listen. All your life you have thought you listen, but you have heard only about one hundredth of what was said to you because you don't understand that true listening is something that comes from your soul, your blood, your concentration, your mind.

Listening is a very difficult thing. You must acquire the asset of listening with all of your instinctive abilities.

If you speak about the English actors, you would say that Olivier has a lot of craft, which means he has the essential beginnings with which to interpret. If you have the craft of the piano, you have the beginning of being able to play the piano with talent. There is no profession without craft, except yours.

Do you understand the difference between craft and the result of craft, which is talent? Nobody says "I want to play the piano at Carnegie Hall" before they take some lessons. You can imagine what it would sound like.

As an actor you need craft. Mr. Olivier can hold the curtain up. He knows how the play is built. He's thought about it. You could say he knows how to act. He knows how to handle the part. If you talk about Ralph Richardson, you'd say he knows how to handle the part and you don't have to worry about him. Sometimes you have to worry about Mr. Olivier, because his craft is bigger than his talent, greater. But once in a while he will give a great performance.

Craft is the basic thing in the beginning of this work for you to understand: it is your handle. It is not your talent. But you must have it. The pianist has it. The flutist has it. The painter has it. Everybody has it except the modern actor. We don't have it, and therefore we have very few actors. We have nobody that we can send to Europe. Well, we can send a type to Europe. De Niro would be a very good type to send to Europe.

But everybody is suited for more than what they look like. For instance, you know what I look like. You'll tell me the truth, and I don't want to hear it: I look a little like an ex-Hollywood star. I'm rather pretty and graceful. I have a lot of assets, but I'm really a character actress. I played servants, peasants, secretaries, queens. I played every goddamned thing they could think of when they couldn't give it to anyone else.

It was terrible. If they couldn't get a character actress the right age, they gave it to me. When I was ten, I played my father's mother. I was in London, I had to do it. It was all right. It's all right to have scale. Your scale has to be large enough. But I'm afraid your scale is "I *am* me and I *like* me and I'm going to *show* me!"—hoping that they'll buy you, the way they buy the cloud or the rain or the river they need for the shot. "That's a good rain, let's photograph it! It's a wonderful river—the best river we ever found—we'll photograph that! That's a good actress—she's short and fat"—or "tall and thin"—"exactly what we want!" She is what they want. So's the dog they choose. I played with Asta—and he was the best actor in the company.* I told him to sit up—he did it. He did everything right. That's very good, but it's not acting. So we can't just say about you, or anybody, "He's got a lot of craft. He studied with Stella Adler"—or Uta Hagen or Lee Strasberg. "Give him a try at King Lear."

Once there were auditions in California for *King Lear* and a thousand people came to read, and one man with a Yiddish accent said he wanted to play Lear. They said, "You can't. We won't give you an audition." He said, "You give me an audition—you'll see." The director said, "But you speak with an accent." He said, "Never mind about the accent." So they let him audition, and he got up and said [*with perfect accent*], "Once more unto the breach, dear friends, once more!" The director said, "You speak perfect English!" He said, "That's acting."

---

* Adler co-starred as an impostor-villainess with William Powell, Myrna Loy, and Asta, the wirehaired terrier, in *Shadow of the Thin Man* (1941), the fourth of the Nick and Nora Charles detective films.

He was right. The accent must be perfect. It must not be "worked on." It's got to be perfect. Your job is mid-Atlantic English. [*Speaking affectedly:*] This is not American English. This is a British affectation which is peculiar to their culture. They do very well with it. They conquered the world with it.

It's a façade and they can't get rid of that façade. That's why they can't play modern plays: that façade keeps away the truth, which is a very bad thing to keep away in our modern time because that's what we're after.

We have other faults. [*She mumbles:*] Nobody knows what we're saying. We're sloppy and vulgar and miserable. I was starring in London once, and I went into an expensive store— Black, Starr & Frost—and asked for something and they said, "Yes, Miss Adler, where should we send it to you in England?" I said, "I'm awfully sorry, I don't live in England. I live in America." They said, "Oh, we thought you were English." I said, "No, just affected."

The affectation may or may not work in life. On the stage here, it's mid-Atlantic English. I can work in all the other plays because I can play the accents. That's craft.

But it's not talent.

We really don't trust the talent because of the lack of craft. We trust the craft more than we do the talent: "Maybe he won't be great, but at least he won't let us down." It's very important to keep the curtain up.

We're going to the American playwrights. How many people here are just interested in literature? A bunch. You don't want to act; you want other things. I'm glad. I wish there were more. To take the course because it's about literature is fine. If you're here because you're interested in being a stage designer, that's fine, too. I'm not speaking only to people who want to act. To interpret means to interpret stage design, lighting, scenery. All this is part of acting. The actor has to train himself as soon as possible, as soon as he's smart enough, to understand directing; to understand the other characters; to understand sets, lighting, costumes. Don't come to just show yourself on the stage 'cause you're special. You're not. You're a dime a dozen.

What I'd like you to get is a kind of size where you know your profession in the way that Stanislavsky did. I can't tell you how much he knew. I'm the only American who worked with him. God did it. Once in a while, God does something; he put Adler together with Stanislavsky and a great deal came out of it—for me and for you.

Stella Adler as mob moll Claire Porter in W. S. Van Dyke's *Shadow of the Thin Man* (1941). Her hat rivaled Myrna Loy and her perfume ruffled William Powell.

The audience is interested not just in acting but in the literary side of the playwright; that has to come through. There are statements in every play. Get to know how they work. Every play is external. It isn't internal. It isn't in you, and it's not going to be—not if *I'm* around!—until you pay a real price for it. A lifetime's price, like every poet or writer pay.

"Lovely play," you say. "Brilliant!" But what are you going to get out of its words? Nothing. So we start with the outside. It starts outside, on the page. You begin with those externals. There's no other way to do it. The externals come partly in sentences, sometimes in monologues, but finally through the two things YOU have to bring to it: study and instinct!

I went up to Harvard to study psychology once. A very interesting course was being given there. I did my homework a little. My blood told me it was necessary, and I believe in blood. I believe in that thing in us that is eternal and true.

My husband, Mitchell Wilson, was a physical scientist, an assistant to Fermi, the great physicist at Columbia, and he told me a wonderful story. Once there was an equation up on the blackboard, and Fermi and three of his Nobel Prize colleagues were standing there, looking at that equation. The three said, "It's right." Fermi said, "No, it's wrong." They said, "How do you know?" He said, "I feel it."

I feel it. I sense it. I know when something's true. I know when it's a lie. I told you that story because we think of science as being cold. It isn't at all. By the way, Einstein didn't have his physics books or formulas handy when the fourth dimension came to him. He was sort of having coffee when it suddenly came to him. "My God, that's it!" Then he fainted. It put him to bed for weeks.

Thousands and millions of years are in us. I'm going to treat you as if you were millions of years old, not just *pishers* on the street. I want you to know that the most important thing in opening the play is to know the circumstances.

Where does it take place? Is he writing in Venice? Is he writing about the Venetian war with the Greeks? Are you in a garden in 1870 or 1970? Is there a thunderstorm? In 1970, you have something that diverts lightning from striking your house. In 1870, you could not divert it. It struck your house, and your house burned down.

Time and place give you a great deal—the social circumstances. An actor who doesn't know where he is is crazy. You must know on the stage that you're in the garden, in prison, in an insane asylum, in a house, if it's 1870 or 1960. You've got to know where and when. This is a crucial part of craft.

The only person who doesn't know where he is is an actor. A girl got up the other day to do a scene and didn't know where she was. She went from there to here. She started sobbing. I said, "What are you doing? Don't you know that the cheapest thing in the world is beauty and temperament? Don't you know that every stinker has temperament? Every cab driver has temperament. You've got temperament. So what?" She didn't know where she was stepping. She didn't know if she was in a room or a garden or an airplane. She was "acting."

You have to know what class you come from. You have to know the season, the ethic of the time, the morality of the time. You must know that every play starts with the present but every play has a past. If you don't know the past of your play, you don't know your play. This is technique. This is craft. The play is in the present, but it deals one million percent with your past.

There's a doctor who comes to you because he wants to make money, and there's a doctor who comes to you because he's interested in science, and there's a doctor who comes to you because he works for the poor. It's not in the play. It's behind the play. The past is the actor's job. That is where his talent is.

When Karl Malden came to the class, I said, "The actor's job is to provoke himself and his own talent. For that, his character has to have a past." He said, "That's all. I got it."

A big part of that is knowing your social situation. You are now in a situation where there is 10 percent unemployment, there's rampant divorce and sleeping around. It's a change in morality. Mugging in the street is a big change in America, compared to when I was young. You live in a highly industrial, capitalist society. Reagan's in the White House. We are gearing ourselves up to spend an unprecedented amount of money so we'll have enough armaments to wage another war. The reason we need another war is economic. We can increase our economy by making enough armaments to sell to the world.

What is your attitude toward that? Toward the church? You have to know. You have to know what job you're in, what education you have. The social situation is what makes the writer write the play. In Odets's *Awake and Sing!,* the mother had to work because the father had to go to school. He was weakened. The son didn't have money, so he didn't go to high school. The girl slept with the boarder because she no longer had the home training of discipline.

Work on the social situation of the play. If you don't know it, you can't work on the stage. Don't be dumb. You have to develop enough technique to be able to handle the play.

You are in a different time and situation because you have something new: you have movies. Movies are mostly action. You are mostly interested in what's going to *happen.* Is the guy going to win or lose? Escape or get caught? Live or die?

It's fine. But it's not going to help you to understand Strindberg or Pinter or the American playwrights. There is virtually no writer in movies who has a signature. Hitchcock, maybe. But usually you don't know or care who wrote it. There is not one playwright who does not have a signature. The signature is the size of the man who is giving it to you as a collaborator, and you must become as big as the writer because you will be with his ideas, with his mind.

Who is the most important element in all theater history? It is the actor. "Did you see Kean in *King Lear?*" The growth of the actor is what people want to see, and what you should want to see in yourself.

You gave this up for movies. Take it back again. Take it back so that we can work together.

EUGENE O'NEILL

Eugene O'Neill, photographed by Alice Boughton (c. 1921)

TWO

OVERVIEW

AFTER SHAW'S HEYDAY came an international war,
and this war had a profound effect on the theater. It's impossible
for you to know how to work in a postwar theater unless you understand the new nature of it. Our American theater—the theater as a
big force—started only after the First World War.

You live in a moment where you don't quite understand what
happened to America in World War II, let alone World War I. It is
impossible to act in the American play unless we go back and see that
the American play really starts with O'Neill. But in order to get to
O'Neill, you have to know what was before him.

Before O'Neill in this country, the play was for business, for success,
for the star who brought in money, for its fashionableness to an audience. The theater was nothing more, and not thought of as anything
more, than a place of amusement.

The theater had already cracked through in Europe, but Europe
was very far away—it took seven or eight days to get there. In Europe
the play form had already arrived somewhere; Europe was always able
to articulate in the arts what it wanted. It had a kind of theater that
didn't exist in America.

The world war came along and something happened. Americans
interested in theater became aware of an enormous movement that
hadn't touched them before. New ideas hit our playwrights and intellectuals. The result was chaos—complete chaos.

O'Neill understood for the first time that the theater was a platform that could be used to express modern sociological ideas. Should

the family stay together? Should we overthrow the king? Should we undergo psychoanalysis? All this was modern. Nobody had ever thought or done anything about it before. Realism was modern, anti-realism was modern, surrealism was modern, expressionism was modern. All these things overwhelmed the new American theater man, who said, "If I have the possibility of a platform like this, I have to really *do* something with it."

These new ideas, new forms, new styles coming into American theater challenged the deepest thing in American society, which was materialism. Theater was the first art form that challenged the "goodness" of the fact that America is the richest, the most successful, the most powerful country in the world—and that challenge has never stopped since.

There were no big differences in the society here. There was no king, no peasant, no aristocrat, no huge gulf between the middle and working classes. Our play form therefore could not grab hold of the revolutionary idea "Let's get rid of the upper class, up with the lower class!"

But the society had one great thing: it had unprecedented energy, energy that went into making money and to holding on to what it got—what we call rugged individualism, a fantastic, unprecedented belief that every man can *make good.* It did not go to manners, it did not go to elegance. The American writer wrote about Americans; he did not write about the idle gentry or any subjects that didn't affect his life. The thing that affected his life was that enormous energy, strength, vitality, desire to grow, enormous everything, but not much tradition, not too much hanging on to fixed things. The world became unfixed.

This is the key to American plays, which expounded what we were: nothing is fixed. No religion is fixed, no family is fixed, no property is fixed—nothing gets rooted long enough for it to hold on.

The European theater at this time had five or six aspects. There was a tremendous movement for realism, which is the social play that says, "Let's fix society," the play that says, "If I show you this problem, then you'll understand and maybe fix it." In reaction against it was the counterrealism that flourished all over and said, "Let's put poetry back! Let's put *everything* back, because realism is pulling us down!"

These were large things. What happened in Europe, especially in

Germany, was that the war provoked strong ideas in every writer, not just to alter the form but to find new forms—"Let us exhaust what happened to us in the war!"

In Germany they found expressionism; in France they found surrealism; in Russia, constructivism; in all the countries they found symbolism—all coming out of a need to find form. They had the content, but the old forms didn't work as a way to express themselves anymore.

Those postwar styles are what you have inherited: a lot of impassioned speech, a lot of propaganda, a lot of sex, the real and the surreal—now you're walking on a cloud, now you're in a room, now you're not in a room. The shifting sets, the plays about half-reality, half-fantasy. Another kind of play dug into the inner situation: "What's the matter, what's the matter?" "I don't know, nothing can fix me up."

All this self-revelation in the European theater finally hit America. You have inherited all the schools. We didn't create any one school. You can't say there is any American equivalent of Brecht, who made an absolute new form called the epic theater.

We can't say, like Meyerhold,* that we created constructivist theater, in which every actor had to be an acrobat. But we can say we mixed them all together, and *that* is our contribution. Any play in America can go from realism to the other forms. The American didn't care what he did, and in that way he made a form. No American playwright feels he fits into any school. A man like Maxwell Anderson wrote poetic plays, then alternated naturalistic plays, then propaganda plays in between—he wrote in every form. Odets tried most forms. He tries out everything in *Waiting for Lefty* and *Awake and Sing!*

You must understand this historically so that you are not ignorant of what's happening. Every one of these plays *wants* something—"I want social reform!" "I want psychoanalysis!" "I want poetic prose back in the theater!" "I want realism!"

Why realism? Because the authors had not been able to agree on or invent a single new dominant form, individually or collectively. The

* Vsevolod Yemilyevich Meyerhold (1874–1940) was an actor and director on the staff of the Moscow Art Theater, where he pioneered many avant-garde productions, staging symbolist plays, using constructivist sets, and employing all manner of futurist experimental techniques.

realism most of them settle for is not a high social realism. It is not Ibsen, it is not Strindberg, it is not in that big tradition. It isn't the realism which warranted the breaking away from artificial drama into something that was going to reshape the world. But the subject matter is new, and realism permits the audience to understand it.

Now, suddenly, all these "issues" are bombarding you. You can't sit in a room for five minutes without somebody trying to explain their insides. It is not a very logical procedure. It's not an orderly process. If you say "I'm sick inside," that "inside" is not something everybody understands. You try to follow a stream of consciousness, and it's hard. If you go in to your grocer and give him your stream of consciousness, he won't know what to do. He'll know what to do if you cry.

All these new ways—the psychoanalysis, the breaking away, "I don't care about objectivity, I'll make expressionism! I'll say what I feel!"—it was something big that hit painting, music, and theater at the same time.

Now, how are you going to *act* those forms? There is nothing the matter with the theater. There is only something the matter with the actor, who doesn't understand that he has to deal with *form.* You must understand that acting is only valid if the form is there. For you to be real is not to be realistic. It is to understand that Nora's problem is universal. All wives all over the world are going to solve this problem if *you* solve it.

O'Neill does very good realistic plays like *Anna Christie* and *Beyond the Horizon.* His issues are large. But he is pessimistic. He says there's no way out, every man is groping blindly, nothing and nobody can save him. That's why he is so passionate. The thing that holds you together is smashed. There's no religion to hold on to, they don't do what the Catholic playwright in France asks or what Gorky prescribes for society in Russia. Sometimes you get propaganda, but the great American playwrights write with tremendous energy, tremendous darkness, tremendous pessimism, tremendous hope.

Don't approach O'Neill without giving him his size. When you read O'Neill, I want you to see he recognizes the futility, whereas the Europeans say it can be straightened out. To be lost in Ibsen, to be lost in Strindberg, is to be groping to solve something. O'Neill is very influenced by Strindberg.

But Mr. O'Neill doesn't do it like Mr. Strindberg. He vomits it through layer and layer and layer until the deep sickness finally comes out. He digs and digs and digs until the person says, "YES, I WANT TO SLEEP WITH MY MOTHER!" and has to kill himself.

The style of O'Neill touches all forms. There is no other like his. O'Neill writes in an extreme form. Don't always demand a term. "This must be naturalism," "That's expressionism." The signal to look for and obey, to be able to act it, is knowing what provokes it: these are characters who are fighting, struggling to break through!

O'Neill is looking for the form as much as you are. In his every play, he's looking and trying to break through. The difference between him and the Europeans is that O'Neill's dumb American—the hopeless one, the one that doesn't know, the one who can't talk—is articulate. That's what makes the drama. This is a marvelous thing for you to know, and I'm giving it to you: up here you must be able to express your inarticulatenesss. In life we are often inarticulate victims, but on the stage we articulate.

The king used to speak like a king, poetically. Take the king away, and you have a new kind of grotesque king talking on the stage. Don't be afraid of talking it out, of finding a way out of it, of saying, "I don't know, and because I don't know, I'm going to talk to you about it." These are plays where you speak! The author makes you struggle for your voice. The common man has a voice. You can't go into O'Neill without knowing his sociological and historical moment in the theater.

That moment gave birth to Greenwich Village, Off Broadway, the Provincetown Playhouse, the little theater that became the big theater. And then came another theater—"I'm going to say what I want, I'll do Ionesco!"—and from then on, it's a fight for form and content and a mixture of both.

With the emergence of O'Neill and Provincetown, you got the American onstage in every form, the American man, woman, child, goof, southerner, plantation owner, worker—everybody got onto the stage. You would never have had all these classes and the desire to explore their concerns before Mr. O'Neill. There would be no small art movement in the theater.

You belong to a movement that became articulate. For God's sake, educate yourselves so you are not somebody who just wants a job on Broadway! Know what you're headed for. When we started out in my day, we knew what we were headed for. You knew you weren't going to make 5 million dollars playing Ibsen. You wanted to go to Greenwich Village, you wanted to lose yourself. The artist was against Main Street, against Babbitt, against settling. The aim of the artist was to live dangerously, not securely. The aim of the actor was not to be recognized quickly but to find his theater, his way, what movement he belonged to, not the solution to his economic problem.

There is nothing money can buy for O'Neill or an O'Neill character, no security you can provide by giving him property. He and his people knew they were only able to accomplish what they wanted a little bit, by knowing that is was their destiny to fail. If he was in love, it was doomed, because love couldn't succeed. If you find your sweetheart at the end of *Anna Christie,* the sea is against you, the cosmic fate is against you. Nowhere do you come around the corner and see the light. The audience in O'Neill's time connected with the idea that neither the iceman nor anybody or anything else could really be saved.

Your American audience aims at success, meaning money. It's not a natural ally to the playwright. There's a big mix-up. The playwright represents a minority voice and always will. The audience, by nature, is against what the playwright says, by virtue of being in a business that says, "Gee, to be successful you don't go against, you go *with,* the tide." The playwright says, "You're a schmuck! You have to break away!"

O'Neill got drunk, from an actual and an intellectual point of view. On the one hand, he was influenced by European theater. On the other, he was brought up in a melodramatic theater—his father played the Count of Monte Cristo—and understood that he had to be theatrical. "Theatrical" means all kinds of tricks—lights, music, thunder. O'Neill uses every trick. He is theatricalized. He comes with his bag of tricks and says, "I'll use masks, drums, inner stream of consciousness, everything. I don't want to take out the theatricality, I like it, I love it!"

O'Neill draws character better than anybody else on both continents—better than Shaw. He doesn't trust you to your own devices, like Shakespeare. He tells you how to speak, what kind of accent, what clothes to wear, how your lipstick should look—everything he can do to draw a sharp characterization. Read the opening of *Mourning Becomes Electra* for character. Then read the opposite of it in the opening of *Anna Christie.*

This is the key to opening up O'Neill. You need to open up in acting, to be aware of what produced the style. Explore it, dig into the historical need for the style. In a quieter period, where a style lasted a few hundred years, the actor was settled. He didn't need to ask questions. But in an unsettled theater like yours, no style can last that long. You must be responsible or you'll play all plays as if they were the form you know. When you had a little horse and carriage, you knew the road. When you can travel to the moon, you know that something else will come soon.

The only thing that's the same is having babies. The emotional things that tie you to life are not different. But the author wants to break out of those things. The plays we'll deal with revolted against unpoetic expression. They use what we call *poetic prose,* which is higher than poetry and needs a fuller thing from you—it needs more.

Poetic prose in our time is a great deal more veiled than verse poetry, because it has size. It has elegance, the beauty of language, depth of soul, magnificent ideas—don't belittle it. It creates the enormous characterization O'Neill gives many of his small roles. He likes salty speech, he understands better than anybody else that small characters must all be very sharply drawn and have an ear for language.

O'Neill feels everything that's going on underneath. It isn't just a plot, it's what's going on farther down. A lot of the plays are terribly in torment, which comes out of the need for some solution and not knowing how to find it. He's groping in the dark—without a church, without a neighborhood, without tradition, without security. His plays reflect that more and more as they move closer to the Second World War. Nobody is anchored. It's as if a wind were blowing them all around, with nothing to latch on to. Bring that out in O'Neill.

He couldn't solve anything, but he's a fighter. He had this devilish Irish insight: "I know what's going on here, and I know there's something else going on, rumbling underneath." He says the social problem is a matter of fate, of struggle, of inner torment. It's unsolvable, and he becomes violent and emotional about it. It will help you to know this in the plays. He uses common people. The characters are symbols. They talk a lot about roaming. Many of his characters have no place. They don't know if they should stay or go back and risk being wiped out. In *Long Day's Journey:* "I'm only at home if I become like the bird."

You can't play that unless you understand that O'Neill says *man is displaced.* At one time man said "I'm going to God," but now he doesn't know where he's going. So he runs around like a chicken with his head off. He is a restless wanderer of the earth. He can't settle—and won't settle—for a social solution. He is trapped.

If you understand this, you'll understand a lot about the American theater.

THREE

BEYOND THE HORIZON

(1920)

SYNOPSIS OF *BEYOND THE HORIZON:*
Robert and Andrew Mayo are totally dissimilar but
bound by strong brotherly affection. Frail young Robert, so fond of books and dreaming, feels "the far places
of the world beckon alluringly." Andrew's hopes flower
in the homely tasks of the farm. Both of them love
Ruth Atkins, the pretty daughter of a neighbor. At the
outset, Robert is on the eve of departure for a world
voyage on his uncle's ship, but when he learns that he
is Ruth's choice, he promptly if regretfully gives up
his plans for sailing. Elder brother Andy announces he
will sail in Robert's place. But Rob is unfit for farm
responsibilities.

The family sinks into poverty. In a fit of anger, Ruth
confesses to Robert that Andrew was the one she really
loved. Soon after, prosperous Andy returns for a visit
and tells Rob he is over his old affection for Ruth. She
reacts hysterically to that news. When their child dies,
Robert loses his last interest in life. His own death
from tuberculosis is near. Ruth confesses to Andy that
Robert knows the truth. Andrew makes her promise
to tell Robert she really loved Rob all the time. But

when she enters the bedroom she finds that Robert has already passed beyond the horizon to the fulfillment of his longings.

—B.P.*

O'NEILL WAS A GENIUS, and *Beyond the Horizon* is the best representation of human passion and restraint in American playwriting. It is his first full-length play. There is a great amount of hope in it. O'Neill goes full circle from *Beyond the Horizon* to *Long Day's Journey into Night,* his last play—from hope to night, night symbolizing darkness and death.

O'Neill got born in this country and knew that the big problems here deal with the human being. You will learn from the play how human the being is. You don't have a chance to learn that in your own personal life, because nothing means anything anymore: the boss doesn't mean anything, the children don't mean anything, the parents don't mean anything, God doesn't mean anything, living alone doesn't mean anything. It's all crumbling.

The plays mean something because they remind you of who you are and what you are. An O'Neill play is a teaching form. It teaches the truth.

This play is going to be about family life (most modern plays from 1860 on deal with family life). The circumstances: it's rural America, a farm. It was written about 1920. Every play takes place in the present. Every present has a past. The play is as valid as the time in which it is written—the playwright experiences his own time.

The actor must redo the creative work of the author in developing the past. The play will lead you to think about the past—to arrive at it. Knowing the past life of the character makes the actor own the

---

* *Beyond the Horizon* premiered at the Morasco Theater in New York on February 2, 1920, running for 111 performances, with Richard Bennett (Robert Mayo), Robert Kelly (Andrew Mayo), and Elsie Rizer (Ruth Atkins).

part. Every play exists in a social situation, and the most important thing for the actor to work toward is understanding that situation. It shows you the way of life—creates the plot, conflict. It includes the political structure, economic structure, religious structure, family structure, morality, ethics. Know the period! Go into the literature, art, music—research. Get pictures. What do the houses look like? The clothes? The land? Understand the land. The farm belonged to *you*. The connection between land and man is mystical, biblical.

In O'Neill, it doesn't matter what you give the land; it gives back nothing. There's a knowledge that you are alone—you are not social on a farm. There is isolation. Women work—they chop wood, milk cows, feed chickens, wash, cook, clean. Man and woman work together to survive. Read Chekhov's peasant stories. Get close to peasant life—the body of a man working difficult land, the difficulty of getting food and water. Life is involved with death. We have lost the sense of physical pain, physical difficulty, the physical life—outhouses, getting water in pails, no telephones, no communication. The work leaves no time for thinking. Don't identify peasants with mind. Think on a very simple level. What are the appetites of family life? Where do the food and drink come from? What do they need money for?

With *Beyond the Horizon,* we have a poetic play where sickness is a symbol. It's not good to make a poetic play too literal. Give it a sense of size. Tackling this too realistically is not right for O'Neill. He is beyond the real.

In this play there are two forces that belong to each other, symbolized by the two brothers, Robert and Andrew. Robert is a dreamer, a poet. He is described as a "sickly specimen." This is the way O'Neill says he is special. To know what special is, you have to know what average is: in O'Neill, it is the desire for material things, mindlessness, unselectiveness, lack of awareness. What is special? Being ethical, not driven to materialistic things—being selective, disciplined. Robert says, "I can remember being conscious of it first when I was only a kid." Conscious of being different. He is a dreamer. An exceptional man needs to dream. When you dream, you lose the reality, the pain. Robert's mother pushed him aside—he didn't exist for her. He didn't bother anyone. He was always quiet, even before he was sick. What didn't he do that other children do? What did sickness keep him from? He didn't learn how to deal with other people; he didn't play with other children. He was left to himself, and his self had to find other things. The structure of pain in man has so many levels. Don't make it small.

You are responsible for knowing what is different and special in his set of circumstances. What did he withdraw from? He withdrew from the smallness of his surroundings. He lives on a farm. The humdrum of farm life is revolting to him. He has visions of adventures. In his monologue, Robert says, "I used to be sick and Ma used to take me to the west window and I looked out beyond the horizon." The west symbolizes distance, and endlessness. Being at the west window gives him a vision.

The opportunity to go on the voyage with his uncle is the answer to a prayer. It's the only thing he really wants. The sea is a symbol of endlessness, as opposed to the rooting of a man tied to the soil, to the daily routine of the farm, to being landlocked. The land is a symbol of the material, the taking of the dream away from man. Robert says he was always alone and he always needed to be quiet. He lived intensely in his own world. He made pictures of faraway places—pictures that are very large and have to do with the mystery of the world: the sky, the sea, and the road. Those are symbols. "The road leads me beyond the horizon." He recognizes the long road and interprets it. He says the long, long road of life leads you to the sea. O'Neill says the land eats you up, destroys you. All corruption takes place on the land; cleanliness of soul comes out of the sea.

Robert's interpretation of the world is not the usual one. Don't pull it down, don't make it pedestrian. He is not looking to build a railroad. Robert is comforted by the beauty of clouds, the sunset from the west window. There are voices calling him to go. The illusion of going is part of that dream. He is reaching for something that means more but is not conveyable. He always knew his destiny. That's why he left college: his vision and the voices calling to him were so clear.

Robert has a special way of talking. In American literature, it's poetic prose, prose made poetic through ordinary speech. But it is not done in poetic form. The poetic character is intensely aware of the world, of understanding what there is out beyond. He understands in depth, not in facts. The poetic character goes with fantasy, playing with fairies, little people he creates to speak to him—and he does this without shame. It is very hard for someone overhearing that to connect with it. His brother, Andrew, says that is just nonsense. Robert has a part of him that connects with another world, and so has O'Neill—always looking, always dreaming, connected with nature. He has no time to be "here," with what is going on around him. He connects over "there," loses himself in a world that is far away. He chooses the road for company because he and the road are going to search for life together. It is mysticism. It is very hard for him to convey his thoughts to another person. That is why he ruminates: "When I was a child, I looked at that road, and it called me and I wanted to go out and I promised that someday I would go out, and those voices didn't leave me. I still hear them calling, and I go out to see the sunset—that's the road I'm going to take. I'm not just going to die, I'm going to go beyond."

The play is about how America ticks. Andrew is a very American type. In the first scene, he comes in and says, "Gosh, you do take the prize for day-dreaming! And I see you've toted one of the old books along with you . . . What is it this time—poetry, I'll bet." The book falls and Robert says, "Watch out that it doesn't get dirty." And Andrew says, "That isn't dirt, that's good clean earth." His eyes catch something and he reads: "I have loved wind and light, / And the bright sea, / But, holy and most sacred Night, / Not as I love and I have loved thee." This is because he is in love, and everything reaches out in this expansive feeling.

Notice the difference between the two brothers. Andy says it isn't dirt but good clean earth. Who "belongs"? When man knows that it's earth, to grow grain, what kind of a man is that? The earth means something to him—life. Robert is alien to running things, fixing things—against the grain. Andy *is* the grain. He loves the earth. But he leaves the earth and then loses that thing which is deepest in him. When you lose that thing which is deepest in you, you go off on a false road. You have lost your way in life. If you lose your way, then you substitute other things for it.

O'Neill deals with that: people lose their road because the country has sold out for money, advantages, cars—things, things, things. Materialism does something to people—to the soul—from the Bible on: Moses took the golden calf and smashed it because it pushed his people down, vulgarized them. Robert doesn't understand the earth. How could he, when he calls it dirt? He understands two things—truth of life and, beyond that, the spirit. People like that cannot be rooted down to a job. They don't know how to cope with that material side of life.

Ruth and Andrew grew up on farms as neighbors. They were like brother and sister, brought up together. She doesn't have much education, but she talks a lot. You get her class from the way she says "Maw"—she's a rural, middle-class farmhand. At one time Andrew was in love with her. How did he love her? The period didn't have sexual permissiveness. It was an innocent love. In the twenties, if a man wanted sex, he went into town and saw a whore. There was no sex before marriage—you held hands, walked together, maybe gave the girl flowers. Man and woman did not easily embrace. "I love you" was a declaration of marriage.

The father, Mr. Mayo, represents a tremendous force: he's head of the family. He is America. The land is America. He says, "You're a Mayo, and I have inherited this land from my father." He foresees that this handing-down from generation to generation—the chain—will be broken because Robert doesn't belong to the land. Andy did. The father is angry when Andy leaves the farm, but he is not just angry about that. You must find out the epic size of that anger.

There is a tremendous love between the brothers. The passionate way Andy responds, the restraint of Robert: we have lost this tragic sense of family life being split up. Today you don't stay on the farm—we are a mobile society. Ruth doesn't want Andrew to go away. Their inarticulate farewell and Ruth's emotional outburst are crushing to Robert's dream. Ruth and Robert make a fatal mistake when they marry. His failure is to love somebody who doesn't like him. In the first scene she says, "Let's go, let's not look at the stars, let's go—dinner is ready." The minute you hear that, you realize Robert is making a fatal mistake. She doesn't like books, she doesn't understand the spiritual side of him. What does a woman do in a marriage when she doesn't love the man? Does the man continue to love a woman that doesn't love him? You eventually learn in your life who is emotionally on your side and who is not, in spite of your feelings.

Sex or love is to O'Neill a force, but it's a dark force which leads you away from yourself. It can lead you right into death. Love has a side of it that is sexual, the love mate, which leads you away from your goal, from your true nature, and we see invariably in these plays that it is a destructive force. It will destroy you unless you are able to control where it leads you. Robert has a sense of the marriage bond—his ethic or relationship to her is on such a high level that he can't just break away and leave her. He couldn't make himself do that. He had promised himself to her in the deepest sense, which is the sense of marriage. Falling in love here is different because of the nature of family life in the twenties. The meaning of love was marriage, not sex. Love is on a very high plane.

One of the things that happens in the play is Robert's struggle against Ruth's nagging at him, belittling him. It is very American for a woman who is dissatisfied to nag. The mother, Mrs. Atkins, nags at Ruth, blames everybody: "The idea that you let him come to meals at all hours, I never heard of such a thing. You're too easygoing, that's the trouble." Ruth says, "Do stop nagging at me, Ma, I'm sick of hearing you, I'll do as I please about it and thank you for not interfering." This you don't get in Europe. You get a fight between a man and a woman, yes. But the American woman is irritating to the end. This nagging gives her husband the sense of inadequacy. His only consolation is his books and his daughter. No modern play ends on an up note about marriage.

With the infinite possessiveness of the mother over the son, the relationship between the wife and mother-in-law is very difficult. The daughter-in-law feels great isolation. It is not pleasant for her. Think about the conflict between incompatible people living in the same house—the anger that accumulates from incompatibility. It's not really living. You feel poisoned inside. Ruth is *angry,* not sad.

Ruth talks of the farm being run-down—what does that mean? When something is run-down, there is trouble. She talks about losing land—what does that mean? The farm is not running properly. That makes a big difference in attitude to husband and wife. If you lose the land, your whole existence, continuity of family, is threatened. Inheritance is very important. Unity of land is dependent on the unity of parents. Woman is abandoned if land is abandoned. Allegiance is big to the land.

Robert has betrayed the land. If a man doesn't know how to fix anything, but reads, how much respect can Ruth have for him? Either you work or someone has to feed you. She has no patience with him. If a man doesn't work, he is a bum. The whole basis of respect for peasants is in what you produce. O'Neill introduces the creative artist as not understood by the peasant or the middle class or the farm family. The artist didn't mix. Always look for the conflict of classes. Ruth knows a man has to be strong, but Robert is weak, it's his own fault, something has to destroy him. The artist has killed the land, from Ruth's point of view, with his self-involvement.

Never play an artist weakly, only with strength. Not strength of money or things. The tradition of strength is in our minds—the handed-down idea that a man has to be virile, able to fight. Ruth is a victim of the pioneer tradition. The artist has the potential to know, expressed in his art. Books, music, etc. involve the emotions—the artist is always emotional, never cold. Money is not emotional—"cold hard cash." The artist takes the world in and gives it back, using his senses. He is passionate, sensitive, perceptive, vulnerable, intuitive—but it only adds up to weakness from the point of view of the money man: if it doesn't sell, it isn't creative. The great aristocrats of the past knew about artists—the Medici, the Renaissance men. But the modern money man doesn't; he's limited. It's a difference in culture—American muscle, European finesse. This play could be called *The Power of Weakness*.

Ruth is an old-fashioned woman who wants strength from the male. She is very angry. Her anger comes from the misplaced value on strength. Stretch this to epic size—a man and woman must understand each other from what they do, otherwise the relationship is finished. Rob is good to the baby, cares for her. To Ruth, Rob's weakness is that he stays up all night with the sick child but can't fix the leak in the roof. She is dispossessed by his care of the child, who loves Rob—he is loving, kind. He has no escape from his life—there's no tradition of leaving the wife.

Ruth has a hope that Andy will return—a kind of romantic hope that love lasts, that Andy loves her. Romance played no part in marriage at that time. You lived with someone and made the best of it. The love came with the children. What Ruth didn't get out of life was romance.

Robert speaks in the second act about Andy going beyond the horizon and coming back and talking strangely about it. You must know why Andy can't take in the far horizons. There is something in the character of the American traveler that doesn't really communicate with the past, with life, with the whole cycle of life. It was unusual to travel in the twenties. At that time, one never expected to see someone again if he was going six thousand miles away. Leaving is connected with death.

Ruth keeps silent for years but finally vomits out the truth in the most Greek-tragic and dramatic scene. Robert almost kills her. "You love my brother and are living a crime!" The bond between brothers must be so eternal, so strong, that this incestuous thing, when it comes in, is a tremendous shock. Now, sense the situation five years later when Andy returns, a totally worldly man. Ruth is in a state of exaltation. Her exuberance comes from the improbability of his coming. It gives her wings. God has sent him back. The mother is cooking all day in honor of his arrival. How much has she suffered, too, receiving no letter, wondering if he would come back? Andrew has been away from the farm for a long time. Build a background of separation for those years: what happened on all the birthdays, Christmases, holidays?

Andrew speaks about the farm in a take-charge sense—he knows how to save it. He knows how things work. They need "a man to work for salary and a percentage." If a man can look ahead, he is smart to Ruth. The big men in those days were country men—not Harvard men. The country man had a certain primitive power. The country doesn't hold you back because of education. You get ahead with shrewdness, intelligence. Power in America has not been in the mind. America is not about intellectual power, but individual power.

Andrew wants to go into the grain business. Even if he's not educated, an American can get into the grain business. He is "ripe for bigger things"—it gives him size, the size of big scientists or big industrialists, like Ibsen's Brand and Master Builder. O'Neill was influenced by Ibsen and Strindberg—he dedicated his Nobel Prize to Strindberg.

Andrew has a godlike ambition. His aim is to compete with God: "I am man, I can make something." His vision is so big that the farm is too petty—the grain business is big. He is America saying this—America is not content with making a little pile. Andrew is speaking to Ruth, someone who hasn't seen the world, so that she will understand he's godlike. That's what Brand says to his wife, too. All big men think they are understood.

Robert talks about how his brother belonged on the land; what is he doing trying to make money? Because he left, he is suffering, and through his suffering he should understand how Ruth suffered and maybe the both of them, through suffering, can help each other. It is beyond sex, it is beyond love, it is Christ—it's Christian. It is mystical.

Andy says his passion for Ruth was gone a few months after he left.

It didn't last at all. That was Andy's capacity for loving. He might have loved her, they might have made it—but once he got out in the world, all relationships evaporated. He is interested in facts, money. Andrew has been around the world—the size of ambition reduces love. Capitalism trumps the emotions. Love is nourished by loving, and industry is not an object of love. The love instinct shrinks in the face of the power instinct. America is not considered a romantic country but a powerful country.

Andrew has the ethic and the spirit of American manhood. He keeps a certain form. He does not say "damn" in front of a woman. He calls himself a fool about his past behavior. Ruth's horizons haven't changed. They have two different attitudes. Andrew levels with her—puts his cards on the table: he thinks of the past as foolish, he makes that clear. In his effort to clear up the love situation, he takes every ounce of romance out of it.

Andrew's relationship with his brother is not concerned with Ruth at all. She doesn't see that she hardly even enters into their lives. Robert and Andrew are not going to talk about the home element. The sense of her not existing is dramatic. For Ruth, that is the end of hope. What happens when a person loses hope? When you lose love, you lose something. When you lose hope, you lose everything.

Their little girl has died and they are down to poverty level because Robert doesn't care . . . He has a fatal disease, but in the last scenes there is a tremendous reaching out beyond death for the future. The last speech is very epic. Robert breaks away and goes to the hillside and watches the horizon that will never be crossed by him—but he goes beyond it. The last keynote is hope against death, against all odds . . . for an eternal voyage after death. This is the optimism of O'Neill. It is some kind of mystic hope against fate. He says, "I can hear the voices calling me to come, and this time I am going; it is a free beginning, the start of my voyage, my trip, the right of release beyond the horizon. You ought to be glad, very glad for my sake."

There is nothing bigger in all literature. O'Neill was in his twenties when he wrote this play, and he knew everything. When a genius knows everything, he knows everything in his twenties. The exaltation of the spirit in O'Neill is what made him great. It is the exaltation that you get from the Greeks—the severe test of tragedy that has come down from them. Tragedy purifies through suffering. O'Neill met this test. O'Neill believes fate traps people in impossible relationships because of the sexual impulse. And he is right. In this play, we have the dreamer vs. the conditions of life that have to be endured in the commonplace world of earning a living.

Now, that is your problem too. Your dreams of acting, playing and creating characters, are not far from this. They come out of your poetic imagination. The character of a poet cannot make a farmer. Here you see Robert on the farm—after three years, he has aged, his eyes are lifeless, he has lost his spirit, his hope, his dream. He is grounded, imprisoned with dirt.

There is an irrational search that the poet, the artist, has from which he cannot free himself. That is his destiny. It was mine in act-ing. It was not my destiny to be a housewife—it was my destiny to have this irrational search. In the play, Robert's love for the wrong woman imprisons him on the earth from which he couldn't move. The inadequacy between them could never be fixed in a million years. They belonged far apart. She learns to loathe him. He is such an irri-tant to her. There can be no fulfillment of the dream. The character of Robert doesn't know this and doesn't blame God. He is caught as most of us are.

The play is a drama. Make dramatic choices. Don't take anything that is in the middle. Facts lead you, but there's a difference between a fact and a dramatic choice. The dramatic choice is creative, it goes through the imagination. Be specific in your choice. In your choice lies your talent. Work on knowing the character that existed before the words. Agitate the past—and once it is in you, trust it. Dialogue comes out of character—you must understand the character before you open your mouth. *Then* take up the words. Don't push them, just make sense. Start with the title, *Beyond the Horizon:* it's something large. See how your life and the play come together. The statement doesn't make it yours; the *experience* of it makes it yours. De-fictionalize it. Build the experience so that your character has a foundation. What you take in as the character has to have depth, truth.

The truth of art is not *your* truth. It is in the truth of the play's cir-cumstances, not your own truth.

FOUR

MOURNING BECOMES ELECTRA

(1931)

Mourning Becomes Electra is a trilogy, adapting the basic myths, characters, and structure of Aeschylus' *Oresteia* to the saga of a New England general's family just after the Civil War. The themes of murder, adultery, incest, and revenge roughly correspond to those of Aeschylus' *Agamemnon, The Libation Bearers,* and *The Eumenides.* Each of the three O'Neill components comprises four or five acts, which makes *Mourning Becomes Electra* an extraordinary five and a half or six hours long in toto.

HOMECOMING

In late spring in New England, war-weary General Ezra Mannon (the Agamemnon figure) is about to return home to his wife, Christine (the Clytemnestra), and adoring daughter, Lavinia (the Electra). Seth, the gardener, tries to warn Lavinia against Adam Brant (the Aegisthus), a mysterious clipper captain who is coming to call. Lavinia's suitor, Peter Niles, and his sister, Hazel, arrive. Lavinia tells Peter she cannot marry anyone because her father will need her.

Seth observes that Brant resembles the male Mannons. He believes Brant is the son of Lavinia's uncle David and a Canadian nurse, who were banished by Ezra's father (the Atreus) for fear of public disgrace. Brant enters and, provoked by Lavinia, confirms Seth's story: Ezra cheated his father of his inheritance, and Brant has sworn vengeance. He exits.

Lavinia tells Christine that she saw her kissing Brant in New York. Christine defiantly admits she has long hated Ezra and says Lavinia was born of her disgust. Christine loves her son, Orin (the Orestes), because he, unlike Lavinia, always seemed hers alone. Lavinia says she will keep her mother's secret for Ezra's sake, if she promises never to see Brant again. Christine accuses her of wanting Brant herself, but is forced to accept Lavinia's terms. Later, Christine proposes Ezra's murder to Brant.

A week later, Ezra returns, telling Christine the war has made him realize they must reconcile. Christine assures him of her fidelity, but later, when she tries to slip away from him, Ezra catches her, saying he knows she awaits his death to be free. Christine angrily admits she is Brant's mistress. In fury, Mannon threatens to kill her but falls back in agony, begging for his heart pills. Christine gives him poison instead.

Realizing her treachery too late, Ezra calls Lavinia for help. She rushes in as he gasps, "She's guilty—not medicine!" Christine collapses in a faint, dropping the poison container. Lavinia picks it up and sees in horror that her mother has murdered her father.

THE HUNTED

Two nights later, a Greek chorus of townsfolk comments doubtfully on the irony of General Mannon's sudden demise. Peter and Lavinia bring Orin home from the train station. Orin complains that Christine is not there to greet him. Lavinia cautions him against

Alice Brady as Lavinia and Alla Nazimova as Christine in Eugene O'Neill's *Mourning Becomes Electra* (1931). Behind the Greek columns lies a tomb with many ghosts.

her, but when Christine enters, mother and son warmly embrace. Lavinia leaves. Orin asks about Brant. Christine says Lavinia has gone mad and is making insane accusations. Orin recounts his idyllic dreams about Christine and the South Sea Islands. Lavinia calls Orin inside to view their father's body.

In the study, Lavinia proposes they watch Christine until she goes to meet Brant. Orin agrees. The night after Ezra's funeral, Brant's clipper ship appears at a wharf in East Boston. Christine and Brant meet and go into the cabin to speak privately. Lavinia and an enraged Orin listen from the deck as the lovers decide to flee. When Brant is alone, Orin shoots him and ransacks the room to make it seem he had been robbed.

The following night Christine paces the drive before the Mannon house. Orin and Lavinia appear, revealing that they killed Brant. Christine collapses. Orin kneels beside her, promising they can leave Lavinia and go abroad together. Lavinia orders Orin inside. He obeys. Christine glares at her daughter with hatred and marches into the house. A shot is heard from inside. "It is justice!" says Lavinia.

THE HAUNTED

A year later, Lavinia and Orin return from a long voyage to the islands. Lavinia has lost her stiffness and now resembles her mother. Orin has grown thin, with the statuelike look of his father. Orin grimly remarks that Lavinia has stolen Christine's soul. When Peter Niles enters, Lavinia greets him eagerly. Orin mocks her, with dark jealousy.

A month later, Lavinia finds Orin working madly on a manuscript and demands to know what it is. Wracked with guilt, he says that they must atone for their mother's death and that, as the last male Mannon, he has written a history of the family crimes.

He accuses Lavinia of sleeping with one of the island natives. When she taunts him in reply, Orin threatens to kill her.

Hazel arrives and Orin gives her an envelope to be opened only if he dies—or if Lavinia tries to marry Peter. When Lavinia enters, Hazel tries to hide the envelope, but Lavinia sees it and begs Orin to make her give it back. Orin complies on the condition that Lavinia never see Peter again and, once Hazel leaves, expresses a perverse desire for his sister. Lavinia in horror says, "For God's sake!—No! You're insane!" and rashly wishes his death. Startled in and out of madness, Orin decides she is right—his death would be another act of justice. He exits. A shot is heard.

Three days later, Lavinia is again dressed in mourning when Peter arrives. They pledge their love anew and she flings herself into his arms, crying, "Take me, Adam!" That slip of the tongue leads to her realization of futility. She orders Peter away and, with no one left to punish her, declares she'll do it herself—by entombing herself in the hated house with her hated ancestors' ghosts for the rest of her life.

—B.P.*

* *Mourning Becomes Electra* premiered on Broadway at the Guild Theatre on October 26, 1931, running for 150 performances, with Alice Brady (Lavinia) and Alla Nazimova (Christine). It was briefly revived in May 1932 at the Alvin Theatre with Judith Anderson as Lavinia. The 1947 film version, directed by Dudley Nichols, starred Rosalind Russell and Katina Paxinou (after Louis B. Mayer refused to let Katharine Hepburn play Lavinia, and forty-two-year-old Greta Garbo declined to play the mother of thirty-nine-year-old Russell).

Is it possible to play a man and a symbol at the same time? This is what O'Neill made actors do. When a dramatist uses a figure to typify an epic idea, he necessarily minimizes the human element. O'Neill does not deal in trivialities. He gives you man's struggle with his fate against superhuman forces. His struggle used to be with the gods—the Greeks. Now, he struggles with himself and his own past. This is the underlying theme in all O'Neill plays, in one form or another: Man struggles with all aspects of life on an epic plane. It is not lyrical. It is melodramatic.

You must have a large size in order to act him. O'Neill said it was unbearable to write for actors because you had to give them so much and tell them what to do, because they can't do it for themselves. He didn't like actors, and he didn't usually like what happened to his plays. I don't think his plays are particularly actable. He makes you speak prose, poetry, blank verse, couplets, dialects, sing songs . . . He'll go into anything when he wants or needs to.

If a character is a symbol, you have to build it very carefully. You must have a technique for it. If you play Zeus, you need some kind of cloud to float on and some way of sitting other than crossing your legs on the sofa. O'Neill tells you exactly how to walk and gesture. He is as clear as Shakespeare. He is an intense playwright with an intense desire to crack open big ideas. But he builds slowly. His passion is what appeals to us. Someone once said he writes as if no one else ever wrote before, as if he discovered writing.

In the twentieth century, the old boxed-in theater changed. Authors like O'Neill wanted something else. The artists became disgusted with the new materialism. Their experience in World War I said, "It has all failed." Freud came along and said, "Nobody can 'solve' your problem, you just have to vomit it out." German theater became violent, doing that. O'Neill was the first American playwright to use

European expressionism—almost like Wedekind*—in *The Emperor Jones* and *The Hairy Ape.* But his intensity is pure American. He had enormous culture but no eighteenth-century traditions around him, so he is wild. The vitality, the size of his problem and his characters, are fantastic. For common people he uses reality, but not for big people like those in *Mourning Becomes Electra.*

What is tragedy? In every tragic situation, something terrible happens. It is tragic because nothing more comes of it than one's personal suffering. You cannot play O'Neill without probing and arriving at impossible depths. It is not everyday life. So O'Neill puts you in circumstances that feed the large idea. He describes the Mannon mansion as like a morgue. You can't behave in a morgue like you do anywhere else.

Mourning Becomes Electra is a very modern play. Like everybody after Dostoyevsky and Strindberg, O'Neill deals with this enormous question that can't get an answer from modern morality: what do I need to save myself? As I try to save myself, I destroy myself. It's about the destructive and constructive forces in man. One or the other wins. You have no Bible today, only what goes on inside you—and you cover it up. "It's a godless society, I will judge myself." There is lunacy in modern man. Hitler is a lunatic. If it's in the man, it's in the society, says O'Neill. Every individual illness is a social illness. Man is stuck. He can't go back and can't go forward.

Of the many forces in *Electra,* the most powerful is Lavinia's to protect the Mannon family. But underneath there are murderous, incestuous relationships. You can't win with those; whether they're conscious or unconscious, forces like that will kill you. Mr. O'Neill warns you in each play about some destructive force. In *Dynamo,*† the machine kills man; in *Anna Christie* the sea kills—it's so powerful, it sucks the life out of everyone until there's no life or love left. In *Strange Interlude,* it's that Nina can't win if she wants love—that love itself is too possessive;

---

* Frank Wedekind (1864–1918), German dramatist who pioneered the declamatory, hysterical, expressionist "epic theater" style, notably in his Lulu plays, *Earth Spirit* (1895) and *Pandora's Box* (1904). Their then-scandalous depiction of sex and violence pushed audience and censorship limits to the max.

† *Dynamo* opened in February 1929, with Glenn Anders and Claudette Colbert, and ran for fifty performances. The plot pitted a superstitious religious family against their atheist neighbors—operators of a hydroelectric plant. It was considered a failure for O'Neill and is rarely revived.

even if you love, you kill yourself, because you don't know how to live with it. O'Neill is pessimistic.

When an O'Neill character represents an idea, the playwright eliminates detail and puts you into an enormous conflict right away. The actor and the play must be one. With O'Neill, and from now on, acting is not words, it is not literature, it has nothing to do with the novel. Acting is a space that the actor has to fill with everything the play needs.

You have a hard time getting to what the playwright wants, because as an actor you are victimized by interior psychological sets. You are still in the realistic school in a form that has cracked wide open. O'Neill needed to crack it open, because it no longer served him. Realism is logical: you can solve the problems. O'Neill was the inheritor of the insoluble: man can't solve his problems—he tries but usually fails. With O'Neill, and after him, you got a whole new school of playwrights: Odets, where the social-political situation must be saved; Tennessee spills out of it, but nobody's saved; with Miller in *A View from the Bridge,* Eddie the longshoreman's inner chaos can't work itself out until it's too late. Most of the plays after Ibsen deal with that chaotic soul of man.

These forms need the truth, but not a realistic truth. They need a truth from underneath, that opens up and reveals—not the closed-up realistic thing. When you dig from the soul outward, you're no longer in realism. The form breaks open and the actor must fill the new space with this enormous American thing, which was restless and energetic, stormy and violent. This American thing has a vitality you find nowhere else since the Elizabethans. O'Neill's plays are not about temperament; neither are Anouilh's or Giraudoux's* or any great twentieth-century playwright's. They are about ideas.

---

* Jean Anouilh (1910–1987), one of the major figures of French theater, was a master of many forms. His trademark techniques include the play-within-a-play, flashbacks, and role reversals. *Antigone* (1944), *The Lark* (1953), and *Becket* (1959) are considered his greatest. He rejected both naturalism and realism in favor of "theatricalism," the return of poetry and imagination to the stage.

Jean Giraudoux (1882–1944), a prolific French novelist and dramatist, employed a fanciful, impressionistic style. Most of his plays, including *Amphitryon 38* (1929), *Tiger at the Gates* (1935), and *Electra* (1937), are imaginative remakes of Greek myths, ridiculing man's greed and selfishness. *The Madwoman of Chaillot* (1944) is a bitter satire on twentieth-century materialism.

With every new idea, O'Neill uses a new form. Each large theme, he says, needs its own form. He is unique in this way. He was always searching for the right style. He says form and content are inseparable. After he wrote a play, that particular mold was broken. He had used it up and didn't want it anymore. He is the first great American playwright who has no consistent style of his own but creates a different one for each theme. If you know the form, you can act it.

Mourning Becomes Electra is O'Neill's most ambitious play. He uses aspects of the epic Greek form of the *Oresteia,* but he changes it. The house and the people in it are doomed before the play opens. He says it was the father's original sin, not the gods, that did it. He wants to prove the modern psychological idea that men and women lead themselves to self-destruction. He says that to avoid falling into those Oedipus and Electra patterns Freud described, you must treat life objectively or you'll destroy yourself. Fate controls the characters in Greek tragedy. O'Neill says you need to make your own fate.

O'Neill is one of the few writers who never leaves the local scene. In *Electra,* he doesn't make you into a Greek, he doesn't give you a crown or a cloak. He keeps you local and puts your ideas in common speech—but he gives you a mask, which makes you even more responsible for revealing what's beneath it. His poetry is in the idea more than the words.

For the classical distance between people, you don't want to be in small space. You need to be in vast space, by yourself. You don't have to face each other. You can practically face the audience. When O'Neill puts a mask on you, he doesn't want you to just stand there fiddling in your pocket for change.

* * *

I would like you to see how Mr. O'Neill builds the atmosphere in *Electra* from the start. "It is shortly before sunset," he tells you, "and the soft light of the declining sun shines directly on the front of the house, shimmering in a luminous mist on the white portico . . . intensifying the whiteness of the [six tall] columns." Right away you get that it's not some bungalow. You get something large, beyond a normal house. He says it's like a Greek temple, and that "the temple portico is like an incongruous white mask fixed on the house to hide its somber gray ugliness"—like a mask on a prison wall. Even his sets have mistakes.

He says we hear a band in the distance playing "John Brown's Body," a somber Civil War dirge about death.

The first person we meet is Seth, the Mannons' gardener and handyman, "an old man of seventy-five with white hair and beard, tall, raw-boned and stoop-shouldered, his joints stiffened by rheumatism, but still sound and hale." What do you get from that? Weather-beaten, like an old tree that's battered but still standing. Get an image for this character right away so you can play the inside from the outside. Don't play him as you "feel" him. O'Neill didn't trust the actor, so he describes Seth very precisely: "He has a gaunt face that in repose gives one the strange impression of a life-like mask. It is set in a grim expression, but his small, sharp eyes still peer at life with a shrewd prying avidity and his loose mouth has a strong suggestion of ribald humor. He wears his earth-stained working clothes."

This is a fine and very typical O'Neill description—the hair, the beard, the stooped shoulders. Does someone with rheumatism move easily? No, he's like a tree moving around. His expression is like a mask; only the small eyes are working. O'Neill is giving you a big man with small qualities. You must build him from impression. You can't build an O'Neill character realistically.

Seth's job, here at the outset, is to fill in the townsfolk (and us) on the Mannon family background, how they made a big pile of money in the shipping business: "They been top dog around here for near on two hundred years and don't let folks fergit it." The townsfolks' job is to be the Greek chorus. Let's look at a couple of them—Amos the carpenter, for example, who is "dressed in his Sunday best."

Build Amos. What does "dressed in his Sunday best" mean? A carpenter dressed in his Sunday best instead of his working clothes feels uncomfortable, so Amos behaves according to the clothes. His high collar gives him a stiffness that restricts the way his head moves. O'Neill tells you he is "the townsfolk type of garrulous gossip-monger who is at the same time devoid of evil intent," like someone striking up an acquaintance on the train. "Where do you come from? Oh, Minnesota." He gets information. O'Neill gives you the key to his character: He uses gossip as a way of communicating and entertaining. If he's sitting on a porch and someone comes by, he'd say, "Gee, he looks drunk." He'd tell you some detail that would hold your interest. "Gosh, she looks pregnant."

Then there's Amos's wife's cousin Minnie—"a plump little woman of forty, of the meek, eager-listener type, with a small round face, round stupid eyes, and a round mouth pursed out to drink in gossip." She's like a piece of fruit, with her outside mask of roundness. Does she have any inner life? Only the life you give her. You can't play her unless you find her. Minnie is round and plump and takes things in. She has no brain. You see this a lot in servant girls—nothing upstairs. She's not a city type, she's in the country-bumpkin culture. These people are like fish, swimming around to see what there is to eat.

In the second play, you get a chorus representing a different class—the minister and his wife, the doctor, the manager of the shipping company. O'Neill gives you wonderful things with them. The manager's wife, he says, is "a typical New England woman of pure English ancestry, with a horse face, buck teeth and big feet, her manner defensively sharp and assertive." He calls Reverend Hills "the type of well-fed minister of a prosperous small-town congregation—stout and unctuous, snobbish and ingratiating," and Mrs. Hills "a sallow, flabby, self-effacing minister's wife." It is wonderfully vicious.

O'Neill is a little like Lavinia—he hates them all: "These . . . are types . . . rather than individuals, a chorus representing the town come to look and listen and spy on the rich and exclusive Mannons." He gives you the archetypes; it's your job to heighten them. O'Neill was very good on dialects. Seth has a ribald humor: "I used to be noted fur my chanties"—his dirty limericks. He has beady little eyes, but they always see what's going on: "If that news is true, there won't be a sober man in town tonight!" What does that mean? It means they'll all be celebrating General Mannon's return. He's used to talking to men, women, rich people, drunks, preachers—he's not humbled or intimidated by anybody. Get his attitude toward the class he serves —and the class he comes from. They live by laughter, sex, liquor. Seth is very salty.

This is New England Puritan, not southern. It's tight and thin, with a rasp in it. It comes out like cold New England weather and church steeples and an owl in the night, screeching in a barn—strong, primitive. O'Neill gives you their dialect, just as Shakespeare did. Seth is just like the Gravedigger in *Hamlet,* a reprobate. Minnie understands him and all these other salt-of-the-earth drinking men, too. In the way she talks and walks, you see the peasant—a rough class.

Seth gets quickly to the point: "They're strict about trespassin'." What does this tell you? The Mannons don't let outsiders in. They don't like people knowing their business. What's behind those pillars and that stone wall? The Borgias. They're shut off from the outside, with their tradition. I once talked to one of the Lowells, an enormous doctor. It was like talking to stone. Even their speech is stony. There's a wall around it. This Mannon house is a prison for its inhabitants. Nothing comes in. It's theirs alone.

In every O'Neill play there's at least one character—a mother, a wife, a mistress, an adulteress, a materialist, an idealist—whose real name is Woman. This thing called Woman which he puts on stage is very Strindbergian. She is a very life-eating, heartbreaking, adventurous type. The central women in his plays are man-eating creatures. They love deeply and they destroy deeply. Love, murder, poison—how do you play that? They are epic creatures. You cannot touch O'Neill without this epic size. They are big enough to lead an army.

Lavinia is the general. O'Neill tells you she has "a stiff military bearing" and a "hard voice" that sounds like an officer giving orders. But she's a general without many troops, and most of her battlefronts are unprotected. The house is open to attack from outside. It is surrounded by the enemy, besieged. The servants belong to the lower class, and she has coopted them with money, to some extent. But nobody is above suspicion. She listens with the back of her head, without confronting. She is twenty-three but looks older; "tall like her mother, her body is thin, flat-breasted and angular, and its unattractiveness is accentuated by her plain black dress." She has eczema, she is all pulled tight. The outside reflects the inside. There is so much rage in Lavinia, she has to work constantly to hold it down. You must find for her the opposite of womanliness.

Christine brings a different kind of bigness, the more European, more cosmopolitan type. "Folks all hates her!" one of the chorus women says. "She ain't the Mannon kind. French and Dutch descended, she is. Furrin lookin' and queer. Her father's a doctor in New York." Christine is forty but looks younger. Her background was not claustrophobic, like Lavinia's. It was more open, more human, more Old World. O'Neill makes that distinction, all the time, between what is American and what is un-American. Lavinia is thin, narrow, the essence of an unreleased woman. Christine has the essence of a released one. She speaks differently. She has that other kind of female strength that says, "If I don't get love here, I'll kill somebody—I'll live with love, or die!"

In Christine we have this queen, constantly with her royal colors and human passions. "Each time I come back after being away, it appears more like a sepulcher!" she says. She calls the house a monstrosity, a temple for the ancient Mannon family hatreds. How can you get to this Cleopatra? What is this strong, voluptuous thing that's being drained of its life? The sap is running out but it's still upright, like an oak tree cracked in the center. If you play her, I want you to be able to walk the way she would. Christine is the only one who moves like that in the play, the only one who makes men want to sleep with her. The village laughs at her, the waves are hitting her, the storms are all around, she's knocked over, but the sap is still pumping from somewhere—you don't know where.

Her husband, Ezra, is not a talking man. That's one of the things that always drove her crazy about him. He never talked—until now, when all she wants is for him to shut up. You often get the key to a character from what other people in the play say about him. You get an image of his bigness from the rural class. Old man Rockefeller was not like any other millionaire. He was old America. That old Rockefeller quality of money and strength had nothing to do with the Renaissance man. Part ape, part shrewdness—no fourteenth-century tapestry behind it. Ezra is an American giant like that. Every branch of life in America has this type of giant, a Carnegie or a J. P. Morgan. Old man Mannon is like Morgan—a cannon, enormous and indestructible—but inside he is chaos.

Brant is thirty-six, very open—a soldier of fortune. Lavinia says "his trade is being romantic!" "Where's my battleground now?" he wants to know. "Can't you take on this battle?" Christine asks. "I can!" he says. What makes him so able to go wherever he has to go—a lack of belonging? He's a bastard in the literal sense. There's probably only one thing he *really* wants to do, which is get a good crack at old man Ezra. Maybe he's deeper, but I don't think so. I'd say he's a pretty shallow fellow. His character is weak in the Giraudoux *Electra,* too. But he is physically strong. O'Neill gives him to you in amazing detail: he says Brant has "a big aquiline nose, bushy eyebrows, swarthy complexion, hazel eyes . . . He wears a mustache, but his heavy cleft chin is clean-shaven . . . always on the offensive or defensive, always fighting life. He is dressed with an almost foppish extravagance, with touches of studied carelessness, as if a Byronic appearance were the ideal in mind."

He even tells you the eye color!

Brant says, "My only shame is my dirty Mannon blood!" He is actually Lavinia's illegitimate first cousin, since their fathers were brothers, right? In their big confrontation scene, Lavinia accuses him of merely using Christine as a means to get revenge against Ezra.

When everyone wears a mask, you can't use an ordinary voice or ordinary gestures, you can't have an ordinary attitude, you're not in ordinary circumstances. Lavinia speaks as if she were in a Greek temple, praying and lighting candles for a solemn ceremony. It is not Dumas *fils*. It is epic. You must fight to get the mask.

* * *

This trilogy is so massive, we could spend a year on it alone, but we haven't the time. So what I'm going to do is to examine with you, in depth, certain scenes—which O'Neill usually calls "acts"—from each of the plays, starting with the most descriptive characterizations and first encounters of the key figures. You remember I told you at the beginning that O'Neill doesn't trust actors—or directors, for that matter—to do what he wants, so he makes things crystal clear. His directions are often more revealing than the dialogue itself.

"HOMECOMING," ACT I. After the opening with the townspeople chorus, you have a first action with Seth and Lavinia together. It's a tough one, very moving. The idea is that it's easy to rescue a situation that isn't divided, but to save something that's divided is murder. "You can count on your paw comin' home," he says. She says, "I hope so." Instead of answering, O'Neill tells you, Seth avoids her eyes. Now, that is an excellent direction: he glances away—something you do when there are no words, as a way out of talking. He knows she's been spying on her mother in New York, but she doesn't know he knows. They are in code, like two spies working for the same side but at different ends of the room, giving each other signs. There's something going on underneath. You get it between a nurse and a doctor in front of a patient: they never say the word "cancer," they don't say what they mean. They put it in code and extend feelers. O'Neill's instructions are splendid: "slowly as if admitting a secret understanding between them." Seth doesn't ask or need to ask where she's been. He just says, "It's durned hard on you, Vinnie. It's a durned shame." It's to feel her out, because they are working together, like two animals in a jungle on the scent of the same prey.

But in the middle of that, just when Seth starts telling her about Brant, they are interrupted by Peter and Hazel, and Lavinia has to receive her guests. The intrusions of life, just when she needs ammunition for the big battle! Her rejection of them is not so much "I can't stand you" as the need to be with what interests her. What does someone on the verge of a breakdown do if an old beau turns up? You get rid of him.

Once I had a terrible crisis in my life, and just then a famous sculptor arrived for tea. I said, "Not now!" What is Vinnie going to do with these people arriving in the middle of her crisis of needing to save the family? They're outside the orbit. It's "Go away, foreigners!" If you're dying and suddenly a child wanders in, you'd say, "Don't come here, darling, this isn't for you." Did you ever have somebody show up and deliver coffee at a moment like that? They are foreign to the darkness of her needing. She doesn't want to think about marriage. Peter is thinking about the ring and Hazel's thinking about the cake. Lavinia is caught, but she won't deal with any lie. She won't accept anything alien to what's in her guts, and what's in her guts is ownership.

"HOMECOMING," ACT II. Lavinia and Christine had a skirmish outside the house in Act I, but that was just a prelude to their big confrontation scene in Ezra's study at the start of Act II. Lavinia is fighting to control herself when Christine enters. What is the difference between them? Lavinia is a woman with a purpose. Christine has an air of disdainful aloofness toward her. It is not an "intimate" scene. They are sworn enemies. That has to be established right away. But it is indirect. "I know you hate me, but I am going to pretend I don't know it." Find the action that is not intimate. She has put her lover up to seducing Lavinia so the girl won't be suspicious, but she's suspicious anyway. Christine watches her and sees—but pretends not to see—that.

Lavinia owns this place; she's the head of it, and the responsibility of defending it is on her. She's just been dealing with this deadly enemy Brant, attacking him with poisoned darts. When he said, "Let me walk with you, let me touch you"—it was horrible to her. Her response was, "You cheap, vulgar outsider, did my mother tell you to kiss me? You think you can undermine me with that?" It's the Greek thing of protecting the dynasty: you can't *do* that, you can't bring the enemy in! But at least, from these demoralizing forces coming onto her home ground, she's getting evidence of the crooked game her mother is playing. If you play Lavinia, you must be on her side, in her attitude, dealing with these intruders coming into her world.

So Christine is up against the boss. She is surrounded, doesn't know where to turn; they block her way, spy on her. What is Christine's attitude toward these thin people who are putting her on trial? It's a plea for justice. It's as if you walked into a group of Nazis and knew you had ten minutes to live: "I'll face you directly—what do you want? Do you know whom you are persecuting? I am a five thousand-year-old race, who are you?" Lavinia's attitude is, "This is father's room, you whore!"—to try to keep her in line. Has Christine got a chance in this place? What is it that aggravates her here? Who's in control in this room? Lavinia is.

Lavinia stands for the house. She is the prosecutor. Christine is on trial. Think of a Jewess under arrest, being interrogated. What makes them enemies? She's worn out. Does a woman need to rest? Christine is saying, "Listen, I've given birth, I have a human heart, I'm in conflict—leave me alone." You must build her as humanly as possible.

Christine should not use her voice so realistically. Use what we call a classical voice. If I were you, I'd walk as if I were in a cell, or some other place where you're waiting to be beheaded. There isn't much space. You have to find something for how to do it there. Transfer it from the imaginative to the reality. We must get this high drama of her being judged. If she sits in a chair, she must think, this is the chair I'm being interrogated in—use it like a throne. "I'm a queen being put on trial here!" Let that motivate the fact that she is so insulted. If Lavinia says "Sit down," force her to come over to you, make that a struggle. Don't just give in. Don't use the room realistically. It's like being dragged into the Senate to testify: you're a foreigner there, they own it; you're on trial. When I went to Washington to the Capitol, I walked through those marble halls. It was so big, and I got so little. But I was all America walking. I said, "All America is here, and me too." If I were Christine, I would not show my daughter that I was afraid or on guard. They are instinctive, preordained enemies, two forces meeting. Talk from your belly, not from your head. Lavinia's action is "I've got you trapped." She caught her lying about going to see Brant. "So how was poor Grandfather in New York?" "Oh, much better . . ."

They are *acting* with each other.

O'Neill builds slowly. The description, the clothes, the background, the voice, and the movement must all add up to equal the symbol. You can't play him without doing that. He builds slowly to the kill, each action leading up to the destruction: "I am going to try to destroy you. Now I will do it this way, and in the next act I'll do it another way." Lavinia's aim is to lure her, trap her until she has her by the throat: "I've got you—in my own thin little way!" It's what Christine hates about her. Being a fuller woman, Christine can come out in the open and say, "I love him!" Lavinia has something that doesn't permit her to love, but permits her to hate: "I can't love, but I can take revenge!" It suits her temperament—it's mean, it's cruel. Christine is equally cruel with Vinnie. If you play Christine, you must see yourself in royal clothes and be able to say, "I love men, I love my son—and I'm against you" like a queen would be!

Christine is being cornered. You need something as an actress to help you in that situation. Look for a piece of costume to pick up and do something with. At that moment, do something to reshape her. It's not about the words; it's about eternal things in a temple that can give you the mask. Here's a hint: every corner in that temple is rounded; you need to make an angle. O'Neill is about the use of stage space. There are precious few props.

Where does the Pope get his sense of size and importance from? Look at what the ring and the robes do for him. Get a sense of Christine as queen until she's down in the last act. Everything you do or wear in a play must filter through your imagination; use it to make it work for you. Motivate it. A king is made by a crown; the clothes and chair and how she sits make her a queen. Don't use them in a contemporary way. This must be your technique in O'Neill.

So they move, they walk, they posture. He builds the play and the characters by having them feel out each other's secrets. O'Neill doesn't build conversation, he builds *tension*—in each scene. They're all asking, "What are you up to?" until finally Christine says, "I know you, Vinnie! I've watched you ever since you were little, trying to do exactly what you're doing now! You've tried to become the wife of your father and the mother of Orin! You've always schemed to steal my place!"

Remember, you're not in a room, it's a courtroom—it's judgment. For Lavinia and Orin, the portrait of the judge in that study *is* the judge—a constant reminder of guilt and punishment. That goddamn portrait is in all three of the plays, always watching and judging everyone. It's there when Lavinia confronts Christine about Brant. It's there when she terrifies Christine by putting the pillbox on Ezra's dead body. It's there watching Orin write his history of the family crimes.

Find the style and don't be so realistic. Don't just do what comes naturally. Don't just use a chair as a place to sit, or a table as a place to eat. When you do it on Broadway, the poor director will kill himself if you give him a realistic reading. No wonder he wants a European actress instead. Find an image to make you act it the right way. "I know you went to New York! Why did you go to New York?" It's cat and mouse. If I put this card down, which one will you play next? In a chess game, you move one piece, she stalks you on her next move. What is that second move? The third?

These two are fighting it out to the death.

"HOMECOMING," ACT IV. O'Neill tells you that when Ezra kisses Christine at the end of Act III, Lavinia appears at the edge of the portico behind them and "shrinks back from their embrace with aversion." Do you realize what Lavinia wants when she sees the mother and father together like that? Christine was right when she said Ezra is really the beau Vinnie has been waiting for in the moonlight. It's no secret. The incestuous guts are opened up here to be seen. Its power is in its passion, and the characterizations must be very strong, otherwise it will look foolish.

I remember being at Mount Sinai Hospital once, when a remote second cousin of mine was dying. It was four in the morning, and his mother was there, trying to keep him alive—another minute, just another minute at a time. At that moment, his mistress appeared. I wish you'd seen the mother. She was like a wild Indian. She was ten Clytemnestras at once! She flew in between this other woman and her son—her "other man." The ferocity was amazing. "I don't want you with my son!" The attachment was more than that of a healthy mother. It was pure O'Neill.

Ezra has an hour to live, he feels death all around him, he's going to make his last confession, Christine is going to kill him—what possible reality can you establish with such things going on? His action at first is, "Let's have our last five minutes together be soul to soul, let's feel out each other's souls here, I want to reach into your heart, which has been closed to me." But she doesn't want that, doesn't do that, even though she sleeps with him, and then he gets vicious: "You let me take you as if you were a nigger slave I'd bought at auction! . . . as you've done since our marriage night! I would feel cleaner now if I had gone to a brothel!" It's a great line.

So is Christine's "Look out, Ezra!" It's the low growl of a lioness.

He is pushing her over the brink. Speak to this and use your epic voice, not a little, intimate voice—use it with a gulf between you. She is not afraid once she speaks out. She is not a girl, she's a woman; that's why she is so loved. She is talking to a statue as big as the house. At first she tries to appease: "Please tell me what it is you suspect me of." The action is to hold off the storm, the war. But this man is highly alert in war. What does he suspect? It is great tragedy—big-time. It's rough, it's rude—he's a rude stone monument sitting there.

What are they talking about in this death scene? What is the big truth inside of these people? It's: "You want the truth? Here it is, look at it!" But when he finally gives himself, she breaks him. The moment his sick inner life is fully revealed, she gives him the false pill and destroys him.

"THE HUNTED," ACT II. When Orin returns, wounded and shell-shocked from battle, he's twenty but looks thirty. "Sometime in some war they ought to make the women take the men's place for a month or so," he says. "Give them a taste of murder!"

Christine tries to soothe—and seduce—him: "We had a secret little world of our own in the old days . . . which no one but us knew about." It works for a while. Orin says: "I won't pretend I'm sorry father is dead!" That's just what Christine wants to hear. She replies, "I'm glad, too!—that he has left us alone! Oh, how happy we'll be together, you and I, if you only won't let Vinnie poison your mind against me!" Orin says, "Oh, Mother, it's going to be wonderful from now on! We'll get Vinnie to marry Peter and there will be just you and I!"

You get her clever psychological manipulation of him. She builds it up. She says, "I haven't told you the most horrible thing of all! Vinnie suspects me of having poisoned your father!" It has just the effect she intended. "By God, that's too much!" Orin says. "If that's true, she ought to be put in an asylum!"

It is not "real." O'Neill loves melodrama and uses it for purposes of large cosmic ideas, as he uses the storm in *Anna Christie*. *Mourning Becomes Electra* is a peculiar combination of classical tragedy and sensational melodrama. It must open up for you as a style. You must get the real sexual ecstasy when Orin grabs his mother by the hair later and basically tells her, "You're my woman! DON'T MOAN LIKE THAT ABOUT BRAND'S DEATH! A man is talking to you, Mother—I'm a man and you're a woman, stand and face it!"

Man is speaking to Woman, and that woman is destroyed by evil and by her own son's passion for her. O'Neill reveals things no one else reveals except on an analyst's couch. He finds the form for it, gives you the words for it, and unleashes it even though there is no sense in unleashing it.

If you do O'Neill, you will be able to act. You must catch that part of yourself which is wild, that large, insane thing that Shakespeare catches for characters like Lear and Lady Macbeth, who want to win and to rule in a truly pathological way.

Lavinia has taken on something that's terribly divided—the whole Mannon family through the ages. You patch it here, it opens up there. You patch it there; then Orin comes back. You patch him up, and the mother brings in a lover. You patch that, and the father has a heart attack. You patch that, and the enemy turns out to be a cousin of yours. So the whole essence is of falling apart. All these things all undermining the house of Mannon, and Lavinia reveals it, opens it up. She represents the family's division and the counterattack to its enemies. What have she and her brother done by the end of "The Hunted"? They have murdered Brant and driven their mother to suicide—and that, in turn, has driven Orin insane.

"THE HAUNTED," ACT I. At her entrance in the third play, Lavinia speaks to the portraits on the walls of the house of Mannon: "The dead! Why can't the dead die! . . . Love isn't permitted to me. The dead are too strong!" Orin has been speaking to the ghosts—between reality and unreality—ever since and he and his sister killed Brant in the second play, when he looked at the body and said, "By God, he does look like Father! . . . This is like my dream. I've killed him before—over and over . . . He looks like me, too! Maybe I've committed suicide!"

Orin is truly between two worlds, grabbing at Lavinia's soul in an effort to hang on to something: "Vinnie, you're changing, you're turning into Mother! Where is Mother? Where are you?" How do you behave on stage between these two things, when everything is so strange and unreal? Look for elements that intensify. He can't go to the "real" Lavinia. That's too logical. He goes to the Lavinia in his mind.

You have to act the situation as if this whole cathedral is on fire. Lavinia has never loved, never opened her heart to anything, except to say "It's mine!" She has the possessiveness of a child: "I want this or that, and I'll break it if I don't get it!" Lavinia doesn't have—can't even think about—love and life and children and flowers, while Christine was someone who had all those things, all the colors of life.

Christine had a certain feminine weakness in her human armor; Lavinia doesn't. Lavinia has a different problem: she can kill, but she can't bend. The battle between them was: Who owns the father? Who owns the brother? Lavinia feels, "I must control them—all these things—or it will all go to pieces." She's convinced of that to the end. It's classical, but it isn't Greek. It's American: everybody here is breaking down.

Once his mother is dead, Orin shifts his mad jealousy to Lavinia. "I won't stand your leaving me to marry Peter!" His way of keeping her there in that tomb of a house is to blackmail her with his history of the Mannon family's crime and punishment.

It's not really that hard to do, as I've said, because the author doesn't trust you, he tells you everything. O'Neill gives you the exposition, the characters, makes it all clear before you even get to the stage: this one's a judge, that one's the mayor, this one inherited wealth, that one's a pompous ass . . . Ibsen doesn't do that. In Ibsen, you don't know who anybody is until and unless you figure it out for yourself. In O'Neill, it's all clear from the start: the first moment Lavinia sees Christine, it's "Vile woman!"—like the devil seeing a cross—"You've always hated me!" It's shattering, this unmasking, this violent tearing-out. O'Neill says one evil unveils another. Lavinia loves the father, Orin loves the mother, then he begins to desire Lavinia . . . O'Neill got this from Freud: he says if it's not redirected, you'll be wiped out by these forces in a society where there are no gods anymore. It is psychoanalytic drama going on behind all the killing and suicides.*

---

* Some forty characters in O'Neill's fifty completed plays meet violent ends, including ten suicides and two dozen deaths by pills, poison, drowning, electrocution, strangulation, and incineration. O'Neill's own suicide attempt (by pills, at age twenty-four) is replicated in *Exorcism,* a one-act autobiographical play thought to have been destroyed by him but recently unearthed.

O'Neill uses the Greek family-feud model that says the house—the society—is fated to go down through revenge and murder. Lavinia tells Orin, "Face your ghosts right now, and me, too." She wants the house of Mannon to survive and go on, through her, or die. Play it from yourself—from the need to keep what is yours. You fight and fight until you cross the boundary and kill, like Raskolnikov in *Crime and Punishment*. Plays either entertain you or they talk about something. If they entertain you, they don't really change your life. If they talk about something—are you being eaten up from inside by inner problems?—they might.

Inner conflict leads to external conflict. O'Neill piles up horror after horror, and the play lives on those theatrics. All the characters are in conflict, inside and out—conflicts meant to be understood in modern psychological terms, conditioned and motivated by the past, which holds on to them. That conditioning keeps their animosities and hatred alive, suppresses and perverts their sexual instincts, fans their inner conflicts. Passions and emotions that stem from repression are *violent*.

O'Neill understood these crafty, property-owning people. Their capacity to hold on to wealth and property is ferocious—to hold their ground like a battlefield, to catch and remove any force trying to undermine it. O'Neill says this whole class is doomed. Why? Because they are greedy and intolerant and violent. Seth says, "That durned nigger cook is allus askin' me to fetch wood fur her! . . . That's what we get for freein' 'em." The pride, the life-denying Puritanism, the possessiveness of these sealed-in people—it seals in all the hate and seals out all joy and love.

* * *

A play like this—a trilogy of such plays—had never been attempted in America. The style is detached, magnificent, august, opulent in its way—not concerned with life as we know it. You have to go somewhere else to get it. Why does he set it in the Civil War? To give you distance, a perspective on it. A good metaphor-image for it is architecture: the details are lost because of the size. If you do a Greek play, play marble, not cement!

The magnificence must be in O'Neill. It is all so filled with villainy, desperation, diabolically gloomy situations. The psychological gods are coming down on you! When Christine asks Ezra why he keeps talking about death, he says, "That's always been the Mannons' way of thinking. They went to the white meeting-house on Sabbaths and meditated on death. Life was a dying. Being born was starting to die. Death was being born. How in hell people ever got such notions!"

Orin delivers the title line in "The Hunted" for you: "Death becomes the Mannons."

In this play, it's the New England Puritan tradition itself that shatters the moral code. One brother destroys the other; that brother has a son who wants vengeance. The daughter has a passion for revenge, too, but eventually the dark truth comes out and she finds she is sexually involved with her father and brother—and in a sexual rivalry with her mother.

It's a modern play where people are trying to discover themselves and uncover everybody else. O'Neill thinks in public. He wants the actor to think out those problems as well. Sometimes it is direct, most times indirect. Don't try to make an O'Neill soliloquy "natural." If there's no God, people have to find themselves through psychological digging, which is not particularly natural if you're the product of generations who have hated.

How do you win? In Christine's case, by deceiving that Puritan general Ezra and finally declaring, "I love Brant and I'm proud of it!" When she does that, it's as though Lavinia sees her naked in bed with him. "Stop it, don't do this to Father!" Christine will be smashed on this business of love and freedom because Lavinia can't stand love or the talk of it. At the start of the very first play, when Peter asks her if Orin loves Hazel, Lavinia has an amazing answer. She says, "I don't know anything about love! I don't want to know anything! I hate love!"

Sex is especially dirty and awful to her. I remember a real-life scene once when some crazy man went into Notre-Dame in Paris during a high mass and started screaming dirty words. There was chaos! People covered their ears. That's what is happening inside Lavinia when her mother says, "I love another man!" It is sacrilegious. It's an abomination. She goes berserk.

Lavinia gradually realizes why this disaster is happening, but as she figures it out, she begins to unravel. That technique holds in almost every play from now on when a playwright articulates cosmic themes that have nothing do with logic. "I see now I was born out of the disgust of two people," Vinnie says, "—so *that's* who I am." Your job is to dig up the O'Neill technique from within. Emotions are not logical. When Lavinia tells Christine, "You've loved Orin," it means, "You didn't love me and you've made me a motherless cripple." It's an accusation without pity or self-pity. Christine: "I tried, I tried, I wanted to be a human being, but you were his child, not mine—I loathed you." The scene builds to where Lavinia is left without a world. Get the mounting tension of it. You must be very frank and three-dimensional. That's the kind of person the sanatoriums are full of.

Use gestures in a big way, never the commonplace thing. The circumstance is bigger. In a Greek play you must say to yourself, "When I talk, two thousand years of my Greek relatives are standing behind me, listening—I'm not alone here, I have a long tradition, all of Athens and Troy are behind me."

You're a human being in your own century, looking to establish your own truth. Lavinia is the rugged American individualist without sentiment, whose aim is to conquer. She has marvelous, murderous qualities. With Brant, she wants to tear his nails out—"You! Born out of a servant girl, you don't belong here!" I'd murder him for even being near me. "How dare you be in my presence? I'm a Mannon, you cheap bastard! There's a moat around here, how did you even get in? And just because you did, you think you are part of this house!"

Lavinia is like an Indian putting his ear to the ground, listening for hoofbeats: "Are the buffalo coming? The cavalry? Does so-and-so know this? Does so-and-so know *that*?" She puts out feelers, like an animal. Her whole business with the servants is indirect. Your habit of always talking directly comes only in realism. O'Neill's technique is to heighten reality, not replicate it. In plays where there is fantasy, you take a certain license listening for the sound of information and responding to it.

These plays are theatrical. You are not supposed to produce "reality," but you are supposed to produce a real human being within the style. It even has bits of humor now and then, to help you. When Hazel says, "Ezra is at peace," Christine says, "I was like you once, I believed in heaven. Now I know there is only hell!" Lavinia has an even better line about Hazel: "I hope there is a hell for the good somewhere."

In the ancient Greek versions of *Electra,* mercy triumphs over justice in the end. Not in O'Neill. Lavinia's last speech gives you his awful message: "It takes the Mannons to punish themselves for being born!"

The gods no longer punish anyone; you're your own judge. It is a hard road Lavinia takes to get to that. She is destructive; she is driven. Her salvation cannot come from anyone but herself. No god or priest comes in. The chorus and the Furies are pursuing her. Every tragic Greek figure carries his burden, and the burden is not relieved until he is sacrificed or killed. Nobody can really absolve you. If the gods forgive you, the Furies don't. Lavinia has the size of a monster. She is her own monster-god inside. "I forgive myself!"

This is the big play, the big time. There's nothing bigger. This is modern tragedy. O'Neill creates a universal character who stands up for dignity's sake and says, "I must destroy myself and my house." It's not "I am Lavinia!" It's *"I am the house of Mannon!* I stand for the human trapped. Despite my sin, I announce to the world that I can rescue myself through my own destruction."

Creating and experiencing this deep human need to rid oneself of pain through destruction—this has a certain joy for O'Neill. He says it is better than a happy ending.

FIVE

LONG DAY'S JOURNEY INTO NIGHT

(1956)

SYNOPSIS OF *LONG DAY'S JOURNEY INTO NIGHT:* The action takes place entirely in the family room of the Tyrones' summer home in August 1912. James enters with Mary, who has just returned from a sanatorium for morphine addiction. We learn that their son Edmund has been away, and that his health is bad. Edmund and his brother, Jamie, enter, but the men's bantering turns into arguing. Tyrone calls Edmond a socialist and anarchist. Edmund, much annoyed, goes upstairs coughing. Mary refuses to believe Edmund is truly sick. When she leaves, Tyrone says Jamie lacks direction; Jamie accuses Tyrone of miserliness, blaming Mary's addiction on his father's bargain-hunting for her medical care. When Mary returns, Edmund tries to talk to her frankly about the morphine problem, but she deflects the subject.

In Act II, Edmund chats with Cathleen, the hired girl. Jamie comes in to sneak a drink. Mary enters, and her strange demeanor confirms she's been taking morphine again. When she and Edmund leave, Tyrone tells Jamie that Edmund has consumption. Jamie worries Tyrone will send Edmund to a cheap sanatorium. Mary returns and reveals she bore Edmund to com-

Bradford Dillman, Jason Robards Jr., Fredric March, and Florence Eldridge in Eugene O'Neill's *Long Day's Journey Into Night* (1956)

pensate for the death of an older son, Eugene. Edmund reenters and urges his mother to fight her addiction, but she feigns ignorance of what he's talking about.

In Act III, Mary plies Cathleen with whiskey while musing about her childhood dreams of being a nun or concert pianist and how in love she and Tyrone once were. Edmund and Tyrone come home to find Mary lost in dope. Mary says Tyrone's habits have set both their sons on the path to alcoholism. She reminds him of the night they met and, in a brief moment of tenderness, speaks nostalgically about her wedding dress, which she has long since misplaced. Tyrone goes out for more whiskey. Edmund tries to tell Mary how sick he is, but she won't listen.

In the final act, Edmund enters at midnight to find his father playing solitaire. They have their normal round of fighting and drinking but also manage a soulful conversation in which Tyrone reveals that he ruined his career by staying in a lousy role for money. By playing the same part for years, he lost his nascent talent. Jamie comes in drunk. Tyrone leaves to avoid another fight. Jamie confesses that he loves Edmund more than anyone but wants him to fail. Jamie passes out but, when Tyrone returns, he wakes up for another fight. Mary comes down, doped to the max, carrying her wedding gown—hopelessly lost in the past. The men watch in horror: she does not even know they are there.

—B.P.*

IN THE SAME WAY Chekhov was the great innovator of the nineteenth century, O'Neill was the first master of the twentieth. *Long Day's Journey into Night* is his single most powerful play. It was never performed in his lifetime. It was much too intimate and would have been much too painful.†

* *Long Day's Journey into Night* opened at the Helen Hayes Theatre on November 7, 1956, running for 390 performances. The production, directed by José Quintero, featured Fredric March (James Tyrone), Florence Eldridge (Mary Tyrone), Jason Robards Jr. (Jamie), Bradford Dillman (Edmund), and Katharine Ross (Cathleen). It won Tony awards for Best Play and Best Actor (Fredric March).

† O'Neill presented the manuscript of *Long Day's Journey into Night* to his wife on July 22, 1941, with this note: "For Carlotta, on our 12th Wedding Anniversary. Dearest: I give you the original script of this play of old sorrow, written in tears and blood. A sadly inappropriate gift, it would seem, for a day celebrating happiness. But you will understand. I mean it as a tribute to your love and tenderness, which gave me the faith in love that enabled me to face my dead [loved ones] at last and write this play with deep pity and understanding and forgiveness for all the four haunted Tyrones." When first performed in 1956, three years after O'Neill's death, it won him a posthumous Pulitzer Prize.

Strindberg is the biggest influence on O'Neill. Strindberg said there were many reasons why people were unhappy, not mainly because there was an increase of unemployment but because there was an increase of inner chaos. It is dark inside you, and you don't know where to go to clear it up. Nobody knows what's wrong. If the outside doesn't have any pleasurable aspects and if you don't get any pleasure from your work, then where do you go to make sense out of life? You go inside to what really is the meaning of life, because the outside is a cheap disappointment.

Strindberg writes about the mix-up in emotions of loving and hating. In *The Father,* a man loves his wife and also hates her. She loves him and hates him, too. In Strindberg, it's the Dance of Death: they *more* than hate each other; they want to kill each other. In O'Neill, they forgive each other.

We touched on compassion in *Beyond the Horizon:* there's no attainable horizon on this earth, but maybe there is a horizon beyond. Despite all the passion and cursing, we must take care of one another. That is very O'Neill. His compassion for life is unequaled.

In O'Neill, people are full of anger, even if it isn't "motivated." If I'm angry because Nixon disappointed me, that's one kind of anger—external, political. If I'm angry because my boss is trying to cheat me, that's external social anger. But if I'm angry or disappointed in myself—I've been given the world but I'm still depressed and dysfunctional—it's an internal thing, and that internal thing is not easily solved. It makes you mad, makes you love and hate without any solution. You go wherever it leads you.

What O'Neill does more than any other American playwright before him is delve into the inside, which is complicated. Although his speech is vernacular, down-to-earth, with no pretense, the text has something mystic about it. It conveys the idea that there is nothing real outside, but that's where I want to be—somewhere out in the fog. The answers are hard to get in a fog. One of the messages of the big writers is that we are lost in the outer world. It's an expression of the mystical spirit, the thing man has in him that leads him away from reality.

O'Neill gives you a chance to be bigger than yourself, which is your job as an actor. It's a puzzle in need of an explanation. It takes a great actor to say to his brother, "Don't tell me the truth, because I want you to die. I love you more than I love my own life, but I'm rattled inside and I'm bitter and I'm a failure."

There are things about *Long Day's Journey* that you don't get immediately. First of all, it's written with a great deal of blood and tears, dedicated "to my dear dead ones." It is tremendously autobiographical, containing all the formative forces at work in O'Neill's own life. Like his character Edmund, O'Neill went to sea for years and spent six months in a TB sanatorium. But more than that, this play is an infiltration deep into a certain ethnicity—unparalleled for understanding what it is to be Irish-American. It's a key part of our cultural history.

You need to know that O'Neill, like Edmund, was the son of a well-known Broadway actor. The O'Neills were Irish, like the Tyrones. Both families were Catholic, with an old-fashioned father upset by sons leaving the church. O'Neill's father, James, like Tyrone, was an alcoholic who gave up his dream of being a great Shakespearean actor for the security of a lifelong run in a silly popular melodrama.* O'Neill's mother, Ella Quinlan O'Neill, like Mary Tyrone, became a morphine addict after her last child was born. Jamie in the play is based on O'Neill's real-life older brother, Jamie, a hopeless drunk who failed at everything. O'Neill's other brother, named Edmund, died as a baby; in the play, he calls the dead middle son "Eugene." The O'Neill character in the play is Edmund, the younger son.

It doesn't get any more autobiographical than that.

He's dealing with New England Irish Catholicism as a family strain in America. There is a great deal of disaster in terms of what each member of that family experiences. They are failures—all of them—but it is written in tremendous sorrow and forgiveness.

Don't you think the Kennedys have a kind of fate like that? The Joe Kennedy family was just first-generation American, too. Old man Joe was an immigrant's kid who got rich being a bootlegger during Prohibition. He and his own kids had that same kind of Irish clannishness. He was determined to make one of his boys president. It didn't matter much which one. When the oldest one died in the war, it would be one of the others. They didn't kill themselves; other people killed them. But no matter how much they got killed or fought with each other, that family—those brothers—were together.

What made them stick together? It was a tremendously complicated love—an attachment and isolation apart from everything else. In the

---

* *The Count of Monte Cristo,* first performed by James O'Neill (1847–1920) in New York in 1883, and repeated by him countless times thereafter.

play, the Tyrones fight constantly. They hurt each other a lot, but their family relationships are so intertwined that nobody else really gets in their way. There's the mother, and the children are wound around her. There's the father, and—with strife—they are wound into and around him. They are knit together. The brothers are made to love each other, like Bob and John Kennedy. The Kennedy boys must have had real Irish-American fights, but we don't actually know how their private truth came out. In the play we know, because people say, "I love you and I hate you," or "I'm jealous, but I love you more than I'm jealous of you," or "I hate you more than I love you."

O'Neill makes them come out with the truth. In O'Neill, you have this vomiting out of the complex truth of relationships. In all family life onstage after O'Neill, there is a complexity of truth winding in and out. It's a tortured route to get to a certain feeling that has the opposite feeling in it at the same time.

The sense you get in the play is that the Tyrones are Irish and they live in America without being American. They do not mingle, they do not associate, they don't have neighbors, they don't identify with the bigger structure of American life. They come as foreigners and stay that way, but they are more complex than other foreigners. They speak our language, but they don't really want to. They'd rather speak Gaelic. They would rather be Irish. The fact that they speak English fools you into thinking they're American, but they're Irish-Catholic against a Protestant society. Their society is built on different cultural, religious, and psychological values. They feel apart, they feel insulted, they feel foreign. They *are* foreign. And if you keep on being foreign, and feeling you don't belong to the mainstream, you naturally become belligerent, angry. You're constantly living as a stranger. You feel that strangeness, and it's justified.

America is not just foreign but also a country of fools and sinners alien to the Irish. Emotionally, they can't communicate with outsiders—only with one another. You get this inner thing: in the play, they seldom leave each other. One brother goes to the bar, and the other brother goes too; they all meet at the bar. The only people they meet there are other Irishmen. They're gleeful when they hear the story about the Irishman who let his pigs go into the foreigner's field. It's a triumph that the American who owns the oil is beaten, and that the Irish are going to sue him to the last drop of blood.

That antagonism toward "native" Americans ran deep for the Irishmen who came here. The father in the play says he arrived starving and remembers that his father starved in Ireland and committed suicide. You find there are three people already in this Irish-American family that tried or succeeded at suicide: Tyrone's father, his wife, and one of their sons. You get a sense of an enormous unhappiness in their lives stemming from what they are inside due to the social situation. They drink or take drugs because reality has disillusioned them. O'Neill says, and so does Tennessee Williams, that whatever illusion you can grab out of life in a tough society like this—grab it! Be disillusioned, but try to hold on to what's left of your illusion. In that sense, O'Neill is not pessimistic. These characters may want to commit suicide, but they still hold on.*

Tyrone, the father, is the biggest failure, because he couldn't live up to his talent. He has all the money in the world, but he knows he's a failure. He's stingy about money, he built a cheap house, he bought a secondhand car. He is constantly sick—sick with the insecurity of life that was born when he first had to support his family at the age of ten. He tells you that in a monologue—it's one of the great speeches in the play.

When people have that kind of experience, their souls are shattered. He's living in a foreign country. His father deserted them and then killed himself. That's a terrible burden. He's doing the best he can under the circumstances, but he betrayed himself. Stinginess is just a fear of death—fear of going to the poorhouse. We in America don't really know what the poorhouse is now. But there was such a thing here and in England and Ireland, and people would rather have committed suicide than go there. It was an institution everybody feared more than death. People were hired out from the poorhouse to work for five cents a day, children and old people included. They were frightened and hungry and terribly mistreated. It was unbearable.

---

* Domestic sorrow and suicidal tendencies were grimly replicated in O'Neill's own immediate family. He disowned his daughter, Oona, in 1943 for marrying actor-director Charles Chaplin (she was eighteen and Chaplin fifty-four), never laying eyes on her again. He had equally problematic relationships with his sons. Eugene O'Neill Jr. (1910–1950), a professor of Greek literature at Yale, said he never even met his father until age twelve. Eugene Jr. committed suicide at forty by slitting his wrist and ankle. Shane O'Neill (1919–1977), a heroin addict, likewise killed himself. Shane's son, Eugene III, died at the age of two months, "showing evidence of neglect," according to a doctor's report.

"Over the Hill to the Poor-House" was the name of a famous poem.* It was a fearsome thing. Do you understand Tyrone's fear? It's not superficial. It's very psychological. He's sixty-five, and when you get to that age you're frightened of many things, especially of death and of being poor. O'Neill goes into it deeply. He's not writing about a *poor* man who is afraid to be poor, but one who is fairly well off. Yet all the money in the world doesn't give him security, because, underneath, he betrayed himself. He has that sense of self-betrayal, and the sense of what he did to his wife. He tried to make it up to her, but there's nothing to do now. He didn't realize the marriage would be such a big mistake on both their parts. He loved her.

A father is a patriarch—he's supposed to be the star of the family. Yet you find there really is no father figure here. There are three boys. There is no separation in the sons' attitude toward the father as someone they respect. He has the image of being another boy in the family, which leads to all the fighting amongst them. On the other hand, you have the image of the Virgin Mary in the mother. You see the protected convent girl, and the misalliance. She should never have married an actor. She couldn't take the life.

Who could take such a life? It was rootless. It was without any desire to have a home. It was children brought up without a base or a nest, which makes for unhappiness. The father is a terribly disappointed man. He got sucked in by American materialism— thirty thousand dollars a year in those days was like thirty million today—but he didn't become the star he wanted to be. That means spiritual failure. He's still a Catholic even though he doesn't go to church. Somewhere inside him is a leftover of "If you do what the Bible says, you'll be better off." He tries to teach his boys that, but they are already alienated from God. They've both been reading the new literature—Nietzsche, Ibsen. What do Ibsen and Nietzsche teach you? That God is dead. What does Ibsen teach you about the idealization of the home? That it's a fantasy.

The father gives them liquor practically from the day they're born. They got used to the father and the liquor early on. Liquor is the center of the play. There should be a big spotlight on a bottle—there usually is. What is liquor? It's a symbol of deep unhappiness. The liquor,

* Written by Will Carleton in 1872 about the plight of the indigent elderly, the poem was made into a popular silent film in 1920.

the needle, the morphine all give you an illusion of escape from your misery. Tyrone is a failure, and when you're a failure you are angry with yourself and life and the world. People who truly want to become artists and poets don't give in to the instincts that drive them down. Tyrone recognizes that, but he doesn't have the strength to resist. He both wants and doesn't want to rise above it.

In the society O'Neill talks about—American Protestant capitalist society—the aim is money. That confuses a man who has other standards for success. The standards that exist in Edmund are too hard. Art is too hard. Tyrone has the inner turmoil that Strindberg saw—that darkness, that internal fight. People are pulled down inside all the time by what they do. To be pulled up, they go to money, fame, success. They go to church, not to God. Marriage in this society is built on sexual, romantic illusion. This illusion can mislead you. O'Neill says it can kill you; it has destruction in it. If pursuit of material gains is the goal every day, you lose the better side of your nature.

Artists interpret this within their time. O'Neill sets the rhythm of the uselessness of materialism in America. He felt it was a lost cause; he felt alienated and alone within that thing, and he put it in his plays. The literature of this time is built on being alienated from the drive of America, that relentless drive for the biggest industry, biggest buildings, biggest homes. It's about the end of the American spiritual drive, replaced with the money drive. The writers defined their characters, their novels, their poems as a revolt against this way of life. In every O'Neill play, look for the revolt. There will always be some rebellion against the given conditions of American life.

Jamie, the older son, sees all this. He is very smart and groping inside with this mixup. Jamie's view is that the church doesn't represent God. Something inside Jamie, in his Irishness, makes him rebel. It is natural for the minority group to have a fight. The majority doesn't have that fight. This Irish minority sees the society for what it is, but they don't go and join a group to make a revolution. They are in isolation. Loneliness makes you angry; you can't go out and mingle. Any minority person is in a big spiritual tangle about what he accepts and what he doesn't accept. Given his standards, given a Shakespearean father, a mother who plays the piano, a brother who is a poet, Jamie isn't going to accept what's in the bar. He is turned off by the outside world.

Jamie tries to show Edmund how to live. Jamie lives realistically;

he knows it is very hard to be a poet. If you're going to be a poet, you will pay a price; you may starve. Some poets did actually starve to death. American poets of Irish descent had nothing. You are in a moment of change in twentieth-century history when there was no poet laureate—no Tennyson, no Byron elevated and respected anymore. It was down to the guts of things. Jamie saw that Edmund was going to have to make money and that if he just wrote little poems for some out-of-town newspaper, he was going to be a failure. The paper doesn't give him a chance to write much. Jamie ridicules his writing, out of anger and love.

But within that, Jamie is jealous of Edmund's making the attempt. Edmund's trying is like what you're doing here, with acting: you make an honest effort. In spite of all the things people say to discourage or belittle you, in spite of all the failure and defeats, you're trying. That is what people are jealous of—not of your success but of your *trying.*

Jamie is saying to Edmund, Do you want to know what reality is? Reality is whores. You'll never get a nice girl, because if you find a nice girl you're going to fall in love with her, and your Irish-American tradition is unfit, unable to love because it is so inhibited. You're afraid to cross that border, and so the only time you can love is when you are drunk with a whore. When you are free to love, you love something that is depraved. Sex is dirty—something to be hidden. That's the inherited taboo.

You must make it real for yourself. You must be affected by it. The state of the family in this country is broken, but families stay together because they can't accept what's outside—the social condition. People are mixed up inside. The mix-up is something that happened to you and modern society. It's in everybody. The battle you got from Strindberg is what you'll have from now on. The analysts like O'Neill were born out of that. The base of *Long Day's Journey* is that everyone is struggling with an inner lack of clarity, lack of problem solving, lack of finding a road.

Jamie's internal truth has no logic. He is vomiting out something that is going on in him without reason. Identify with that. I can say for myself, logically, that I'm very nice, but internally I'm aghast at what goes on inside—at the mix-up in me. That's our inheritance. Some people inherited God and the way to live and pray, but most of us in the twentieth century inherited internal confusion. We hang on to something logical—work or studies or becoming something—but the rest is in turmoil. If you dig down too far inside, you might go insane; we can deal with the outside much more logically. If you go inside, there's a great deal of anger, depression, belligerence. All of O'Neill's characters have this. He was a pioneer of that new sense of confusion.

"I'm dead inside," Jamie says, but he has the capacity to make his peace with it. In the last line of *Beyond the Horizon,* Ruth says she settles for the lack of hope with a calm that is beyond hopelessness. Jamie is still fighting. What is dead in him is that he will never be able to get the other side of himself going—the poetic side. He finally gives up trying. You know about writer's block—"I can't go on." That's why Hemingway killed himself. That's why writers in America don't produce for eighty years the way European writers do. They give up. Something in the way of American life defeats them. They are after the next best seller and if they fail, they give up.

If people give up something very organic in them, they die. There is nothing to take its place. The pregnancy of an artist is the desire to fulfill himself through his work, not just his mind. "I have a passion for this work!" When that dies, they may have all the money in the world, but they're dead. All of Hollywood is dead. The only effort that is valued there is the moneymaking effort. But success is just an accidental aspect of a person's life. The man who works and tries and fails is to me just as much a success as someone on the marquee.

Jamie has seen more reality than Edmund. He calls Edmund a "big, overgrown kid." O'Neill is saying we're all big, overgrown kids, beaten from the start even if we try to play the game. Jamie says the way to go is you write for a magazine and then you write a book and then you become a success. If you do that, then you're not a ghost of this society; you're part of it.

In fact, if you do that, you're a Frankenstein—part ghost and part society. Is it better to be a zombie or a ghost? I don't know. But at least Edmund has a job. Jamie is jealous of that, even though he doesn't want to do what Edmund wants to do. Edmund is already a Frankenstein—partly in the fog and partly what America is. Jamie's the one who gave birth to him that way, taught him how not to get gypped in this world, taught him about whores, gave him Strindberg's lessons. Edmund can exist with what Jamie gave him—it's a road. But Jamie himself doesn't believe in that road. He believes that you may sell a poem, but you don't win. The bigger the success of an artist, the less secure he is. Something in him demands more.

From practically being born on the stage and being brought up with a father that played Othello, Jamie imitates the father's postures. They both have a sense of the grandeur of the theater in a house where there's no grandeur. They are theatrically inclined. O'Neill likes that. They fight and then they forget that they fought, and then they come together and then they fight again. It's a wonderfully exaggerated theme.

What kind of minds do they have? Very excitable, which is Irish. They are on fire instantly. Most other people don't have this immediate flare-up, this immediate need to justify everything, where the blood rushes to your head, your face gets red, your eyesight gets blurred—and then you come right back down again.

I had a student once who was in a jam, and he came to see me at my house and in the middle of our talk, all of a sudden, there was a terrific outbreak between one member of my family and another. I said, "I'm sorry this happened"—I was a little embarrassed. But not too much. He said, "Well, it happens." He saw he was in a climate where tempers could flare up in a second, which is an Irish climate but can also be Russian or Jewish or Italian.

Mary Tyrone had a father who told her to go out and buy anything she wanted and a mother who said that was wrong and complained that he spoiled her. The father was a businessman; buying things was the best he could do. O'Neill didn't put that in by accident. James Tyrone lived in the theater; Mary lived in the hotel room. She didn't have his spiritual satisfaction of being an actor. He didn't need anything else. He was right in doing that for his own soul; he had a place to express himself. But those surroundings didn't give Mary a way of expressing *her* soul. He had no right to be with her without giving her what she needed. For him, it was husbandry vs. poetic license. In that sense, no man who is an artist or actor can give a woman what she needs—a home. Mary waited, but all she got back was a man that was drunk. She had been brought up protected and wasn't accustomed to that kind of life. It made her angry. When there is no reward in waiting, in the life that you make an effort for, you get angry.

The illusion of romantic married life was over. You got that in Ibsen, where people were told that honeymoons and orange blossoms and white dresses would all be a permanent part of it. The honeymoon didn't last. Mary was hit with the reality of sex, the reality of childbirth, the reality that James's real life was the theater and that he didn't entirely belong to her, the reality that there would be no home. She had no outlet as an artist, a mother, or even as a housewife. If someone has no identity, she gets depressed. At least in Ibsen, when the honeymoon is over and the husband is away working eight hours a day, the woman takes her place as a mother and becomes necessary to the home. She has as big a job there as he does at the office. But if even that is taken away, you get sick. You have no exit. You sit around waiting, for Godot or something else.

When Mary talks to Tyrone, she does exactly what O'Neill characters do in every play—she vomits out her truth, or her anguish as the truth. From now on, everyone goes inside to express what they feel: it's not that the society owes me more, it's that I owe *myself* more. I'm living without anything to reinforce me, living without God, living in a materialistic society without my identification. It goes to self-examination and sickness: I have no purpose, I don't know where I'm going.

The two sides of the coin are "I love you" and "I hate you." The chaos results from this parallax view that both sides are operating with. You're in a revolt against the inner situation. It is not the outside that is guilty. If it were the outside, you could do something about it; you would leave him or divorce him. In Ibsen, Nora went out. That was no inner revolt, it was social revolt. After Ibsen, you get the chaotic inner revolt, which is much more painful and difficult to resolve.

Mary holds on through hope. What is her hope? She wants to get back. Why can't she go back? What was it that hurt her so much that she lost her faith in God, in herself? The thing she experienced was the shock of reality. She was protected at home by her father. Her first exposure to reality was sex, drunkenness—things that jolted her to the core. She was incapable of dealing with childbirth, with the guilt of losing a child through carelessness, with a husband she loved very much but who mortally shocked her by his life.

Tyrone is a shocking character with panache, who came from peasant stock. He wasn't gentle in introducing her to sex, because he was drunk when he did it. She has a terrible sense of failure from living in dirty hotel rooms with cheap food and no decent surroundings. The first time I read the play, I cried bitterly when I saw that if you're born into a family of actors, you really never have a home. I realized I never had a home. It was a house, but there was no mother or father who took care of you. They were too busy. Their home was really the dressing room. That's where they really "dressed for success." As a child, I was left in dressing rooms. Later, when I tried to create a home, it was completely an illusion of theater—a stage set.

Mary's love of lace on her shoes and gowns—everything she needed of aesthetic beauty in life—is gone. She has lost the music. What is she holding on to? She has no religion. You can't pretend to be the Virgin Mary if you're a dope fiend. You can't pray. If only she could! If only the dope would feed her enough so she could believe in something! But it doesn't, and she doesn't.

It is really *her* long day's journey into night that the play is about. She can't face reality anymore, with all her conflict inside. The thing that's really Irish-American about it is that her boys are twenty-three and thirty-three and they're still at home, not married. Mary says to Edmund, "If you hadn't been born, I wouldn't have this rheumatism and wouldn't have been so sick. It was when you were born that I lost my life in worrying, caring, suffering." She has a lot of idealistic illusion about how beautiful life was when she first married. She's in a terrible state. Nobody can give her back what she had. She can't help herself. She needs very much to believe in life, but she can only believe in life through religion, and that's a curse.

Edmund knows and understands his father and still demands that he *be* a father. He calls him a "stinking old miser" yet wants to be supported by him. The relationship is complicated. Both the children and the family ties are weak. James is weak in terms of Edmund, but there's still a sense of "I won't desert you because I'm your father, even though you don't treat me like one." That is pure, emotional, in-depth O'Neill. Edmund is his baby, his son. It's umbilical. It is not so much "Papa, you owe me" as "Papa, I'm not grown-up—I *can't* grow up."

Edmund is a poet, and the poet recognizes he is detached from reality; he knows about life, death, love—the secrets that no realist can explain. O'Neill knows that something in such a man either lifts him up or pulls him down and kills him. The drive of the artist reveals those truths that are buried so deep but must come out. Every artist has that need to find out—that inexplicable aim to go beyond the "real" to the mystical experience he doesn't know. That kind of groping and talking is O'Neill's version of "To be or not to be." It is not realistic dialogue; it is spiritual. It is man with the question most people don't dare ask themselves: "What am I living for?" Nobody can really answer. But O'Neill questions it, and his answer is that you have to go into the "ghosts"—have to go as far beneath them as you can and discover whatever it is you can get to.

These are ideas that have to be dealt with. Edmund does so. He deals with the mystical things, and understands them. He sees that the spiritual side of life lets you identify with the sky and how it meets with the ocean. If you begin to feel it, understand it, something happens to you. That is O'Neill. The literal side is where the chaos is, and the blindness. But the sky and the sea give you a freedom of identification with something above and beyond and apart. Edmund vomits out the truth: man has inside the capacity to be bigger than he is on the outside—that capacity to rise higher than his fears and his material desires. O'Neill is telling you that man is capable of more than just being "a success." O'Neill needs big actors, not ordinary ones. O'Neill says society is bankrupt—you don't see it in yourself. He says fate intervenes, and that fate is not about success or failure. Fate draws you deeply into the fog, where there are no answers. It is scary but reassuring at the same time.

Jamie and Edmund feel responsible for their mother in a tribal way—responsible for her being sick, for making her give birth, dragging her down. They know they've hurt her by the way they've lived. Edmund's sickness is making her more of a zombie. He feels it's his fault. There's a tremendous sense of guilt. These sons are cynical about the reality of their lives but sentimental at the same time. There's an enormous amount of betrayal in the play. The boys feel Tyrone betrayed them by not being able to be a real father. They feel betrayed because they had no home, no roots. They feel betrayed because they can't function. And, of course, they betray each other. Edmund knows his brother showed him a life that wasn't true, even though Jamie insisted it was.

I want you to understand how powerful the play is, how powerful the father is, how much they can't relate to him and can't leave home but—being thrown together—they have this extraordinary *talking*. O'Neill says that to say something is not necessarily to understand it. It must be repeated. You must know things about this play: Where does its size, its theatricality come from? From the father. What makes Mary so shattered? Her sheltered life, her piano career, God—all those things that were taken away from her. In exchange for what? Pain, childbirth, drunkenness, vulgarity. What happened that the sons can't rely on the parents? What were the betrayals? Does James really want to send Edmund to a cheap sanitorium? Did he really do that to his wife? How does the mother betray them? She lies, even though she says she won't.

If you can't trust your father or your mother, who can you trust? Now, the mother loves each of them in a different way. What's special about her love for Edmund? She finally takes her husband's word and realizes Edmund is going to die. That's quite an unusual situation to put a very sensitive woman into. She tries not to take the drug, but the pain she suffers is so great she has to get relief. A lot of people run to a psychiatrist to get it. How many people do you know who can't live their life without an outside force helping them? If they don't get help, they destroy themselves.

Mary needs to get rid of this psychological pain. There is nothing inside to sustain her. There is no help for Edmund, either. He lives in a time when most consumptives die. Where can he run? He wants to be happy, he wants to live, but he feels death coming. Jamie knows that and, if anything, it makes him a little jealous: Jamie wants to die, too, and is in the process of drinking himself to death. The situation is pretty hopeless. The men reprimand and scream at each other for drinking, and then they give each other a drink. The boys know what they're doing is destructive. Somebody in the play says, "The alcohol will kill you." It kills Jamie in the next play, *A Moon for the Misbegotten.*

You need keys to discover these people. You have to dig down into the social facts of their lives in order to understand their relationships. Since the only thing they connect sex with is whoring, it means that they don't look for love; they look for something to take away the pain and failure in their lives. Drink releases them and makes them angry; they can have sex only through anger and the destructive idea "She's a whore!" That's enough to make anybody psychologically sick. They have a family life, but they all feel abandoned within that life; the father feels the boys have abandoned him, and that the wife is abandoning him; the mother felt abandoned long ago by all these drinkers; the boys feel that they don't belong, that their father is stingy, even though they love him.

It's complex. They know life is tragic. That's the most important thing. They see the tragedy of life and can turn it into a joke. There's that awful guilt, but their suffering brings out the truth. The big scenes—as when the mother breaks out with her truth to the father—are all fight scenes. But as soon as they attack one another, they hear themselves do it and they feel sorry afterwards, which makes them give in. It breaks them. When the father lashes out, he regrets it. He sees the death on Edmund's face. When Jamie strikes out at him, he knows his father is doing the best he can—he starved as a child, he's frightened as an adult. You can't change people who grew up with poverty. The Tyrone boys understand their father and understand that they're stranded, too—out of sync with American life. They can only work sporadically, and they loathe it. It's "I can't do it! I can't take a job for eight hours a day!" The father is talented, the mother is a musician, both boys have certain gifts, but their talents aren't focused. Jamie is paralyzed by infantile ways, which he resents in himself. He is the bitterest of all—bitter about his own inability to grow up and lead a life on his own. Edmund is in an absolute frenzy of wanting to escape this house and go into the world, but what would face him there? He is going to die, and with no life in front of him, he sees that he can't be a poet. "I can only use the ashes," he says. "I can only stammer through."

Again, these brothers remind me of the Kennedys. Forget about wives—they don't matter. What matters is that the brothers be together. They can't break away, because then they would be exposed to strangers, to living the way strangers do. The thought of that frightens them, so they keep going back to being together—unhappily, but loving each other. If you reject what the outside society is trying to force on you, you do what the Indians did: you keep on being tribal, no matter what. It's a primitive security instinct. If you break away from home, you don't count. You're a deserter.

What's special about these Irish sons' love for the mother? How does the shattering of their mother illusion affect them? They can't face it. The reality is devastating. What happens to them emotionally? Why do they feel guilty? Does Jamie believe he killed brother Eugene? How did he kill him? He is fated not to be helpful. Jamie brings failure into life. He has that sense of himself.

In every Irish family there is a bum, a ne'er-do-well—the black sheep made helpless by that clannishness, who can't hang onto anything. It was in my family, too. Because of the strength of the father, Jacob Adler, there was a black sheep. Nothing could help him. My father tied him to a bedpost and whipped him, but nothing he did could stop him from being overpowered by the sense of being useless in that clan. Still, that boy worshipped my father more than anybody.

But in my whole family, there was always this sense that nobody could ever really break away from that powerful father.

Long Day's Journey is built on that. This Irish family is waiting for something to happen. Waiting is a human situation. An individual is made up of the past, which is clear, and the future, which is not. You see their sickness. If one of them falls and skins his knee, the others sympathize, but at the same time it becomes a joke. The more of a joke it is, the more insulting. Tyrone never understands that he's not really stingy, just afraid. He is stung and strikes back at his son for calling him a tightwad: "You've never earned a dollar in your life! You don't have one goddam idea what a dollar means!" He remembers when his mother brought home her first meager wages and for the first time they all had enough to eat. It's a tremendous memory, but at the same time it triggers the tremendous anger that he wasn't wanted and that people said he destroyed his mother. She was weak, she got sick, her eyes went, she was crippled, she was bedridden—she had a hard time when he left and went off on his own.

All that shame and blame from the past comes back in the present as suspicion. Everybody in the play is suspicious, skeptical, critical of everybody else. They spy on each other, constantly wondering what the others are saying. "They're talking about me outside," says the father. "Jamie's coming in—he was talking to Edmund about me!" Edmund comes in and says, "Who were you talking about, Mother? Well, *don't*!" They all feel belittled. The father wants to deal in real estate, but it's another illusion. He's an artist. What did all his talk about business do to the family? Mary says, "You're no businessman." The sons say, "What are you doing? That's an insane investment!" He dresses shabbily. They're deeply offended to see their father, whom they love, in such a threadbare suit. He won't buy a new one. Yet he has this fantastic voice and this fantastic theatrical size.

Their arguments start in easily, out of nothing. She says, "Papa snores so much." He says, "I don't snore. Jamie snores." She says, "Yes you do." He says, "How do you know? So you were just pretending to be asleep? I thought so. I heard you go into the spare room." She says, "I just went in to see how Edmund felt." That leads to the fact that she's taking morphine even before sunrise and ends up in a big suspicious fight among them all. They worry each other; they upset each other.

Now, Mary must not worry; that's the one thing she mustn't do.

She says Edmund has a bad cold. Underneath, her inner voice says, "He's going to die, I see it in his eyes; I'm his mother." But out loud, "It's just a cold. Now, you take care of your cold, dear. I'm not going to worry about you." But in fact she has tremendous apprehension. There's nothing worse than the understanding of something deep down inside you that you can't express because you're trying to fool yourself. Deep down you feel your child is going to die, but you say, "Oh, he'll be fine."

Why does Jamie lash out so much? Out of loneliness. He's isolated and looked down upon. He doesn't respect himself, has no will to do anything. He stays home and gets money from his father, who has to use his influence to get Jamie a job he can't keep. It's a play about deep inner failure.

Do you see that it's not about *external* success or failure?

Elizabeth Taylor is beautiful and talented and extremely successful, and she married a great and beautiful and extremely successful man.* But she is not someone I envy. Something tells me she's dying inside. It has to do with her standards. Burton is drinking himself to death. I'd accept an invitation to dinner with her—I'd look forward to it. But I wouldn't think of it as a special treat. I'd rather have dinner with Marlon. Marlon is different. Do you recognize the difference between Taylor and Brando?

Marlon is in deep, deep agony all the time. That's why he identifies with the Indians and the blacks. His spiritual side is kept up by taking part in the social disaster around him. He identifies with that. That's why in Hollywood they don't know if they should give him an Oscar, because they're afraid he'll send in another Indian or bring up some other cause.† He is always struggling to keep up with something bigger than he is.

O'Neill says every man has to struggle to keep up with being a man. It's hard; most of us fail. In *Long Day's Journey,* he is trying to

---

* She, in fact, married seven successful men. Stella is referring to actor Richard Burton (1925–1984), whom Taylor married and divorced twice (1964–1974, 1975–1976).

† Adler is referring to Brando's second Academy Award, for *The Godfather* (1972), which he refused to accept in protest against the plight of Native Americans and government violence at the Pine Ridge (Oglala Sioux) Indian Reservation in Wounded Knee, South Dakota, in February 1973. Sacheen Littlefeather made a controversial statement to that effect in accepting the award on Brando's behalf.

come to grips with his own failures as a man and as an artist, trying to make peace with his past, trying to forgive his family as well as himself. We are all trying to do that, or should be. In doing so, we go to the sources that can nurture us—to the people who struggled before us—and we find there is an eternal yearning in man to keep himself high through his work, through his thought, through his inheritance. Man has inherited property in art, in literature, in science, in philosophy. It is there for you.

Unless you take and use that, you are not just a failure; you are truly lost.

THORNTON WILDER

Thornton Wilder (c. 1948)

S I X

OVERVIEW

YOU LIVE in a moment when there's not much to say about the
American theater. You are part of a society that doesn't take the
theater seriously. "Let's go see *Hello, Dolly!* Oh, that's sold out? Should
we go see Tennessee Williams? Is it fun? I don't want to go if it isn't
fun."*

If I want to go to the theater today, I don't know where to go. Do
you? Somebody says, "Off Broadway." That's too general. If you say,
"I'm going Off Broadway," you might as well say you are going to a
whorehouse. It might be good, it might be bad. Who knows?

It is important to take the theater seriously. There are important
people involved. I'm going to make clear to you that the theater is
an art. It's hard work, because there is no clarity, no road leading you
from one author to another. You are in a mess. Let's find out how it got
itself in such a mess.

Americans think of theater in terms of success or failure. If a play
is successful, we say it is good. If it fails, we say it's bad. When I was
living in California, I heard a couple of stars talking about a movie:
"How much money did it make? Did it bring in eighty million?"
They just immediately look at the figures, which are on the front page

* This chapter is condensed from Adler's lectures of February 28 and March 7,
1983—a time when she was more agitated than usual: several days earlier, on February 25, Tennessee Williams had choked to death, on the cap from a bottle of eye-
drops, in New York City at the age of seventy-one.

of the *Los Angeles Times.* "Gee, this one got great ratings and has a big star in it. That one doesn't."

"Is it making money?" "Did it get good notices?" That's American. That's our way of looking at it. That is the way we are. We say, "I'll go to *Sophie's Choice.*" Why are you going to *Sophie's Choice?* "Because I heard it's going to win all the awards, so it must be great."

Sophie's Choice is a lie from beginning to end. It's a fake. If it wins ten thousand prizes and ten thousand critics say it's great, it's still a lie. I was down in Florida taking a walk and what I heard was, "You didn't see *Sophie's Choice* yet? I saw your sister there last week. I called her about it, and she said her husband is going tomorrow." *Sophie's Choice* is suddenly something the country is obsessed with.

It wasn't like that for the playwrights. Our three biggest writers are O'Neill, Wilder, and Tennessee. They are the three big ones. And there were others—I knew some of them.

There was a man called Maxwell Anderson. He was a very important influence in America, our first wrote verse plays since Schiller. I'm going to mention these names to you because I'm terribly hurt: Robert Sherwood wrote magnificent plays. Paul Green was one of this country's great writers. He was influential in making the black-and-white race situation clear. You know more about Turgenev than you know about Paul Green. Marc Connelly was a man of stature. George Kaufman, Moss Hart, S. N. Behrman wrote wonderful plays. Philip Barry, Clare Boothe, George Abbott, Lillian Hellman, John Steinbeck, Sidney Kingsley, Irwin Shaw, Archibald MacLeish, Clifford Odets, Edna Ferber . . .

That is not a cheap set of writers. They are your playwrights and you don't know anything about them. You know more about English literature, because somehow or other they made you read Dickens and earlier stuff. But about the Americans and modern Europeans you know nothing.

I'm scolding you because these are writers who spent a lifetime writing plays and most of them were failures. They are forgotten, unknown, unplayed. There are fifty volumes of Shaw, twenty-five volumes of Behrman. There is all this work that you think is just old "show business." It's not show business but art business.

This is the only country that discards its own writers.

From the 1700s to the twentieth century, we had ordinary melodramas, comedies, musicals—but no great dramatic writers. Not even the

Civil War produced one. Can you believe that no playwrights came out of that? Our first great playwright, O'Neill, came to us around 1916. After a few years, he was forgotten. Then he came back and then he was forgotten again. Hardly anyone speaks about O'Neill now.

I was thinking about that today, thinking there would be millions of people mourning Tennessee's death. But there was nobody. One or two people. There should be millions of Americans paying tribute. We've had two or three great playwrights in the two hundred years since this country's inception. One of them was O'Neill and one was Tennessee. Nobody was there. What is the matter with us? How often does a great poet come into the world? You can count them: Keats, Shelley . . . and you're finished real fast. I am very upset. I lectured for eight weeks on Tennessee last year in California, and the audience—maybe 150 people came. So I am upset.

Thornton Wilder had better luck. He had economic advantages that Tennessee didn't. His education was mostly in Europe. He saw Brecht; he saw a lot of plays. He was our one writer who understood all the different contemporary styles of realism that were around. Some said, "I want poetic realism." Somebody else said, "I like inner realism"—very strong for a while, very dark. Others liked the intense naturalism that was big for a time.

Modern realistic theater is psychological and philosophical, with many sides. It deals with many aspects of people's problems. Realism was a kind of partnership, able to embrace and share many forms.

This made it hard for the actor. I'll give you an example. The opening of *The Seagull* is hysterically funny. They are having tea and joking and it is a completely funny thing in a very serious play. Chekhov opens this really serious play with funny business, for clever reasons.

The style of the previous one hundred years was to do a play straight. Now, no play was completely straight. The tables turn, the lights turn, everything turns. It is so trimmed. It is so mixed up with excitement in a variety of styles.

What is the actor to do? What is the director going to do? You have turntables. You can turn a whole theater upside down. One director told me he was doing a play and the inside of the theater had to be excavated. Imagine a style where the producer has to excavate a whole building in order to do a play!

There was a transition in the 1930s. You could taste it. It was a transition that created people like Thornton Wilder and William

Saroyan, who had a lighter quality and did a little what Chekhov did. They didn't bemoan the political dissolution of America, or that the war was going to destroy us. They were not politically dedicated like the Group Theatre playwrights in New York who said we had to change, had to become socialist or communist—people don't have jobs, the culture is going down.

Wilder and Saroyan came along and said, "If it goes down, it goes down. What can we do? Try to survive by the skin of our teeth and have the time of our life going down."

Nobody else has Wilder's style. It is not to be found elsewhere. It is the poetry of life. Thornton Wilder wrote four plays and got Pulitzer prizes for two of them. He wrote a novel and got a Pulitzer for that.* Do you have any idea what that means in literature? It was unprecedented acclaim.

You must be aware of the difficulties faced by playwrights like Wilder. It is very difficult to make a transition from one period to another—to go from horses to cars, boats to airplanes. It means that something long accepted has lived out its life and must be replaced. Most great American writers were caught in a transition.

Read *Happy Journey to Trenton and Camden* and you'll see why Wilder is the most important contributor to American drama, even more than O'Neill, up to that time.

Envy me because I knew him.

I'm going to quote from his biography by Gilbert Harrison: "Thornton Wilder's life is distinguished from many of his literary compatriots by its rather unadventurous stability and normality. In his youth he was not a hobo, nor a dishwasher, nor a cotton-picker, nor a stevedore . . . His father owned a publishing company and published a paper, but Wilder was not even a journalist. He had the typical career of an academically trained teacher. It is difficult to determine which was his greater passion—teaching or writing."

Do you know what a housemaster is? It's the man in charge of the university building you are assigned to. I was assigned, as a teacher at Yale in '66–'68, to a residence where Wilder was the housemaster. A delightful man! He loved being with young people. Everybody in his house could come and talk to him. If you were in a room with him, he

---

* Wilder's first Pulitzer was for his novel *The Bridge of San Luis Rey* in 1927. The second and third were for his plays *Our Town* (1938) and *The Skin of Our Teeth* (1942).

made you laugh. He sang, he danced. He was absolutely unique in his liveliness. The author you thought you were going to meet—the man who got the prize for *The Bridge of San Luis Rey*—receded. He grew up in a puritanical Midwest environment, but nothing could be less puritanical than his *Skin of Our Teeth* burlesque. His father was consul general to Hong Kong. Wilder spent his early years there, attending a mission school. At Yale from 1917 to 1918, he studied languages and published essays and short plays in the University Magazine. In World War II, he became a captain and then a lieutenant colonel in the Army Air Force, serving in Africa and Italy—where he picks up African and Italian history. So he's now at home in *five* cultures. No other American playwright had such a thing. He is a man of unparalleled culture and knowledge.

He had an introspective nature that he wanted to—but couldn't honestly—attribute to an unhappy childhood, something he felt was essential to artistic development. The isolation of an unhappy childhood awaken things in you which later on develop your gifts. Happy children should not try to be artists. You have to be born with a broken heart and a sense of loneliness inside. I never had a happy moment as a child myself.

It's very important for actors to know that loneliness is the center of your profession. You are alone, whether you are rehearsing or acting. You are alone in public. When you are acting, you are alone with many people. Loneliness is at the center of the creative artist's emotional life.

Wilder highly respected the avant-garde. Gertrude Stein was a big influence on him. So was James Joyce. In the preface to *The Skin of Our Teeth,* he says he is deeply indebted to *Finnegan's Wake*. I want you to know about him. You've got to know more. You've got to read and know and understand the writers you intend to interpret.

Wilder said the dangers of success are as great as those of non-success. He knew how to avoid those dangers because he was smart. Only an idiot takes success personally. He recommended keeping a diary—not for publication, but for inner concentration. He advised young writers to discipline themselves and learn from a master. In your case, that means me.

Learn from a master, whether it is architecture or painting or whatever you study—whereupon, originality will come of itself. He warned against trying to fake originality. The key statement from him is: "I consider it best to write about things that lie on the boundaries of the unknown." He created the universal man, woman, girl, boy in every play he wrote. He is the most universal writer, but also, in a way, the most American—very attached to American traditions, despite his cosmopolitanism.

Wilder isn't anxious for traditions to be broken. The groom isn't supposed to see the bride before the wedding. In *Skin of Our Teeth,* the mother can't saw the wood—it's too hard for her. The father says to the son, "You know, I was sitting here and I heard a noise outside, somebody sawing wood. And guess who it was? It was your mother—your mother, who cooks for you and me and the children and cleans the house and irons the shirts and dresses." He doesn't say, "You do it." But the son gets the message.

You live in your present culture without realizing that there's an older culture that still exists. The playwright of *Our Town* is extremely careful. His newspaper editor is knowledgeable. When they ask if the town has any history, he says, "Yes, indeed, we do. Families have been buried up there on the hill since the 1600s."

Wilder gives you a tradition of three hundred years. They ask, have you got any art? He says, "Well, we know 'Whistler's Mother.' " Not too much art in America. But we know seasons, how the leaves look in autumn and how the flowers and the sky look in spring.

That's tradition. That's the universality of life. Wilder does that all the time. The son must be taught by the father. The girl is going to put rouge on. The mother is going to slap her.

He knows the truths. Not Harvard truths, not courses in developmental psychology: the truth of people. What Wilder didn't admire was overintellectualization. He wanted, in his plays, the kind of truth that would go on for generation after generation. There will always be families. They'll always have a boy and a girl. They will die and be buried in the same cemetery where their parents are buried.

Those are universal truths. We don't have to know about Nietzsche's conflict with Strindberg. It's not necessary. Go to Harvard for a few months, if you like, and then forget it. Wilder says, "For God's sake, live your life! Live it with as much joy as you can muster because it won't come around twice. There will be sorrow—but pass on the joy!" That's why he puts in the horse, the milk, the beans. He says life is made up of small things. In the end, Mrs. Antrobus says, "Will we ever know what it means to take a hot bath or drink hot coffee?"—all the things people take for granted.

Wilder didn't like living too much in America. He lived minimally here. He said America was dominated by an elite that posed a danger. Much as he loved our way of life, he said Americans don't really know who they are.

But he believed Americans were committed to developing a new human being whose chief characteristic was the ability and willingness to regard every individual as equal. He had very much the democratic sense: an American is friendly to all, not out of goodness or condescension but because he realizes that every human should be free to live his own life. This attitude wasn't characteristic of all Americans, but it was characteristic of Mr. Thornton Wilder. He was absolutely available—in his life and in his plays.

With Wilder, and thereafter, you are in the form of theatricalism. No scenery or props are necessary. Anything can happen. Don't try to pin some other pompous name on it—"Oh, this must be expressionism." If anybody asks what it is, say Stella says it's "theatricalism"! If they say that's not definite enough, ask them where expressionism ends and constructivism starts, or vice versa. Nobody can do it. It's good enough just to call it the transition from realism to theatricalism.

That's what we're in, and what you are the inheritors of. Me, I like a nice set where I know where the sofa is and how deep I can sit in it and that I hid a handkerchief that didn't belong to me under the cushion. I know how to play that. I know an awful lot about the logic of psychological acting. My own talent runs towards this.

And yet I love illogical plays. I was trained one way, but my talent led me another. Never think that somebody who gets bad notices is a bad playwright. Chekhov got bad notices. Criticism is an extremely unrealized form today. We have no great critics. Jack Kroll [of *Newsweek*] is perhaps the best. Frank Rich [then chief theater critic of the *New York Times*] is not a critic. Please don't take him seriously.

I'll say it again: The biggest writers are O'Neill, Wilder, and Tennessee. These are the three great ones. The difficulty of the modern theater is that after the advent of realism, playwrights had to mix in all the other styles in order to create and keep their new ones going.

America did not create a great theater like the Comédie-Française or the British National Theatre. There was no "big" American theater. Its successes came from small corners of the country, from forgotten geniuses like Wilder. It was the job of Behrman, the job of Miller, Inge, Kaufman, Saroyan, Wilder—their plays of the twenties, thirties, forties, and fifties—through the blood of those authors who worked all the time but had mostly failures.

Only Wilder "succeeded" in commercial and critical terms—with his three Pulitzer Prizes. But that's not what's important. What's important is that nobody else has his style. It is not to be found. It is the poetry of life. He left you alone onstage, without scenery or props, and left you to make great theater. That's Wilder. He took away scenery, props, costumes—everything—and created great plays without them.

When we get to *Skin of Our Teeth,* you'll get Wilder. That is where we are heading, kids.

SEVEN

THE SKIN OF OUR TEETH

(1942)

SYNOPSIS OF *THE SKIN OF OUR TEETH:* George Antrobus and his wife, Maggie, have been married for five thousand years. They reside in Excelsior, New Jersey, with dysfunctional children Henry and Gladys, oversexed maid Sabina, and a pet dinosaur and mammoth. Past houseguests have included Homer and Moses. They've lived through fire, flood, locusts, plagues, depressions, and Ice Ages—but a new one seems to be coming.

The play opens with an announcer intoning "News Events of the World": top stories include a glacier moving south over Vermont, and the recent invention of the wheel (by Mr. Antrobus). Sabina then delivers a parody of the standard opening expository speech, breaking character to complain that she doesn't really understand or like this play—she's just doing it for the money. The stage manager—very different from the one in *Our Town*—comes out to reprimand her.

Son Henry has anger-management issues. Sabina says he killed his brother in "an unfortunate accident" and, for some reason, has had a nasty red mark on his forehead ever since. Daughter Gladys is promiscu-

Tallulah Bankhead as Sabina in Thornton Wilder's *The Skin of Our Teeth* (1942), objecting to her lines and tending to the Antrobus family's pet dinosaur and mammoth

ous. Mr. Antrobus's motto is "Enjoy Yourselves!" Mrs. Antrobus's is "Save the Family!"

Act II takes place in Atlantic City, where George is being installed as new president of the "Ancient and Honorable Order of Mammals: Human Subdivision." Sabina is now Lily Sabina Fairweather, Miss Atlantic City 1942. She again drops character and refuses to say her lines for fear of offending a friend in the audience. Mr. Antrobus abandons his plan to leave his wife for her because a big storm is brewing and he must get his family and two of every animal onto a boat.

Act III begins with an announcement that several actors have fallen ill and are being replaced by dressers and extras drafted against their will. It ends with

Sabina, back in maid costume, beginning her first soliloquy again but then interrupting herself to say, "This is where you came in. We have to go on for ages and ages. The end of the play isn't written yet." The Antrobus family, in the cyclical nature of all mankind's existence, has survived past (and will survive future) millennia—by the skin of their teeth.

—B.P.*

WILDER KNEW the atom bomb was coming. He knew we were in trouble. One of the most famous lines in America is "We got through the Depression by the skin of our teeth." People got through the Ice Age and the Flood by the skin of their teeth, too. But Wilder wants to lift the atmosphere. He doesn't want it to be so heavy and dark as O'Neill—not deep, deep tragedy. The other person who wanted to lift the playgoing atmosphere was Chekhov, because he also knew what was coming—the revolution. Everybody could have his head knocked off. So he lightened it up. When a man finds a way to laugh, to lift it, he has universality.

Wilder says we'll get through it. He loved the theater. He said, "Let it breathe!" Life during the Depression had great cruelty. The country was in passionate difficulty. People wanted to push the great passions down. They wanted their theater to be soothing. Thornton Wilder was an intellectual. He resented the middle class's strength, and so what he did was to break it open and write the most middle-class play ever written. *The Skin of Our Teeth* carries to a logical conclusion the relation of what is apparently trivial to what is very grandiose.

Mr. and Mrs. Antrobus of Excelsior, New Jersey, are Adam and Eve.

* *The Skin of Our Teeth* premiered at the Plymouth Theatre in New York on November 18, 1942, and ran for 359 performances. Directed by Elia Kazan, it starred Tallulah Bankhead (Sabina), Florence Eldridge (Mrs. Antrobus), Fredric March (Mr. Antrobus), and Montgomery Clift (Henry).

They become renaissance figures but they are also the neighbors next door. Wilder is capable of merging huge periods of history with the present. He depicts the rise from primitive ignorance and connects it to the continuing problems of survival.

In the first act, the characters are pitted against destructive forces of nature—the Ice Age. Everybody's asked to help. The audience is asked to give them chairs to keep the fires burning. In the second act, man is against the moral order. In the third act, against himself.

A typical American family serves as the model. This allegory, the sense of story, is a theatrical expression of incredible fantasy. At the outset, man—Mr. Antrobus—is very, very excited as he arrives home from his office because he has invented the wheel and the alphabet. Wilder puts man into situations in which there can be burlesque and vaudeville, combined with anything else you like. You move from period to period. Man learns very little from experience, but he has the power to go on laughing and hoping. He cannot just retire from it all and permit chaos to be triumphant.

Now the Ice Age comes right down to 1940, with the Depression. All the characters play actors as well as their characters. From time to time, they break and stop being characters and come down and say, "I don't know what this goddamn play is about. I just don't understand what he wants. I don't know whether we're in the Cave Age or whether we're in 1939. I wish he'd tell me. I can't figure it out."

So the play confuses the actors, which is funny. An actress is painted as a yo-yo, a dumbbell. There's a great Shaw story about a young sot who could find no profession. His father asks, "What would you like to be?" He doesn't know. So the father says, "I think we'll make you an actor." Which is to say, "You're a dumbbell." Actors and playwrights in other parts of the world are given state funerals. One great French working-class actor was given a state funeral in the sky—in an airplane over Paris—with the president on board. Europe understands the importance of the artist. We don't. The artist gets a very, very tough deal here.

The Skin of Our Teeth is based on European sensibilities. You can call it surrealism or expressionism: the changing of sets, the switching of characters, going from young to old, talking to the audience, stepping down to the front. We have used all these things since the 1930s—but not before.

What does Wilder use in the play? He uses burlesque and *com-*

media dell'arte. The father, for instance, has five or six characters. Nineteenth-century plays were conventional, with single characters and boxed-in sets. American theater stayed in the nineteenth century well into the twentieth century, until the thirties. We were boxed in. The Europeans weren't.

I went to see an English production of *Cats* recently. My God, what they did. There's no stage, no audience, no walls. It is all for the cats. The cats are up on the ceiling. There's a scene when one of the people-cats dies and they take her in a chariot through the theater, right up through the roof. The ceiling opens, the clouds come out, and she steps into heaven. It is just fabulous, the scenic part of what they do. Technology happened early in the European theater. They used it. We didn't in America. I don't understand why. We saw it but didn't use it.

The title of Wilder's play gives you the whole thing: "We got by, by the skin of our teeth." There was no food, no fire, no jobs, nothing to eat. The only way they can have food is if the dinosaurs help out somehow. Somebody asks the maid if she has milked the mammoth yet. It is all without any sense of our reality. Then, in the second act, it goes to our reality. It goes back and forth, back and forth.

You must always know your playwright, always. If not, you will not know your play. Wilder thinks man has behaved in an absurd way—not in a rotten way, not in a stinking way, not in a filthy way. He just says absurd. He softens it. Man has behaved that way, but Wilder thinks he is worthy of surviving. Even with the Depression, even with the war. He knows Hiroshima is coming. He still thinks man is worth survival. But instead of putting it in drastic terms he puts it into funny terms, as an author and as a citizen of the world. He feels that man has to be saved. He is deliberately old-fashioned. His characters talk like old-fashioned actors did in America. That was considered good acting. It could be considered great acting.

What has man done? He cheats, he steals, he tries to beat his neighbor, he makes war, he sells armaments. He sends our boys to Japan. They're going to be killed by the steel we sent to Japan because we wanted Japan's money. That steel is going to shoot our kids. That is what is absurd. Do you know this? We send armaments to countries all over the world, and they kill us with our own armaments. We want to be rich, so we do that and we don't stop doing that. It's absurd.

Wilder is very worried about the coming extinction of man. He is able to put it into funny words. The play has a lot of old-fashioned vaudeville, very risqué. It's low comedy, and a little on the vulgar side sometimes.

First we have the characters Adam and Eve. Who else would we have first? The name Antrobus means all mankind. Maggie Antrobus represents Eve, and Sabina is Lilith. In the old rabbinical literature, Lilith was the first wife of Adam, who refused to be subservient and ran away from him. That's why the name Lilith is never given to a girl. You will never find a boy named Cain or a girl named Lilith or Medea. The baggage is too much. She was Adam's first wife, but she was banished and became a demon, and a demon can't be a wife.

The second wife remembers when he wedded the other one. She says, "You married her, you son of a bitch!" So they represent Adam and Eve and Lilith. Eve is the legitimate wife. But he took Lilith, some time during the second marriage, and put her back into the house. He really screwed around. And Maggie is mighty pissed off about it.

From one side of each character to another, they are very difficult, very interesting, very human, very intense. There are moments when they reach great tragic heights, as in *Our Town*. The comedy doesn't disturb the tragic element. George Antrobus is Adam, but he is also a burlesque comedian, an American businessman, and a scientist. He invents the wheel and the alphabet. When things get absolutely terrible and the whole place is going to pieces he says, "Break all the furniture." He even takes seats from the audience and the audience has to stand up and doesn't know what's happening. He says, "We gotta build a fire—burn everything except Shakespeare!" He has a sense of scholarship. He has the time of his life and then, in the second act after there's the flood, he has to rebuild the whole world. He's very proud of his inventions, very proud of culture. That's Wilder. He says Antrobus is cultivated. The intellectual side of man's nature he never leaves out of any characters, except in the working class, because he doesn't think the working class has a chance with culture. If you're farming or working all day and night, you don't have time to take in anything cultural.

The other side of culture—the instinctive, intuitive understanding of life—comes from Adam. If you really wanted to ask a very tough question, you used to go to your grandmother. That's the tradition. Your grandmother would tell you the right answer. She understood. That's a culture that comes through living, through doing, through having been a girl, a mother, then a grandmother. You accumulate a certain kind of knowledge.

Sabina doesn't accumulate any knowledge. Just give her a hat, she'll bleach her hair, and she's happy. She's the woman who has no mind and doesn't acquire one. Give most actresses a bauble and they're happy. Look at Elizabeth Taylor. Elizabeth's the smartest girl in the world but not very cultured. Yet she knows things nobody knows. She knows how to get her first husband back to be her third husband. She has the wisdom of the great-great-grandmother with seven children and twenty-two animals. She has accumulated wisdom of the peasant kind.

Wilder remembers and laughs at that kind of wisdom when he gives you the speech of the professor. You don't understand a word. It's convoluted. It's said with crazy words people don't understand, so they put it away. He says they take it in without finding the truth. Culture is finding the truth in science, music, theater—the truth. Scholars don't necessarily find the truth; that's why they are limited. A scholar will tell you a lot about the one aspect he's majoring in or teaching, but chances are he can't really tell you about the whole thing. A scholar in the university can talk about the literary side of a play but not about the histrionic side, the acting side. They just can't do that. They don't know it, which is why studying theater in a college is a waste of time. They don't know how light affects an actor; they don't know how a partner affects a scene. They don't know how to bring that out.

Wilder is a scholar and a drunk. He's an Irish bum. He's a businessman and he's afraid of the police because he does crooked deals. He's like many men. So he doesn't paint Adam the way we think of him, or Eve as the homemaker. She keeps the home, but she's tough about it. She's the mother of Henry and Henry killed his brother. Cain killed Abel. There are two sides of man. One is the good side that wants to create a good world. The other wants to destroy people and make wars and steal and rape. The papers are full of the other side of man. We buy those papers because most of us don't use that side of ourselves, but we like to read about it. That's what sells. The public doesn't usually want or get a chance to rape and steal and betray and plot wars and be a spy. All of us are respectable except the business people. They understand what they're doing. You tell them they sold more ammunition against El Salvador and Nicaragua than against the Nazis, and they'll say, "Yes, we know that. So what?"

The home now is the same as before. Maggie is Eve and she's like other mothers, only she's more intense and not as civilized. Her family is not civilized. So, you have to play it with vaudeville, burlesque, and all that. You don't come in with a housedress and an apron that was invented by a servant. You don't dress like ordinary people. You dress like the actors *think*. Adam comes in; he's just been whoring around—he's late. Do you remember that the man is always late, how Wilder puts that in every play? They say he's late because something has happened to him. Nothing has happened to him; he's just been out whoring.

In France there's the hour called *l'heure bleu,* from five to seven, in which a man leaves his office and disappears for two hours. That's when he goes to the other little house where he has the other little girl and he has the other kind of sex and all the other things that he can't get at home. It's better than our way.

Home is now called Excelsior, but it's still Grover's Corners—a lower-class Grover's Corners, where the struggles go on in the lower side of man. The Greeks call it the Dionysian side. The Dionysian side is when you want to give in to your rotten impulses, and the Apollonian side is when you want to create poetry and music and the brotherhood of man.

Sabina is a descendent of Lilith, who was thrown out because she couldn't make a home. She didn't have the children and she didn't do what was supposed to be done. But the one thing she could do was put on a hat and rouge and get all the fellows—and become an actress. She didn't want the home. She hates being in the house. It's like poison to her because it has furniture and windows to clean. She's a coward. She's frightened. She has no intellect. She just needs things to make her happy. Her philosophy is, don't worry about anything. You've got ice cream on your plate? Just finish the ice cream and that's it. Enjoy yourself, have a good time.

That's what Wilder wants, too. Go to the movies. Be happy. All the lower instincts are represented by Sabina. She goes into the husband's tent and tries to seduce him. We get to a monologue where she describes her feelings, which are Wilder's feelings. By making her so lowbrow, he makes you understand that there really is no time for serious drama anymore. When you use lowbrow characters, serious drama is finished. Ibsen, Shaw, Strindberg all say that. You can't make a country from the intellect of the working class. Sabina says she could be a star—not in a crazy play like this, but in all the "great" commercial plays. You just don't get them anymore.

Catastrophe is always there, or lurking. Something always goes wrong. The Ice Age or death or divorce or the failure of your business or the government. The banks go bankrupt. There's no way to buy anything. People really are just getting along by the skin of their teeth.

Wilder shows you another side of the middle class and how they live: all of these people are different and they fight, but not like in other plays. Sabina and the lady of the house really go at each other. But they have to be together in the end. Nobody can live alone, and Sabina is such a coward, and the Ice Age is coming. It's very melodramatic. What does Wilder say a man has to have in order to survive?

Wilder's idea is that man has to have a *mind.* He must develop his mind. He has to love in every way that he can, but he also has to lust. This means he has to pick up a girl and take her somewhere. In Paris, they have these two-hour rooms: they give you a towel and whatever you need, and then you go home. In France, the pickup is done very nicely, because you go to a very clean place and have your sex. Wilder thinks man has to have that. He says that although God made the world, he left the running of it to man.

Man then had the problem of making a world psychologically, which meant that he had to use his feelings, his heart and his mind. He had to be responsible. That is the activity of a human being that is determined by his psychological dimension, but he makes mistakes, because inside he's very confused. Man has made every mistake possible to destroy himself. But he's also gone to the moon. I think that is the greatest event. It's worthwhile having lived with the atom bomb just to have seen that. I watched it on TV. I saw Armstrong stepping down and going on to the moon. My husband, Mitchell Wilson, was a physicist and understood the inner workings. How he cried because of the complexity of it! I didn't cry, but he cried because he understood what that performance was. I cry when there is a good Hamlet.

Wilder says, difficult as it is to admit, man has a destructive impulse and it's always there. We have in us destruction and we have to work like hell to keep it down. A man wants to get drunk and he wants to study and he can't study if he's drunk. He can't go to work if he's drunk. He wants to love one woman and there's another woman there and he's just as attracted to the other woman, and now he's limited. It's complicated.

My father was incredibly handsome, not to be believed. Big, tall, white hair. When he went on the stage the whole audience got up and cheered. My mother said, "When your father first put his hand on me, I felt a reaction that was powerful. And if I felt it, then other women feel it." That's the wisdom of a wise mother. Not "He's a rotten son of a bitch!" Then you're jealous—another murderous thing. Shakespeare wrote a whole play about jealousy as a lower instinct. You've got to get over that, because it still exists—my God, it's one of the things that exist in your crowd and age bracket especially. The jealousy of men and women ruins any home. When you are jealous, you see signs that aren't there. He says, "I'm going out to the grocery." She says, "Who are you going to meet?" He says, "I heard you talking to that man in French. What did you do, make a date?" She says, "He only speaks French, so I talked to him in French, for chrissakes!" It's a sickness; a lower sickness, in Othello. Shakespeare kills him off.

When the flood comes, this is what's funny—by accident there's a boat there. It just happened to be there. And it just happens that the two-by-two animals are all there, too. He didn't actually do anything or arrange anything. There's a flood, so he just takes in the animals and, being a very nice guy, takes them and his family. So there you are with Noah's Ark. That's the way Wilder handles history—by accident. He doesn't say it's the Bible, just gives you that little reference. It's so lowbrow that it's interesting. He's such a great liar. Oh, there's a boat? Let's get in.

There's a certain part where the actors don't want to act. They're supposed to play Socrates and Euripides and all the Greek philosophers, but they don't want to act, so the wardrobe mistress and the ushers and the dressers have to act. They're happy to serve because they're needed; they're the saviors. That's very funny, because they don't know how to act. Can you imagine an usher getting up or a maid with a duster saying, "I'll be Romeo—or Lady Macbeth—tonight"? The actors get sick, so the others take over. Why not? It's the end of the world, and you have to make it look as if the world will go on.

That's burlesque. Henry is trying to make clear that there is a base aspect of man's drives. He tries to clear himself and say that's just a part of man, an inner power that drives him. The fight against the parents is, "No, I don't want to be like you." In this play, they even deny who their parents are when they're on the street. The first anti-social drive is to break from the parents. Wilder shows you that it's serious; there is a plea to you, begging you to understand that side of him that killed his brother. The side of you that wants to lust, cheat, sell out. He is pleading for you to see that side, too. The intellec-tual Wilder is saying something that should emotionally move you: "Understand me, I'm bad."

There is a great deal about the glaciers. The play opens with the Ice Age. The ice stopped at a certain point. Where I live in the country, there is one side that the ice didn't touch—the side you can grow flow-ers on. There are trees. On the beach side, you can't grow anything. They call it the scrub side. The Ice Age was real and it did affect us.

A great deal happened from then to the Second World War. So unforgivable, the First World War. Wilder went to war. We had a real political civil war of our own here, before that. The North wanted to free the slaves? No, we just wanted to get them for one cent more than the South; they remained slaves. They were called niggers. They still are. That's part of the absurd side of man. Other people call it the crooked side of the North or South. All wars and revolutions are political. How does Wilder deal with it? When things get very bad he says, "Make coffee, build a fire, burn the furniture, get the strang-ers in, and let's sing!" It's Excelsior, New Jersey, but it's also the Cave Age. He says you have to use common sense to overcome the disasters of the world. The flood, the storm, the atom bomb? We'll see what we can do. Make coffee and try to get it together again. He thinks man *will* get it together. Part of the defeat of your generation is your subconscious feeling that you could be wiped out. That's why you have no enthusiasm. Certain things happened in the last generation with the war and the bomb that have affected the eternal belief in God, in oneself.

Mrs. Antrobus is proud of her husband. She is very insulting to his opposition. The play opens up with the Ice Age coming over. They are scared to death. The walls are closing in on Sabina. One wall comes right up to her.

Sabina has lived under these difficulties since Adam. She has gone through all of them. But she still has a good time if she goes out: has an ice cream soda, a couple of drinks, has a guy, has some sex—that's what she wants. The living room has literally no scenery. You could draw a door. Get used to drawing it, so you know what the characters can do. They can walk out of the windows; not naturally look out the windows—they can just walk through them. We get in this play none of the usual reality.

Reread Sabina's monologue to get used to the style, the language in which he wrote: "Oh, oh, oh! Six o'clock and the master not home yet. Pray God nothing serious has happened to him crossing the Hudson River. If anything happened to him, we would certainly be inconsolable and have to move into a less desirable residence . . . I don't know what'll become of us. Here it is the middle of August and the coldest day of the year. It's simply freezing; the dogs are sticking to the sidewalks."

Then she gets angry and says, "Does anybody understand this?" The audience says no, and she says, "Neither do I." She's so angry with the playwright. She's an actress. She sat in her room. She didn't have a job for a couple of years. She took any part they gave to her. She took this crazy job and she hates it. She has to play it in this style. She doesn't know this style. So she goes in and out and does terrible things.

"The whole world's at sixes and sevens and why the house hasn't fallen down—Ahhh!" It starts to. Then the scenery goes back. She says, "Why the house hasn't fallen down about our ears long ago is a miracle. I don't understand it." She doesn't like the way the scenery is behaving. "In the midst of life, we are in the midst of death . . . Ahh!" She's paralyzed because another piece of scenery falls down. She doesn't know if it's going to kill her. The scenery goes back in place and she feels a little better.

She begins again. But she hates this play. She hates what she has to say: "Of course, Mr. Antrobus is a very fine man, an excellent husband and father, a pillar of the church, and has all the best interests of the community at heart . . ." Now the bitch comes out. She doesn't want to move to a cheaper neighborhood. That's Sabina's character. She thinks the playwright is crazy. She doesn't understand this one bit.

Wilder puts you first in one period and then in another—it's insane. "The whole world is at sixes and sevens." This is the kind of a drama—more than any other I know—that will teach you not to play only one side of a character. Every author has quite a number of sides and Wilder gives you all of his. He was a writer, a great teacher, a linguist. He wrote plays, novels, many things on different subjects. Don't just know one side of him. And don't just play one side of his characters.

Sabina says she understands both sides of man. She understands that Mr. Antrobus is very respected—he invented the wheel, after all—but he's many-sided. It has to be done with charm. Light—even when she falls against a proscenium arch and screams. When she crosses herself, she gets mixed up. "What is it—how do you . . . ? I don't know how to cross myself. God, which way does it go?" Slow down for those things. She shows her bosom to the audience. When she gets down by the chair to dust, she's in a little lacy skirt; pick it up so they see your backside. Look at a big mirror that isn't there. Take time to find her needs. He has given you the part; you have to fill it. Don't think the words are the part; the words are nothing. In a monologue like that, you must do fifty things with the duster. You must be able to take it and make a hat out of it—"Oh, I'm so worried!"—using a duster for a hat. You don't know where the pole is? Then you dust without a pole; it isn't necessary to *have* a pole in order to dust it! Find the pole in your imagination, and then dust it and the world. It's important to burlesque everything. I don't teach burlesque, but if you can find somebody to come in and teach you, you should. Learn about the speech. "The master is not home yet!" People don't talk like that. That's phony talk of another period. Wilder is making fun of the way they used the English language. It's camp.

You find out a lot about Mr. Antrobus from Sabina. He is a big shot. He goes to meetings. It means he's not home anymore, which makes her angry. You get the dangers of the big town when he goes to the meetings. The son is as stupid as he always was. You get the daughter right away: she wants a handsome, stupid, rich man—she's the historical "other woman." When you see prostitutes in Paris, you get a clear sense of what she is: she is where she's supposed to be—where the wives can see her. Since the men go to the museums with their wives, that's where they see the prostitutes. They're not in corners. They are very handsome, charming girls, very well made up. Something in the way they stand around—the men know that's a prostitute. The girls have signals.

Fredric March and Florence Eldridge as Mr. and Mrs.
Antrobus with Tallulah Bankhead as Sabina—now Miss
Atlantic City 1942—in Act II of *The Skin of Our Teeth*

I remember when I was in North Africa, the women all had long
curls. The man I was with said, "Oh, that girl is a prostitute." I said,
"How do you know? She's dressed like everybody else in a long skirt."
He said, "Don't you see the way she's swinging her bag?"

Great signal!

Man is stupid. He has a smart side but he has the other side. He
enjoys disaster. He likes going to war. It's exciting to a man. I asked
a student once, "How did your father become a general? Didn't he
know he was going to lead people to war? What kind of a profession is that?" "Big men" understand something I don't understand. I
wouldn't be in a profession where I had to teach men how to go to war.
But I suppose if you don't have a general, you don't have a country.
Every country has an army.

You understand in *Skin of Our Teeth* that the family situation has
been the same since Adam. You can't break it up. The children are the
same. Sabina is the same eternal maid-mistress who has no problem

but to go to parties and seduce men and get telephone calls and go out to lunch. She does that at twenty, twenty-five. If she does it at thirty, she's going to end up being the maid for good. She could get a job but she doesn't want to work. She's an actress. Why should she work? Wilder says Adam pulls through because he is Everyman, and Everyman is a superior being. What does Sabina do that infuriates him? She lets the fire go out, the fire that keeps the inside safe from disaster—the children, the husband. That's why he built the home. That's why he made the fire—to keep them all alive. If she lets it go out, is she fit to be in a home?

He says, "You have done the worst thing in the world; you have exposed the inside—it's the family's death. You will never understand what a wife does. A wife, in order to keep that home going, will go out and borrow fire and risk death to keep the family alive." Sabina falls to her feet and says, "We'll die without you." She can't live without the person who knows how to keep the fire going. She begs Maggie not to go out, but the wife has no fear. She will risk her life for the family. The mistress won't. She has no responsibility. She has nothing but herself to take care of. Sabina is very young and doesn't grow up. If she plays in Ibsen, she grows up. If she lives long enough, she grows up like her grandmother; she grows up by the simple experience of life.

But at the end of the play, when Antrobus has lost the most important thing of all—the desire to begin again, to start rebuilding—it is Sabina who is life and virtue and sex and self-interest and love and deception: everything that woman is. She is the one who prepares to go to the movies, and she will work with him if he has any ideas about improving the crazy ol' world. Forget that it was—and is—such a struggle.

"All I ask is the chance to build new worlds and God has always given us that second chance"—always made us struggle. Although we forget, he reminds us. All these years, one struggle after another. "We've come a long ways."

Sabina comes downstage to tell the audience good night. She assures everybody that they have plans and are sure to start again.

Wilder deals with the most commonplace, the most trivial, in many ways but is enormously profound at the same time. His work has a very simple philosophy: live every moment of your life, because life is beautiful—the tragedy is human wastefulness. He is a writer who is comfortable in a comic vein, but his plays have a grand scale. He uses theater to make clear our mistakes from birth to death. Let's finish with a statement of his that I love:

"I am interested in the drives that operate in society and in every man. Pride, avarice, and envy are in every home. I am not interested in the ephemeral—such subjects as the adulteries of dentists. I am interested in those things that repeat and repeat and repeat in the lives of the millions."

CLIFFORD ODETS

Clifford Odets

EIGHT

WAITING FOR LEFTY

(1935)

SYNOPSIS OF *WAITING FOR LEFTY:*
The action takes place in the Depression, unfolding in
eight episodes. In the prologue, taxi drivers are debating a strike. A union official, Harry Fatt, is against
it. One of the men calls him a "red" and says he will
betray them. A war veteran, Joe, says he favors a strike
and wonders if everyone involved will be labeled a
Communist. Others ask where their real elected leader
is—the mysteriously absent Lefty.

A flashback reveals Joe and his wife arguing about
the strike in their home, where all the furniture has
been repossessed and the children have gone to bed
without supper.

In the next episode, industrialist Fayette informs
Miller, a lab assistant, that he's getting a raise, a promotion, and a new boss, Dr. Brenner. They'll be working on poison gas for chemical warfare in preparation
for "the new war." Miller is agitated; his brother died
from being gassed in the last war. Fayette also wants
a weekly confidential report on Dr. Brenner. Miller
refuses. They argue violently.

Florrie is going to a dance that night with Sid,
but her brother Irv objects—saying Sid doesn't make

enough money driving a taxi. Sid arrives and tells Florrie he knows her family hates him and that she no longer wants to marry him. He's sick of being poor and at the mercy of powerful men. Florrie pledges her devotion. They dance, and when the music ends, she weeps.

Back in the strike room, Fatt introduces Clayton to the group. He was part of a failed strike in Philadelphia and says Fatt is right about not striking. A man rushes up and denounces Clayton as a spy and a union breaker. Clayton denies it, but the accuser has proof—and says Fatt knows it.

Next comes Dr. Benjamin, an intern upset to be taken off charity-ward surgery and replaced by a bad doctor. He is summoned by Dr. Barnes, who has even worse news: the charity ward is to be closed; the hospital is losing too much money. Staff will be fired, including Benjamin, because he is Jewish. Barnes gets a phone call: the woman Benjamin was to operate on is dead. Benjamin says he now sides with the radicals.

An old man named Agate Keller speaks to the drivers, chastising them for being weak. They must unite and fight. "What are we waiting for?" he asks. Lefty may never come. A worker rushes in with the news that Lefty has been shot to death. Agate exhorts them to make a new world. The workers in unison yell, "STRIKE!"

—B.P.*

---

* *Waiting for Lefty,* produced by The Group Theatre, opened at the Longacre Theatre in New York on March 26, 1935, running 144 performances. Co-directed by Clifford Odets and Sanford Meisner, it featured Lewis Levitt (Joe), Russell Collins (Fatt), Elia Kazan (Agate Keller), Paula Miller (Florrie), and Odets himself (Dr. Benjamin). The production moved to the Belasco Theatre on September 9, 1935, playing there in repertory with *Awake and Sing!* for 24 additional performances, with Luther Adler taking over the role of Dr. Benjamin.

O N   T H E   F I R S T   R E A D I N G , read for the anatomy of the play. This is Odets's first to be produced. It was very important. It still is.

It opens with Fatt trying to show the failure of strikes and to sell the idea that the government is right—the strike breakers should put their bets on the government. "All we workers got a good man behind us now," he says, trying to convince them that the situation is taken care of, that the country is in good shape. The other side is arguing to destroy that order, to say they are being trapped by the government and they can't get out. They all belong to this world that they want to preserve or destroy.

When some disgruntled guy says the country is on the blink, Fatt has a new purpose: to show up that bum! Then there is a transition where he wants to get them all out. So you have Fatt's action: to kibosh the strike, to prove the country is in good shape, to expose the bums, and to get everybody out of there.

Another voice says "Says you!" and Fatt's gunman says, "Sit down, punk!" and another voice says "Where's Lefty?" Fatt says, "That's what I wanna know. Where's your pal, Lefty? You elected him chairman— where the hell did he disappear?" The men yell, "We want Lefty! Lefty!"

The crowd is made up mostly of people who want to strike, and Fatt gets excited about putting them down, telling them to leave, trying to establish order. There is a platform with people on it, and they are talking a kind of fouled-up language—strong, rough and tough. It's English, but not as properly spoken. Here's a fresh guy who can't speak English, and he's talking about very big subjects: governments, strikes, steel. It's great ideas in the mouths of Tenth Avenue taxi drivers: "Hey, look out there, you son of a bitch!" It's got a slogan quality. A slogan is theatrical. It's bandwagon and barker stuff, like "Uncle Sam Needs You!"

That's your impression from the text. Fatt doesn't respect people.

"Who the hell are you?" A man like that will punch a woman in the jaw if he gets angry. He does what he wants. It isn't so much what he says; it's his whole approach to the individual—showing up "those lice" who disagree with him. It lets him degrade the bigness. He can take the biggest thing in the world and crush it.

From impressions like these, you will be able to find what to do, not just what to say. Fatt is the kind of guy who throws rocks at you. He's got brass knuckles. What kind of body does a man like that have? It's not loose. Nothing about him is loose; it's tight. "Your mother is a whore!" he'll say. You never heard such language in your life. It's a stream of dirt connected with men, family, religion. He tears down, he destroys. But when he starts to "expose" the bums, something happens. There is a sudden transition. At this point, the mass is coming at him. If I played the part, I'd imagine the men as lions and tigers coming at me.

So then Fatt gets more conciliatory: "Now listen, we can't stay here all night . . . You boys got hot suppers to go to." Different tune. "Where's your pal, Lefty? . . . Where the hell did he disappear? . . . What the hell is this—a circus?"

Animals aren't a bad choice of images. It's a circus with the animals breaking out. You have action and characters dealing with a large subject; it's a mass of wild, untamed elements here. The opening night of this play, after the curtain went down, the audience stood on their chairs and shrieked and threw things for a solid fifteen minutes. To control that thing happening in the audience would have been like controlling a zoo. The play has a rabble-rousing quality that is very dangerous. It tries to address one idea: should they strike or shouldn't they?

From the technical blocking of the play, you get the impression; from the impression you get character; from character you get reshaping of the action. You cannot play the bare thing, to mock or belittle them. Corner them—do something physical. When you analyze the style, you see there is very little detail. You get an impression or two from the slogans. Use them. This form is very economical. The American playwright didn't create a brand-new form or style of writing. Odets took all the forms, put them together, and used them.

Fatt is trying to sell them the White House. To peddle the White House is a very different thing than to reveal the White House. It loses its epic nature. You are conning. Pick the action that gets them; sell them the pipe dream. He's reducing the White House to his terms. What is the White House to him? It's a place where you get money. His name is Fatt—the greasy stuff that runs out. It's symbolic, no?

It's that cunning, that real gangster thing, that has to be revealed. He's trying to slip out, ease his way out. You have to corner him. The action should be physical—he has to retreat. In the action lies the doing; in the doing lies the character. He sees that the workers are starting to get violent. "Where's your pal, Lefty?" He does there what the man in the middle of the fights does—he referees. You use them and leave them. Steal from them, but get out of the circus. It'll lead you to Bellevue if you stay in a circus.

They are getting ready to attack him. To reestablish order comes from his character, which is snarly and dirty. He wants Lefty, too—but to kill him. He's going to arrange to have a lot of these fellows killed. He knows these boys. He knows his enemies. It's about life and death. People aren't striking for *pizzacaca.* They're fighting for their lives. The single man represents everything. Fatt is the symbol of the gangster. The little man has inherited the big struggle. Expressionism has in it the largest form for the smallest individual. Every individual has in him the cosmic burden of the world.

When the girl Florrie says, "I want to love, I want love, I want to go out with Joe," it means Odets has him set up as all the lovers of the world—with all the love there is. "I would bring you fifty dozen roses—tall ones!" It's not realism. He gets down, he plays music to romance her. Get the background, get the family of workers.

When you speak of Lefty, think of a man and a family that have been on picket lines, in the rain together, at the kid's funeral when they all had to chip in money to bury him. It's the family, it's the class, it's everything about him. This is what we use as background to stimulate the actor. Learn how to use life for the play. These people don't go to museums or libraries; they don't talk about makeup or "relationships." There is nothing really individual about them. There is a sense of personal catastrophe within the group, but there is no sense of privacy. It's as if all these workers never had any place where they were just one person alone.

The thing you get from the middle class is family interiors and picnics. Here you get only a group thing. With Florrie, there is no place for two people to be together. They steal their private moments.

The leadership, by comparison, is way different in proportion. Nothing about these "big men" is human. As a class, they are wounded, clubbed. If I were a worker here, I would do what Odets wants: I would appear as a scarred man—the sense of wounded, beaten up, mutilated. The workers have the mass energy that any mass has, but as individuals they are wounded. They have a mass uprightness but an individual feebleness, brokenness, an ability to get themselves messed up. They are destined for personal violence.

The individual is not a force. It's only the mass that is a force. The play says, "Get together and do something about it." Clifford makes them strong when they're all together as a mass, and individually he makes them fight for an individual life. The boy lives with the fact that he and Florrie are cornered. He knows it. It's like living with one arm missing. He knows that they're cornered in this way.

When those people are left alone, they drift off. They are the dreamers. The boy who says, "Gee, Ma, I wanna be a drummer"—it's no good offering him concrete things. He's a talker. If you give him something real to do, he'll drink. He dresses differently. He has feeling for life. He isn't ashamed to say, "You'd look beautiful in roses!" He's shameless. He's high on his dream. When John Garfield played him, he had that thing. He was naive. You could tell him anything. He trusted everything. He had this free, wonderful, open-hearted, childish smartness. Otherwise he couldn't play the game with her. For a brief time it's like they're in a dream.

The poet may not be very useful in the trade-union movement, but he's part of it. Odets reveals to you that the union was made up of people like this, too. It was "agitprop"—a Bolshevik term in the twenties and thirties for agitation propaganda. By putting in the off-center character, he captured the poetry of a taxi driver. They have dreams, too. He knew their language and their poetry. Paula Miller played Florrie in the original production, and when she argued with you, it was as sweet as toothpaste. She got angry and nasal, but it was soft, touching. You can't play little Florrie as a fresh girl. Be careful how you build that part. Odets builds very well for the actor. He constructs a part so well, you can't get out of it.

Take the Lab Assistant Episode. Something happens at the mention of "poison gas"—a change in action for Miller. He comes out of his ethereal world to the dirty details of life. Fayette brings him into his office from a laboratory. Miller says he's never seen an office like that outside the movies. He's never even been in the office—he has been kept in the background before. If I had to dress him, I would make him look like a drugstore man in a pharmacy—they have the uniform and the faces of men who deal with chemicals, they're neutral-looking. He's straight. Anything a little bit off, he sees. He doesn't laugh at it—he just remarks that it looks like a movie set.

You see that this man speaks simply and truthfully, that he lives in a simple world and that the other man's world is made up of fancy talk that isn't true. Fayette feels he can expound large principles whether they're right or wrong. He goes off into the possibilities of steel, that whole impersonal world—Mr. and Mrs. Consumer, big business, advertising, sales volume, market's up flush against a stone wall . . . big gateways ahead. You decide whether he is just naive or whether he really knows. I think Fayette is a man that knows. He deals with large entities—"workers . . . pollacks . . . niggers."

But there is a switch in Miller at that point. The moment he hears Fayette say "poison gas," the whole cover comes off. He's in an area he understands. He is a symbol of how much a man can contain and not show. He's almost a zero in the beginning. You can play him as totally detached then. He's been functioning like a dead man. But at the mention of poison gas, from now on, he's analyzing.

One day I was walking in an alley in Venice and I saw an old man coming toward me and said to myself, "If that man didn't look so tired and old and poor and neglected, he could be Stravinsky." And it *was* Stravinsky! He looked so beaten up by life, but it was actually Stravinsky. Until you touch off the intellectual understanding, he is nothing. He's just somebody off into his own world, and the rest of the world is ping-pong.

The game of spying—to get a man to do that seems easy, but it's not. Miller reads nothing but Andy Gump.* Fayette handles him like a baby for a while, until the poison gas and spy business. When a man's real power rises, all that came before is nothing. "You're dealing with sneaking, and I'm dealing with an American force!" Fayette is on the floor by the time Miller leaves. Don't play it just for sentiment, because Miller is not sentimental. You can't know how to build the beginning unless you know how the scene is going to end.

When we get to the romantic characters, you see that what they

* Henpecked hero of cartoonist Sidney Smith's popular, long-running (1917–1959) syndicated newspaper comic strip.

want—their quest for happiness through love—is a romantic ideal. Clifford says romantic idealism is part of the structure of the society he's dealing with. But you have to build the characters without sharp outlines. There is nothing sharp in ambition. It is not attainable. The experience of it is not realizable. Love, too, is something you can't take hold of. I want from love some of the perfume of a baby. A romantic attitude rather than a realistic attitude is what's in this form of play.

In the Interne Episode, Dr. Barnes is sitting in his office when young Dr. Benjamin bursts in and says the dying woman he was attending is to be operated on by the wrong man. He wants to fight and not take it lying down. The author's intent is to reveal that everybody is a victim of the corrupt society and that if you're in it too long, you acquiesce. If you are young, you can break through.

Dr. Barnes isn't young. He is involved with board meetings and policies. But Dr. Benjamin is concerned with real, inside "guts" medicine. He's involved personally, emotionally, and completely without all the structural stuff. If you're rushing to get your mother off a sinking boat and someone stops you and says, "You can't go on the boat," you say, "But my mother's on that boat! Don't you see my mother's on the boat?" And he says, "I'm sorry, the Cunard Line does not permit visitors; read that sign."

It's not human anymore, it's what the Cunard Line says—not what any human being would say. You've been removed from things. Barnes is talking rot; he is absolutely removed. You get the juxtaposition. It's like a kid knocking his head against a wall.

Benjamin is talking about medicine: that replacement doctor is "incompetent as hell." Barnes is talking about politics: "He's the Senator's nephew and there he stays." Then Barnes changes the subject to brain surgery. In a very English fashion, he says, "Let's stay with generalities." The business of medicine is a different thing from medicine. But Barnes finally snaps into medicine with, "Her life is in danger?" Benjamin gives that to him; his action is to get the doctor to *do* something.

Suppose you walk up to a director and say, "How dare you let that actress go on—she's lousy!" He says, "Don't talk to me like that. You don't have thirty thousand to put in the play and she has!" That's it, and the play goes on. You can't fix certain money things. That's just the way it is.

In order to play a queen and really play her, it's important to have an itch—something that humanizes, some human contradiction. Barnes becomes humanized. Finally, he says, "Someday it might cost you your head." He goes back to the personal as he did with "You mean she is in danger of dying?" The play changes. When the large aspect is opened to a man, he doesn't let go. He sees it. It's not just about "reasonable" anymore. It's bigger. Dr. Barnes's façade has been ulcerating in him. He needs whiskey to shake it off—and you need to find him. He is not a ready-made type.

For Dr. Benjamin, a whole way of life is now open. A complete switch from before. He's a universal man. Barnes now has in front of him a man called JEW. His size makes Barnes bigger, too—now they are both on epic terms. This is the play. It says that medicine is run by big business, and they've made something dirty out of me and they mustn't make this out of you. You see Benjamin rally to the ideas of a new world. This is the epic, colloquial power—a really great moment in the expressionistic theater. Benjamin takes the gloves off and Barnes says, "Go and fight! Do it!" It's a challenge to action.

How to costume the play? You have the dirt of the street in your hair; part of your job remains on you visibly. You never rid yourself of the work or the worker's body. You have to get a kind of rudeness into your body. I wouldn't handle a cup properly in this play. Your selection is very important. If you don't use the play's world, you are not an actor, because the play is taken from that world, not yours, and you have to go there to find it.

These are not brainy people, but they are people with enormous feelings. The eye is what they think with. It's hard for them when they take things in. Go to workers that you know. I would never, never show ankles in this thing. If I were young, I would wear cotton stockings that would give me a little thickness. Dirty nails would help me. Even if I were manicured, the polish would be chipped or my lipstick would be smeared.

Let's go to The Young Hack and His Girl episode: Florrie tells her brother Irv she's been working hard to take care of her sick mother but needs more out of life—from her boyfriend, Sid, who's coming to take her to a dance. Irv is dead set against the romance because Sid doesn't make much money as a cab driver. Sid enters and says he knows he is like "rat poison" to her family. Poverty has made him a defeatist.

With her mother, brother, bad working conditions, no money—she is trapped in every way. Her action is not really to get love, it's to get out of the trap. The things trapping her are small, and she wants something cosmic: to escape the family trap, the factory trap. She has a right to get out of that.

How are you going to act her? I want you to expose yourself from your affective memory—by stealing from your own life. "What are you watching my soul for?" Florrie says. As an actor, I can use that. I'm not ashamed to expose myself. From that I can go to, "Leave me alone, I want to get lost. It is not the boy that is trapping me; it's the *ideas*. I am fighting for a bigger life."

But don't play "fighting" as much as just "getting out of the trap." It's about not being able to go forward. She is a bird in a cage who can't fly out. Her voice is diminished. She has one tiny little corner she can run to. She has a cancerous mother, a boyfriend who brings home eight dollars a week. How can she fight? She doesn't want much out of life, just a little. She's a good girl. She talks about love—the most ephemeral thing in the world. She wants the atmosphere of it more, really, than the body of this cabbie Sid.

What is her brother Irv's action? Words are what you do, not you think. Why does he want to turn her against Sid? He is trying to take an action that he thinks is good for her. Their lives are fragmented, and each fragment has its place. There's the Mama fragment and there's the eight-dollars fragment—pieces of life. Don't act Irv as a lawyer trying to convince a jury. You have to be very humble to act. If you bring in any irrelevant action, you will be murdering a fine play. His whole thing is little. It's about their little life that can't be messed up. They can't have another person in the house—there's not enough food or coffee or milk. They're fighting for survival. Don't choose a big action for this boy. It's not what you want. He's on almost a baby level. They are two children. You can't play the brother or sister too hard. He knows she is dominated and under the rule of men. She knows she is not his equal.

When Sid comes in, she flies. This need to fly—to flee—has to be expressed in such a way that you can act it. Florrie wants to dance and love. "I don't smoke or drink," she says. Odets is reminding you that she wants a dream world, the dream things of life—the sweet things. She doesn't say, "I want a career" or "I want a fur coat." She wants dancing and love. She wants the myth.

With Sid, you get the opposite: he loves Florrie, but he knows the real world and his love are poisoned—rat-poisoned—by poverty. He feels bitter and beaten down about it. "The cards is stacked for all of us," he says. "The money man deals himself a royal flush and gives you and me a phony hand like a pair of tens." Sid lives in the stark reality. Florrie lives in her fantasies. Their two worlds can never get together. It's a conflict of elements and character. The conflict isn't, "I want things you don't want me to have." It's, "I want things you don't even understand."

Her outlines are soft, not sharp. It is difficult for her to face facts with him. This is a social play. Odets isn't saying she is the only one trapped. He says all girls are trapped. He says nobody in the working class really has time for love. The worker is about striking and fighting and maybe getting killed. The nuances aren't for him—love, babies, ball gowns, roses. She says, "You promised me a life, but you can't give it to me." Maybe you in the audience can achieve it, but she can't. Her wanting to get married and have a baby and a nice house is impossible—like Masha and Olga and Irina saying, "I want to go to Moscow."

Odets gives you an unsentimental boy and a very sentimental girl. What makes them so compelling is that earnest clash of sentimentality and honesty. The scene is embarrassing. It has a realistic feel, but it should not be played realistically. When two people talk like this, don't look for psychological motivation. The author is pushing you around. The style of the play suddenly goes from realism to something where you're free to do anything you want. You are playing characters that aren't real. They have taken their values from the movies, in a way. There's something oppressive and not nice about this game. It's almost like camerawork. Odets is giving you the culture through a camera, not through psychological motivation. You have to find it. They try to get out of the realities, so they go to something unreal, but they are trapped when they think romantically. It's not charming—there is something sickening about it. This whole class wants something out of life it can't get. The author says these people are dreamers who are not fit for the working class. They are sensitive, and if you take love away from them, you paralyze them. Odets says it's not in the cards for them to be down to earth. They are in a romantic quest, to get off the earth, to go higher than reality—which is not realistic.

If love is the chief thing in your life, it goes against the proletarian polemic. The polemic of the play says you've got to strike to make a better world. But these characters need more than money. Money alone can't save them. Florrie needs this illusion of love and romance. If you take that away, you kill her. These people get killed by their romanticism. The brother runs away. In not being able to carry out the dream that every man and woman has, they are victimized, crawling alone in the dark. People in love are "in the clouds," not on the real earth. These people are on the movie earth. It's sad, and Clifford is skillful to do it that way. He is in high gear.

Let the words lead you to character impressions, to actions, to situations. Only situations give you the value of the words.

Take the Labor Spy Episode: Fatt has an action without words. He's giving Clayton the floor. "Let's hear from someone who's got practical experience." His hope is for Clayton to win them over. There are lots of people, lots of voices. Everybody's action after the introduction—including the audience's—is to hear him out.

I once heard Roosevelt campaigning in Philadelphia, and one of the most important components was the audience listening. The other important action was of the bodyguards—guarding. When Clayton takes over to speak, somebody yells, "He's a spy!" Fatt's action turns to keeping control. He doesn't want a fight to start. Fatt tries to keep order, but the truth comes out.

What can he do now? He and his main witness have been exposed. He's trying to find a way out. It's like being told you have cancer in public: horrifying. Trace his emotion through the whole thing. The main thing you must do is relate to his circumstances. The style of the play calls for something very graphic. You can't just do an inner change. It's not Ibsen. You must always choose in terms of the style of play. It's as if somebody threw a pie in Fatt's face. Would he say "Oh God, what'll I do?" No. It's not that kind of play. In expressionism, you have to find that thing which is graphic. It's a heightened thing that you do. Fatt wants to keep control but he is beginning to lose it.

When a man goes into the ring to fight and takes a few punches, those are steps in a bigger situation. If you play it all separately, you'll need four plays. Fatt has one aim, which is to keep control. He's using Clayton to help show that he is right and the crowd is not right to interrupt him. Fatt's action is to keep them in place. Draw the steps together. Don't play them as separate things.

Who is Clayton? He gets up in front of a very rough crowd that is booing him. He's afraid the ax will fall. He must be a nervous wreck. It's hard to get up in front of an audience that is against you. He knows the situation. He's seen strikes before. He could get killed. Is he a strong man? Is he cornered? He's a yes man in a dangerous situation. He's a rat. You have to characterize him very strongly. He's got watery eyes, he's unattractive to women, he runs away when he is in danger. He's fanatical, in a way, but fanaticism needs size.

I saw a lot of those guys around progressive movements. They're the underminers. Big things always have little things around them. He's like a louse on a horse. He's fighting for life with "You're a liar!"—like a fish out of water, gasping for water instead of air. Once he is exposed, the lines can't be played logically anymore. Both sides are inflamed, now that everybody knows about him.

The Young Hack and His Girl are caught in a world they can't get out of. Fayette, the industrialist, has something he's preserving that is heading toward war. Fatt is trying to preserve the world in which he can be a racketeer and dominate the trade union. In each case there's a racket to be preserved. There's a war; the general is in it to get the promotion, the government is in it to make money—everyone is in it for a reason. You have to join the war, but you don't quite know what you're joining. People are expecting something wonderful to happen from this war, but they don't know what. The action for all of them is either to fight their way out of the trap or submit to it.

They all enter the scene as if they don't know what came before. They are caught in something that they don't know. That Lab Assistant Episode opens with a man who is working in no direction. He comes in already blocked out mentally, with the futility of work already instilled in him. He is released from his trap only when he says, "Now I see . . . the poison gas. . . . Now I have a reason to fight."

When you are consciously in it, you can fight. When you're unconsciously in it, you are a victim of something you don't realize. Once you have established the theme, draw from it. Miller exposes the whole situation—the big American principles of salesmanship and war. Fayette is aware of all aspects of it, too, but poison gas has a different connotation to him. He reveals the whole setup, very much as Fatt does.

The play isn't "I have my point of view, you have yours." It's about people who see society in its confusion and do something or nothing about it. You can't be in that world without fighting it or being a victim of it. You have to be pushed further and further until you say, "I've had enough." Your destiny is being laid out by the war. Other men have your destiny in their hands and they're playing with it. "You're making a spy of me and you want to give me twenty dollars?" What is the play about? "Stay in this trap, god damn you, and we'll use you!" Some people say no, we don't want to be used. Others, like Florrie, say we can't get out. Nobody can act in this play as though there weren't a trap, because the spine of the play—of every character and every situation—is to examine that trap and make a decision.

Fayette says, "I want you to rat on somebody . . . Niggers are good for digging ditches . . . You get a twenty dollar raise not for being a scientist but for being a spy . . . " All of which is un-American. If the group in control is in a trap, they want you to be in it, too. Everybody either challenges it or gives in. Benjamin says, "I don't give a damn, I've seen this at Harvard, but I'm going to be a doctor." He's going to join up. He says, "I've tried as an individual scientist, as an individual Jew, but now I'm going to get all my brothers together because I can't do it alone."

There are various tactics available. One is used by Marc Antony in *Julius Caesar,* when he says, "But Brutus is an honorable man." It's a way of exposing. How do you fight the stooges' tactics and expose the rat Clayton? Exposing is at the heart of much of the action here. Florrie and her boyfriend expose it. Barnes lays it bare and Benjamin says, "I see, it's clear to me now." They go from the trap to fighting it, after they take stock of the situation.

Every character in the play is caught in some situation. The situation is forcing them to change the world. What does it mean to fight, to strike, to struggle through to victory? The other side needs to control, to manipulate, to hold you in place. Fatt needs to keep them in line for himself, the agent, as well as for the industrialists, who need to hold on to their money and authority.

That's the conflict. It's not a conflict of individuals. It's bigger. The conflict and the climax have to flow together. If each scene is played differently, it's very hard on the audience. A great example of that "holding it together" idea is *Dr. Zhivago:* in the end, the crucial thing was to be part of the revolution. That had to happen with them all.

You have to get one thing that makes you act—not fifty things—to set it straight, to put the pieces in place for the whole story, which is bigger than any single character.

You have to know an enormous lot.

GOLDEN BOY

(1937)

SYNOPSIS OF *GOLDEN BOY:* Fight manager Tom Moody and Lorna Moon, his girlfriend, argue over the fact that Moody hasn't yet divorced his wife. "A youth," Joe Bonaparte, enters and says Moody's fighter Kaplan has broken his hand and can't fight that night. Joe offers to replace him. Moody laughs at first, but is desperate and agrees to it. Later, at the Bonaparte home, Joe's dad plans to give him an expensive violin for his twenty-first birthday, but Joe says he might want to make some real money fighting instead of making music. Mr. Bonaparte holds off giving him the violin.

Two months later, Moody, his partner Roxy, his trainer Tokio, and Lorna worry that Joe is holding back in the ring, afraid to hurt his hands. Lorna is enlisted to convince him to give up music for boxing. Joe wishes he could get even with people who've made fun of him, and Lorna tells him boxing would be a good way to do that. Joe wants a fast car. Lorna says if he fights he'd get the money to buy one. Later, Mr. Bonaparte tries to give him the violin, but Joe says to return it and asks his father's blessing on his boxing career. Mr. Bonaparte refuses and tells Joe to take care of his hands.

Act II opens, six months later, with Joe training and gangster-gambler Eddie Fuseli saying he wants to help manage him. Joe tells Lorna he loves her and wants her to leave Moody, but Lorna says no because Moody rescued her from the streets: she wants peace, not love. The next day, Moody tells Lorna his wife is finally giving him a divorce and he can now marry Lorna. Joe walks in and catches them kissing. Lorna confesses she loves Joe.

Six weeks later, Joe leaves the dressing room for a fight just as another boxer, Pepper White, comes in. Mr. Bonaparte sees Pepper's deformed knuckles and realizes if Joe continues, his fingers will be useless for playing the violin. Joe returns from his bout with a broken hand—his "official" conversion into a fighter.

Act III begins, six months later, with everyone congratulating Moody on his engagement to Lorna—which is news to Joe. The next day, Lorna waits in the dressing room while he fights the Baltimore Chocolate Drop. Joe wins—but his opponent dies. Joe is horrified. Lorna decides to leave Moody and flees with Joe in his sports car. At the Bonaparte home, Joe's managers await his arrival to celebrate his victory. They are stunned when a call informs them Joe, their Golden Boy and prized possession, has died in a car crash.

—B.P.*

* *Golden Boy* was first presented by the Group Theatre on November 4, 1937, at the Belasco Theatre, under the direction of Harold Clurman. The legendary cast, headed by Luther Adler (Joe) and Frances Farmer (Lorna), also included Morris Carnovsky, Lee J. Cobb, John Garfield, Robert Lewis, Elia Kazan, Martin Ritt, Howard da Silva, and Karl Malden.

M ARGARET M EAD, the anthropologist, said the first generation of immigrants who come to America want to be American, but they can't be because they don't have the language. The second generation wants to be American even more. They're ashamed of the first generation's accents and culture; they go to schools and learn to speak English better, and they turn against their parents. The third generation is told that Washington and Lincoln are their relatives. The fourth generation finds out they're NOT related to Washington and Lincoln, so they go back to Europe to find their real relatives.

Moral of the story: it takes a helluva long time to become an American.

Young people in the 1930s were children of immigrants, for the most part. They wanted to do and be something—especially to be American. Success and fame are the goals. The mechanization of life is taking out its pleasure. The fruit peddler is being destroyed by technology. Technology kills pride. If you put all your energies into making money, whatever you gain in dollars and success, you lose in your soul and your spiritual awareness.

The feeling of not belonging made these kids angry. Their communities were pockets unto themselves. In Italian neighborhoods like Joe's, there was a great deal of brutality. "Weren't you ever a kid?" Lorna asks him. "Not a happy one," he says. Why not?

Because he was born into an émigré Italian family—the "wops," the "dagos"—Joe Bonaparte belongs to a section in America that was used and abused like the Puerto Ricans or any other minority in this country, brutalized by prejudice, by the lack of union wages or trades or respect or acceptance. Joe wasn't and isn't a happy kid. You must come in with an understanding of what it means to have been brought up in America without feeling for one minute that you really belonged here. As Mead said, it takes an awfully long time to become integrated into this country. You wanted to be American, but you couldn't be because you were still a wop, a sheeny, a mick, or a spic. America has always mistreated its minorities. They're finally fighting back now, but back then they had to be very careful.

This kid Joe is a symbol of every boy and girl in every foreign pocket in America in the thirties. They had no sense of childhood. Their schools were lousy and overcrowded and full of prejudice and gang fights. While their parents worked, the kids had to sell newspapers or do some other menial jobs—maybe be up all night—to help bring in a few pennies.

Joe's father was good. He bought him a violin. But when and where was Joe going to practice on it? He had to go to school, fight off the bullies, help his dad, make some money, look after his aunts and uncles. He is bitter about it. It wasn't easy being named Bonaparte. It wasn't easy to be named Cohen and Lipschitz in this country. It didn't get any easier until after six million Jews were killed, and even then—even in Hollywood—it wasn't easy.

I'll tell you a little story to illustrate that: I did a film in Los Angeles.* I was starring in it. But my film couldn't be screened if I was billed under the name of Adler. You may not believe this, but it's true. Paramount couldn't release it. They said, "It's not good in the South for a marquee to have the name Adler on it. People might think it's Jewish." Eddie Robinson changed his name, and Muni had to do it, and Sylvia Sidney—all the "ethnic" stars had to change their names, otherwise there was no way you could be on a marquee.† So they told me to change it, and I said, "It's not mine to change, it was given to me—I can't change it." The lawyers met, but the studio refused to budge, and I finally had to say, "Spell it any way you like, but I'm saying it's Adler!" And so they released it with my name as *Ardler*!

I'm not making this up. They thought Ardler sounded more gentile or less Jewish or some goddamn thing. When I told Luther about it, he said, " 'Ardler'? Why didn't they just change it to 'Beverly Wilshire'?"‡

---

* *Love on Toast* (1937), for Paramount—coinciding with the Group Theatre's premiere production of *Golden Boy*.

† Edward G. Robinson was born Emanuel Goldenberg; his cousin Paul Muni was born Meshilem Weisenfreund; and Sylvia Sidney was born Sophia Koslow. From 1938 to 1946 Sidney was Adler's sister-in-law, married to Luther Adler. The two women remained lifelong friends.

‡ Luther Adler (1903–1984), Stella's younger brother, was one of six children of Jacob P. Adler and his third wife, Sara Heine, founders of the great New York Yid-

So that was the mentality and the reality in America, and that's what Joe Bonaparte is going through—that kind of mindless prejudice. I experienced it, and I can tell you, it wasn't a very good thing in America then to be either a Jew or an Italian. It didn't make you American. And you got angry because of it. Joe Bonaparte is very angry. He wants revenge. He's the angry young man in a transitional society who says, "I want the big time—nobody is going to keep me down." There's no stopping him.

There was no stopping Odets, either. *Golden Boy* was a big departure from the social plays he wrote before. This one focused on personal issues. He wrote it after he got back to New York from a scriptwriting job in Hollywood, when a lot of his friends on the left were criticizing him for "selling out." I think he was torn between the Hollywood movie scene and the New York theater scene in the same way Joe is torn between boxing for big money and becoming a great violinist.

---

dish theatrical dynasty. (All six siblings—including older brother Jay and sisters Frances, Julia, and Florence—were actors.) Luther first appeared on stage at age five and made his professional debut at eighteen in Theodore Dreiser's *The Hand of the Potter* (1921). His first notable Broadway success was in *Humoresque* (1923). He was an original member, with Stella, of the Group Theatre, for which he played in *Night over Taos* (1932), *Success Story* (1933), *Alien Corn* (1933, opposite Katharine Cornell), *Gold Eagle Guy* (1934), and Odets's *Awake and Sing!* and *Paradise Lost* (both 1935) with Stella. His greatest role was as Joe Bonaparte in *Golden Boy,* but he lost that part in the 1939 film version to the more WASP-ish William Holden.

His stage directing work included Ben Hecht's propaganda play *A Flag Is Born* (1946), starring Paul Muni and newcomer Marlon Brando, which ran 120 performances and raised money for Jewish Holocaust refugees seeking sanctuary in Palestine. He last appeared on Broadway himself in 1965, when Zero Mostel left the cast of *Fiddler on the Roof* in a contract dispute and Luther took over the role of Tevye.

Luther's most memorable film appearances include the gripping film noir *D.O.A.* (1950); *Kiss Tomorrow Goodbye* (1950), as the unscrupulous lawyer for crook James Cagney; Joseph Losey's remake of Fritz Lang's *M* (1951); *Voyage of the Damned* (1976); and Sydney Pollack's *Absence of Malice* (1981), as Paul Newman's mobster uncle. He was often seen on TV in the fifties and sixties on such series as *General Electric Theater, Studio One, Playhouse 90, The Untouchables,* and *Naked City,* and in the seventies on *Mission: Impossible* and *The Streets of San Francisco.* One of his mordant claims to fame was being the only Jewish actor to have played Hitler three times: in two films, *The Desert Fox* and *The Magic Face* (both 1951), and an iconic *Twilight Zone* episode, "The Man in the Bottle" (1960).

Stella "Ardler" and John Payne in Paramount's *Love on Toast* (1937). Studio executives thought the name sounded "more gentile or less Jewish" than Adler. Luther said, "Why didn't they just change it to 'Beverly Wilshire'?"

Clifford didn't want to be in two worlds, but he got caught up in them. He was driven in two directions—art and money. That division was in him and all of his friends, and it was something audiences understood. Odets created this morality play about the artist in America at a time when each group was trying to make sense out of the social chaos, and materialism was not so automatically accepted as a choice. Mine is the generation he is talking about. We were all subjected to that same choice of directions, and some of us survived and some of us didn't. Faulkner went to California, they gave him an office, and then he got sick of it and left. That thing of running out to Hollywood and, after a while, suddenly saying, "Take the desk, take the chair, keep the files and the movies, keep everything!" The artist goes back where he came from, to be naked with his inspiration, but then he runs out there to do a commercial and stays again, then he divorces his wife and says, "Keep the kids, keep the house, and keep yourself." There's no solution for that running back and forth. It's a serious problem for every artist who does it or tries to do it, and it's how a lot of them go down. Certain types of artists can't handle it. In some ways, it killed Odets. It certainly killed Franchot Tone. He

Luther and Stella Adler during their early
Group Theatre days (1933)

couldn't live with that divided spirit. He couldn't live with that—or
with Joan Crawford.*

It never touched Luther or me, because we had a strong heritage. We
had a line given to us. We wanted it. We could always do whatever we
could—this stage, that stage, the movies. But with someone like John

---

* Franchot Tone (1905–68) was a founding member of the Group Theatre and a big
success in its *Success Story* production of 1932. Later that year, he became the Group's
first member to defect to Hollywood, where he made a record seven movies in 1933,
including *Bombshell* with Jean Harlow and the smash hit *Dancing Lady* opposite
his difficult wife-to-be Joan Crawford. Tone got an Oscar nomination for *Mutiny
on the Bounty* (1935) but later played mostly second leads, often typecast as a society playboy—which, in real life, he was. Facing the blacklist in the 1950s, he left
films for New York television work and character roles on such shows as *Bonanza*
and *Wagon Train;* from 1965 to 1967 he co-starred in twenty-seven episodes of *Ben
Casey.* The high- (or low-) light of Tone's chaotic personal life came in 1951 when he
suffered disfiguring facial injuries in a fight with actor Tom Neal over actress Barbara Payton, another wife-to-be. Tone was the most egocentric and confrontational
of the Group's early members, but for the rest of its existence sent much-needed
financial aid to the company.

Garfield, it was the destruction of both his personal life and his art. That division—who am I inside? what am I?—is the most destructive thing that can happen to anyone, but especially to the artist.

You may not know who you are, but you know who you are not. You know that if you're writing a script in Hollywood and the producer comes in and says "Change that line" and you do it—you know you are not a creative artist.

* * *

Let's take a closer look at the characters in *Golden Boy*. Besides Joe and Lorna, there's Joe's brother, Frank; his father; Mr. Carp, a friend of Joe's dad; and Moody, the fight manager. In the lower-middle-class world of the Bonaparte family, we find the different roads they can all take. Frank's road is a political one. He is part of the labor movement, trying to organize unskilled workers. Any big political movement in America involves violence; trying to organize means killing or being killed. Joe understands that, and he could go brother Frank's way or he could go the milder way of his father, who is a socialist. Unionism and socialism are both responses to industrial capitalism—big business. Or he could go his own way . . . The question for all of them is what and how to choose—how to live in their social situation.

Joe is aware of his situation. He was hurt in childhood. He's proud, sensitive, complex, isolated, and tough. He's Italian. "Joe Bonaparte"—my God, what a name to carry! We know about Bonaparte. He was the biggest, most dictatorial ego in the Western world. Napoleon was a fighter and Joe is a fighter. The symbolism is obvious. You don't have to read a book on it. How brilliant Odets was to pick the name of a man who was defeated because he had the arrogance to think he could conquer the world. Joe Bonaparte wants to do that, too.

If you want to conquer the world, you are not an ordinary man. Joe is an extraordinary man with an extraordinary will and vitality—everything about him is extraordinary. We get his temperament from his name. We get a young man with a talent for fighting, and there's no other profession where you win or lose so clearly as the fight game. I never watch anything violent, but I know that for men in America, everything stops for the fights. They love that savage gamble on who will win or lose. It's big. That's the world we enter in this play, the thing that fixates everybody into paralysis: who's going to beat whom?

Lorna is not known to you, but her symbol is. Why isn't she called Sun? I like the fact that she's named Moon. A name like that is a key for you to her character. The moon is a dead place. I think the author is saying she's dead, in a society that produces a prostitute with no understanding. She thinks success and fame are the answers to all problems. Lorna is not safe. She is being kept by a married man who has a child. She could be thrown out at any moment. She is nostalgic, but also realistic.

Names can sometimes be a tremendous lead for you. If it's Kennedy or Blumenfeld, you don't have to worry, but if the names or titles don't reveal useful things or if they come with just a park bench or a table, you need to start looking for symbols to interpret. Why do you think Mr. Chekhov gives you a cherry orchard? The orchard hasn't functioned for one hundred years; it's just there and it's beautiful. So are the people who own it: they haven't functioned for one hundred years, either, and they are too beautiful to function in an oncoming society that wants to chop it down, sell it, and put little houses on it. The cherry orchard is a symbol.

You get that with *The Seagull*, too. Mr. Chekhov isn't such a bad writer. The seagull gets killed uselessly, for no reason. And you find, in the play, people who are injured for no reason. And what do you think "Uncle Vanya" means? If we want to call somebody the typical name for an American, we say, "He's a regular Joe." A soldier, we say, is GI Joe. Joe is the name for all men. So Vanya is the name of all ordinary Russians. He's not somebody's particular Uncle Vanya, he's *all* the Uncle Vanyas, unable to save themselves in a society that's going down.

Traditions change in a transitional period, and that produces alienation. Alienated humans feel hollow inside. Artists don't have to worry as much, because they have a path, but Joe doesn't have a path, because he hasn't made his decision yet. It seems like he's going to be a fighter. But then suddenly he says, "Music means more to me." That comes out of left field. I don't understand it, or him, because nothing leads me into it. That side of Joe is completely different from fighting—the side that says, "With music, I'm not afraid of people and there's no war or mean streets. But music can't help me there anymore."

It's not simple language. "Golden boy" means one of two things:

either a prizefighter or a child of gifted heritage. The hand that makes music is the same hand that can kill, and Joe has to choose what to do with his hand. Every artist has to decide what to do with his hand, and with his soul. Is he going into the competition and the brutality of boxing—to kill and "win"—or into music? Mr. Odets wants you to see that if you leave your room, there's war. If you stay in your room, there's music. Do you want war or peace? Odets says you have to be what you are, or end up in the bughouse. But Joe doesn't know who he is. He's tortured. Joe is big, and so are his choices. Odets says every man is divided and must choose.

His fine writing clarifies those choices from the moment *Golden Boy* opens. The first big choice you get is the prizefighting world. Odets establishes that atmosphere perfectly in a minute. But one scene in particular is so beautifully written, and such a crucial key to Joe's choice and the whole play, that it needs your special attention. I'm going to pull it out and dissect each line of it with you later.*

For now, you just need to see, in the whole first action of that scene, there is a lack of logic. It's unrealistic; there's nothing for you to hang on to. In a play like this, everything is important, yet not necessarily connected. The more you fail to connect, the more you work against the circumstances.

This scene takes place in the park. There's nothing onstage except light and a bench. Joe is nervous because he's not home practicing. Lorna is there because she has nowhere else to go—no home or children. She just sits there having nothing. She belongs to the boxing world, a kept girl, sitting with a boy named Joe Bonaparte in a park. They are not together. They have no real idea why they're next to each other. They have nothing in common. But there they are, each in their own world.

Lorna is talking about success and fame. She sees women dressed in beautiful furs and fancy cars. In America, on the street, you don't feel like a real person without money. It's bigger and stronger than personal values. Lorna thinks Joe will be a fighter—choose success and fame. She is terribly innocent. They drift . . . he to the cars, she to the carousel. They talk from different points of view. The scene need not go anywhere. But it is tense. There is a sense of urgency in it; you can't

---

* See chapter 10, with the complete text of *Golden Boy's* Act I, scene 4, and Adler's interpolated motivational breakdown in a line-by-line exegesis.

play it like you have all the time in the world. The key to Joe is that tension. The key to Lorna is that nothing can touch her.

They don't really communicate until they get to criticizing each other. "For chrissakes," she's trying to say, "why don't you do what you're supposed to do? Go fight, and you'll make a lot of money. That's what you want, that's what the world wants—go do it. You want to work in a lousy factory eight hours a day? You're going to be famous!" That's the plot. She tells him to go fight, they criticize each other, and they go home angry. The scene is not so much logic or action. It's about creating a mood.

Now, we know it's idiotic to tell anybody else what to do: "I think you should go to Hollywood" or "You should go to New York." You can't think for somebody else. You just mustn't. I do it all the time: "Oh yes, here's what you should do!" But right off, she tells him what to do, and what she tells him to do is exactly what he can't do, which is *make a decision.*

Joe has to commit himself immediately. The guy scheduled to fight broke his arm. This is Joe's big chance—to replace him. He's in a state of panic because he has to make up his mind right now. Lorna knows all this, but she's not particularly interested. These two people don't know anything about each other. People generally don't.

Joe's thoughts come to him like darts. His nervousness stems from having nothing to hold on to. He doesn't know where to put his energy. The action is unfocused. The rhythm is staccato. Joe is a moral family person. Lorna is an orphan. Up to now, their relationship hasn't been clear. We don't know if it's romantic or not. They don't seem to get along. She says, "I don't like you." He says, "Why?" This girl is from the wrong side of the river, her father's a bum, and *she* doesn't like *him*—a musician of Napoleonic size and intellect?

Joe's attitude toward anybody who's small, who's lost, who isn't guided in a big way, is "You don't know what you're talking about." He's ruthless with her, with no concern for her humanity. "I'll tell you why you're living with Moody," he's saying, "—because you're a whore, that's why." But she says one thing that catches him up short: "Tom loves me." Moody is a lousy fight manager and a loser, but he's the one person in the play who can love. She may be dead, and Joe may have everything going for him, but the one thing he doesn't have is love.

No ambitious man can have it all. We know Napoleon is not going down in history because of whom he married or divorced. We know that Talleyrand, Einstein—none of the "great men"—will be remembered for being Pelléas with Mélisande, or Romeo with Juliet. The big thing missing in any really ambitious man is the ability to say, "I'm gonna lick the world AND be a great lover!" Joe knows that. He knows what he lacks. He doesn't love.

He's a big man who understands the contemporary world and belongs in the framework of the working class. And here's some little whore who belongs in no framework at all. You can't put a whore together with a Napoleonic man and think they're going to make it. They might make it under certain conditions—but not from the point of view of love.

This is not a love story. It's a hate story.

*   *   *

What, exactly, is Joe's idea of success? He says, "My nature is not fighting, I know music." Yet he also says, "I'm going to buy a car." Now, any *pisher** can buy a car. A man of his size wants to buy a car? When you sit in a nice car, you can look down on the world. Joe is in a long tradition of strong men who want to be important, and that's his symbol of success.

Lorna's idea of success is the same as yours. Who do you think of in your world—what rock singer, what movie star—as successful? Give me names! [*Class responds: "The Rothschilds!" "The Fondas!"*] All right. When we say "Who's successful?" we mean "Who sold the most records?" "How much did *Star Wars* make?" In our community, I never heard anybody define success except that way. This play is about that—and it's about you and me.

That beautiful singer who came here before she was so successful—what's her name? [*"Diana Ross!"*] You know her as successful. You don't think of Einstein as successful or Walter Piston being a great musical success. Who did you speak about this week as successful? [*"Farrah Fawcett!"*] Right. Now, don't laugh. It's not funny that success and fame are just what's advertised most—nothing else. Who's the most advertised success in the world—that fighter? [*"Muhammad Ali!"*] Yes, that's the one—the one who says "I'm the greatest!"

Lorna is like we are—brainwashed to think of success in terms of

* Yiddish for a phony or small fry, lacking the status or power he pretends to have.

popularity. In our world, we don't really know or care about quality; it's all about money and publicity. It's a sickness. Lorna's idea is really a whore's idea: if you have money and everybody talks about you, what the hell have you got to worry about?

I had another instance of that yesterday when that little girl came . . . Catherine O'Neal—what's her name? ["*Tatum O'Neal!*"] That's the one. She was in the room, and everyone was absolutely overwhelmed with the honor of her presence. She's about nine years old! I'm not making this up. If your name is Tatum O'Neal and you're on the marquee, everybody loves you.

Now, Joe understands that notion of success, but he also knows a different kind of ethic. He doesn't necessarily accept what's advertised. His value system didn't come from boxing, it came from the *Encyclopaedia Britannica* and from being a musician and from the working class. He is isolated because he is so different. It's a play about emerging values in a society where ambition conquers all during a period of greatest distress. Joe is a tough Italian kid who wants to get ahead in America, but his values are stopping him.

You get the same kind of confusion in *Awake and Sing!,* where lower-class people try to elevate themselves to the middle class, and the family is the breeding ground for revolt. The destructive mother wants respectability and wants her daughter to marry a rich man. The daughter is frustrated and doesn't solve her problem by running off with a gangster. The father lacks any force. The old socialist grandfather let himself be trapped into compromise. All sorts of troubles due to the social system. The conflict comes in people wanting both worlds.

For Joe, it's the world of music vs. the American dream of success in the fight world—becoming a capitalist. Being part of America for him means, "They won't keep me down in this corner of Little Italy, I've got too much. I want what I can get, and I'll get it, and I'll still read the encyclopedia and appreciate the difference between a Horowitz and a Jack Dempsey who gets half a million for stepping in the ring."

I'm very much like the Golden Boy—I want both worlds. How many of you want both worlds? But what do you do when the world you want to be part of doesn't want you unless you're already a part of it? And the Golden Boy isn't. He is typical of the split in most of us who don't know who we are, or what to do with who we are. He's a troubled soul.

So there's inner turmoil, and there's turmoil outside—represented by Joe's brother. Frank is an organizer for the CIO. That makes a tremendous impression on me, Stella. I immediately say, "Wow, that rings a historical bell!" I suddenly remember all through America there were moments in unionism when people were persecuted. The first man they jailed was Debs.* Working-class leaders in America were always being put in jail for something. Debs was an organizer with a political point of view, like Frank. The playwright wants me to know the period and that brother Frank is an organizer. My whole instrument must be awake to the impression that it's a big political moment in America so that I know where I'm situated historically. Nothing is bigger then than the labor movement, which is represented by Joe's brother, Frank. I don't know much about Joe, but I know he knows about the CIO.

You can't understand Joe in *Golden Boy* unless you understand his historical past. He and Biff Loman in *Death of a Salesman* are contemporaries. They both experienced the disenchantment of the Depression in similar ways. Biff tells his father, "You blew me full of hot air when you said America was so great. You told me this and that about how great I'd be, but I've been a dollar-an-hour guy for twenty-two years." The tradition Willy handed down to his sons did not work for them—or, really, for Willy. That same kind of tradition was given to Joe.

The Depression was a chaotic period when the middle class collapsed. Their homes were foreclosed, their businesses closed, their children couldn't go to school anymore. There was no money, no jobs—even the theaters closed. The country was paralyzed. Men who used to be rich were selling apples. "Brother, Can You Spare a Dime?" How many know that song?

Joe, the Golden Boy, is faced with a society in transition. Despotic political parties are developing. If you have a depression, you will have a revolt. In a country that preaches freedom, you have a right to revolt. You also have a "right" to be policed if you revolt. In order to get to

---

* Eugene V. Debs (1855–1926) was co-founder of the American Railway Union (ARU) and Industrial Workers of the World (IWW) and a five-time Socialist Party nominee for president of the United States. He was jailed during the Pullman strike of 1894 and again in 1918, under the Espionage Act, for denouncing U.S. participation in World War I. The last of his Socialist presidential campaigns (1900, 1904, 1908, 1912, 1920) was conducted from a prison cell.

Golden Boy, you have to understand there was an outburst of political activity in America such as we never had before. The Communist movement was on the march everywhere, so why not in America?

Communism is a desperate philosophy: the ends justify the means. If we're going to do something, let's use guns—violence. We've got to have change. That was a terrible period, around the time the play takes place. The CIO was trying to organize laborers who were working for a dollar a week—steel workers, shoe-factory workers, every goddamn kind of worker you could imagine. It was infiltrated, naturally, by many forces, including the Communists. The AFL was more Socialist and didn't want unorganized labor organized.* So you had two groups, with strong movements of overt socialism and covert communism behind them. The Socialist Party in New York was enormous. When you voted for president in New York, you had a choice of five parties. Now you have two. You had a split Liberal Party, the Republican Party, Socialist Party, Communist Party, Democratic Party—you see how complex it was.

If you have a political situation like that, you have an enormous reaction on the part of the writers, the intellectuals, the playwrights. Out of this period came Clifford Odets, Lillian Hellman, Arthur Miller, Maxwell Anderson, Irwin Shaw, and a flock of other writers. They were political—the scene was political. They came out of the need to talk about what was happening in America and the world. You had musicians like Marc Blitzstein writing *The Cradle Will Rock*—an enormous uprising of Americans with something to say. Then you had Mr. Roosevelt making the WPA, putting people to work, creating a theater for them, public mural projects for painters.

* The Congress of Industrial Organizations (CIO), proposed by John L. Lewis in 1932 and formally founded in 1935, was born out of a bitter dispute in the labor movement between craft and industrial unionism: whether to organize workers by specialty skills, such as the carpenters' and railroad engineers' unions of the American Federation of Labor (AFL), or by CIO umbrella unions of all workers in mass-production industries like steel and autos, where craft distinctions weakened bargaining power and left the unskilled majority unrepresented. Their violent rivalry got fiercer as the Depression worsened, causing big membership drops in unions such as Lewis's own United Mine Workers. In the postwar Red Scare, the Taft-Hartley Act required union leaders to swear they were not Communists—a provision later declared unconstitutional. The CIO merged with the AFL into the current AFL-CIO in 1955.

Golden Boy Joe comes out of that upheaval. He has fifteen philosophies to choose from—he read them from A to Z in the encyclopedia. He is a boy from the streets, and the streets are crowded with hungry, murderously angry people. Steel was on strike, and the army was called out and shot a number of the strikers. It was like bringing out the militia at Kent State: when you have a strong left movement, you get a strong right reaction to it. In Joe, we have a young man who knows the political situation: Who will beat who in this phase of American history? People are moving fast, in competition. It is muscular, it is tense, it is loud, it is brutal. Who am I aiming at? And who's aiming at me? Who do I have to kill? He knows there's a war out there on the streets, and he treats Lorna as if she were a war, too.

In Lorna, what do we have? She is much like you: "What the hell's the CIO? I know the CIA, but what's the CIO?" Lorna is not part of the political scene. Joe knows about factory workers, even though he isn't one. Lorna says she's a butterfly, and butterflies don't work. She makes no sense to him. She knows nothing about politics; she talks in an obscure way—you can't really tell what she thinks. He gives you factories, but she gives you nothing to hold on to. He has a tremendous need to understand what's going on, and it makes him angry . . .

I want you to see that landscape, that America he's angry at, and why you have Trotskyism, Stalinism, right-wing communism, left-wing communism, every kind of ism. And if you had twenty different political parties to choose from, you also had twenty kinds of theater: the Broadway dramatic theater, the musical theater, the workers' theater, the Group Theatre, the labor-movement theater, *Pins and Needles*—every imaginable kind.

I especially want you to understand the naturalistic play. A writer uses its different forms—realism, expressionist realism, impressionist realism, surrealism—to make you travel where he wants you to go, because he does not want the logic of life, he wants the inner truth.

Acting in the modern theater is not a way for the actor to sell. It is a way for the actor to tell the truth. If he doesn't have the truth in him, he's back in the old theater, where the lines or the plot would carry him, but where he would not need to expose his soul.

Playwrights express themselves in certain forms because they have certain ideas that are best conveyed that way. You must learn the styles that go with the ideas. The style—whether it's poetic realism, psychological realism—is essential. Every author takes liberties with this

thing called reality. Ibsen's plays are connected with water; his characters come from island to mainland. O'Neill had his fog—getting lost
in it. O'Neill's passion centered on the Irish being doomed, isolated,
unable to find a way out—and the closeness of the family. The fact
that you are inland in *Golden Boy* makes a big difference.

Golden Boy is written in a stark, not-so-realistic style. The passion in
it is different from that of other playwrights. Odets's passion says it's
not enough for some of us to be together, we have to ALL get together
and unite forces. He doesn't think aloneness is good. Alone, you go
under. Odets wants to help you find a road, and the road he gives you
is the social road. The road he took for himself as an artist was to join
the Group and the Communist Party—"Together we fight!" Odets's
characters need to live higher. His plays are epic in the demand for
life, and the battles in them come out of that demand. Odets watched
history and wrote this play about a specific time and social situation.
He wrote it in the contemporary vernacular—a very American kind
of street talk—that places us clearly in the late thirties.

It was not a good time in the American theater for drawing-room
comedy. The theaters were empty and there was no money. There was
one play in which six stars and myself got out in front of the stage
with guns—I mean really big guns—and said, "We're going to kill
you!" The audience was scared to such a degree that one critic died
a little later, after seeing it and being subjected to that—he actually
died!

The more I think about it now, the more I think somebody *should*
have died.

* * *

Joe is thinking along those lines, too. "People have hurt my feelings
for years. I never forget. You can't get even with people by playing the
fiddle. If music shot bullets, I'd like it better—artists and people like
that are freaks today. The world moves fast and they sit around like
forgotten dopes."

I, Stella Adler, can absolutely confirm that. This boy of twenty-one
knows something that I didn't figure out until much later, and that I
still don't know how to deal with: the artist doesn't move fast, and the
world does. Whenever a character in a play is an artist, you're going
to have trouble, because the artist is written by an artist. So you'll

always find the author terribly caught up in the complications of the artist, what he is, his point of view—he bothers very much with the artist because he is one, and he wants the artist character to interpret the society.

Being an artist, Golden Boy is looking for the truth in himself. I've told you that modern plays do not deal so much with set characters as with human beings struggling with their own inner truth—not explaining life, but trying to find out how they feel about it. That's what Willy Loman is trying to do. We have to know how the character feels inside. They are not ready-made characters talking about things that are taken for granted. They have their own point of reference in the past, and they try to orient themselves in the present from that past.

Golden Boy says, "My truth comes from a thousand years ago. I do not lie when I create a work of art or play the violin. I am not conditioned by anything from the outside to make me compromise. I have only myself, and must obey my instinct to express what I believe in." If an artist has to compromise, he stops believing in himself. This is a very dangerous moment for Joe. Part of the creative process is to trust what is given to you. Could Beethoven or Mozart possibly not believe what was given to them? They had to. Joe is a first-generation American who got culture and a political sense from his family. His brother deals with the masses, but Joe—as an artist—can't. An artist should be of some use to society, but Joe doesn't know how to put his art into action and make it do good. "I can't play Mozart for the masses," he says, "they don't need it." Joe doesn't want to give people something they can't use. "They're hungry, brutalized, without work or hope. What good will it do to bring them Bach? I'm a musician, but I'm also socially displaced in my historical moment."

The Golden Boy is out of place in this political upheaval. He understands the masses, but he doesn't like them, because they don't help themselves. He's not like Tolstoy, who loves and goes to them, or his brother, Frank, who organizes them. The Communists say, "Take it now." The Socialists say, "Wait a couple thousand years—man will evolve." Joe examines all that and says, "I don't think men will evolve. Something has to happen, but I don't know what."

Even in good times, the actor is never really part of the world. I don't know any society where the lawyer and the doctor sit down and have dinner with the actor, if they can avoid it. They just don't. Actors, poets, painters think differently, feel differently; their judgments are different, their passions are different. I'm thinking of my brother Luther. Luther, in the house, is a ghost. He is not companionable— typical of the artist. It's not an accident that he's not a hail-fellow-well-met. It is not by accident, it is by choice. Luther does not belong to a house.

If you don't belong to a house or a neighborhood or a club, or if you're not a citizen or don't have a family, and try to stand alone, you're crazy—you can't do it. Identification is one of the most crucial aspects of life. But Golden Boy Joe doesn't identify or belong to this, that, or any other thing. He has the sickness of wanting to choose how he lives. He's even fighting his own family. He doesn't want his father to sell fruit fifteen hours a day and keel over in order for him to play the violin. He wants to be an American here, not a foreigner, and the way to do that is to get what's most American: "money and cars—they're poison, but I want them!"

And he has something for sale, to get them. His Italian name isn't saleable; his music and his individuality aren't saleable. He is arrogant and unsympathetic because he's educated—none of that sells. But he has one saleable thing: "I know how to box. Nobody can beat me, I've got it sewed up—I can be the champ. That's what America will buy. That's my truth."

Joe doesn't want his father's truth or the political truth. If you belong to a party and do the wrong thing, they kick you out. If you write the wrong play or the wrong music during the revolution, what do you think those revolutionaries do to you? You can't do what you want in a communist country. In a socialist country, they say you can, but he's not so sure about that, either. Joe says, "I know who's a whore and what they want, and I don't like them, I don't like anybody whose aim isn't big. I don't like Moody. He's in a racket—an exploiter who lives off other people. He's a liar, by necessity—he's got a wife here, a sweetheart there. I'll use him, but I don't respect him." Everybody around Joe is judged by him. Early on, he tells Lorna, "I'll know you the way nobody knows you." It is not a realistic play about a unique artist. It's about every artist looking for truth in a world that only the artist understands.

Joe wants to live up to his name, Bonaparte—to conquer in a big way, not be sucked into some movement. So he stands alone, but it's too emotionally difficult. There's an enormous tension on that stage—the mood, the scenery, even the lighting is tense—which you must deal with as actors. Joe's tension is permanent. Nobody can talk to him, nobody can steer him, nobody can influence him—he can't be touched. Everything makes him mad. What makes a man whole is being in harmony with himself—a balance between his spirit and materialism. But this is an unbalanced period in America, and the spiritual aspect is failing. Materialism leaps ahead much faster than the spirit. Most people in America are spiritually behind their capabilities.

How do you get characters like that off the page?

If you just go to the words and say, in a whiny or pathetic way, "People are hurting me and artists are forgotten dopes"—you're a *schmuck*. That's not a dirty word. It means stupid.* You have to say it the way Joe means it: "I need to get revenge and conquer, and artists don't know how to do that anymore!" You use tone and movement. Schopenhauer said you can tell a man by a gesture.

The way to find the right thing is to concentrate first on impressions, not on the whole play. If it gets born through too much logic instead of the creative instinct, it's no good. It is not important to take the whole work at first. It's better to do that later, only as you develop it.

We established the impression that Lorna has a whore's idea of success and that Joe doesn't think much of her or really relate to her at all. But don't underestimate her. She catches on to certain things from his face and his tone—not from the text. She knows she's on her own with a guy that's giving her the dirtiest looks in the world. He does the same. When she hears a tune and says, "That's the carousel—did you ever ride one?" Now, he's probably written a paper on it; he won scholarships in music. All he says in the text is "That's for kids." But what he's conveying is, "You need kids' music, and you need Moody to hold you up because you don't have legs to stand on. You don't know what you're talking about, so shut up."

It's not in the text. It's in the acting and the understanding. It can only be revealed through the creative side of the actor—through himself. All Chekhov is that, all Tennessee, all Miller . . . The inner truth of a human being has to be so big that finally the audience catches on. You have to get him off the page, and in doing that, you have big work to do. You have to take and experience areas where Joe lives, in

---

* Adler is clarifying for the gentiles in her audience: *"schmuck"* is a Yiddish word for "prick," both literally and in the English pejorative sense of "dumb jerk."

an Italian ghetto, and build them in such a profound way that you can say when his mother's funeral took place, how they threw fruit at the coffin, how his broken-down father couldn't work anymore—the helplessness and anger this boy felt watching him. In the anger is where Odets makes the transitions. Those transitions are more interesting than staying with the logic, and it's your creative duty as an actor to find them.

Every play starts with words. The words are outside, on paper. Sometimes they can stimulate a reaction in you, but it's more essential to get the rhythm of the play. Wait for the attack, don't wait for the line. The most important thing you can pluck is yourself. Pluck yourself by saying, "I react too fast." If you choose the cliché, you're going to pick up the banality. You will pick up what is obvious in the words and say, "That's it." The main pitfall you must avoid either saying or thinking is "I know the character."

Now, stop taking notes. How long have you been taking notes—since high school? college? all your life? How many of you ever use any of those notes? They lie there quietly in a drawer, and sooner or later you throw them away. I think this note will be more valuable for you—put it in your mind, not the notebook: to understand something is not to experience it; it's the *experience* in the actor that gives him the privilege of saying he is interpreting the play.

I experience everything, because I'm a very good actress. I don't trust the goddamn text. I work with what's inside me. I want to activate and agitate myself until I know this boy, know what he went through in school. I want him to be full of hate. That's your job. If you take something that doesn't affect you, you're mediocre. You have to work and work until what you take affects you. You must learn how to make the part alive in you by agitating yourself so that you're emotionally alerted to his experience, not so much his mind. If you build him up intellectually, you will be able to write a very good paper about the Golden Boy, but you will not be able to act him, and you won't get the part.

Understanding for the actor is living it. Don't take anything unless you know it and have it in you. It's easy to say in principle, "I understand Golden Boy and I understand his father, too," or "I understand Willy Loman and also Biff." It may be within your mental comprehension, but it's no good onstage unless you take something that works in your guts. I respect the director, but not more than I do me. It's I, not he, who has to give birth to it. I'm the one that's going to pay with my blood.

There are no ideas in the theater of entertainment. It's not art. So there's the theater of ideas, which requires a different sense of discipline. The difference is "I am responsible to create a character through my craft." When I was in the Group Theatre, there were many people in it, and I thought, "They all feel fine, they're all together, but I'm alone." I said, "You know, I don't feel as if I belong here." And they said, "Neither do I." Each one felt separate from each other one. In a company called the Group! Because each person came from a very different area in life—one came from the East, one from California, this and that. It's terrible to feel like an outsider. You all look as if you belong. I never felt I belonged to anything or anybody. I think that's the nature of an artist—to feel he's crazy and isolated. Do you feel a little isolated?

Of course you do. But it's not necessary to put *your* alienated feelings in Joe. It's necessary for you to say, "Where is *he* alienated? How does *he* feel?" He still feels like he's in the streets, and he's angry to not be part of it. At school, they put him at the back with the other kids who had accents . . . put him in fifty different situations where he withdraws. Discover it for yourself. Find only what is do-able, not what is feel-able. Remember, Stella said so: never take what you feel, only what you can do, and from that you can steal the action. Instead of thinking "Joe must feel like I do when I'm alienated," leave him in his circumstances. Mr. Stanislavsky said: "The truth of acting is the truth of the circumstances you are in on the stage, not your personal circumstances." Otherwise, it just becomes your own psychological pathology.

When Laura in *Glass Menagerie* says "I am a cripple" and her Gentleman Caller says, "I wouldn't have taken that too seriously," it shows he doesn't remotely understand her. When Joe mentions his cross-eyed problem, Lorna says, "Oh, well, your eyes don't matter," meaning, "Just fix yourself up, just make yourself American." Odets uses it like Tennessee, to show you how utterly callous people can be. She's telling a man who could be Napoleon to get his eyes fixed and forget about it? She doesn't realize his whole life has been affected by it.

So he leaves her at that, in anger. He sees he can't reach her; nobody can. "I'm an Italian, I'm different, I'm educated, I'm cross-eyed, I'm sick inside because I'm alone, but here I am anyway, my name is Bonaparte!" When Lorna calls herself a butterfly and says "butterflies don't work," it's an insult to his mother. He'll avenge her. The whole of *Golden Boy* is about revenge—revenge for the insult, for the indignity, of not being understood.

Grab that truth. Take your time, but grab it. The truth is not in the lines. I worked personally and arrived at it, so that when I said the line, it was mine, it didn't belong to the author anymore. It must always belong to you. Always do it in terms of what you can bring to it. You have to build it. I don't want to see so much logic, I'm bored by it. If I can pull the inside of the character from my impressions, I'm closer to it. The playwright doesn't talk about Joe's mother. I've got to find her by myself; I've got to find everything. If I had to work from the text alone, I'd be naked, I wouldn't know about the mother. I have to find out. I've got to have everything about his life in me in order to be able to say anything.

Later on, in the second act, for instance, I can find that his father's old Jewish friend, Mr. Carp, must have been a tremendous influence on Joe—he's a philosopher, he plays chess, never goes out . . . I think he's the one who introduced Joe to anarchism, because he was from the old country and brought over a ready knowledge of political factions. He must have discussed this with Joe. When I did *Resurrection,* I read a great deal about Herzen, a great idealist who influenced Tolstoy, to try to understand the political implications.* I needed to round myself out, which I'm trying to make you do. Start on a script with some recognition.

Recognize in Lorna, for instance, that a key to her character is the objectivity with which a whore approaches sex. She lets herself be experienced, but she doesn't experience it or go to the experience herself. People experience her. That's the oldest profession—the professionalism of watching it more than participating in it. Lorna has watched men through the ages—men using life, taking it, grabbing it. But she is deadened to it. Yet she sees; she's able to judge. After

---

* The stage adaptation of Leo Tolstoy's last novel (1899), dealing with the social injustice of laws and the hypocrisy of institutionalized religion, was a staple of Jacob Adler's Yiddish theater in New York and of Stella's repertoire. Alexander Herzen (1812–1870) was a radical agrarian populist known as "the father of Russian socialism."

all, nothing is more intimate than the sexual experience. Nobody can judge a man better than the woman who's in bed with him. She knows the differences between men, and she knows she's sitting next to one who is different.

He knows he's sitting next to a girl who has seen her father bum drinks, who knows a burn* when she sees one, knows different kinds of burns in all strata of society. She knows men; she knows the ones who are kind and the ones who are brutal. I'll tell you something: I'm sorry I missed that profession. I'd give my life to know as much as Lorna does about men. For some reason, I think every man's good, I always have. I still think so. It's very childish, not to say romantic. But Lorna has real insight. That's why it's interesting to put her and Joe together. Each knows the other to a certain depth. Lorna has some size in that through her way of life and age-old profession, she can judge Bonaparte almost as viscerally as he judges her.

Joe has to deal with what's inside himself, but has a hard time facing it. The truth of him has to be dragged out. The modern play is built not on what I say but what truth I can pull out from my character. These playwrights deal with the soul—what modern man is stuck with.

* * *

Odets had a soul he was stuck with, too.

I think the most important line he gives Joe is: "When I play music . . . I'm not afraid of people and what they say." It was written by a writer who is talking just as much about acting as music—about how you feel when you create a part and it opens up and you know exactly how a character feels and thinks.

I've created that kind of human being, and I know the feeling of accomplishment. I know Clifford, I've worked with him: he has the enormous sense of conquest the artist has, as a writer or an actor, when he can say, "I am part of that universe, of that tradition. I am able to create." Whether you do it on a stage or a typewriter, it makes you a whole person with the biggest harmony the world can provide. Only God can give you greater harmony. And since we don't deal with God in the modern age, art is the biggest satisfaction that man can get out

* 1930s slang for a swindle

of life. Every author and actor knows that and tries to express that joy of creating.

Joe and Lorna aren't very eloquent, but somehow the audience gets them. The modern audience is connected in a cosmic way with their inarticulateness—otherwise we wouldn't have had *Golden Boy*. We would never have had Chekhov or Ibsen or Odets or any of those writers who deal with problems that are not very logical. The audience and the actor must feel and respond to the same things together.

When Joe says "You have to be what you are," it's an idiotically large statement. Neither of them knows who they are. You've got to reach further out in every direction and break it down. Who is he? How old is music in the Italian soul? In Italy, if a man is digging or driving or cooking, he's singing an aria. He is brought up with music the way we are brought up with baseball. Joe is saying, "I've got music in my soul, I'm the Italian boy my Italian father bought the fiddle for!"

When Lorna says "You don't have to be just one thing," she means "You have such an ego, you could probably kill half the world AND play the violin." This maniac Joe is familiar to her from being in the fight game and from knowing how the world works. She's saying, "Why not be a winner, fight your way to the championship? For christsakes, get a bank account, fix your life by doing something about it—that's how it's done!"

I'd like to play her because she has that age-old wisdom in her. He's a man, understandable to a woman like Lorna. "Is your mother dead?" He says yes. "So is mine," she says. That's it. She gets him—or thinks she does.

He does the same thing, only more brutally: "Where do you come from? You look like you don't have parents." So typical of him. I think that's the cruelest line in literature, to tell a girl she doesn't even look like she had parents. You get a lot about both of them from that line: he's so empowered, she's so destroyed. Not physically but in her soul—the result of no parents, no nurturing, no love. He sees she's pretty dead and knows her profession. She sees his indifference and self-involvement and says, "I don't like you. I've seen 'em all, and you I don't like." He says, "Why?" She says, "Because you don't ever need anybody." She's got him. That's Joe: "I don't need the party, I don't need socialism, I don't need you, I'll give up my family tradition, I don't need anything or anybody anymore—I'll make it alone."

Golden Boy wants to guard his talent. He doesn't want to get mixed up with people or parties or theories that would distort or influence his talent. She nails it: "You want all the money and all the beauty that goes with loving, but you're so involved with yourself, you will never love." He is modern man—the man who has no time to come home and play with the children. The last one to do that was Willy Loman, and Willy was weak. Anybody with Joe's strength has no time to love. No really big, ambitious man is going to be able to love; and if he tries, it's pretty much in a minor key.

In breaking down middle-class life in the last hundred years, the ambitious man in industrial society has been dealt with and nobody has let him off the hook. In *The Master Builder* and *John Gabriel Borkman* and *Golden Boy,* it's all about the man who wants to conquer. It's the same man with the same problem, and always there are victims, and the victims are whoever is nearest him. Lorna says, "You want what produces music, which is love and harmony, and you want to be the big man who conquers. But whenever you want all the money and fame and conquest, your soul starts to bother you."

It's the first time the word "soul" is used in the play, and the second she says it, he knows what to kill: his soul. That's it! He always left room for that soul, but it bothered him inside. It held him up, the way it holds up every ambitious man. You can't win with that. The *truly* ambitious man gives it up. She has given him the key, and he finally makes up his mind. "By God, she's right! If that's what I have to do, I'll do it." His big transformational moment comes from the partner.

I'm very proud that I got it. I asked myself when and where he made up his mind to fight, and it's that one line when she finally reveals it to him. In a flash of the word "soul," he knows. Now he's in control. She says Tom loves her and he says, "Fine—your job is love. Mine is to get the car. It's poison, but when I'm speeding in it and looking down on the world, nobody will get me—in or out of the ring!" He has to make up his mind, and the actor has to know how he gets there. You can't get there from the lines. You get there from understanding the scene. I'm telling you, you don't need the whole play. This is a better way to work. It's fun. It can be honestly funny if you get it and deliver his line right: "When you're lying in his arms tonight, tell [Moody], for me, that the next World's Champ is feeding in his stable."

Golden Boy is closer to us than any other Odets play because we're still very divided in our society about where and how to make it, and what "making it" means. It could be called *The Rise and Fall of Joe*

Bonaparte. Joe's moral conscience is in agony and paralysis. The price a man pays for freedom in America is a terrible uncertainty about what to pick. Odets wrote *Golden Boy* as social criticism of the artist—the fate of the restless spirit who wants it all and can't make a choice. It was his most successful play. He wrote it to create a hit and give the profits to the Group Theatre, because the Group produced his first plays. He knew the audience would like it. Audiences, then and now, understand the difficulty of the choice. They understand that Joe cannot be dictated to, and that because of his education he can see the fallacies in each of the roads he has to choose from.

Joe Bonaparte stands crucified by his separateness.

Great play, absolutely. It gives you such a kaleidoscope of political, emotional, and spiritual ideas. Clifford is writing about his own time, and at this time all artists are talking about America's conflicting spiritual and material aims: your inner spirit is searching for how to put yourself together into a whole man. Society is neutral to whatever choice you make.

In *Golden Boy,* the society is utterly indifferent. Joe doesn't realize that if he chooses the fight game, he'll be in the hands of people who know how to use him better than he knows how to use himself—just as if you go into a studio, they use you much more than you use them. Joe doesn't know the strength of the gang, the power of the management. The gang consists of prizefight managers and the Mafia. I've met them. It's one of the few professions that deal with human flesh. What other profession does that? Producers. What do you think the whole play is about? Can't you guess? It's about Hollywood.

Do you want to be a great actor, or do you want fame and success? What is your choice today? You notice I don't give it away easily. Do you like this? You like that we solved it?

TEN

GOLDEN BOY

TEXT ANALYSIS

(1937)

Of all the scenes in all the plays in all of Stella Adler's script-analysis lectures, none was better or more thoroughly explicated line by line than Act I, scene 4 of Clifford Odets's *Golden Boy*. Below is the full text of the scene (indented), interspersed with Adler's exegesis—a remarkable set of in-depth actor's notes and character insights—beneath them.

—B.P.

ACT I, SCENE 4

A few nights later.

JOE and LORNA sit on a bench in the park. It is night. There is carousel music in the distance. Cars ride by in front of the boy and girl in the late spring night. Out of sight a traffic light changes from red to green and back again throughout the scene and casts its colors on the faces of the boy and girl.

Art Smith as promoter Tokio and Luther Adler as boxer Joe Bonaparte in Clifford Odets's *Golden Boy* (1937). "Bonaparte—my God, what a name to carry! It takes a long time to become an American."

> LORNA: Success and fame! Or just a lousy living. You're lucky you won't have to worry about those things. . . .
>
> JOE: Won't I?
>
> LORNA: Unless Tom Moody's a liar.

The unintended irony that motivates Joe's line is that Tom Moody *is* a liar—by definition: he has a wife and kid and is keeping a girlfriend that his wife doesn't know about.

> JOE: You like him, don't you?

"You like that world of being a gangster's girlfriend, don't you?" He's indicating their totally different sets of values: the independent artist vs. the dependent person, who must lean on "the gang" or somebody else for her life.

> LORNA [*after a pause*]: I like him.

She's saying, "Don't dig into my relationship. Mind your own business." A subtle fight begins now. Lorna gets by with the bare minimum of feeling.

> JOE: I like how you dress. The girls look nice in the summer time. Did you ever stand at the Fifth Avenue Library and watch those girls go by?

By bringing up and talking about other women, he's showing that he doesn't have a real interest in her. He's drifting off into his imagination and fantasy: he likes the artistic impression of the way girls dress. He observes girls, but not sexually. He studies them.

> LORNA: No, I never did. [*Switching the subject.*] That's the carousel, that music. Did you ever ride on one of those?

She's being sarcastic. She's not a girl who goes to the library. She's never been there in her life. He is out of her reach. Neither of them is on the make for the other. So she changes the subject to something more comfortable, the carousel. The tension is strong. A man is on the rack, being torn in two directions about what he's going to do, and she's nostalgic for the rinky-dink music.

Why? Because the carousel is what she didn't have. She had no new shoes, no birthday party, no dolls. Make choices that give you Lorna's loneliness—in your choice lies your art. She has no past, no morals. She symbolizes the lost children of America, thrown around, not asked to join the parade but watching it longingly from around the corner. She's a drifter. She didn't know what road to take. How do you get lost like that? Because you don't care what happens to you. She belongs to nothing. She has had to use sex to survive. Life runs you down. Her clock is run down. It must be rewound to give her some hope. She is numb. The carousel is a good symbol for her: it moves but it doesn't go anyplace. It just goes in a circle.

JOE: That's for kids.

He's saying, "Yeah, I know, it's kid stuff—that's about your style, that's all you can handle." He knows Brahms and Beethoven and every opera and sonata and spent his lifetime with music. It's the carousel vs. Mr. Music. He didn't have time or money to ride carousels as a kid. He was mature at ten, special and different. He played the violin, played chess, read the encyclopedia. His father is a workman with culture. How did Mr. Bonaparte get the violin for him? He scrimped and saved. Joe knows the social conditions. He feels he's an artist with values, sitting next to a girl that has no values.

LORNA: Weren't you ever a kid, for God's sake?

JOE: Not a happy kid.

Joe was beaten up and had to defend himself on the streets. He got nothing positive there—just bullying. It was a jungle. He didn't fit in. He couldn't partake of that world, so he partook of another world and was isolated. In America, we don't feel we belong. Joe is angry. He wants revenge. Lorna doesn't belong, either, but she doesn't understand why—or what he's saying.

LORNA: Why?

JOE: Well, I always felt different. Even my name was special—Bonaparte—and my eyes . . .

LORNA: I wouldn't have taken that too serious . . . [*There is a silent pause.* JOE *looks straight ahead.*]

No artist gives up his or her life for politics unless there is a war. You have to fight in the streets. He has no friends. He doesn't trust people. He doesn't trust Lorna. She knows he is isolated, but her life goes a different way. Joe knows how to defend himself against the world. Lorna doesn't. A silent pause means they can't communicate.

JOE: Gee, all those cars . . .

Cars in America are the single biggest thing. He wants the thing the rest of America is obsessed with—the car. Why does he look at a car with passion? It is a symbol of power. He recognizes the power of money. One can recognize it but still refuse to accept it. They are not really talking to each other. They're both off into their own imaginations. Joe sees the fancy cars—

> LORNA: Lots of horses trot around here. The rich know how to live. You'll be rich . . .

—Lorna sees the Central Park horses. She thinks that being rich solves all problems and would solve all of Joe's. It's a mistake. She doesn't see his conflict. Joe takes this as an insult. She has no understanding. Joe is antagonized in the play by almost anything that is said.

> JOE: My brother Frank is an organizer for the CIO.

No, the rich don't know how to live—they're just rich. My *brother* knows how to live. It is a very meaningful thing in the society to be with the CIO, demanding better working conditions. Frank is a person of great esteem in Joe's eyes. He knows his brother's life is at risk. Frank can be killed for his union activities.

> LORNA: What's that?

> JOE: If you worked in a factory you'd know. Did you ever work?

She is oblivious, and he is saying so. "If you broke your back, you'd understand." Inside, with his depth of respect for work, he's ready to kill her. He has contempt for her. He comes from the working class—you don't go out with girls that don't work.

> LORNA [*with a smile*]: No, when I came out of the cocoon I was a butterfly and butterflies don't work.

She's being sarcastic again, but also coy. He doesn't understand anything about women in general, and her in particular. She was raped by society and had no road, so she ran to a safe harbor. Joe has a road—music, morality, ambition—but no compassion, because his work ethic is so strong. All he knows is that she's a kind of whore and leads a stupid life.

> JOE: All those cars . . . whizz, whizz. [*Now turning less casual.*] Where's Mr. Moody tonight?

He has no use for her. So he ignores what she says and changes the subject, going back to what's in his blood, back to wanting his piece of the power that cars give you on the street. But just for a second. Then there's a major change of action. "Where's Mr. Moody?" means "Where's your pimp?" It's not in the line; it has to be in the voice: Moody buys and sells flesh, like a pimp. It also means Joe is asking Lorna, "What are you doing here with me?" and asking himself, "Why am I sitting here with someone else's girl?" It's a little line that signals a big shift.

> LORNA: He goes up to see his kid on Tuesday nights. It's a sick kid, a girl. His wife leaves it at her mother's house.

That information is very revealing. Moody is married and has a sick child that he visits at his mother-in-law's place once a week.

> JOE: That leaves you free, don't it?

"Free" meaning unattached, no loyalty. You don't have that if you're a mistress, whoring around with Moody. People in the fight game are primitive. "So you don't have any kind of loyalty—you can do anything you want with your life tonight." She's free. But he is not free. He's in a jam. He is in this complicated emotion of not yet making his decision.

> LORNA: What are you hinting at?

"You can do your thing then. Moody is busy on Tuesday nights. Fine triangle, nice setup—you and Moody have a smart little arrangement."

> JOE: I'm thinking about you and Mr. Moody.

"Are you going out to solicit or something?"

LORNA: Why think about it? I don't. Why should you?

Lorna is alone, like a piece of leftover apple pie. She doesn't want this angry man to touch her. "I got you from the first moment. You're a son of a bitch and a cold bastard. I've seen your kind in every hotel. I don't need you, I don't want you, I'm injured enough without you."

JOE: If you belonged to me I wouldn't think about it.

LORNA: Haven't you got a girl?

"Miss Nobody" is talking casual nonsense to an artist. Why doesn't he have a girlfriend? He is an artist with music in his soul. That's his flame. He is not *burning* for a girl.

JOE: No.

LORNA: Why not?

JOE [*evasively*]: Oh . . .

He is the boss. What girl would be good enough for Joe? He's an oversized man.

LORNA: Tokio says you're going far in the fighting game.

This is a big transition. Fighting vs. music is what his life is about, and he must solve it for himself. She calls it a *game*. It's not a trade, not a profession. His talent is for something insecure—a win-or-lose game. He hears her and there's an explosion inside his head—

JOE: Music means more to me. May I tell you something?

—but we—and the lines—are missing the transition. How does he get from the fight game to "Music means more to me"? It's "I don't need Tokio to tell me I can be a champ—I know that. I know what I am. I've got music." He's talking about his soul. He is not responding to what she says Tokio says. The actor must put that in, otherwise it's impossible to make that transition. You must know what to *do* in this play, not just how you *feel*. What is the action of spilling your soul? This is the biggest psychological action, and it comes from the inside. Inside, Joe is screaming! He asks permission to speak his mind—to spill out his soul.

> LORNA: Of course.

> JOE: If you laugh I'll never speak to you again.

"So be careful of me." This character is a killer.

> LORNA: I'm not the laughing type.

> JOE: With music, I'm never alone when I'm alone— Playing music . . . that's like saying, "I am man, I belong here. How do you do, World—good evening!" When I play music nothing is closed to me. I'm not afraid of people and what they say. There's no war in music. It's not like the streets. Does this sound funny?

"I'm not alone when I'm alone" is mystical. Don't try too hard to make it logical, because it is not. Tennessee does it all the time: "I didn't go to the moon, I went much further. But time is the distance between two points." Who the hell knows what he's talking about? He knows, but it's hard to penetrate. He's trying to tell the truth, which involves trying to express the inexpressible. "I'm going to tell you how I feel inside" is almost impossible to do, but Joe is trying, and when he talks about music, he is eloquent. He has tremendous passion. He's the artist vs. the warrior. The two strengths are in conflict.

> LORNA: No.

Finally, she's listening a bit.

> JOE: But when you leave your room . . . down in the street . . . it's war! Music can't help me there. Understand?

To stay in the room means music; to leave means war. The street has power, but it's vulgar and dangerous. He is revealing what a man needs: to express himself. Take away music and art, and man becomes no different from any other animal. America makes you violent.

LORNA: Yes.

The passion, the eloquence—not the logic—reaches her.

> JOE: People have hurt my feelings for years. I never forget.
> You can't get even with people by playing the fiddle. If music
> shot bullets I'd like it better—artists and people like that are
> freaks today. The world moves fast and they sit around like
> forgotten dopes.

The power and cruelty of the world are so overwhelming. Artists go
to their own tiny little corner. That tiny corner makes their soul work,
and they are safe there. But that's impossible for him. He's too big to
fit in that small space, in that one room. He was a freak as a kid, and
he doesn't want to be a freak or be forgotten anymore. He's going to
be *remembered*.

> LORNA: You're loaded with fireworks. Why don't you fight?

His battle is with him all the time. He's like the Fourth of July, so
explosive. He is burning up! Look for all those symbols of passion, fire,
anger, fighting, and killing in the play.

> JOE: You have to be what you are—!
>
> LORNA: Fight! See what happens—
>
> JOE: Or end up in the bughouse!
>
> LORNA: God's teeth! Who says you have to be one thing?

Interesting that Odets gives her such an old-fashioned phrase. It's an
old Elizabethan thing like "Forsooth!" No longer in style. A mild
form of profanity—less profane than "For God's sake!"

> JOE: My nature isn't fighting!

In an Italian family at that time, to be a fighter was to be a bum. It
was not quite civilized. She is telling a respectable boy to fight—a boy
with a tradition of honor and learning handed down to him.

LORNA: Don't Tokio know what he's talking about? Don't Tom? Joe, listen: be a fighter! Show the world! If you made your fame and fortune—and you can—you'd be anything you want. Do it! Bang your way to the lightweight crown. Get a bank account. Hire a great doctor with a beard—get your eyes fixed—

Her new action is to size him up. She begins to see he *could* win—he could be anything he wants. This is a revelation for her. But it creates even more of a distance between them. Don't make her explosive. He's the explosive one.

JOE: What's the matter with my eyes?

The moment she gets intimate, he gets angry. The kids always teased him about his eyes. It's his instinctive reaction to get angry.

LORNA: Excuse me, I stand corrected. [*After a pause.*] You get mad all the time.

Everything he does is full of passion. It scares her, and she pulls back.

JOE: That's from thinking about myself.

He knows he has a "big problem" but feels it's okay to think about himself in this lousy world. It means "*take care* of myself."

LORNA: How old are you, Joe?

She can't handle him and thinks it's because he is young.

JOE: Twenty-one and a half, and the months are going fast.

LORNA: You're very smart for twenty-one and a half and the months are going fast.

She's recognizing that he's a killer.

JOE: Why not? I read every page of the Encyclopaedia Britannica. My father's friend, Mr. Carp, has it. A shrimp with glasses had to do something.

The street drove him inwards. People out there on the battlegrounds ridiculed him by talking about music as something dopey. But he had a compulsive passion to *know.*

LORNA: I'd like to meet your father. Your mother dead?

JOE: Yes.

LORNA: So is mine.

She longs to know what his life was like. She thinks maybe he's softening a little.

JOE: Where do you come from? The city is full of girls who look as if they never had parents.

He's not softening. He's not kind or sympathetic. He is brutal. He feels he's too good for her. She had no good influences. She is "loused up." Now, what does she feel when he says that? A man doesn't talk like that to a woman. You see his ruthlessness.

LORNA: I'm a girl from over the river. My father is still alive—shucking oysters and bumming drinks somewhere in the wilds of Jersey. I'll tell you a secret: I don't like you.

Her side of life is lonely, abandoned. She is untouched by love. She is hiding. She is with the lowest of people, betting and gambling. That's her gang. She sees that Joe thinks she's pitiful. She feels his anger and superiority and lack of sympathy. She can't take that kind of truthfulness. So she abruptly changes the action and insults him.

JOE: [*surprised*]: Why?

LORNA: You're too sufficient by yourself . . . too inside yourself.

Which is true, of course. But the more personal reason is that he treats her like dirt.

JOE: You like it or you don't.

"Take me or leave me the way I am."

> LORNA: You're on an island—

> JOE: Robinson Crusoe . . .

> LORNA: That's right—"me, myself, and I." Why not come
> out and see the world?

> JOE: Does it seem that way?

> LORNA: Can't you see yourself?

> JOE: No . . .

He's being honest about a weakness, and vulnerable, for once.

> LORNA: Take a bird's-eye view; you don't know what's right
> or wrong. You don't know what to pick, but you won't ad-
> mit it.

She knows men viscerally, from experience. She's saying, "You're an
egomaniac, you're neurotic, you don't know who you are. You want
two irreconcilable things, and you're wasting your time trying to reconcile them." It's a pretty damn good analysis.

> JOE: Do you?

> LORNA: Leave me out. This is the anatomy of Joe Bonaparte.

> JOE: You're dancing on my nose, huh?

That's a rare expression nowadays. It means to annoy somebody, like
a fly buzzing around your nose. Today it would be "You're fooling
around with me?" or "Don't mess with me!"

> LORNA: Shall I stop?

> JOE: No.

> LORNA: You're a miserable creature. You want your arm in
> *gelt* up to the elbow. You'll take fame so people won't laugh

or scorn your face. You'd give your soul for those things. But every time you turn your back your little soul kicks you in the teeth. It don't give in so easy.

JOE: And what does your soul do in its perfumed vanity case?

He's saying that she is a whore with the little overnight valise women take when they're traveling or a whore takes when she's going to a hotel.

LORNA: Forget about me.

JOE: Don't you want—?

"Don't you want *me to tell you about yourself?*" That's what he was going to say. But they are already perfectly knowledgeable about each other.

LORNA [*suddenly nasty*]: I told you to forget it!

JOE [*quietly*]: Moody sent you after me—a decoy! You made a mistake, Lorna, for two reasons. I made up my own mind to fight. Point two, he doesn't know you don't love him—

It's dawning on him that she is a spy, trying to seduce him into fighting. "You are whoring for that pimp. You're so cheap you don't even love the man."

LORNA: You're a fresh kid.

JOE: In fact he doesn't know anything about you at all.

LORNA [*challengingly*]: But you do?

JOE: This is the anatomy of Lorna Moon: she's a lost baby. She doesn't know what's right or wrong. She's a miserable creature who never knew what to pick. But she'd never admit it. And I'll tell you why you picked Moody!

He's mocking her, using the same words she just used to describe him.

LORNA: You don't know what you're talking about.

JOE: Go home, Lorna. If you stay, I'll know something about you . . .

LORNA: You don't know anything.

"You don't know anything about my situation. You only know your own passions. My passions were destroyed. Life killed them."

JOE: Now's your chance—go home!

LORNA: Tom loves me.

But she doesn't love Tom. If she did, she would have added that. It's a brilliant line for the omission. By what she *doesn't* say, she's revealing herself and her relationships with men: "I'm dead, but he loves me. I'm being honest, no cover-up: I need to be protected." Jackie Kennedy needed Onassis's money and strength. Lorna represents millions of women who lost their way and settled for something less, for what life gives us. Moody's love sustains and also drains her. But she's realistic, she can afford to be truthful, and she is shooting square with Joe: she had to compromise, and Moody's love is what she got. Compromise is the American way of life. Joe compromises too, but differently, by trading love for power. Joe is without love and hasn't given any hint of loving her. From those three words of hers, he gets all this—and it really hits him.

JOE [*after a long silence, looking ahead*]: I'm going to buy a car.

He has a split second of defeat. That, plus the long silence, is Joe's final, most *crucial* transition. Again, a silent pause means they can't communicate. So he goes back to his fantasy.

LORNA: They make wonderful cars today. Even the lizzies—

JOE: Gary Cooper's got the kind I want. I saw it in the paper, but it costs too much—fourteen thousand. If I found one secondhand—

Why would a potential Napoleon or a potentially great musician choose Gary Cooper as a role model? Because Gary Cooper is the American commercial success symbol. They've broken the ice. They are now on the same level: cars—they move, they go places, they have power!

> LORNA: And if you had the cash—

> JOE: I'll get it—

> LORNA: Sure, if you'd go in and really fight!

> JOE [*in a sudden burst*]: Tell your Mr. Moody I'll dazzle the eyes out of his head!

He has made up his mind now. He's already lost love, and he knows it. So he'll "achieve"—he'll be bigger than Gary Cooper ever dreamed! Tremendous power is lurking in him.

> LORNA: You mean it?

> JOE [*looking out ahead*]: Those cars are poison in my blood. When you sit in a car and speed you're looking down at the world. Speed, speed, everything is speed—nobody gets me!

The rhythm of art is too slow for him. He cannot be held down to it. Speed is mindless—it excludes the creative power—but it feels more exciting.

> LORNA: You mean in the ring?

> JOE: In or out, nobody gets me! Gee, I like to stroke that gas!

> LORNA: You sound like Jack the Ripper.

It's the image of a killer: he has a drive to power like a murderer's.

> JOE [*standing up suddenly*]: I'll walk you back to your house—your hotel, I mean. [LORNA *stands.* JOE *continues.*] Do you have the same room?

He is leveling with her. He understands about sex. He's lived in a slum. He knows life.

LORNA [*with sneaking admiration*]: You're a fresh kid!

His concept is one of size. He wants the power and speed of fighting—or of Beethoven. He doesn't want a tin lizzie to drive, or in bed. Golden Boy has big things to work with and for.

JOE: When you're lying in his arms tonight, tell him, for me, that the next World's Champ is feeding in his stable.

He has a tremendous arrogance of power. He's a fighter—ruthless, demonic, angry.

LORNA: Did you really read those Britannia books?

JOE: From A to Z.

LORNA: And you're only twenty-one?

JOE: And a half.

LORNA: Something's wrong somewhere.

The hand he uses to play the violin is the hand he uses to fight. He is not just a musician, not just a fighter. His tragedy is that he's going to kill himself or be killed. He is aiming at something that will destroy him.

JOE: I know . . . [*They slowly walk out as . . .*]

Fadeout

ELEVEN

THE COUNTRY GIRL

(1950)

SYNOPSIS OF *THE COUNTRY GIRL*: The title character of this backstage story is Georgie, married to the once-great theater star Frank Elgin, who is now down on his luck. She is a faithful, loving, forgiving woman whose years of devotion to her husband have almost obliterated her own personality. In their New York flat and his dressing rooms, most of her time and energy is spent bolstering the morale of an actor whose long periods of idleness are filled with drink and despair.

Suddenly, the proverbial Big Break materializes: Frank gets a major comeback chance from hotshot young Broadway director Bernie Dodd, who picks him for the lead of an important new play. But only Georgie knows how hard it will be to pull Frank together, constantly reassure him, and keep him from slipping at the inevitable moments of discouragement.

Act II's action takes place backstage of the Boston theater, where Georgie continues trying to perform her morale-building job on Frank under the watchful eyes of nervous director Bernie, whose reputation depends on this production. During the stress of rehearsals,

Paul Kelly and Uta Hagen as Frank and Georgie Elgin in
Clifford Odets's *The Country Girl* (1950). "It's about the
theater—the great actor is never supposed to fail. If somebody comes in from the outside and starts meddling, you
want to kill them."

he doubts her good influence, and comes to believe
Frank's alcoholic lies: that Georgie and her lack of
confidence in him are responsible for his decline. The
pressures created by a high-stakes out-of-town tryout
bring the complicated relationship between husband
and wife to a crisis point. Life backstage becomes the
ultimate emotional and psychological battleground for
all three characters.

On opening night in Boston, the strain proves too

great. In the dark light of Frank's relapse, Bernie finally recognizes the country girl for what she is—a magnificent woman whose self-sacrifice wasn't appreciated until too late.

—B.P.*

PUT A BLANK PAGE in front of every script you approach, to write down the essential things: What is the theme of the play? What does it say? What is the style? What is the time when it was written? What is the music of the period? The dancing? The books and paintings typical of its time? That is the culture of the period that you need to know.

Once you have that, then draw a line and ask: What is my character? What class do I come from? You are responsible for knowing that—or finding it out. Put down the clothes, the manners, the kind of rooms you live in. Most of all, you must ask, "How do I think?" And then contrast your own thinking with that of the character. In politics, sex, money, ethics, morality, religion—how do you think differently from the character?

As you steer away from yourself, you'll get closer to the way the character thinks. Unless all this goes through your imagination and you create it, you are not an artist. That's the difference between photography and art. The tendency of the photographer is to capture the personality of the tree. The tendency of the artist is to also capture what the tree is saying.

There is no one single Truth. But there are a couple of truths in every play. The conflict is about one person's truth vs. the other

* *The Country Girl* premiered at the Lyceum Theatre in New York City on November 10, 1950, directed by Odets, with Uta Hagen (Georgie), Paul Kelly (Frank), and Steven Hill (Bernie). The 1954 film version, directed by George Seaton, won Seaton an Oscar for Best Screenplay Adaptation and a Best Actress award for Grace Kelly as Georgie. Bing Crosby played Frank and William Holden was Bernie.

person's truth. You must think your way and the other character's way. Both are true. You may not personally believe in abortion, but there are an awful lot of people who do. If you play a character that believes in abortion, you have to get all the reasons why that character believes—and why the other character doesn't. Gradually, you will feel, "I know the other side of my thinking."

I remember once meeting a multimillionaire in English political life, and I thought how clever he was, because he knew all about communism and how the Communist system worked. That's what made him capable of being on his own side—the fact that he also knew the other side.

Begin to create your character from the outside. Does he have an accent? How does he dress, how does he wear his hair? See and observe him in different situations, under various circumstances. Watch him walk down the street, buy a paper. Watch him eat. Only then can you begin to get a sense of the particular character you are playing.

What are the circumstances he lives in? If my play takes place in a New York rooming house, then New York is the larger circumstance. Read more of the playwright's work, not just the one play you're working on. First you get impressions, and from the impressions you get the plot. How does the play develop? From that you get the character and the ideas. You have to work on the play from the past. And you have to figure out how to use the stage. Don't wait for somebody to say, "Now, walk over here." It's not a good idea.

Bernie's large action in *The Country Girl* is to control the difficult machinery of the theater. That means first he has to control the front office, which is Cook, the producer. Go through all the rest of the machinery he is in charge of: the directing, the scenery, the stage-hands, the company, the costumes, the lighting, the various actors' problems, and the playwright's concerns. You see that Bernie's mind has to go in many directions. He also has to manage the dressing rooms and all those things the actors bring in from outside of the stage. Controlling the complex mechanics and problems of putting on a play is his job.

I'm going to take you to what I think is the pivotal moment in the play, a few minutes into the first scene of Act II, in Frank's dressing room in Boston. The opening is getting closer. It's two o'clock in the morning, everyone is fatigued, and the mood is intense. Bernie's problems are mounting. He's got a script problem and a wife problem. He and the playwright have been rewriting the last scene yet again. That's an actor's worst nightmare—even a secure actor, let alone an insecure one: they keep changing his lines. Frank has already been drinking a lot and having trouble with the old lines. Getting new ones at the last minute could put him over the edge.

Georgie has been trying to keep him under control, coddling and reassuring him and trying to keep the alcohol out of reach. Frank's not there—he's out shooting publicity photographs on the stage—but other people keep coming in and out of his dressing room with their own problems, and she's got a splitting headache. Finally, they all clear out and she gets a breather for a minute, flips on the radio, and starts waltzing to some soft music, Odets tells you in the script, "as if it were possible to waltz herself back to a better time."

She doesn't notice that Bernie is standing in the dressing-room doorway, watching her. When she sees him, she stops dancing abruptly, embarrassed. Bernie says, "Excuse me, the both of you." It's sarcastic. She's been waltzing alone, with an invisible partner.

That's very typical of the theater today. I don't mean the sarcasm; I mean that you don't knock on a dressing-room door, you just walk in, and if you see someone there who's not an actor, you say, "Excuse me," meaning "What are *you* doing here?" In the dressing room, there is no rapport between somebody from the outside and somebody who belongs there.

So you get the attitude, as Bernie comes in, that there are two very different people in this room. You get the sense that they are not together, that they don't really want to speak to each other. She's in the middle of a reverie, maybe looking in the mirror, turning around, reaching for something . . . He's barging in on a mission, looking for Frank, but Frank is not to be seen—just Georgie with her headache. Bernie reaches in his pocket, hands her a little tin, and says: "It's the Age of Aspirin."

He says that because he is very philosophical, and critical—he's saying, "Everybody takes too many aspirin these days." She's struggling: "A splitting headache . . . too much stuffy dressing-room . . . "

He's moving again, always moving, and he says, "I have to get Frank. Where's Frank?" She says, "On stage." He's up and down to the dressing-room entrance and back. He can't find Frank, he has things to do in the office. His whole action is to find Frank. Georgie's whole action is to struggle with this mess. It's not do-able, but she's trying.

This man, Bernie, is against her; the office is against her; Frank has a cold and has already polished off one bottle of cough medicine and is looking for the other one, which Georgie hid. He smashed the empty bottle and threw things down on the floor because she took the other bottle of cough mixture away. She swept up the pieces when he went off—she constantly picks up the pieces for him.

The mess is not something she has just visualized when the curtain goes up. She has it from deep in her past. "I can't take it anymore, I have to get out. I can't take another outburst, I don't want him to break another bottle, I don't want to be here when he breaks things again. I have to get out." She is tense as well as intense.

Get her intensity. Get her realization that it's all too much for her. When he says "Where's Frank?" she turns and faces him. It's the first time she is actually "with" him, and she needs a cigarette to do it. In this particular theatrical style, you don't just "use" props, you let the props clarify you and the text. It is not for you to be busy with irrelevant things. The things you do must help create your character, create the style and help the text. If it doesn't help the text, don't do it.

So where are her cigarettes? She glances around, looks at the table. She locates her pocketbook and picks it up, but doesn't open it yet. She is maybe near the washstand or near a chair and table with a lamp and a pitcher of water on it. She turns to him and says, "His cold is getting worse, Mr. Dodd. He shouldn't be kept up this late. It's more than flesh and blood can stand."

With that, maybe she opens her pocketbook, takes out her hand-kerchief and wets it, to get some cool water on it. She dabs her face a little. He watches her do this. We see she's in a state—she has a headache, she is not well, she is with her own body. He takes this in. He feels she can be of no help to him or her husband—taking aspirin, drinking water, wetting her face. He sees a very womanly woman, doing feminine things.

His disrespect for her is not only in his mind but is made visible by what she does. You can't imagine *him* ever needing aspirin or cold water for his head. His attitude toward her as a man is, "For chrissakes, what are you doing here? We don't need you, we don't need sick little wives around." It has to be established right away that his attitude is superficially tolerant—he doesn't throw her out—but he's not *with* her.

So after taking the aspirin and the water, she could notice there's a new script on the table—that's trouble. She goes over and picks it up, looks at it, puts it down. Dodd doesn't know what Georgie knows: that when there's a new script, Frank can't handle it. Only Georgie knows that. The thing that has to be in her mind—and *your* mind, if you're the actress—is "He can't study and learn this! It's no good!"

In this style, you have to invent a lot from offstage to feed yourself onstage. It is important that you feed off the props, feed off the business, feed off the ideas to agitate yourself. She would get extremely agitated by realizing that Bernie has brought in a new script. She might look at it, see how marked up it is, put it back down on the table, thinking, "He won't be able to do it, there'll be a scandal." The handkerchief, the scripts give her some way to show him what a mess the situation is—why "it's more than flesh and blood can stand."

"Them's melodramatic words," he says, patronizing her. "Look, we need production pictures . . . How's his spirit?" She looks over at where Frank threw the empty bottle of cough syrup, lying there in the garbage can. She knows he's getting drunk. She walks around her table, knowing he threw everything off it that she had arranged so nice and clean. Bernie sees only the clean table. She looks at this man, who knows nothing about what is happening, and then answers: "Low." Her attitude toward Bernie is, "You're a boy, you really don't know what's going on here—you only know what you're told happened." Nobody knows a drunk except his wife.

Frank's "low" spirit means "You can't possibly reach this man except through the things that I'm going to tell you." He says, "Why is he low? The play's in good shape." He is only judging from the outside, not from her experience. They are in complete conflict, which is what you need in staging a realistic play. It's not in the text. The play takes on many dimensions if you do it this way. That is what every realistic play needs. It needs not to be spoken like Shakespeare.

Bernie leans on the edge of the dressing-room table and says, "The show's in fair shape." She takes that in, looks at him, and sees that he's with the show and the new text, while she is with the fact that Frank has had cough mixture with liquor in it and wants more liquor. She goes for her pocketbook, takes out her cigarettes, and says, "Ask the Boston critics. Everyone doesn't have your confidence." She has a cigarette in her hand but no matches. He sees that, and throws her the matches.

Now, the throwing of the matches reveals two things: one, his basic disrespect for women, and two, his class. He throws her the matches instead of lighting her cigarette. You know everything about this man in that one gesture. She lights her cigarette, looks for the ashtray, picks it up from somewhere, and puts it down. "And while I'm on the subject . . ." she says—now that she has the cigarette, she is more pulled together. Smoking, she looks at him: "While we're on the subject, let's talk about *you.*" On that she is quite direct: "On the subject of confidence, I'm going to say that you have a lot of it, which makes you push." Give him back the matches. "It makes you into a bully." He gets it.

The cigarette and the play of the matches will give you a lot of drama that is not in the text. It will give you character and a sense that they shouldn't be in the same room together. If any man threw matches at me, I'd kill him.

"That makes you a bully." He takes the matches back, lights his own cigarette, goes back to a chair, and says, "That's true, too"—meaning, "How clever you are! My God, when did you discover that? When did you find out that I'm aggressive and like to take charge?" She says, "Don't minimize what I say by agreeing with me." It's the first time she really makes up her mind to tell him the ugly truth—that Frank has lost his confidence.

Bernie can walk upstage, open the door to see how the photo shoot is going and, from the back of the stage, say, "What else is bothering friend Frank?"

While the pictures are being taken Georgie says, "You didn't come back after the show tonight. Neither did Mr. Cook." He can grab the script and shake it practically in her face when he says, "Look, this last month I've spent ten, twelve, fifteen hours a day with Frank—fifteen hours a day!—and nothing bothers him except through your mouth. Why?"

This is the first outbreak.

His action, again, is to keep things going—to keep the rehearsal going and make sure everything there is straight. He has the script and the rewrites on his mind. He's spent an endless amount of time with Frank, and the way he sees it, nothing's upsetting Frank except Georgie. It's the first time they move closer together in their confrontation. She wants a way out of this mess, and he wants to keep it all going. They have two different ambitions.

Georgie tries to warn him about a few things, tries to give him an insight or two into Frank. "He thinks it's a crime to lack a sense of humor. He doesn't want to be disliked. He hides when he's nervous" about the script. She picks it up, puts it down. "No humor, so he drinks." Maybe she picks up the cough-syrup bottle and shows it to him. Find elements on the stage that show what she's saying. Find things she can use.

There's no humor in the script—new or old. She picks one or the other one up. "He doesn't want to fail, to be disliked. So he hides and jabbers away, or he sits in silence and rots away inside." She's trying to make it clear he is headed for a bender.

Georgie goes back to her chair. Bernie, now, decides to get rid of her because he thinks she is belittling Frank. She is dealing with Frank physically, with his body, and she's talking about this artist in personal ways. But there is something about a director in the theater that doesn't want to know those things. "I don't want to know what happens when you go home, Stella. I just want to know that you know the text!" That is absolutely true of people in the profession. They don't want to hear that you have rheumatism. "Don't bother me about that."

So Bernie gets very angry. "I have to get rid of this bitch. I loathe her!" Getting rid of her becomes his main action. He says, "Women always think they understand their men. What women know, my God, what great theoreticians they are, aren't they?"

She gets it. "I won't fight with you, Mr. Dodd. He expected you after the show last night." She's right at him with the facts. "He wanted you backstage. He doesn't want you to tell him he's great, but he wanted you backstage. I'll tell you what he really wants: he wants little compliments from you, Mr. Dodd. That's what he needs." This is very upsetting to Bernie, and his anger increases.

She sees that he doesn't understand and says, "Do you know anything about drinkers?" She gets more and more direct. Maybe stuff out the cigarette, move away, walk around the room. She has got to get to him—to make him see that this is a patient, not an actor.

So her action changes, too. The second step in her action was to warn him. Her third step, now, is to try to get him to understand the patient—to penetrate his infernal difficulty in understanding the problem. She gets more intense. "Have you ever had a drunk on your hands? I'm diagnosing this patient for you." How can she get through to him? She tries one thing after another. "He's got a bad cold," she says. "That's a respectable reason for any drinker to jump down the well. If you're not careful, you'll have him full of whiskey before he goes to bed tonight."

She's really an expert doctor. He watches her intensity in trying to explain the anatomy of this drunk, but he only sees her trying to be a mother or a nursemaid. He says, "Why do you work so hard at this marriage? Why not take a rest? You wear your husband down! You make him tense, uneasy—you don't stop 'handling' him. You try to 'handle' me, too . . . You called your own husband a cunning drunkard!"

Because it's *true,* she says—because "it is necessary for you to know it!" The impasse is complete. They both think they know what's best for him. She's at her wit's end. "In God's name, what exactly do you want me to do for Frank?"

He finally hits her with it: "Get out of town!"

* * *

Georgie is sick. Her headache is just a symptom of the deeper sickness of not knowing whether she can handle another opening and another drunken brawl with Frank. "I can't take it anymore. I don't have the right to go, but I can't stay." Right from the start, look for her deeper problem. It's not a headache; it's whether to go or stay. This is the spine of her action.

Isn't that the spine of the dilemma of most modern women who haven't accomplished what they want in their lives? Isn't that what most modern women talk about? "If I'm not fully aware of where I am going, how can I keep going there?" This is what she is worried about. After ten years, does she have the right to think about that? If you play her, build that up.

Does Bernie understand a thing about her? All he knows is that stage life is tense and she's in the way. All she knows is that she's in a place that is killing her. She is in a room without air—a place where everybody's on a first-name basis. This is modern. It is absolutely a new way of life. But she is somebody who has not made that transition. She calls him "Mr. Dodd," and from that one phrase alone you see that she is traditional. She is still called "Mrs. Elgin." She is not called "Becky" or "Sadie" or "Jenny" or "Georgie" by anyone except her husband. She is a Mrs. The fact that she is a Mrs. gives her a certain standing in the society. That's part of what "Mrs." is—it establishes you, gives you a base. But she has nothing to show for it. The "Mrs." is empty for her.

Bernie knows this. He knows she has no home life, no kids—and he knows Frank's temperament. "What the hell are you calling yourself Mrs. for?" he wants to know. "Why don't you just get the hell out of town, for christsakes. You're a misfit here!"

She's saying, "No, I am not a misfit. I've weathered this storm for ten years. I am what stays when *you* go. I am the permanency—the permanent center—of this man's life. He will die without me." It's the attitude of the committed "Mrs." toward the world then. The world changed in the sixties, not in 1950. But it was starting to.

She is saying, "I have been the wife of a drunkard." Bernie is saying, "He's only a drunkard to you with your small, boring, middle-class values. To me, he's a great actor. If you keep calling him a drunkard, I'll break your neck."

He is talking about Frank's soul. "That's what he gives you," she says, "but he gives me his body—his colds and coughs, his vomiting, his taking pills at night, his not sleeping, his nervous tension, his sneaking away and drinking. This is what he gives me; this is what I'm reporting on. It's more than he can stand. I'm talking about his body, Mr. Dodd! I tell you, unless he brings you his body, you won't have his soul."

Can she leave? No. She is a Mrs.—Mrs. Suffering—understanding her role in life biblically, for better or worse. I don't blame her for having a headache. Bernie says, "Them's melodramatic words." A melodrama is a cheap form of theater—a false play with a false plot and false characters. When he says, "Them's melodramatic words," he means, "I think you're a fake. You're not a liar, but your class lies. You exaggerate. You have an exaggerated sense of your value in the society. Whereas I'm a left-winger. I'm the one in the marches. I'm against you and your stockings and your alligator bag. I'm against your white gloves and your way of slandering this great man!"

I would say the same thing Bernie is saying. I'd tell you that a paralyzed actor will get through, that people around him know he will get through, and that there is no such thing as "I have a headache" or "I'm sick"—for God's sake, shut up about that! There is no time for an actor to say "I'm tired." I can't stand it whenever any actor says he's tired, because I don't get tired. No fatigue, no toothaches, no headaches, no "My feet are tired" or "My back hurts." I'm not hungry, I'm not thirsty. *I am working.* This is a play about the theater—take it from the horse's mouth. It's about discipline. If somedy comes in from the outside and starts meddling, you want to kill them.

Georgie is bringing in her own kind of discipline as the Wife of All Time, saying, "I don't trust you and your art. I'm the wife, and I know when he will give in and give up." And Bernie's response is, "You don't know a goddamn thing. You are a cheap slut who is intruding." From the first, he views her with suppressed or unsuppressed anger. "Get out of the dressing room!"

She says, "Yes, he is an aristocrat and an artist. He won't show you he is angry. He will joke with you. He will never reveal any weakness except to me, because with me he is a man, not an artist. With you, or on the stage, he does this whole shtick because you demand it from him. But with me, he is sick in body and spirit. He knows he is defeated. He hears through the door—hears you talking about him and needing him to be a success. But he is not going to be a success. He's a man as well as an artist, and he has a right to fail."

Once I went to see Gielgud.* It was his last attempt in *King Lear* at Stratford. He was very good in the last scene, but he never really had the power for the "Blow, winds, and crack your cheeks!" monologue in Act III. I went backstage, and he was very charming. "This is the third time round," he said. "You see, I fail when I do this play."

The great actor is never supposed to fail. He simply puts the role aside. After my father failed as Othello, he played Iago. He gave Othello to another actor, and his Iago was a great success. Great actors know when they fail. But even then, they don't fail their audiences. If you play twenty or thirty great parts, some of them will succeed and be remembered historically, and some of them will have to be given up.

This thing of telling an actor, "If you fail, the play is finished, the show and the theater will close down"—this is something new. The theater used to be open year-round. You didn't go into a theater for a few days. You were engaged for thirty-eight weeks, and the rest of

---

* John Gielgud (1904–2000): the great English Shakespearean stage and film actor and director, renowned for his Hamlet (performed more than five hundred times), Richard II, and Prospero in *The Tempest,* and an Oscar winner for his sardonic butler in *Arthur* (1981).

the time you filled in with concerts or stock company and things. You were always engaged for the season, and you still are—in every other country.

An actor's spirit is deeply affected by what Strindberg called "the rumor"—by threatening his performance with failure. Georgie says, "His cold is getting worse, he shouldn't be kept up late, he needs rest and quiet and peace of mind. You're asking about his spirit? It's low!" "Low" doesn't mean he isn't feeling good. It means he is on the verge of cracking up. She is taking his part from a middle-class point of view that understands he has a right to fail.

But Bernie says, "If he's low, it's because you're *making* him low." Bernie is in trouble too, and he knows it. When he says "The show is in fair shape," it means "We're in trouble, but I will pull it out and make it work somehow." As a director, he owns the actor in a real sense. "Give me Frank's body, because I can inspire him. He may fail, his way, by drinking himself to death or collapsing onstage, but not your way, by taking him home and nursing him, you bitch! Get out. Leave him alone. Give him to me!"

You cannot play a big play from the words—you have to play it from the conflicts. *The Country Girl* is a very well-written play about an actor who's in trouble because other people need him to be a success. He is thinking, "Leave me alone and I'll give you the performance, but don't whisper about me, don't tell me Mr. Cook is out there depending on me to cook up his money. I don't care—and I can't deal with it."

An epic struggle is going on for possession of this man's body and soul—the struggle of two classes for the artist. Odets deeply understands that the American artist is going down, that he is being killed by commercialism. What's left of courage and fairness in American life is personified by the country girl, facing the new element that says, "I will save the theater, even if it means killing my star actor and myself."

Bernie tells Georgie, "Don't weaken him, don't do what women do. Don't give him the sense that he needs you. Leave him. Let him be with the part. Let him be with me."

There is enormous tension there.

Do you understand the anger between them?

WILLIAM SAROYAN

William Saroyan (c. 1932)

TWELVE

OVERVIEW

I MUST TELL YOU what Bill Saroyan did. I knew him because we were producing his play and he was around in the theater. He was creative and optimistic and desperately sentimental and childish. I was very pretty. Saroyan came up one day in the afternoon and knocked on my door, and I opened it and there he was, completely naked, standing there looking at me with his arms out. I screamed! I ran out and got the elevator man and said, "Do something!" Saroyan got dressed and went away.

Now, that's pretty innocent. I didn't encourage him. I was then like I am now. Men are not apt to go up to me and say, "Come on, kid, let's go for a tumble." I wasn't that kind of a woman. I was a sort of young royalty. Bobby Lewis* said, "Stella will go to Moscow and become a Communist if they will make her the queen."

In America, going from the 1920s to the 1930s, people no longer behaved in predictable ways. That was gone. The disaster of the thirties changed everything, including the theater. It threw the old theatrical

---

* Robert Lewis (1909–1997) was an actor, director, author, and co-founder of the Actors Studio in New York in 1947 and chairman of the acting and directing departments of the Yale School of Drama in the 1970s. He was a founding member of the revolutionary Group Theatre in the 1930s along with Harold Clurman, Lee Strasberg, and Cheryl Crawford. Lewis and other Group members such as Stella and Elia Kazan championed a new form of truthful stage acting based on the techniques of Russian director Konstantin Stanislavsky. Lewis's Actors Studio students included Marlon Brando, Montgomery Clift, Maureen Stapleton, Eli Wallach, Mildred Dunnock, Karl Malden, and Patricia Neal.

forms for a loop. Very little inhibition was left on the stage; you could go far out if you wanted, in formal changes and in language. After the crash of 1929 and the Depression, many new styles emerged. Maxwell Anderson had been writing about fancy society. S. N. Behrman wrote about women who wore high-heeled shoes. That disappeared. The playwrights who had been around in the twenties—Anderson, Behrman, George Kaufman—all talked about (and against) society, but now they were beginning to see a changing society and a change in playwriting.

The one new society that existed then was in the Soviet Union. I had played in the fancy plays, all of them, but suddenly I had a gun in my hand—for Lenin. I didn't know how to dress or act like a soldier, but I had to learn. I went to a Communist school in Moscow to find out what a Communist girl thinks. I found out. It didn't hurt me. You don't have to become a Communist to learn how a Communist thinks. It's called dialectic materialism, and it's interesting. You don't need it now. It's not your period. Wait till the next war comes.

Why did we do such things then? Because the country had experienced complete collapse. For the first time in America, the banks failed, businesses failed, worker security failed, "democracy" failed—everything failed. There was failure everywhere. Nobody knew where to go. The American playwright of the 1930s had a sense of drifting. We were isolationists, and everything was in a state of transition. America's way of life was changing, with dirty economic tricks, making munitions for big profits, furnishing other countries with arms, helping create another war.

The playwrights divided up into different groups, and a lot of good younger ones, like Clifford Odets and Arthur Miller and Irwin Shaw, said, "There will be a new world." They were the playwrights of revolt. Miller has a wonderful scene in *The Price* when the wife finds out the bank went bankrupt—they were very wealthy but now they have nothing. It's such a shock, she vomits on the husband, right on stage.

I was acting at the time it hit hardest. I was engaged for a whole season, but the curtain went down one night and never went up again. The theater just closed overnight. I was left with a dressing room and no money—nothing. Do you know what it is to have no money? It was grim. I had a family. The landlord came to me and said, "We want rent," and I said, "It's people like you we want to shoot." I went to live with different friends.

We did a play called *1931*, where we walked out in front of the curtain with guns and said to the audience, "We're going to shoot you." It was a frightening scene. The situation wasn't so playful then. Out of it came the smaller Off Broadway theaters, all full of fight—all tied to the struggle for a new society. The struggle was in everybody—"We have to do something! We have to have a new world order!" Whether it was Marxism or something else, those playwrights of revolt believed that would happen and fought for it.

But another kind of playwright coming out of the Depression said, "That's too heavy. It's too much. Instead, we say it's all right to be a bum. It's all right to starve. What's bad about not having a place to sleep? What's so bad about being hungry and freezing?" Playwrights like Odets and Miller said, "We can't go on like this." But Wilder and Saroyan said, "We'll do the best we can." They had been thrown out and actually lived that way, but they had kept their liveliness, their spiritual springboard that came out of the most crazy, dismal, desperate moments. They were the *transitional playwrights,* who said, "Let's be cheerful."

We have very few good playwrights now, because society's attitude is passive. It's when you have a really active social situation that you get really good playwrights. Some of them analyze the social situation. Others write poetic plays.

Saroyan and Wilder don't want to talk about capitalism. Wilder is too educated to talk about it, the way Chekhov was too educated to talk about the revolution—they were intellectuals. They knew there were always many sides in politics. Saroyan had no education, was brought up in the dumps of Fresno, went through the First World War and then starvation and the Depression. What was Saroyan going to do with capitalism? He said, "Yes, of course, there are capitalists. They're fine fellows. Let them alone. Maybe they'll get better." That's basically what Wilder said, too.

But Saroyan emphasized the underdogs. He is the opposite of Wilder. With his clownish gaiety, living in saloons and being drunk half the time, he thinks everybody is good and life is worth living. We don't get that from Wilder, whose people seem mostly very middle-class. Saroyan writes about the real down Depression people.

He didn't so much write about them as sing about them. He didn't have an answer. He was not political, so he went into poetic fantasies about them. He used symbolic characters, especially the national bum.

That bum could jump onto any train and "ride to heaven!" He was like Saroyan: a complete person who couldn't be grounded. He didn't have a political philosophy, but he felt he knew somewhere there was a better theory and practice of democracy.

The audiences were changing, too, and Mr. Saroyan's audience was prepared for him. Saroyan was the result of new thinking which made him use a very free play form. American thinking would belong for the first time to a new class. The working class, the bum, the disinherited—these are the people now on the stage. The large majority of these plays are not so refined, not so gentle. Women are not much featured in them. It was a man's theater intended for a new class unique to America.

This tradition of the 1930s is now a part of you. You inherited a theater that changed completely from the drawing room, from all the old values and old discussions and old middle-class characters. It called for an extremely new and bold kind of acting—of actor—even though the class that came to see us was a class we wanted to attack.

Saroyan and others of his time showed the upper class in its worst colors. In Lillian Hellman's *Little Foxes,* they are dirty, run-down, nasty people. When you get those characters, remember that they still belong to the "discussion play." It is when you leave the discussion and begin to fight for a new hero that you are really in the young playwrights of the 1930s—and the 1980s. They were fighting for a different world.

Saroyan spoke with a different voice, not like the political playwrights. He had a childlike, old-fashioned understanding of life. When I was working at Metro as an associate producer, I took him onto the set where they were filming *Tortilla Flat.* It was a big set with roads and little houses made of straw and paper, and Saroyan looked and said, "Isn't that wonderful? I think I'll move in." I said, "But, Bill, you know it's a set." And he said, "Oh, it's a set!"

You see from that that he confused fantasy with reality. This was his gift. In life he had the ability to go in and out of reality, anywhere and anytime he wanted, and he put this quality into his plays. When a man has fantasy and reality so mixed up, you must say this is an original mind. From all his tramping around the world, he was the original hobo. And yet he was a king. He behaved like a king, and he had nothing. If a play failed, he said to the critics, "I think you better rest for a while, you need some sunshine!" It was anger tempered by hope.

Saroyan's other gift—his gift as a genius—was the love of man-kind. Mankind loves, and his plays have to have love in their fra-grance. Saroyan doesn't think anybody is ever bad. That's the way he lived and died. His people are innocent and unsheltered and home-less. They are the uncared-for children of the Depression. Children of the Depression wrote unusual plays in unusual styles. Certain play-wrights in the 1930s believed we are going to be saved, and the thing that would save us was political. When most of Americans had been thrown down, they said "We are going to kill you!" to the audience. They said we were going to make a revolution.

Saroyan didn't talk about revolution. He evaded it with a child-like optimism. He is fragrant, he is perfumed, with his old-fashioned optimism. The thirties have this wonderful thing: even in despair, we know a new man is coming, and it's worth it. There will be a brother-hood of man. There is a big difference between Saroyan and the next group—Tennessee Williams, Samuel Beckett, and that crowd. They aren't so optimistic. The "brotherhood of man" comes from a great illusion and a wonderful inspiration. All the young people were ideal-ists then—all fighting and terribly interested in government. I made speeches for President Roosevelt. I went to Philadelphia for the 1940 Democratic Convention to make sure that he looked good, because he was my president and he loved me and I loved him, and there was hope. I don't think you have that now. We did. Our world was the new world. Artists were together in that aspiration. Even when you suffered in Saroyan, there was a kind of glee and glow and poetry and hopefulness and love. You suffered like a broken child—not in your adult guts. You had faith and you shined as if the hallelujah light was on you. It was warm, spiritual, childish. The 1930s man in Saroyan was not a big man but a new man—a man who was developing a big-ness of understanding how to live with pain. He is just being born into his greatness.

In *Hello Out There!,* a young man in jail tries to make contact in his own crazy way with a girl who is taking care of the jail. He says he is going to elope with her and then other people come in to kill him and then in the end they go out and the girl says, "Hello, out there . . . ?" Somehow, you have to make a universal thing out of this. You are not in the tradition of realism. Therefore, there is not much logic. If you are in a realistic play, you have a name and you have shoes, props, etc., and you are a certain type. In Saroyan, there is fantasy, childishness, imagination. A lot of times he uses music to break in and out of reality. The young man in Saroyan's play is the hope of the artist. The artist makes up his own world. There is very little that he uses of the real world. An artist of the 1930s in a play that is not logical is trapped. Who traps him? People who want money. He is the poet of the play.

One of the things this style gives you is the ability to work with your imagination. The man in *Hello Out There!* has a spoon to work with. That's about it. It's childish. It's not much different from "There was an old lady who lived in a shoe and had so many children she didn't know what to do." There is fantasy and reality, and this is fantasy. A man who is alone somewhere—on a hill or in jail—says, "Hello out there . . . Do you see me, will you come and join me?" In his fantasy, maybe he's a cowboy, maybe he's an artist. "Hello out there, this is Bill Saroyan!" He is a young man looking for company—from the past, from the future. This is Saroyan. This is not anybody else.

In all these plays movement is very important. Light is very important. Everything is important but logic. It is better if you just have two or three stools instead of big sets for jumping around the world. The next contact he makes could be the chief justice, the next could be Lenin—"Somebody, save me here! I'm an artist, I'm wandering around, I don't have any money. Listen to me, I've got to go to San Francisco!" The character is a child. He's trapped. Saroyan says, "I've got to put him somewhere, and he's not going to shut up just because he's in jail. So for a moment he is not in jail. He is any place where the actor who plays him wants him to be." The wind is blowing through his hair, and he's playing the guitar and there is God. Saroyan believes in old-fashioned things. He is not a beatnik. He believes in girls and taking a walk at night. His rhythms are forgotten rhythms.

He has nostalgia for the good old days. He is a man with a top hat. He still has the cakewalk in him. He is not modern. He is a clown with leftover melodies. It is no good making him contemporary, because he doesn't make any sense fighting for an answer. He gets killed. He doesn't know what has happened to him. What is his philosophy? He's somebody who knows you are wrong but likes you just the same. This character wants to drift. He doesn't want to get anything the hard way, working like a dog, or the easy way, either. Men like that ride freight trains. They are not rooted. They bum a ride, their movement is light, they don't hate anybody. "I'll be the finest guy you ever saw if I just get a few bucks—I won't be 'wrong' anymore." When you get enough money, you can't be wrong anymore. Everybody says you are right if you have money. We have to have a lot of money, but we don't want to work for it.

Saroyan has completely old-fashioned ideas of family. He lives with the Armenians—lots of Armenians, all around him. He knows about them. Armenians have a sense of themselves that they are bigger than most people. They don't have a sense of their territory as being small. They think they own the earth, and they have a special largeness about their music, food, dancing, women, love, poetry . . . What Saroyan wants to do is to reach out to *all* of his fellows: "We're in trouble, help us! Help us artists, we're going through hell!" Every once in a while in his plots, someone comes in and hits a guy on the head and he dies, and then you go back to the dream.

You are not in a realistic school. Most of the plays you get in this period are outside of the realistic idiom. In *Bury the Dead** people talk to dead people. Here the artist is as lost as anybody else who is trying to become something in this new society. He has been put under cover, locked up. That is Saroyan's theme. The artist reaches out, and one person may hear him and be helped. He lives mostly through his imagination. He has the ability to make things big or small, dramatic or not. He is a magician. He says, "What are you doing here? You are beautiful."

What does he say about the society? The artist is in jail. What does he say about the young person who is not in jail? That he or she has to be born. Is it best to be born through capitalism, through all the things that have failed? No, it is best to be close to the man that is locked up, to be nothing, to be enslaved. Because he is not really a slave. He is just somebody who doesn't know who he is, who is waiting to be born, to discover himself. He or she has no voice, no ability to make contact, no place to go. He or she is frightened of life. He says, "I'm alone here. I'm nothing. I can't free you. I haven't got the strength—but because I love you, I will make an effort."

It's a real birth. "Something is starting in me," says the girl in

---

* In that antiwar drama, written in 1936 by Irwin Shaw (1913–1984) and starring, in its first production, Stella's brother Jay Adler, fallen soldiers rise from the dead to lambaste the living about the horror and injustice of war. News of their resurrection prompts panicked denials from the authorities. Widows and mothers of the walking corpses are brought in to exhort them to return to their graves.

Hello Out There! She's a terrific example of Saroyan's characters. Her first entrance into the world of poetry is frightening and creative—"I feel better now, yes . . . No, I don't feel so good now . . . I'm afraid of poetry . . . I better go back to the kitchen . . . I'm caught between these worlds . . . Will I have love?" It's about her growing into his world, which has many things in it, too—he can become many men. "I'm a bad man, I'm a good man, I'm all kinds of men." He can reach her or lose her, but he is singing! He has a voice. He is really having a ball.

It has nothing to do with realism or with other forms that you know. It is way out but it is delightful. It is light and full of beauty and hope and aspiration. It is full of the joy of acting in a heightened way. She has the movement—and the size—of a mouse peeking out. A tiny thing. It is a little melody that is going to save you.

Saroyan has the melody. He gives it to the Young Man, like a refrain: "Gee, I feel good. Hello out there . . . ? Gee, if you don't let me create, I'll die. Wake me up, I'm sleepy . . ." The artist out there, or inside, says, "Save me." He's part of the brotherhood of man. It isn't tortured. It isn't psychological. It isn't neurotic.

When Saroyan went on the set, he just gave the actors the first line and said, "From now, we'll improvise. We'll just say what we feel." It's pretty tough to work on a Broadway play that way, but that was Saroyan. He didn't need anything. He didn't need a house—he never had a house. He lived in Fresno. He didn't need anything in Fresno—nobody does! His story is un-American; it is completely away from naturalism and realism. It is surrealistic. He takes you anywhere he wants. He was creative and sentimental. Don't ever try to "enclose" his style. Don't try to "ground" Saroyan's plays or his characters. They are not unusual people, just people who were overlooked.

You must be ready for change and not think always in your terms. You can't play Saroyan as down to earth as you are. You can do anything in the world with him, the way he climbs walls, flies—he does everything. Go from chair to chair and travel a thousand miles when you do. Use all the imagination you have. Use the floor and reach out—reach out so far that you reach through the ages. Don't make it so "real."

The point to Saroyan is that he is lively, bubbly, and full of life. Lighter than Miller, Odets, and Anderson. What Saroyan suffered in the real world was compensated for in his dreams, and he put those dreams into his plays. He dreamt that things would have been different—the way a child dreams of going to a new place that will be fantastic. But when the child gets there, it is really not so much different. Saroyan lived like that. He lived off the melodies of the life he experienced, very much like the Irish—like O'Casey. They lived by what they heard—the melody of the language. Saroyan had to find a way to express himself in an American play with an American language picked up in bars.

The melody of Saroyan's language is so fantastic, because it comes out of no education at all. No schooling, no training, just drinking. When he wrote his plays, he says, he was often very drunk. So you do not have to go to the university. Saroyan read after he wrote, not before. "You don't get talent from reading," he said. "If you did, the people at Harvard would be the greatest talents in the world. Instead, they're the dullest."

THIRTEEN

HELLO OUT THERE!

(1941)

SYNOPSIS OF *HELLO OUT THERE!*:
This one-act play tells the story of a Young Man jailed
in a small Texas town and charged with the rape of a
married woman. The accusation is false. From his cell,
he keeps calling, "Hello, out there!" until he finally
gets a response from Emily, a young woman who
works at the jail as a cook. Eventually she is the only
one who believes and sympathizes with him. The two
outcasts are drawn to each other, isolated as they both
are from the real world.

The Young Man says that vigilantes are going to
kill him if they can. He asks Emily's help in escaping
so they can run away to San Francisco together. Emily
leaves to fetch her father's gun, but the husband of the
Young Man's accuser shows up and shoots him. When
Emily returns, she enters the Young Man's cell and
says, "Hello, out there"—just as he did at the start of
the play. The Young Man has bequeathed all of his

money to her. Will she or will she not be able to escape and find a new life?

—B.P.*

So SAROYAN HAD AN OFFER to share plays on the same bill with Bernard Shaw. They came to him and said, "Have you got a one-act play?" He said, "Yes, I think so." He didn't, of course. He was drinking. Somebody at the place where he was staying said, "Hello, out there! Hello, out there!" Bill kept hearing this. So he sat down, dead drunk, and wrote it and said, "Who says you can't write a one-act play when you're drunk?"

With a three-act play or even a one-act play, you must remember the play is divided into the literary side that comes to you from the author and the histrionic side that comes from the actor. I'm going to do this with *Hello Out There!* because it will show you how imaginative you have to be with a certain kind of play. When we get to the next play, you will need another kind of imagination.

This particular play by Saroyan is called "poetic realism." It is a good term for all of his plays. If you say it's "post-spiritualism" or "early symbolism" or anything else, you are going to be mixed up. Since all the forms are mixed up today, you had better not try to say exactly what it is. Just make sure the play you are dealing with can be called "poetic." There is a realistic moment when they come in and kill him. That's where the realism comes in. Other than that, it is just "poetic"—poetic whatever-you-want-to-call-it.

I'm going to spend time on a relatively few lines to give you an idea

* *Hello Out There!* was first performed in 1941 at the Lobrero Theatre in Santa Barbara, California, as the curtain-raiser to a revival of George Bernard Shaw's *The Devil's Disciple*. It premiered on Broadway at the Belasco Theatre on September 29, 1942, running for 47 performances, with Eddie Dowling (A Young Man) and Julie Haydon (Emily). The play was adapted into a short film, directed by James Whale, in 1950 but the movie (Whale's last) was never commercially released. A 1963 revival of the play featured Al Pacino in his first New York City stage appearance.

of your work. You have the dialogue, which is given to you by the author. It is his contribution. He doesn't tell you very much else in this play form. He doesn't tell you how to dress too often. He doesn't often tell you what to do.

He might say, "Go around the table." In this play he tells you practically nothing. He also doesn't give you scenery. He doesn't give you props. He gives you a spoon—that's all. If a playwright says he's only giving you a spoon, you have to say, "All right, that's what he wants to do."

The playwright says in the beginning that there is a fellow in a small-town prison. Now, you expect from that to have a prison cell. You want it to be logical, because you are used to logic. But you must get unused to logic and see there is no logic in certain plays. It is very modern that they've taken the logic away. You can say that in Wilder, too. You must get used to the fact that there is often no logic anymore.

You're stuck, because life is very logical but not very poetic. My father knew this well. When we went with him to California, he gave each child a mountain. He would say "That's your mountain" when we crossed the Rockies. We'd look out and I'd say, "There's mine!" and he'd say, "No, Stella, that's not yours, that's Luther's." He gave us all things that way—the imaginative way. So, we got used to thinking not so logically. It was very good for actors.

Now, I know Saroyan and I know the plays of this tradition, and I know what happened and how they struggled with it. They struggled with it much more than you need to struggle with it. When we do a performance of *Hello Out There!* today, it is by far a better performance than when it was done originally in the Belasco Theatre. Nobody knew what was going on then. They didn't understand and they weren't ready for it. You must be ready.

So it says in the script there's a prison and there's a man on the floor with a spoon. After tapping half a minute as if he were trying to telegraph words, he gets up and begins walking around the cell. At last, he stops and stands at the center of the cell and doesn't move for a long time. He feels his head. Saroyan gives you a lot of things that the man does. He taps. He moves around. He holds his head. Some of it is realistic, some of it is not. The fact that he holds his head might be that he has a headache. We don't know. Some of the things he does are logical. Some aren't.

In an empty space, tapping the floor with a spoon can mean anything. He could be calling the next cell. He could be trying to find out if it is silver or not—if he's stolen the right kind of spoon. Or he might be communicating something. Who is he telegraphing? Saroyan doesn't tell you. This immediately puts you into a non-logical realm, which gives you a creative imaginative source. I can create what I want with the spoon. I can make it do anything I want it to do.

How is the man dressed? He doesn't tell you. The young man just says, "Hello, out there. Hello, out there . . . " And a girl's voice is heard. That's all the author tells you. You could make it sound various ways, depending on how you do it. The literary side of the play has to be brought to life by the actor. The histrionic side depends on the actor's ability to make the play his own. It no longer belongs to the writer. It belongs to the actor. The playwright gave him the words. "Thank you very much, Mr. Shakespeare. Now, *I'm* the boss." If you're a good actor, you won't need too much of a force in the director. There is almost nobody I know in America who will really direct this play for you. They just won't; it's too hard.

There's a dialogue between a man and a girl. There's not much of the logic we're used to. That the cook should be alone with a prisoner is not realistic. In realism, there would be a gate, there would be a cell, and you would immediately know this is a jail. But we don't get that gate. You don't need a gate, and you don't need a lock. We get a space. That space could become a jail by doing what? You must use the stage unrealistically but theatrically. Theatricality comes from *essentializing* the jail. I would say it could become a jail by using black and white paper strips down in the front. Or it could be a jail by having one stripe here and one stripe there.

There is no way in which you can make this clear by yourself. The director, the scenic artist, the lighting artist, the costume artist take over a part of the actor's job. They, together with the actor, are executing the literary side. The scenic artist has to make a real contribution. The lighting man has to make a real contribution—the director, the designer, all the people who put it together. The actor is in collaboration with them and with something other than the logic of the scene. What is this character in contact with? He has no name. That's your first key. Having no name is not normal. If you are in a style that is "poetic symbolism" or "poetic realism," you must live up to the writing and to what the stage director or the costumer might add.

Suppose he was a clown and they put him in jail because they don't want any clowns in the world anymore. You would say that it was unusual for a clown to be in jail . . . You don't know, so what you must do is get first impressions from the play, and this is a tough one. If I started a play with "Hello, how are you? You're an hour late. I'm sorry, but dinner is cold. I can reheat it. Let me have your hat and coat. You look a little tired. Did you work hard? Well, sit down, I'll pour you a drink"—is there anything strange about that kind of scene? No. Is it familiar? Yes. Does everybody know it? Yes. Would you say it takes place in the womb? No. Would you say it takes place in an apartment? Yes. It is closer to the logic of realism. You got a lot of information from what I just gave you . . . You don't get a lot from Saroyan.

What do you get? What impressions do you get about this girl from the first page? You can say she is not well educated. She is a simple person. She doesn't speak English very well; she doesn't know where Salinas is. She hasn't traveled. She is a cook—very low on the work scale. She has a name and it's Emily—an ordinary name. She is very logical.

Now read the page again and tell me something about the man. I don't want you to interpret. I don't want you to say he's starving because "starving" means that then you have to do something. You faint or you beg if you starve. Don't give me general words, because they will mislead you. You say, "I'm desperate to get my subway!" You're not really desperate—you're in a hurry, you just have to wait for your train. Most of your words make no sense. Don't use them unless they enable you to *do* something. Don't be too fancy. What does she want? She wants company, she wants to talk to somebody. That's much better for you. At least we know what she wants.

He calls her Katey. Is there a Katey here? Is he guessing? If I come into a room in a jail and there's nobody there and I say, "Mr. MacDonald? Is there a Mr. MacDonald here?"—what does it mean? If he says "Hello, Katey," either he knows Katey or he doesn't. You don't know which. He finds out her name is Emily. Is that concrete? Yes. Is she a cook? Ignorant? No. Just lower-class. Do we know what he does? No. Do you know where he comes from? No. Does he know Salinas? Yes. What do we know? That he has traveled. That he has no name. That he calls a girl a certain name he wants to call her and then changes it. Is he as logical as she? He is not.

From those impressions, you have two characters. One is logical and one isn't. Now you have something to go by. Emily is logical, she is not a prisoner. She could be a visitor. She could be somebody's wife. She could be the jail keeper. She could be anything, but she happens to be the cook.

Another non-logical thing he does is that he walks around and has no place that he settles into. He hovers in the middle and holds his head, and from there he can telegraph all the boats in the Pacific and Atlantic. He can turn back and forth to see if he sees anybody on the Pacific or Atlantic. Doesn't see anybody. You cannot put him logically in space until there is somebody else who is logical there.

When he says "Katey? Hello?" he hears somebody in the world. If you put somebody in jail, he can be in jail but he can make his jail into a world. He can hear Katey and other friends here. He can think she will get there. He needs contact. He wants to talk.

Get him so he can talk after he says "Hello, Katey." The most important thing is to get him into his own rhythm. His rhythm is not logical. If she's logical, she is going to be in a certain place. If he's illogical, he's going to be all over the place. Put him everywhere. Don't have him say "Hello, Katey" casually. What he hears is an echo of "Hello, Katey!"—"I hear you there and I hear you here. Oh, I hear Katey all over the world in this place, wherever it is. I am running because I hear you."

You are not dealing with a logical play here with Saroyan, any more than you are with Wilder. It's your school; it's what you have inherited. You are never going to have a realistic play again. One, maybe. That's about it.

They need light. Do we have light? Yes. He is the center of light. He has no name, but give him the lighting that would make him dance. Don't give him sad, dismal light. Give him lighting that would make him say, "Katey, I hear you! Katey, *yes, I know,* I HEAR YOU!!" Maybe the voice is far away. Maybe way up above. Maybe very far down. Maybe he has to kneel down with his ear to the ground, listening and hearing a voice . . . If I get that as the actor, I have the world. It is as deep as I want it. It is as high as I want it. It is as wild and crazy as I want it. Now, I am in control.

If I have no name, no logic, no space that is logical, you better have heaven and hell and earth—you better have it all if you have no name. If he is illogical, then make him illogical in all his movements. You see that he likes girls. How does he meet girls in jail? He finds them wherever he is. I wouldn't station him in a specific place where he sees girls. I wouldn't do that. I'd be all over, looking for where she is. Is she up? I find she is down, very far down.

He says, "You'll be just about the prettiest kid in the world and I'd be proud walking around Frisco with you on my arm and people turning around to look at us." Now, I'm telling you that all this is stuff coming out of his imagination. The conversation with the girl—everything is out of a need to talk to people. Imaginary people are there, non-imaginary people are there. He is saying, "You are real, and that's not good enough, so I'll call you somebody else, because if I call you somebody else then we both can have this fantasy together and then I'll be able to sing!" He is uprooted, he's flying around, he's the Man on the Flying Trapeze. He's wherever he needs to be. Part of him is in jail and part of him is free, and he wants to break out.

Now, who is the girl? The girl is a symbol—the victim of the society, and he awakens her. He starts by talking to her, by reaching her through what he says. He reaches her by poetry, through melody. And as he starts to reach her, she starts to speak. When she is just a voice, she is nothing. "Hello . . . " She goes in and out of the plot. Mostly, she is a heightened characterization built on a squeak, a voice—no eyes, no body, nothing. You must build her from nothing. It is through art and poetry and imagination—through love that begins and grows—that she is freed.

He says, "I will not live logically, although I know a lot about it. I will live *this* way. I will say what I want. I will be surrounded with echoes. I will purify them by my own purity. As I live with her, I will make her into something. She is the prettiest girl and she is beautiful and I love her. And as I reach out, through my imagination, I make her hear all the good things so she will be born."

But where is this girl-woman with the two names? If Emily is far down, then Katey might be far up. And the girl might be circling around between Emily and Katey. And where is he? You have to have a tremendous lot of imagination to give him the instability he needs. Don't root him. If he's in a bar, then he's dancing through the bar, dancing on the bar—then he could be scaling the wall of the bar, on the fire escape, singing to the whole world to come into the bar and join him! He sings wonderful songs like "California, Here I Come."

Use stools in the set—one very high, one medium, and one low. Be able to take them wherever you like. If you want to go far downstage, take the little stool and talk to Emily a thousand miles down and away. If you want to talk to Emily and tell her about San Francisco, jump from one place to the other—onto the highest stool.

He doesn't really see Emily. She is a ray, a myth. She is around, but she is not really there until he lets her in. Maybe it's when he says, "Why don't you cook something good?" and she answers, "I just cook what they tell me." Where is Emily talking to him from? Is he glad that he's met Emily? How is she dressed? Let your imagination allow her to be someone he's going to carry in his arms to San Francisco—whether she is Emily or Katey.

How is she dressed if he is going to take her on his arm to San Francisco? Like an angel. He talks about money. Put her in diamonds. He says, "You can't lose with money." She could be dressed all in coins. It's in his imagination. "I see you in gold coins." If it is antirealistic, make it antirealistic.

He is telegraphing, right? He hears answers from the ships, from the sky, from the birds. He runs to where he hears the birds answering, runs around to see where the birds are circling. They are talking to him, and he goes after them. "They must be following ships, so I'll telegraph and find out where the ships are! Hello, out there! Hello, out there!"

It's not just "Hello, out there?" in a tentative way. It's four things that have to answer, that he expects to answer: the clouds, the birds, the boat, and the girl. All these things he is running around, trying to get an answer from: "Hello, out there! Is that you, Katey?" He hears her very far down. What he hears very far down is the tiniest spirit of love that responds. The birds didn't respond, but love responds. A girl responds. This very tiny voice says "Hello?" and he faints with joy. When you hear somebody you like say "Hello?" your heart dies sometimes. He has heard, now, what he needs. He has no name and no social life, but he responds to Emily or Katey when she responds to him. That is Saroyan's key: man finds woman and woman finds love. It is subtle and low-key.

Does it have to be loud? Let it be soft. Why? Because it has to have poetry. It has to be an echo of love. It's "HELLO? *Hello?* Hello? Hello . . . ?" He listens and he twirls and he dances and he's full of love and he answers. What difference does it make if it's "Katey" or "Emily" or "Jenny" or "Billy"? What difference does anyone's name make to a man who has no name? It's all the same. It's love.

She is in the cellar where there is no love. She has been extinguished by work, by being neglected, by being ignored and uncared for. When she says "Hello," it is because he is so loud in his need for contact. She hears it and takes a chance to reply. Her little voice echoes all around. It is so quiet, so low. He says, "Who? Tell me who?" She says, "Emily." He goes to one of the stools—one place in the world—and says, "I don't remember Emily." He jumps to another stool, looking: "I don't know any Emily." He goes to the third. He has a lot of places to go with these three stools. He can go all over the world on them, saying, "I don't remember her in Salinas. I don't remember her on the railroad. But I remember when a girl waved to me when I was riding on the railroad. I took off my kerchief and threw it to her and she caught it. Was that Emily?" It is killing him that he doesn't remember. It is painful.

What is abstract and what is concrete? Emily has to have a last name. "Emily who? I don't know any Emily. Are you the girl I threw my bandanna to from the train? Are you the girl I'll throw all my money to?" He goes from stool to stool. "Which girl are you?"

When she says, "I'm the girl who cooks here," he must see the Madonna, not a girl in an apron. He sees Mary. "Oh, how beautiful! You are the most beautiful girl in the world!" He raises her from a cook to the highest level in a second because he is a poet. He is the poet who doesn't understand "low" or "high" or "middle" because he is not low- or high- or middle-class himself. So he makes her into someone who has not spoken—and who people haven't spoken to—for so long. They have left her in statues. They have left her unloved and unwarmed.

"Why don't you cook us something good?" he continues, always with the kneeling and the praying and the lifting-up of her. A man who has no name is every man and all men. All men love her—this beautiful Madonna. They love her, they raise her up, they worship her. They bring flowers to her, they serve her.

"I just cook what they tell me to," she replies.

Who put her there? Who put her down? We did. We made her into a slave, just like a black slave. You and I did it. He won't allow that. He is a symbol of what a man can do, which is to create love. That is his job wherever he goes. She says, "Are you lonesome?" That's the first thing a Madonna recognizes: "Are you lonesome on earth? Has it been hard for you?"

Remember, the play is symbolic. I remember a very nice thing, once, when *Vanity Fair* ran a big full-page picture of Luther and myself. They didn't bother with last names. They just said, "Luther and Stella, children of Jacob and Sarah." Everybody knew who Jacob and Sarah were. That heritage is what you are supposed to get in Christianity, in Judaism, in all religions—the sense that we are all eternal, that we are forever. The poet gets it. He knows that woman is eternal; he knows that he is eternal. She says, "Are you lonesome?" Has man been lonesome on earth?

Do you understand lonesomeness? Thornton Wilder says there are three professions, three things you can do: you can write, you can socialize, you can love. But you can't do all three. You can only have two out of three. You can write and you can love. Or, if you want to love, you can socialize—but don't try to be a writer, too.

Saroyan is saying that this artist knows one thing, and that is love. This young man says, "I am lonesome as a coyote. Did you hear me hollering 'Hello, out there?' " Have you ever heard a coyote? I don't know why they are so lonely, but there is no misunderstanding that they howl at night and what they howl for is unanswerable. I think it's loneliness. "I'm as lonesome as a coyote" is an image. He's saying, "Nothing can help me except you, your voice."

She says, "Who are you hollering to?" He says, "Well, nobody, I guess. I been trying to think of somebody to write a letter to, but I can't think of anybody." The birds didn't answer. The ships didn't answer. The clouds didn't answer. "I guess if I had a pen I could find somebody to write to. I'd write a letter if I could find somebody to write to." It means he's a writer, and that the writer is lonesome.

She says, "What about Katey?" Now he has to make a switch. He says, "I don't know anybody named Katey." Then he says, "You're Katey and Emily and the Madonna and you're dressed in diamonds. You're going to bring me luck. Katey's a good name. I always did like a name like Katey."

This is Saroyan. He has no logic. It just comes out, and it's beautiful. "Katey's a good name. I never knew anybody named Katey, though." But if you lift her up as high as he has lifted her, she begins to rise. She says, "I know the loneliness—all the Kateys, all the Beatrices. I know them all. I understand loneliness. You have lifted me up and I feel that you are there and you love me."

The Young Man asks, "What sort of a girl are you?" The Voice answers, "I don't know." He says, "Didn't anybody ever tell you?" No.

The Voice says, "She was little." Why is she little? I guess every man likes a little girl. The Voice says, "I've been isolated, I've been alone. I was taken away from humanity. I was put in a cellar, deep down, thousands of miles."

What he does is reach her soul: "Didn't anybody ever talk to you this way?" She says, "What way?" He answers, "You know—the way that makes a human being love another human being. Didn't anybody give you love and say how wonderful you are? Didn't they?"

You can do what you want with it. The only thing you mustn't do is ground it or make it small. Saroyan is saying there is no man who hasn't been destroyed. Over the thousands of years, all men are little. The giant has been taken out of them. He says, "I just need a break." He is spiritually very clear. Very clean, very much in control, very strong in his control. He doesn't feel like he is in jail. He is reaching out with all his heart. He is awakening love in all women who are neglected or forgotten, raising them to his height.

When someone finally comes to kill him—after keeping him in jail, accusing him of rape—the Young Man says, "You are a dirty liar." That is the first time we get serious reality. Play it. Heighten the jail keeper. He is mean; he shouldn't be mild. This is a theatrical play, but there is reality in it. The reality goes in and out, and this is a very realistic scene. The girl says, "Put him down and go away." The keeper says, "Listen to her, listen to that little slut." You can tell by the language that it gets real.

She sobs and then she gets up, no longer sobbing. Now she is the poet. She will begin to meet her world—the brotherhood. She is Saroyan. She starts to be not an echo but a person. She is born. This is the cycle. This final thing that Saroyan does is what makes this little one-act one of our greatest plays. When the Young Man is killed, she says, "Don't touch him. Leave him." They take him away anyway. She is alone, but she stands up and says, "Hello, out there!" She takes his place in bringing love to the world because he gave it to her to carry on.

That is a universal thing. It is big.

TENNESSEE
WILLIAMS

Tennessee Williams (c. 1950)

FOURTEEN

OVERVIEW

THE AMERICAN THEATER is a theater that shows how completely man is frustrated.

Our best playwrights say that man has been wronged by civilization. They're in the Ibsen tradition. Ibsen says the culture was built to produce frustration. The woman in *A Doll's House* had to live a lie. The husband also lived a lie. He couldn't face it. If anything she did touched his ego, he wanted to kill her—take the children away, turn her into a household servant.

Man has an illusion about life, about himself, about his relationship to the community. From Ibsen on, the great playwrights have been struck by the fact that man lives with institutions that wreck him, that give him false values.

Elmer Rice, Maxwell Anderson, Clifford Odets, Lillian Hellman, Arthur Miller—all were playwrights whose characters found out that the society wasn't keeping its promises. In all of their plays, someone says, "It isn't working for me."

The marriage isn't working. The family isn't functioning. The job is degrading. Willy Loman says, "I am the Salesman—I am New England!" but doesn't see that these are illusions. He can't allow himself to recognize the social change going on around him.

Very few people can take change. These playwrights write about the difficulties of giving up one way of life and going into another. One aspect of social life or another is destructive. In Miller, people are destroyed by their values, and then destroy each other. Miller's characters rebel against society. The son says, "I don't want to copy you,

Papa. I want to get away. I don't want to be a salesman! I want to be what I am. I have to find out what I am."

Tennessee Williams doesn't do that. He's very different. His characters don't really want to find out who they are. They cannot face the reality. They run away from it. That is why he so captivates us—because of the romantic way in which he escapes the filth, the dirt, the frustration. His characters don't blame society. They just try to run away from it.

Laura in *The Glass Menagerie* doesn't need anything except her little glass animals. "They live very well together," she says. "They don't fight." She doesn't leave the house at all. She can't go to school. She goes entirely into herself. Neither she nor Tennessee is a realist who solves problems by facing them.

Miller's Biff solves the problem by saying, "I'll find a way, even though I don't know what it will be." Williams doesn't often let his people stay with any reality. But they are capable of doing something that might save them: they create and live in their own world.

That is what actors do. They create a character, and the character is more alive than you are. When you get hold of the character, you know him. Once I said to Tennessee, "My God, she wouldn't do that! She wouldn't let anybody put his hand on her shoulder like that." He said, "Okay, Stella, pipe down. She's not you."

The greatness in Williams is that they have a *right* to run away. What do they run away from? From the monster of commercialism and competition, from things that kill the melody and beauty of life. The old values were killed by the nature of "success" in America. The new values will kill these people if they stay. Most of them can't stay. They go under. They all fail, but they fail their way.

Tennessee didn't concentrate on making money. He was a multimillionaire from the plays, but he went to nut hospitals, went to drugs, went to drinking. Nothing saved him. He could not get any joy from "Hey, I have a Rolls-Royce! I own this house!" I met him when he lived in Provincetown, on the beach, in a little house with a porch—run-down, really run-down. He also had a place in Key West, just as run-down. No difference. The bars and the people were the same. Tennessee was like his characters: he couldn't bear middle-class life; he wanted to escape.

His great theme is escapism—people at the end of their ability to cope. There isn't a Tennessee play without somebody who is unable to deal with life. Mostly, it's women, but a lot of his men are on the brink, too—unable to go on. In *Night of the Iguana,* it's Shannon, a minister who is leaving the church and leaving certain values. He has gone down into the dirtiest hole on one of those really dirty islands, where it is all sex. You find him there, doing exactly what Blanche is doing—seducing kids, raping or being raped. He has a terrific monologue: "So the next Sunday, I climbed into the pulpit and looked down over all of those smug, disapproving, accusing faces, and I said, 'Go on, go home and close up your house, all your windows and doors, against the truth about God!' " Tennessee is using a priest who is cracking up to get to the understanding that he was misled in the society. He became a minister because he believed—and then he didn't believe. This giving up of what was handed down to him as the truth—he had to get out of it and, in getting out of it, go his own way.

That is what Tennessee did. He had a nice southern upbringing and tried to live up to the sermon—until he got drunk and lost himself and became one of the worst alcoholics with the worst breakdowns. He couldn't get to his truth.

Do you think he has a right to this outcry?

They are drunks and whores, these people, but they speak beautifully. They don't take money. They run away somewhere and mix alcohol with poetry and beauty in their imagination when they get there. In *The Lady of Larkspur Lotion,* there is a woman—a prostitute—who is dying. The landlady says, "I want the rent!" and she says, "Oh, soon . . . I own great plantations . . . "

It is marvelous to lie dying and say, "You must wait because I own plantations." It is a great way to go—the escapist way.

Williams has such a sense of failure in himself. Jesus Christ! This man is the most poetic writer we have, but you open up the autobiography and right away he's fornicating. It is just a disaster, because there is nobody that smells the poetry of life the way he does and yet lives the life of a Bowery bum. No money can help Tennessee, no success. In this escape business, he writes really about himself.

Williams has a feeling for beautiful language, and the characters who escape from reality have it, too. They need beautiful language, and language that is so beautiful is not realistic. In a realistic play, Nora says, "I'm leaving you. Here is the ring." She becomes a realist, knowing what she wants, even though she is bound to drown. She needs to go, and she goes.

Tennessee's characters haven't that need. They go into dream worlds, into fantasy, and the language reflects this. When Nora says "I don't want the marriage or the money," that is reasonable. When Blanche says "I must call my friend because, you see, he wants me to come to his yacht and go to his chateau"—that is not reasonable. In this dump of a place, she puts up Japanese lanterns to dim the light on Kowalski's reality. She brings into this ugliness her idea of beauty.

You cannot resist Tennessee. He never says what Ibsen says: "Save yourself by facing reality." Or Miller: "What did your father's idealism do for you?" Miller and Ibsen are very clear. They write about man's fight to survive by finding his own way. Williams and Miller both write about people who are hurt. But in Williams, the characters never say "It's my mother's fault" or "It's the church's fault." In Tennessee, the soul is so destroyed that they just are desperate to flee. It is very close to insanity.

Miller's characters affirm life—they are always seeking. Tennessee is more like Chekhov. He reports failure, but he never says it is society's fault. Even in *Cat on a Hot Tin Roof* with Big Daddy—a fascist of the first order—he doesn't dwell on it. Miller would dwell on it. A lot of Williams's men come with a fascistic power drive, like Big Daddy or Kowalski.

You have to understand these Mississipppi Delta people—men like Huey Long.* Long was a fascist-populist. He could talk to the people on their level, humor them, endear himself to the hearts of poor people and ignorant people in the working class. He rabble-roused all the time, and they were hypnotized by him. Tennessee is terribly aware of that kind of desperado in southern life. He writes a lot about men who'd just as soon cut your throat as look at you, if you don't think their way. He knows all about the cutting of throats and the Ku Klux Klan and the burning—that violent, fascist side of America.

There's a good example in *Orpheus Descending,* with the character named Jabe, a local big shot that married a lady named Lady. Her father was an Italian immigrant, who had an orchard and a distillery during Prohibition but made the mistake of selling liquor to a black man. So the Klansmen burned the place down, and "the Wop was

* Huey P. Long (1893–1935), Louisiana governor and senator, wielded intense demagogic appeal ("Every man a king!") and corrupt, dictatorial control of Louisiana. He was assassinated by Dr. Carl Weiss at the state capitol in Baton Rouge.

burned up trying to fight the fire," Jabe says. What Lady doesn't know is that Jabe himself was the leader of the mob. In the end, Jabe shoots Lady and blames it on another guy, and the vigilante mob burns *that* guy, too!

It's a helluva play. There's another woman in *Orpheus* named Carol, who came from the southern aristocracy and had money and saw some lynchings and became a civil-rights protester. She wanted to improve the social situation by protecting Negroes from being hung, but they arrested her for "lewd vagrancy" and put her in jail—lobotomized her and turned her into a slut. He's making the point that society destroys this girl who wants to improve society. Even now, if you want to serve society, you're likely to be arrested or killed.

Tennessee repeats these characters a great deal, in different variations—the vulnerable women and the crude, violent men. Big Daddy tells his son that he never should have wasted so much of his money and his sperm on Big Mama. "They say you got just so many and each one is numbered," he says. "Well, I got a few left in me and I'm gonna pick me a good new female to spend 'em on. I don't care how much it costs, I'm gonna smother her in mink. I'll strip her naked and smother her in diamonds." He will choke her to death with his wealth.

That kind of wealth—owning all the real estate and the whorehouses and everything else he owns—is something new. There's no more old tradition. This new way of living and thinking throws all the old beauty and elegance away, once and for all. This is Tennessee unfolding the new southern family: Big Daddy, Big Mama, Big Brother Brick, and Big Sister Maggie. He calls them "Big" because he wants you to know they're pretending to size. Some of them were poor, some had some money left; some had nothing left, but by the time you get to Blanche there is nothing left of Belle Reve—nothing.

Maggie is like Blanche. Her family lost their big cotton plantation just like Blanche's family lost Belle Reve. It went down because they couldn't afford to keep it up anymore. There wasn't even enough left to pay for their funerals. Maggie says, "You don't understand how it is to suck up to people you couldn't stand because they had money and I was as poor as Job's turkey. You don't know what it's like to beg from relatives you hate because they had money and all you had was a bunch of hand-me-downs—trying to keep up appearances on one hundred and fifty dollars a month."

Maggie's mother was from the poor aristocracy and had to marry into the working class. "You can be young without money, but you can't be old without it," she says. "You have to be one or the other, either young or with money." She's a young girl already scheming how to get money out of men—with lies. It's the same thing that happened with the DuBois sisters. One of them goes crazy, and the other one marries a caveman completely out of her class.

You need this before you get to Blanche and Stanley in *Streetcar,* even though *Cat on a Hot Tin Roof* and *Orpheus* came later. You need to see how Stanley Kowalski is the son of Big Daddy and inherits his killer instinct. It's the new man who has taken on—and taken in—America. They're both bullies, but they're powerful and mesmerizing. They're both the kind of guys who would have been behind Huey Long politically.

But Tennessee isn't political. He has no real social or political concern. He is decadent. He is in the literary tradition of the nineteenth century. He is a bohemian, and his interest is in the individual. He lives—God, I can't tell you how he lives!

By the way, it was Tennessee himself who wanted Brando to play Kowalski. Marlon didn't have the money to see Williams in Provincetown. But I had a house in Truro, which is a few miles away, so he bicycled there and we took him and introduced him to Williams. Marlon didn't need a car or train; the bicycle was enough. He has in him a great deal of individualness. Individualists are interesting in different ways. I speak about Marlon because he has been able to take success. He lives in Tahiti where there are no walls. The rain comes and you drown in water. Marlon is not really "Marlon," of course. He was called "Bud" when he went to military school. But he created a whole new world when he created Kowalski.

Marlon acts twenty-four hours a day. He has always been anxious to link himself to me. Just last week, he wrote something about me. You can't fool him. How does he work? I was a guest in his house. The first thing he says is, "You take the house, I'll leave." There I am dictating but Marlon is behind a big partition with an arch. Suddenly I hear him saying, "Yes, yes, okay, yes, okay . . . oh, ah, *aha . . . !*" I thought, he's dying—he's dead. I said, "Marlon, what's the matter?" He broke into laughter. I said, "Some joke. What were you doing?" He said, "I wanted to find out how killing it is to be bored."

So he experienced that boredom. The emptiness hit him. A person is emptied by the common life. The actor gets things that way. The good actors see.

I remember, as a kid, my father saying, "Look at that. Tell me what that is. Imitate that. Do it for me." Because the actor lives by what he sees. Ibsen says that in order to tell the truth, you must see, and what you see must come back to you, and when you understand the truth in what you see, you can put that truth into a character. The entire training of an actor is to watch, to take it in, to come back and say, "I saw this, I saw that, I saw houses and stones and ocean and sky." You should write all the time what you see. What does it do for you?

When a person is singularly different, you recognize it. And if he is not like other people, he is alienated and can't find his way in the world of people. Blanche doesn't care about the real world of people. But she is revealed in a way that tells you the truth about life.

The form is poetic realism. The place is there, the room is there, a reality is there. Some live with the reality, but others live as if they are inventing the reality. A conscious soul-ache makes them want to escape. They are individual.

I keep going back to Marlon. He lives with crazy animals. He gave me his house another time, with this terrible animal in it. He lives with the animals. They live the same life. He didn't really want the theater. He said, "If I could have done the great plays like in England, maybe I would have." He didn't want to go into the commercial theater. But he is a great actor. He gets it the way great actors get it: by instinctively knowing what's what.

Marlon, in an arid place like Los Angeles, knows where every stream is. He knows the difference between this stone and that stone, this plant and that plant. He works at it all the time. He lives, he sees. He is awful.

* * *

Williams, Wilder, Miller, Odets, Inge—these playwrights all saw what was wrong. Inge is very influenced by Chekhov and Miller. Miller is influenced by Tennessee, and Tennessee is influenced by Miller. All of them are influenced by where they come from. All of them know each other.

This was true in Russia, too: Gorky was a Communist revolutionary—"Let's get rid of everybody in charge! Let the working class rule!" Yet he was one of Tolstoy's best friends. Chekhov wouldn't touch the working class. He said they have no minds—"They don't interest me. I don't like the way ordinary people think." He writes about the best people in a society he admires, knowing they are going to go under. Miller writes about the best American people, fighting to break through. Tennessee writes about the best southern people who go down.

When you see Kowalski, you know what he represents in America. And you understand that Blanche represents somebody who can't live like that. Blanche is the opposite. Watch for that in Williams—watch for the extreme opposites: the people who can do it and the people who can't.

The style of poetic realism is given to you by the way the characters behave. Blanche says, "Come in, young man, you look like a god that has come down to earth." He's just a boy who has come to sell her a newspaper. But the scene is that she has created a god and treats him that way, and he begins to react to this. A kid comes to sell a newspaper, and she takes him into fairyland.

Tennessee's women are full of self-delusion. Everything about Blanche is "I know poetry and how beautiful the sky is, so I am better than you." That's how she treats Kowalski, and he doesn't like it. Nobody does, because her exalted sense of beauty makes them look ridiculous. If someone comes in and says, "My fantasy is real and your reality isn't," you'll have a fight on your hands. It has reality, it has fantasy, it has prose, and it has poetry.

Williams likes raw life. He doesn't like a beach that doesn't have bums on it. He doesn't like a beach without the bowery. He goes to the rawness of earth, of feelings. Everybody is raw to the bone. *Streetcar* is absolutely a brothel of ugliness, the dark side of the poetry of man.

He is the playwright of failure. He writes about people who fail. He has empathy and understanding for failure, including his own. He says that people fail in order to live. To live at all, you have to create a world, an odd dream, a world of dreams.

Tennessee puts truth and life on the stage by transforming reality through the poetic imagination, by going to where it is beautiful. He is a poet and he knows the truth. He can't find it in 1945 America. But he knows that there IS a truth—and that it is higher than Stanley Kowalski.

FIFTEEN

THE LADY OF LARKSPUR LOTION

(1941)

SYNOPSIS OF *THE LADY OF LARKSPUR LOTION:* In a roach-infested boardinghouse in New Orleans's French Quarter, Mrs. Hardwick-Moore— a bleach-blonde in her forties—sits alone on the edge of her bed in a squalid rented room. She seems lost in thought—or, perhaps, no thought at all.

Her reverie—or stupor—is interrupted by the noisy arrival of Mrs. Wire, a no-nonsense landlady come to demand her overdue rent. Mrs. H-M's response invokes the fantasy that she's related to the Hapsburgs and has inherited a rubber plantation in Brazil, from which she receives steady income. Those daydreams help her cope with her squalid circumstances, but in fact, what meager income she has is derived from entertaining gentlemen in her room at night.

Mrs. Wire knows there's no Brazilian rubber plantation. She has been putting up with the story and the deadbeat tenant—until now. As Mrs. H-M protests the cockroaches and the outrage of living in such conditions, the landlady's demands for money get increasingly shrill. She ridicules the plantation illusion and declares that the use of her boardinghouse as a brothel

must stop. Mrs. H-M insists there IS a rubber plantation, and she'll be getting her check from there shortly.

Mrs. Wire spies a bottle of Larkspur Lotion on the
dresser, which Mrs. H-M says she uses to remove nail
polish. Mrs. Wire knows better. Her merciless bad-
gering of Mrs. H-M is interrupted by the entry of
another boozy boarder, the Writer, who claims to have
a 780-page manuscript tucked away in his own fetid
room—the Great American Novel he's been working
on for twenty years.

In a stirring, wild-eyed defense of dreamers like
Mrs. Hardwick-Moore and himself, the Writer orders
Mrs. Wire to lay off the Larkspur Lotion lady: so she
has invented a plantation fantasy to endure her bleak
existence—so who has the right to deprive her of that?

—B.P.*

I WANT YOU to be aware that I won't let you get away with anything. I'm very happy that you're here, and that I'm here, but I'm
very frightened that you may think of the history of acting as being
related to television. You must realize that television is primarily
visual—it does very well if it has four ducks on a pond and a sunset.
But you can't play a duck or the sunset. So they don't really need you.
What they really need are the ducks and the sunset. They only need
you for a couple of words to be heard—not necessarily to be seen at all.

The stage is the most important form of writing and self-expression
because it is the best way to reach people emotionally and intellectually. There's nothing that comes closer. You can read a great novel all
day and night, but however absorbing it is, you will still remain in a

* *The Lady of Larkspur Lotion* never had a professional Broadway or Off Broadway
premiere in Tennessee Williams's lifetime.

certain more or less neutral, abstract state. A great work of theater, on the other hand, keeps you absolutely gripped—or should.

I want you to do a lot more work than you are inclined to do. Most of all, I want you to know about using your imagination—that you absolutely, desperately need your imagination in studying and working in the theater, and that you must get yourself more involved with working on the play than with showing yourself. What you must show, and what you must do, is called *interpretation.*

No playwright can really give you background. Shaw tried and failed. He rarely failed at anything, but he failed at that. He failed to give his character Candida anything except the valise she walks in with. Candida has a whole life inside her, and much of it is gradually revealed in the play. The author can tell you when it is, where it is, to some extent the social situation—but that's all he can do. The rest is your responsibility.

In this case, with *The Lady of Larkspur Lotion,* it's 1941. The Depression is still dragging on. If you don't know about that, spend some money—steal it, if you have to!—and go buy some books that tell you about it. There are plenty of them. Every art form evolves. It took a long time for music to get to the sonata. It took a long time for the drama to get to Tennessee Williams. Don't try to understand him "by instinct." Instinct is not imagination. Imagination requires that you know something first. I don't know what you know, and I never will—because you're quiet. I see this is a very educated group, but none of you speak forcefully. You're not like eastern actors—they ask a lot of loud, obnoxious questions.*

Anyway, you see why you need the author. Now, why does the author need you? Because an awful lot of Candida's character or the Larkspur Lady's character belongs to her background, which the actress playing her must bring in on her own—as an embellishment or gift to the author—to realize the part.

The first thing you have to do is read the play over and over. I reread *Streetcar* a dozen times before I realized two key things about Stanley Kowalski: that he's the head of his little family, and that he doesn't lie. He's rough, he's rude, he's macho, he says, "I'm not educated—*but I don't lie.*" Blanche lies. Stanley can say, "I tell the truth, and what

---

* This lecture takes place at Adler's Los Angeles studio on June 22, 1988.

you are is a liar." You are inclined to think that she's a fine, frail victim and that he's just a bum. But he is not. He represents a lot of things—including the working class and the men who fought World War II.

The Lady of Larkspur Lotion is a one-act play with just three characters—all symbols: the artist, the businesswoman, and the one who can't make it. I've talked to you about the South and its different classes around this time: the upper class is going down and has to make a transition to the middle or working class. In the ones who don't make that transition, you get the whole of Tennessee Williams: if the women can't be southern belles, they go down. And when they go down, they go so far down that they reach insanity. They substitute fantasy for the reality. That's when you can't be saved.

The moment one of Tennessee's characters fantasizes—"I'll get the money, I have to wait until my friend Charley sends it, he has a plantation!"—you know he or she is in deep trouble. As soon as the fantasy gets over the border of reality, there is no hope for that character. Nobody can get them back to reality.

Larkspur Lotion was a drugstore remedy used for lice and body vermin. You put it on your skin for bugs—it's a lotion to take away the ugliness and corruption of what has happened to your body.

Mrs. Hardwick is beyond communicating. She's on the lowest level. She's someone who thinks she's going to call some guy with some estate and that he's going to send her money and save her life. She's way beyond what you are, Ilse.* You are able to talk about real things, but the thing she's talking about isn't real. But you don't need to scream or run around and go crazy. Just stay center stage. Don't go too far away from there, not even once. *Go deeper.* You are not going to survive the night. You are going to die.

There's a lot of acting going on here—an awful lot. I mean, you could supply the entire United States with this acting. Take it deeper, not broader. I don't know exactly what bag ladies do out here, but in New York the bag ladies on the curbs never look up—they never see you, they never really see anything.

---

* The actresses with whom Stella is working here are Ilse Taurins and Sandra Tucker. The actor is Bill Lithgow, who later taught at the Stella Adler Acting Conservatory in Los Angeles for many years. Part of the exercise, on this occasion, was the advance instruction to choose and wear their own costumes.

Once when I was having trouble with a character I said to Stanislavsky, "You don't understand! It's different with you. You're handsome, you're distinguished, you're gorgeous—no wonder everybody looks at you and loves you! If you looked like other actors do, you'd understand why they have problems. You don't have any problems."

He said: "I'll tell you something. When I walk down the street, however good-looking I am, if there's another man with a crutch, all bent over with rags around his feet—everybody looks at *that* man, not me. There's something about a cripple that immediately draws attention away from what's more good-looking."

So in that sense, you are that bag lady. And we're not getting it. We get that you're secretly all right and that you're just acting. You can scream if you like, but I would like *you* not to exist when you're that lady.

Sandra, you are acting a whole lot, too. Throw it all out! Every bit of it. Don't use the stage to act up a riot. There is such a thing as acting the truth—and that's what Tennessee's writing about. He's not writing about a bad landlady; he's writing about a person who deals with the reality of money, the reality of living, eating. You come in with a ready-made character. Instead of hiding it, you show it. If she's a landlady, why does she dress worse than the scum people on the street? You're dressed worse than your boarder is. Why don't you wear a skirt with a waist and a girdle?

[*"I'm run-down," replies Sandra Tucker.*]

No, you're not. You have money—you manage the place. She's *acting* run-down, she's not really run-down. Anybody with money isn't rundown. Don't act evil. Simply come in with "Listen, I'm sorry you're so pathetic, but I need you to get out." Look around, see what the room is like—pick up a shoe, maybe, throw it in a box—but take the bandanna off your head, and don't be a mess. If the landlady is a mess and the Larkspur Lady is a mess, too, we haven't got a play.

Something else Stanislavsky told me. When they were playing *The Lower Depths* by Gorky, the entire Moscow Art Theater company went to see where the bums lived. They went there and went there and kept going there until they understood what it really was like to be in those lower depths. I saw the play in Moscow, and you would never have thought such distinguished actors could be so completely buried in dirt and aloneness and despair.

Understand that Tennessee is talking about the lower depths, too—the lowest of the low. Which is why there's something about a white, clean nightgown that's not right, Ilse. You're not costumed correctly. I keep telling you, the costume will awaken the part. It will give you a clue or maybe even a key to the part. This play is about *you*—the Lady of Larkspur Lotion. Theatrically speaking, you are the leading lady, so be center stage—always if you're the leading lady. Center stage, and center *yourself.* Take it from an old pro. When you're alone for months and years at a time, you feel like a stray dog, lost and abandoned. Nothing exists for a dog when it's lost. It just wanders around alone. Get more of that sense of aloneness. Really *talk* about those cockroaches. You've been living with roaches and lice! Don't be so logical with the prose, so pedestrian.

Sandra, don't just come on stage and start talking to her. Enter, walk around, look over the place, check things out, check *her* out, before you start talking. Continue talking, maybe wander offstage and come in again, go over to the washbasin, come back—you don't always have to be up front "communicating" the way you do. I don't want you to compete with her. You have a small part. You're a landlady—everybody knows what a landlady is. *Talk*—don't act up a storm. You're acting, but what's your action? You don't know what you're doing. Have an action. Walk in to *do* something, darling. You came for the rent. You came to see if she has whiskey—did she get it from that man you heard her with last night? Look around, see if she has anything worthwhile to pay you with. Maybe look in the bureau, in the trunk—go off and come back again. But don't compete. We won't hear the character who's speaking if the other character is so busy moving that we watch her instead. Please be busy only on your own lines. Don't be busy when somebody else is talking.

I was working with another class on a scene from *Orpheus Descending* the other day, and the actor playing Val kept picking up his guitar during Lady's big speech—the leading lady in *Orpheus* is called Lady. It's confusing, but never mind. I said, "Don't pick up the guitar while she's telling you these things. After she's told you, go get your guitar, take all the pauses you want, walk across with it or strum it, look through the window at the moonlight, do whatever you want to do as the character. But don't walk around and make us watch you while she has important things to say. You can't do that to an actress—if you did it to me, you would be dead! It's the rules of the game." He said, "Why would they be watching me instead of her just because

I'm—" and I said, "Listen, will you shut up? I don't want to go into any more explanations. Trust me. It's just bad technique and bad theatrical manners!"

So let's try the scene again.

[*The actresses do so.*]

There's too much voice, Ilse—too much projection, too much awareness of an audience. Hide from life, hide from Mrs. Wire. She's your tormentor—cover yourself against her. Maybe put part of the nightgown over your face. Try to protect yourself a little. *Then* talk about the cockroaches. You have to do something to show us, to reveal your character through something that you choose to do. The writer doesn't tell you that. The writer tells you she's talking about the plantation, but he can't create the character for you. Your job is to find a way to do it.

I don't believe a thing either one of you is doing. It's a shame. You have talent, but you keep going to those goddamned clichés. Don't handle a prop unless you know the prop and need the prop. The scene on the page is one thing—it's dead. The other kind of a scene is when you act what's on the page, which makes it live. But act the *character,* not the lines. We've got to get two different characters here. We have to get the person who's chosen to live with money and the person who has chosen to drink herself to death and get thrown out. A woman needs to be cared about, that's the center of Tennessee; and if nobody cares, she goes down. She's down and abandoned and cannot lift herself up. He has a central character like that in almost every play.

Know your author. Your author does not like rich people. He does not admire people who don't have pain or psychological inner problems. He understands them better than any playwright in the world, because that's what he was himself. Once they put Tennessee in a good hotel and gave him a steak and chocolate sauce, and he took the chocolate sauce and put it on the steak. He was by nature an innocent man, and he went toward the people who needed him. He writes about the people who fail.

How is the Larkspur Lady failing, Ilse? Show us. Maybe cover one eye at the end. Now that we know she's done, put your head into your bosom—down, in. And quiet—draw into yourself, I don't want so much voice. It's not the text, it's the character we want. She *hates* that word "roaches"—every time you say it, close your mouth against it afterward. When something frightens you, it should be physical.

Run around the room. Run! Never mind the language. Too much goddamned logic! Sandra, why don't you just pick up the bottle of Larkspur Lotion and simply read the label—just say it out loud with some disdain, and then go off?

Separate the language to make the ideas clear. It's not clear to us when you run all the words together. Stop acting—that's an indulgence for yourself. Instead, try just going back, just reminiscing. Do the wonderful thing that Chekhov allows you to do: he lets you talk without having to look at your partner or relate to your partner or even *have* a partner. Anybody and everybody else can be there in the scene, but you can still just talk to yourself or about yourself. You don't have to look around for someone else to bounce it off. The secret of Chekhov's characters is that while one's talking, another is drinking tea, the other one is crying, the fourth one is smoking a cigarette . . . Nobody else on stage is listening, necessarily—but the audience is! Tennessee gives you that same privilege, that freedom of not always needing a partner. You can be thinking and talking about all these profound things, but you don't have to aim them at somebody opposite you. Sometimes they're better when spoken utterly alone.

* * *

Keep in mind that *The Lady of Larkspur Lotion* takes place in the lowest kind of gutter. You can't go any further down than this, not even on the Bowery. It's brutal. The landlady says, "I want money! I don't want to hear 'She's sick.' " She attacks this victim—this "Blanche"—who's lying there, completely down and out, with her insanity of having plantations. You don't talk about your plantation to a landlady demanding the rent.

"I never spy and I never listen at doors!" Mrs. Wire says. "The first thing a landlady in the French Quarter learns is not to see and not to hear, but only collect your money. As long as that comes in—okay, I'm blind, I'm deaf, I'm dumb! But as soon it stops, I recover my hearing and my sight and my voice. If necessary, I go to the phone and call up the chief of police, who happens to be an in-law of my sister's"—and he'll come and kick you out on your behind, you deadbeat!

And, then suddenly, at that point—when this mismatched heavyweight fight between the two women reaches its peak—the Writer from the next room shows up, saying Mrs. Wire's "demon howling" was so loud it woke him up from his sound sleep. She lets him have it: Your *sleep?* Hah! You mean your *drunken stupor*! Don't try to pull the wool over my eyes, you lousy alcoholic!

It's really Tennessee who shows up, in the form of the Writer. It's really just a two-scene play, and this is where the second scene begins. The conflict suddenly goes from Mrs. Wire and the Larkspur Lady to Mrs. Wire and the Writer. He comes in to deliver the ending and the message that gives over and over. *Lady of Larkspur Lotion* clarifies that character of the Writer, who shows up in all of Tennessee's plays. In *Glass Menagerie,* it's Tom, who says, "I wrote a poem on the lid of a shoebox." Here, it's a guy who thinks he has a great 780-page manuscript in a drawer—a writer who's trying to be creative in a house full of roaches. Tennessee does that. He found he was sparked to be creative in places where most people are destroyed. He understands that if you are destroyed—*really* destroyed—you can find another life and live there. It's not real, but you will be able to live there. Or at least you'll try to. You'll fight. You fight to get yourself out of that gutter.

The Writer says to this landlady: "What do you care if I write and it fails? What difference does it make to you? Why do you have to take my dream away?"

Many of you—most of you, I'd say—have experienced your parents or your friends or your husband or somebody trying to dissuade you from becoming an actor. They can't do that. You can't take a dream away from somebody. I don't care what else you do, but don't take a person's dream away. And don't let anybody take away yours. If you want to act, tell your mother or father or husband to go make a lot of money to support you! That's really the brilliant answer to anybody who says, "An actor doesn't make any money."

Is this something that has meaning to you? Is it happening to you? What Tennessee says in a play like this has some social or political value that speaks to the audience, because it's still happening in the world, right now. Artists and dreamers and other people are still becoming alcoholics—there are lots of Larkspur Ladies and Writers and Blanches. There are institutions all over the world for them, because they don't know how to stop, or take care of themselves. I think it's brilliant of Tennessee, as an outcast of society himself, to say something like that.

I think *The Lady of Larkspur Lotion* is brilliant, too. Tennessee is at his best here, in a miniature form that's going to lead to something big, something much bigger. This is a kind of preview or run-up exercise to *Streetcar* and Blanche. It's important. Tennessee is as important to us as Sophocles was to the Greeks.

The Greeks wrote plays—they didn't write novels—to teach people that Oedipus shouldn't sleep with his mother. We're still working on that one. But that's what they wanted to tell their people then, so they found a play for it—and other plays to say other important things. The play form is that old. The crucial thing is for the audience to understand it, and the only way they can do that is through the actors interpreting it.

If you're tense, it won't work. If you try to fool us, it won't work. Try to relax and really *go* to what you're seeing or describing—if *you* see the rubber plantation, *we* see it. If you see the cockroaches, we'll see them. If you don't see them and just talk about them, you will see no plantations or roaches and we won't see them, either, because *you* don't. When you talk about something, it has to be in you, and it can't be if your body is tense. How many of you have tension on the stage? Everybody? Of course you do. Wherever the tension is, let go of it from there and put it somewhere else. Transfer it to another place. If one foot is very tense, let go of that and tense your arm instead. If you don't and you go on working while you're tense in that certain crucial spot, it alters your voice, your movements—you're not free.

Do what I've taught myself to do about nervousness: *Talk* to your tension, put it in its place. "Look, I know you're in me. But you're not all of me, you're just a part of me. I'll live with you, you son of a bitch, but don't try to dominate me." That's a good rule for all actors.

Here's another one: You have every right to make a mistake, any mistake. You're not on this or another stage to "win" something. Write this down: "If I feel I have to succeed every time I get up, I am sure to fail." Put that down and keep it in your memory. You must be able to say, "It didn't go well—I'll try it again." You must not try always to give the great performance. The harder you try, the worse it will be. If it doesn't win the first time, you'll do it another.

Why I felt it didn't win before is that you used the "real" reality. Which means nothing at all. Realism, theatrically speaking, doesn't mean being real. It means being truthful. That's what an actor is for, to bring out the truth of the play and make it mean something for the audience. They might not get everything, but they'll get something as long as you don't bring all the lines down. If you want to say something really big, don't pull it down and make it ordinary, the way you'd say it in television. The play won't get anywhere then.

Now, let's do it again—the whole thing, from the top.

[*The transcript lamentably lacks audio, as well as visual, but reports "loud applause" at the end of this final run-through. All present—including Stella—are evidently enthralled by it.*]

It was a beautiful performance. Ilse, wonderful. Bill, brilliant, it's the best thing I've seen you do. Let's give them an applause for being actors. Did you see how much the play came alive in them this time? It's a big undertaking to act a play by one of the greatest playwrights in the world. I'd rather act than go to the bank—wouldn't you?

SIXTEEN

THE GLASS MENAGERIE

(1945)

SYNOPSIS OF *THE GLASS MENAGERIE:*
It is 1937 in St. Louis, where the Wingfield family occupies a shabby apartment. Tom, the narrator, introduces himself; his mother, Amanda; and his sister, Laura. He works in a shoe warehouse to support them but is desperately unhappy with his life. He longs to write poetry and find adventure. Amanda, an aging southern belle abandoned long ago by her husband, nags Tom to better himself, which only increases his misery and drives him to the movies night after night for escape.

Laura is a reclusive cripple, too shy to relate to anyone outside her family or, indeed, to anything except her collection of glass animals. She quits the typing class her mother made her take because she threw up in class before the first test. Amanda, at wit's end, decides marriage is Laura's only option left and importunes Tom to bring some "gentleman caller" home from work to meet his sister.

Tom invites Jim, a casual friend from high school, to dinner—unaware that Jim is the only boy Laura ever felt strongly about. Laura is consumed with anxiety, but Jim gradually draws her out of her shell. She shows him her favorite glass animal—a unicorn. He

Julie Hayden as Laura and Laurette Taylor as Amanda in Tennessee Williams's *The Glass Menagerie* (1945). "Time is the longest distance between two places."

dances with her but accidentally knocks over the unicorn, breaking off its horn. Laura is not upset. Now the unicorn is a normal horse, she says. In a rash moment, Jim kisses her. Too late, he realizes his mistake, tells her that he's engaged, and leaves, breaking her heart.

Amanda rails at Tom, who is eventually fired from the warehouse for the crime of writing a poem on a shoebox lid. Tom goes off to join the Merchant Marine but will never escape the memory of Laura—or the life he led in St. Louis—wherever he goes.

—B.P.*

* *The Glass Menagerie* premiered at the Playhouse Theatre in New York City on March 31, 1945, directed by Eddie Dowling and Margo Jones, starring Dowling (Tom), Laurette Taylor (Amanda), and Julie Haydon (Laura). The first film version

In the voluminous Stella Adler lecture transcripts, stage directions—ambient noise, classroom action and student interaction—are rarely supplied. Fortunately, the transcriber of her opening lecture on *The Glass Menagerie* included parenthetical details of Stella's grand entrance: polite applause—followed by Stella's imitation of its weakness. "That isn't applause! It wasn't interesting enough. Actors applaud this way! [*She claps vigorously.*] They want to say something. When you do this [*claps weakly*], you're not saying anything. Don't do something unless you mean it. So please, may I have that applause again? [*Vigorous applause.*] Thank you!"

—B.P.

I F   Y O U   K N O W the South and if you know Tennessee, you know he wants his man to fight against being pushed around, against being forced to work in a shoe factory. He's talking about the artist, the poet—that's the special class he's concerned with. This boy Tom in *The Glass Menagerie* is in revolt against what happens to him.

The historical and economic moment in the South is that, by this time, there's such poverty that the structure and manners and elegance of being an aristocrat couldn't exist anymore. The price of cotton kept falling and falling until the landowners were as poor as the black men picking their cotton. The South went to pieces. Plantations got taken over at sheriff's sales, and the situation went so far down that people had to leave in order to survive. Most of them went north.

So we are in a period when people who knew and loved the South and brought memories of it with them now live in big northern cit-

---

(1950), directed by Irving Rapper, starred Arthur Kennedy, Gertrude Lawrence, and Jane Wyman. The second (1987), directed by Paul Newman, starred John Malkovich, Joanne Woodward, and Karen Allen.

ies, because at least they can get a factory job and a cheap dump of an apartment there. Tennessee himself was a young man of twenty-six in St. Louis then [1937]. He understood that what started in Europe with the Spanish Civil War was starting to happen here, with violent disturbances in Chicago and even quieter cities because of hunger, low pay, no unions or minimum wage. He goes to this time and shows you what happened to people who left the South and came to places like St. Louis, where workers were turned into automatons.

But one character here—Tom—understands. Tom is not a middle-class boy. He's a poet. The poet always understands. He understands he can't make much money as a worker in a shoe factory. His real job is not to make money; his job is to understand. In Tennessee, be careful: when you interpret the artist or poet, don't make him weak, for chrissake. He's not weak! He's humble, he's pushed down, he's defrocked, because there's no need for a poet in the society. But when Tennessee writes about him, especially in *The Glass Menagerie,* he is a fighter. He's a fighter against middle-class values, against his mother's values—the southern belle with seventeen gentleman callers. Tom is a revolutionary against the South's old ways.

Change is difficult. This is a family that went down from one generation to the next. From the plantation, it went down and down until they had to move to St. Louis to work. The male either had to give in or fight. He says, "I followed in my father's footsteps. I left the idea that you had to be forever enslaved to things like gentlemen callers. There are no gentleman callers anymore. It's just too goddamn bad, but there aren't."

Williams isn't big on praising the success of the middle class. He loves bums, he's a drunk, and he's the greatest poet we have. He's also a drug fiend. He's all these things of change. He writes about the disaster of change. "I didn't go to the moon," Tom says. "I went much further—for time is the longest distance between two places." He's in a new time, the thirties before the war, "when America was stupid"—but the artist isn't. He's a bright young man with great strength and power.

Memory plays a great part in Tennessee Williams. He lets Tom take the liberty of coming down in front of the curtain, breaking away from his mother and the glass menagerie, to tell the audience what he's going to do. It's not realistic; it's poetic realism—to break the reality of being in a room. Tennessee doesn't care what the rules were in the past. You can go down front and just talk to the audience if you want.

"I went further than the moon, for time is the distance between two points"—his grandmother's point and his point. He would begin to take his own road. He probably won't be successful, because it's just before the war. I think he's going to be called up and killed in it. But he's on the way. "I've got muscle, I've got guts! I'm on the road, I haven't got a dime, I didn't pay the electricity bill, I left my mother sitting in the dark, but I'm on my way to become a poet, even if I starve!" He may well go to his death—but that's the road of the artist.

Tennessee says life is changing. The plantation, the value of cotton—all that is lost. But what isn't lost is the sense of family. Does Tom have southern chivalry? He's torn. It's not that he lacks chivalry. It's that he's been working for eight years in a shoe factory and is expected to spend the rest of his life there. To stay with his mother and work in that factory to keep his family alive—it's too hard. He abandons it, like his father. At work, they call him "Shakespeare." In that dismal factory, he finds a way of writing poems on the lids of shoeboxes. He wants to stop being a victim of his family, strike out on his own, become an artist. He's in rebellion against being enslaved by Amanda, his mother, and her old southern values.

You find Williams's women—Amanda, Laura, Blanche, Alma—all around his plays, essentially the same woman, in different stages of their lives. With Alma in *Summer and Smoke,* you have a version of Amanda: "We had a bad summer here. The clouds aren't going the right way." Amanda says to Tom, "Honey, don't push your food with your fingers. If you have to push your food with something, the thing to use is a crust of bread. And chew—chew! Animals have secretions to digest their food, but we don't . . ."

Amanda goes on and on. She puts on an old lace dress and still thinks of herself as living in a fine house—she won't give that up. She needs Tom to stay in the factory and make money. There's no way she can pay for food and electricity herself. She has a daughter who has no ability to face life in an apartment where you have to come in by the fire escape, let alone deal with the world out on the street. "What are we going to do the rest of our lives, sit here and watch the parade go by? Lose ourselves in a glass menagerie? Keep playing those worn-out records your father left behind? What is there for us? Dependency all our lives? I tell you, Laura, I know what happens to unmarried women who aren't prepared to occupy a position in life!"

Laura can't live like her mother. She knows she has to do something, but the only way she can live is what she finds for herself. She walks in the park. She goes to the zoo, visits the animals and watches the birds. She can sit for seven hours at a time and see such beauty. She has all this love in her little glass menagerie. That is her world. She tries to function in the real world, but she can't. She is not a realistic character. She is a character created in poetic realism.

Pay attention to Tennessee's language. Even when speaking about the most commonplace things, he lifts the language up. Tennessee doesn't write in your speech. He writes poetic realism, to show what it's like to live with people who don't want you there—your brother's wife or your sister's husband. I've seen such pitiful cases in the South: barely tolerated spinsters living on some brother's or sister's life, tucked away in a mousetrap of a room, encouraged to go visit from one relative to the next. Sad women without a nest. "Oh, Laura, is that the future we're mapping out for ourselves?"

What is the quality of this literary language? What does the aesthetic of it give you? Does it strike you as tumultuous? Is it gentle? Does it create a mood for you? It is tender, very tender. It loves. It's very quiet. It's sad, not brutal. It's not just "She needs something and Jim is a jerk." She doesn't have a wholeness of body or mind. On the contrary, Jim has a very whole personality. What appeals to you more, his wholeness or her vulnerability?

In every member of every audience, there is something that can be reached that is not tangible. In each person somewhere you can reach that. Everything about Jim is tangible, but Laura has an intangible, incomplete quality. Think about it as a virtue rather than a failing.

Thank God, that's still left in some of us.

*　*　*

Tennessee understands that the brutality of the times is toughest on those who don't or can't play the game. He didn't want life to be focused on, or lived for, making money. He was a multimillionaire from his plays, but nothing could save him from his abuses. He wants you to understand people who are caught in difficult situations—bag ladies, drunks, people who live in a hole in the wall with no money. The realistic world gives an artist truth.

That's where Tennessee is. He doesn't want to pass that by. His own character was drawn to the misshapen, to those who failed. Tennessee is the poet of failure. He is the man who understands it and seems to prefer it over success. So do most people, as a matter of fact. Putting failure on stage seems to awaken in the audience an identification. To most people, somehow, the man who succeeds is not as sympathetic as the man who fails. It's bigger to fail. It's more universal. Tennessee has to be in Bellevue and the Bowery. He has to be as drunk and as low as anybody in order to write a play. He doesn't have time to wait on tables and become an artist later. He had a place in Key West, where there were only bars and drunks—that's where he chose to live, because he understood those people. Rich people made no sense to him. He thought of the rich as vulgar. Tennessee understood people who couldn't face the music of being poor in the richest country in the world—people who had to escape but found no way to fight it. Ten million hungry on a bread line, with no roof over their heads in the winter—he thought they needed some attention. Was that his weakness or his strength?

People's inability to deal with their situations in life is in all his plays. Whatever their situation is, somehow they can't deal with it. Tennessee became the greatest playwright of our time because he tried to address their ghastly situations. Mostly it's the women who can't face it, but a lot of the men are on the brink, too. The plantations went down, you had a depression, the women were left without money, and the son with no land asks, "What will I do?"

Tennessee writes about the man who answers, "I will survive MY way!" Tom can't accept that he exists just to support his mother and sister. "I want to escape," he says, "but I have to stay because of my tradition." This creates a great deal of anger and confusion. He has to find what he wants to do. He can't just be in a place where there's nothing but eight hours a day in a dark factory—all dirt and blackness, with no air or sun. It's too much for the soul. He says, "Mom, do you think I want to spend my life down there at Continental Shoemakers in that Celotex interior with fluorescent lights? Honest to God, I'd rather somebody take a crowbar and batter my brains out. I go every morning, every time you come in and say 'Rise and shine!' "—which is her southern way of saying life is beautiful. But it isn't anymore.

Amanda still nurtures the memory of that "Rise and shine!" life. But he's the one who has to go to the warehouse. If somebody said to me "Rise and shine! It's six a.m.—time to get up and audition with six hundred other people for a TV commercial!" I wouldn't like it much. Neither does Tom. He says, "I go. I think how lucky dead people are. But I go. For sixty-five dollars a month, I've given up all I wanted and everything I wanted to do."

He wanted to be free.

* * *

What's great about Amanda is that she thinks she's very beautiful.* She could be wearing a rag, but it would be trimmed with something. She would have her hair up with a bow or flower in it. She wouldn't give up that tradition of "a woman has to be cared for, has to be beautiful, has to be feminine." She keeps that up and insists on being treated the way a southern woman should be treated. All the grabbing and clutching and intimacy of today—that's too naturalistic for her, and for Tennessee. What he wants here, in her, is anger kept down. She never stops talking. She goes to a very important problem, which is having a daughter who is crippled but who she won't let be a cripple because it's not allowed to be anything ugly like that.

If a playwright gives you a cripple in the thirties, it signifies that society has produced a type—somebody injured, uncomfortable with herself. Laura has nowhere to go. She can't follow her mother on the plantation, because there IS no more plantation. She can't go out into the world, because she doesn't have the strength to deal with the impossible situation of trying to become a stenographer. She couldn't face it. So she went down. She went to her own way of life. She is very tense, but she takes in all the changes and tones. She is unable to function in society because the society rejects her. The society only accepts success. It doesn't want anyone who is injured. It doesn't like old people or beggars. We don't want them. We don't want anything injured.

Realism is as difficult as dancing. You mustn't hurry it. Jim says, "Don't you like to sit on the floor? Come on, why don't you?" He throws the pillow over to her. Laura gets down on the floor, with her

---

* The actors to whom Stella directs her comments in this section are Anthony Cistaro and Mercedes Shirley.

leg brace. You must understand that she could never do that without pain. But she's the hostess, and if a guest tells you what they'd like you to do, you do it. She knows this, and for maybe the first time in her life, she sits on the floor, even though it's hard. It doesn't allow her the equilibrium to get back up again. You can imagine how difficult it is for her.

You must create a place, create the scene. Create the room and begin to know a lot about that room. There is something about a telephone table that needs a phone book. It's a table that has no love, no life in it. It's something maybe she picked up that was thrown out by someone else. What kind of couch is it? Overstuffed, with washed-out chintz slipcovers. Are the drapes torn? Whose picture is on the wall? Washington? Put something there that's very American. What kind of view does she have? A fire escape. What's on the other fire escapes? The key is "drab"—not just the room, the life. It's lower-middle-class life. The Gentleman Caller is not of exactly that same class. Know the difference in their larger circumstances. C'mon, get going! You can't be stupid if you're a modern actor. You have to be sharp. You don't have to be so intelligent in Shakespeare. He's a giant, so he carries you—if you speak ever so precisely and have lots of good teeth.

Now, what can Laura use in this room? She has her glass menagerie that she plays with—the little animals. That is hers, her collection. She is very good about collecting life. That's what she has. She doesn't have tennis. She doesn't have friends. When people are very closed up, they escape to somewhere else. People in hospitals know more about the weather—if it's raining or if a shower's coming—than people walking around outside. The confined find ways of understanding things: She would find ways of being confined, as children do. She would notice how big the shadows are when the sun goes down. She will watch these things, live within this confinement and find things to keep her busy. Most of her action is not very logical.

How does she think? She doesn't think in terms of cues. If you don't read the papers or leave the house, you have a different kind of thinking. She is given a glass of wine. Does she drink it? She puts it on the telephone table. If I were you, I wouldn't drink it. If the director told me to drink it, I would say, "No, I want *him* to have the wine."

Jim makes this little party. "Don't you like to sit on the floor?" He has his own way, his own rhythm. He creates a little atmosphere. He's used to making himself at home. But what would happen to a cripple sitting on the floor? It would be painful, wouldn't it? In this kind of play, don't think so directly. Think before you speak, and let everything come out of the thought. What the playwright wants Laura to do is to WANT to sit on the floor, but she can't. She tries to give people what they need. Invalids do that. But they're weary of the things they have to do. "Eat something! Did you finish your breakfast?" They learn to say yes, whether they did or not.

Are you interested in this? You better be.

You can't come in without bringing in something from "out there." I'm not talking about Strasberg—I'm talking about "What am I going to do now?"

Tom comes in from the fire escape—there are no stairs. He opens the window and goes over a banister. If they don't pay the electric bill, the lights go out. They're poor. Anthony, you look rich. You look like Byron or Browning. "Oh, to be in England!"—coming in to see your friends. But Tom doesn't have friends. He has something weighing him down from generation to generation, something that produced a crippled sister with no money. Southerners took care of people, they had a tradition, but that tradition was broken with poverty and with moving from the South. Now they're in St. Louis—the worst city in the world to live in. Figure that an audience is stupid. At best it will get half the play, and it can't get what you don't put in—that's majestic work. David Mamet says, "It's bigger than religion, what actors put into the words."

The stage gives you an illusion. When there's a couch and stuffed chair, it gives you the illusion that this is middle-class. If you want a tablecloth there, put it on—but it has to be torn. If you want to give him a cup, give him a mug. If you give him silver or fine china, the prop's all wrong. This family is on the verge of starving.

Amanda, when Tom climbs in from that fire escape—you don't see that he's dirty; you only see that he has to be careful what he eats. You're his mother, but say it as if you were his sweetheart. Don't act out all that drama. She doesn't know she's in a hopeless situation. If you play her that way, we'll get a broken-down family but we won't get Tennessee Williams. I think there's too much couch. It's too rich for a place you have to climb through a fire escape to get into. The table is better naked, without a tablecloth. Later on she might put something on it for the Gentleman Caller. She lives by things "you must do"—"You must help your mother!"—it's on a very feminine level. But don't *act* feminine, just *be* feminine. Get up for a moment and walk around, fix the pillow. You're walking too heavily. You're walking on two feet. Hop a little—lighter on your feet. That's how she behaves with Tom.

Amanda wants Tom to say, "I'll never leave you." But if he did, there would be anger in it. She knows he's angry. He has to come in with what the playwright says about him—which is a lot. He makes him unrealistic, gives him that whole monologue—"I didn't go to the moon, I went much further"—the kind you'll only get in Tennessee. We failed our artists in the North. Tom knows that. He's a poet at heart, but he has to work, obey the old tradition. He wants to go to poetry, he doesn't mind poverty. But he is a man in transition, between two worlds. Tom is a man of words, a man of space. Tom is *epic.*

Tony, don't put your hands in your pocket. If you do that, you can play Odets, not Tennessee. The gestures you use are too improvised. Think about them, and about your clothes. What would you wear if you worked in a warehouse for eight hours? [*Cistaro: "Heavy shoes, heavy pants."*] Bring in the working class from head to toe—make up for your lack of it. You must wet your hair. You can't bring in Cistaro, because if you do, we'll expect the television cameras to come and photograph you.

Climbing up the fire escape, you've ripped your trousers, you're in pain. I want to see you do something when you come in. To just "come in" is boring. Some place you've been has created a certain anger in you—"That goddamn fire escape I have to climb through is rusted!" Come in and notice yourself: "I'm bruised, shit!" Rub your foot, bring over a chair. It's morning, you haven't slept. You were out all night. Come in as if you're trying to sneak in so your mother won't hear you. You had a fight with some guy or maybe a prostitute, about booze or dope. But your mother thinks you just woke up. You have to build it so the entrance is "I am in deep trouble, but I'm going to get out of it. I'm going to be what I am—I'm going to stay up all night and study these low-life characters till I know them." Come in with an idea that you've got to write down—look for a piece of paper, get a pencil, start to write something down. It's morning, but you're still with your writing, with your ideas, with the conflict. You don't want any coffee.

[*Cistaro: "Laura has just asked me to apologize to my mother. I'm coming in to apologize. I thought I should have a certain amount of contrition."*]

No. It's not in your character to do that. The rituals have collapsed.

You know that. You know your mother is living with some idea that she's an American queen, and you're sick of it. When you say, "Laura, let me go . . . " that's the important message. "I want to get out, I want to escape." Escape is your theme. You mustn't just sit on a chair and put sugar in the cereal. Get up and see if she has lit a fire—she might burn the house down. Use the room. Let her talk.

[*Cistaro: "I'm nervous."*]

As a character or as an actor? All actors are nervous. All of us are in trouble when we're onstage for the first time with a new character. What an actor does is say, "I am nervous, but I'm not going to let it dominate me. I'm going to let it live with me and I'm going to talk to it and say, 'Listen, you son of a bitch, you can live with me, but don't try to dominate me. I've got a part to play, I know what to do.' " Don't feature the nervousness. It's not necessary.

The costume is the most important thing to feed the actor. People wear black in mourning—not because black is interesting but because it's the ritual. A wedding is white. Amanda's kimono could be beautiful, but it has to have a certain Tennessee quality about it—old, or ripped. You're living off the past. Hop around, go to the chair—I want you to hop! It's not comedy, it's just the way Amanda moves. Don't be so heavy. [*Amanda piles the plates.*] She wouldn't in a thousand years put one dish on top of another. That's a northern thing, in diners. She'd treat each plate as if it weren't cracked. Don't just take off the old lace tablecloth. Fold it lovingly. "It's so precious!" We need to see a real southern woman on the stage. You have to bring Tennessee in. If you put a vase down on the table, look at it first—put it up to the light. See how pretty it is. Walk around with it a bit, see how it shines in different light. Hop. *Talk* to the vase.

Anthony, take off your shirt, tie it around your neck. [*"I took off the other shirt."*] Take off the undershirt and tie it around your neck so it's sloppy. [*"May I put it on at some point?"*] No. What are you waiting for? [*"I'm making sense out of this."*] You don't have Tom's rhythm. You have the rhythm of a very realistic play.

In scene 4, he says, "I apologize, Mother." Do something with it, Amanda! Take from him. He's made you happy, he's made you sad. Cry or turn away. Girlish things. Girls fuss with their hair when they're agitated, they *do* things. Be a girl. You're so realistic—it's not even good for Odets! You're pouring that coffee so realistically. We need movement from you; we don't need to see you pouring. Don't stay with things too long, because it's boring. You have choices. You can put that tray away, put his cup down on the side or run around the table and put it in the corner, go back and put your own cup on the other side . . . Then you're not so static.

Move the chair over to him while he's apologizing. Keep your own character going. Don't lose your character when his character is going. Use the whole room, never mind him. "I worry so much," she says. Let's see you worry. I don't want you to say it. If you go to the chair and back again, we'll see you're worried. DO worry, don't SAY worry. It's, *Oh my God, what should I do? I don't know what to do next!*—in your actions. Worry DOES, it doesn't SAY.

Anthony, come in with the Rage of Man—the rage through the ages of man. If you don't come in with that and spit on the floor and look out at the moon, it won't work. Let her go on talking and you go on doing. Don't be static, darling. Don't ever stand in the middle of the stage and talk. Maybe in Shakespeare. If you want to talk to her, *really* want to talk to her.

Turn the chair backwards, facing you. If there are things on the chair, throw them off, wipe something up on the floor, maybe the roof is leaking. You come in, you see the chair is all dirty, the roof is leaking, you're sick of it. Be angry. Know your partner's action so you'll know your own: her action is to complain about you, about the situation. You've heard it a million times. When you say "I understand," tear something. Tear that rag to pieces. "I understand, Mother! Every time you tell me, I understand!" That's why you keep leaving home. Use props in a way that makes the action work for you. You're a nervous, intense man. Go to the fire escape, talk from there a bit. You don't have to be on the stage all the time to talk. Run a few steps down the fire escape, she can still hear you. We've seen her nervousness. Let's see yours.

In every part you play, you must know your partner's action and how he or she thinks. You cannot just respond to their words. The emotion and thought behind the words is what justifies putting them down. Empty words are no use. They just blur the play. Respond to his mind, not his words. Otherwise you'll be giving a conventional reaction to something that needs a unique reaction. Amanda does not, at this moment, need attention. Don't give it to her. What she needs is to complain, and so she complains and talks and talks, and she's so busy with that complaining that she doesn't need you. When she really needs you, we'll see what happens.

Until you are able to fill out each word in the text with living feeling and emotion, the text will remain dead. If you activate your characters by doing what the words mean, not just what they say, we will get a quality of character and of language—with a certain amount of beauty in your voice. Harold Clurman said every time he saw Ethel Barrymore, "I never knew whether she was good or bad, I just listened to her." Because she spoke so beautifully. We have to get some quality of voice from you, Amanda. A certain artificiality.

It's in all of Tennessee's women.

* * *

What's in Tennessee's men?

A fine example—even if it's unflattering—is Jim, in the Gentleman Caller scene. It is very American to be a dumb cluck, and Jim's pretty dumb. We eventually get to Kowalski from him. You will see the transition from the doctor who remains true to his heritage in *Summer and Smoke,* to Tom the poet, and then to this boy—to this new America.

Is there anything worse than a boy coming into a girl's house for the first time and saying, "Why don't we sit on the floor?" The floor is where man started a million years ago. He squatted. In North Africa, the Arabs still squat. Gradually, we got to the chair. But now in America, he is back to squatting. Tennessee says the floor and the primitive thing are easier for young people now. Two thousand years of culture have gone out the window because you want to be comfortable. Something about life has made Jim that casual. His formality is gone to the point where he does this naturally in somebody else's home. You get the difference in class behavior: he is middle-class. He is brash. He reaches out but doesn't really see or feel anything. He has lost feeling and understanding. The song is gone, and Laura sees it is gone.

He talks to her about the greatness of America—how wonderful Wrigley's gum and the big buildings in Chicago are. She doesn't answer much. She remembers him from high school, recalls every impression in detail and a great deal about music—but he only vaguely remembers her. A very correct young girl is being visited by a very informal young man. He sits on the floor and asks her to do so, too. She hesitates but gives in. He's very warm and makes himself cozy in the extreme. "I'm as comfortable as a cow," he says—which is *very* comfortable. He talks about the splendor and opportunity of American life. He asks about her shyness; she seems not to know much about it. She recalls her memories of him, his voice, his deportment, his lofty position in high school. She tells him her miserable recollections of being a cripple, how enormously withdrawn she was, her inability to make friends, her total awareness of her own crippled condition. He allows as how it might have been difficult, but he's not sure it's so important. He generalizes and compares his disappointments to hers. He says there are no barriers for people.

Those are the facts you're given. Facts are dead, but from them you can begin to do the work. Once you understand the facts, then—and only then—go to the words. My father, Jacob Adler, said something important: "A lot of actors can get rotten results in a false play. Don't dig too far down, because you'll find shit." It's not good to dig down when a play is false. An actor needs a poetically human situation or a dynamically human one. A good actor can make that happen by himself in a bad play, but in a really good play—like this one—the playwright has done most of the work for you by choosing words that reveal the real social, moral, tragic situation.

Walk around the stage for a little before you start.* Just walk around, sit down, get up . . . You're in a world now that's your world. Get used to that world. It would be very good if the Gentleman Caller saw something that needed to be fixed and fussed with it—that would be creative acting. He's coming from a party, and he brings the party in with him.

Laura, don't *show* your nervousness—*be* it, *have* it. If you really need to twist the handkerchief, something inside will tell you when to twist it. Don't "act" the part. Throw out 99 percent of the acting and you'll still have 100 percent too much when you start. Remember, there is no such thing as "I'm acting Laura." It's "I'm *living* Laura."

Technology, not science—that's what Jim is interested in. It means typewriters, toilets, electric lights. He's not Einstein. He's full of piss

---

* The actors to whom Stella directs her comments in this section are Doug Campbell and Beverly Leach.

and vinegar—a real up-and-coming American. We want to see that when he comes in. Play it into the ground.

Laura, you don't know what to expect. Have you ever heard of a transition? You make transitions in life, and on the stage. He has to *see* that you're shy. All the things he says are commercial traveler's words. Laura hasn't heard about chewing gum or Wrigley. That's out "there." The one time she tried to go outside, she vomited—literally. She went out once to do something, tried to put her hands on a typewriter, and threw up because she couldn't live with chewing gum and typewriters in her world.

Jim is bringing outside American life in to this girl, and he doesn't know that she doesn't want it. When Tennessee paralyzes you, it means that you can't live an ordinary life. When he puts that crippled symbol into her character, it means she can't and won't ever do anything. But Jim *is* America. I want you to play America! Don't just play a gentleman. He's a nice guy, but if he doesn't bring in a lot of noise, a lot of guts, we won't know what the scene is about. Play the kind of a guy who could be in a lousy bar at four in the morning, drinking beer and laughing it up. We have to have a complete contrast between her world and the American world that can't be lived in by this aristocrat of the mind. Otherwise, we have no play. She hasn't talked to a man in years, or really even seen one. Use Tennessee's moment to contrast these two different specimens of mankind. What this American man offers a girl is not a bouquet of roses, not a kiss on the hand, but chewing gum. That's America now. Jim sits on the floor. There was a moment in civilization not so long ago when you didn't. If you sat on the floor, you were in jail.

Don't hand her the pillow—throw it at her! There's nothing civilized about you. Open your tie after a moment or two. I was in a restaurant in Venice once when a Hollywood movie star came in and said, "This is the first time I've had to wear a tie in my life!"—he was so uncomfortable he couldn't eat, he had to leave. This Gentleman Caller is the most realistic character in the play, very much a man you will recognize. You'll recognize his mind. If you know the character's mind, you know the character. You will recognize his aims. It is very important that you know what a man wants to do. Jim has many assets. He graduated with honors. He had the best voice and sang all the time. Music is a symbol of what is, or was, there for him in the world: there's music in him. The last time Laura saw him, he was singing. We see in Jim what was lost in the youthful man who used to sing but now doesn't know what to substitute for that. He is outgoing and hungry for life. Everything he sees and admires is big. Size is important to him.

Laura, on the other hand, couldn't graduate—couldn't do anything—so she built a life for herself of sitting. But she says, "Don't think I don't do anything. I have my glass menagerie, which takes up all my time." That's the metaphor—what she uses in life. She could have used literature or painting and been someone about whom, when she dies, they'd say, "That's Elizabeth Browning, who was crippled," or, "That's Emily Dickinson, our great American poet who never left her room." She might have become an Emily Dickinson. But she didn't.

Jim is sweet but totally insensitive. He doesn't see anything about her. He is direct, aggressive, free with advice. When she says "I have my glass menagerie," he dismisses it. These two people have lost each other. What she admired in him is gone. Therefore it is not a love scene. Don't play it as a love scene. Everybody does. What she loved in him was some glass image of him that she could put in her menagerie collection, but it's gone now.

Strindberg said if you put a countess and a stable boy together in the kitchen, one of them is going to get killed. You can never put two classes together and expect to get a real love scene. You can make it last for about five minutes, but after that it breaks. There's no class difference between Laura and her brother, because he's fighting to be a poet. You fight for it, even though you know there's no guarantee your poems will sell. But there's a big difference in class between Laura and Jim. Everything she thinks about is from the past; everything he talks about is in the future. His idea is "Come on, let's get that smash Hollywood hit! $5 million? Not enough. It's gotta be $50 million!" His attitude explains why *Reds* fell behind the box office of that other movie that won the prize, even though *Reds* will become a classic and the other one will be forgotten.*

Tennessee feels we are drawn to people who play music or write poetry or go off to see the world out of a desire to solve The Problem. Tennessee's audience is drawn to the melody, not the facts, of life. Do

---

* Adler is speaking shortly after *Chariots of Fire* beat out *Reds*—Warren Beatty's epic drama of the Bolshevik Revolution—for the Best Picture Oscar in 1982.

you know people who are attracted to you because you're "offbeat"? Would they be as attracted if you were "onbeat"? In life, there's a stratum of people who are drawn to the unanswerable, the unsolvable. The mystery here is in Laura, not Jim. The mystery is the way she thinks. It's what makes her poetic, and we are drawn to what we can't solve in her. The tendency in the beginning is to think of yourself as superior to such people. But they exist in you and me, too. You have to be damn stupid to feel superior to anybody, because the seed of that other person is in you. Discover that seed! If you do, you will educate yourself about life and about yourself. You don't know yourself. Nobody does. I don't know my own self. You see me as very strong. You don't know that I have a daughter who says, "Oh, Mother, you're so foolish—won't you ever learn?" And I take it from her. That's a side of me you don't see. Where's my revolutionist side? You don't see the side that was in jail. But it's there. Never put yourself above the character. Since there are no heroes or villains anymore, you must ask, "What about him is human? How am I like him?"

Jim generalizes. Do you? Do you talk about things you don't know? When do you talk about something in such a way that later you say to yourself, "My God, how could I have been so stupid?" I, for instance, am very stupid. If I told you my feelings about capital punishment—I don't know a thing about it. I've never experienced it. But I'd say, "Why, I think it's a fine idea!" or "I just think we should abandon it." That is stupidity, isn't it? It doesn't touch me. I don't know it. We all do this. Very few people really examine. I talk my ass off about things I don't know and I'm pretentious and nobody says, "You dumb son of a bitch!" They put up with it.

Understand your character and, even if you disapprove of him, find him in you. The great actors always did that. They played Othello AND Iago. They changed parts, because they knew they had to have that stretch. This play teaches you something I'd advise you to do immediately with every character you play: identify with what you don't think you are—even, or especially, if it's ugly. Work on the technique you need for "stealing." You always steal as an actor. You can steal from yourself, you can steal from life, you can steal from your imagination. You must build it up in you. A good exercise is to ask, "Where am I, in my own circumstances, like that, too?" Let your imagination take you to the experience of whatever you don't like.

Once you do that, it happens. It must pass through your imagination to affect you emotionally.

The first thing we see with Jim is that he's conventional, he doesn't talk in depth about things, he's easygoing and influenced by popular opinion. He could have been a poet if he had remembered the song in him, but he forgot that and exchanged it for chewing gum and money. He doesn't know how to sit or where he is. He does what he wants, wherever he goes.

Jim, use the stage! Move before you say the next line. Never do much when somebody else talks, do it when *you* talk. When she's talking, behave yourself. Laura, wait till he pays attention! You're crippled. The way you're prancing around, I'd think you were a physical therapist. When he asks you to dance, you say, "I can't." It's not a moment to move. It's a moment to TRY to move—to cover up your bad leg because it's got a brace on it, maybe pull your skirt down when he's coming around your way. When you go to the glass menagerie, circle it a couple of times. Stretch it so it's not so horribly quickened by your fear and inexperience of using the stage.

When she gets up and says "I have a glass collection," there are things you could do to sell it. But don't go to him, for godsakes. Understand that Tennessee has written her as a child who is bigger, vaster in her isolation. She is a skeleton—and you have to help take this skeleton and make her dance! Nobody would ever say, "I'd like to lay you." You look untouchable. But you can help this skeleton of a person get rid of her faults. As an actress, you're better than a psychiatrist. But what I get from you is talkative. That's the impression you give. It's bad acting. If Laura can put five words together, that's a lot for her. Jim's a big American guy, he gets drunk, works in a shoe factory. "What is that thing?"—the unicorn—he wants to know. "Whaddaya call it?" He's got to have an answer for everything. Don't go over to him. If she could go to him, she would have done it before. She's not in touch. A menagerie is a place where you keep animals, and Laura is with the animals. It's not, "Gee, I'm beautiful but nobody talks to me."

I'm not here to teach you how to act. I'm here to help you interpret a play. I expect you to be an actor with technique when you get here. The craft of acting is not in the line. It's over or behind the line. You and the line together create the character. That's the psychological side of acting. It's in you, not in the words. The author cannot put the inside psychology into every sentence. What comes out must have your psychology in it, but you can't play it without *her* inner psychology.

Beckett and Mamet and other modern playwrights give you nothing physically to hang on to on the stage. Tennessee doesn't give you very much, either. This isn't a play in which the playwright takes you someplace specific. You don't know exactly where he's taking you. It's more interesting when you don't have that goddamned logic, which is either very comical or very tragic. Look at me when I talk, and put your feet down! I'm asking you for that courtesy. It's tough to listen to somebody else talk; it's very interesting when you talk yourself. I want you to accept the fact that Tennessee says this person is completely lost—someone who cannot deal with the realistic world.

Some of you go to a psychiatrist or a priest for your inner turmoil. Tennessee puts all that inner turmoil, inner fragility, and fear of life into the play. Listen to it, get used to it. The new playwrights do it all the time. They're going to take you out of real space and logic and take you where they want to take you. Go with them.

When *Streetcar* was first produced, the *New York Times* said, "There's no other Kowalski but Brando!"—only Marlon could do it, nobody else. I think that was a terrible thing to say. It's wrong. But my point is, this character Jim is philosophically very close to Kowalski. He's got a lot of the same ego, the same drive Stanley has. This unique vulgarity of the man has to be exploited on the stage—it's the vulgarity of all time! You never threw a pillow at a girl or offered her chewing gum the first time you came to see her. I like this Gentleman Caller—and Tennessee likes him. He admires the outrageousness of strength in men. He writes about strong men, he understands them. Those men have to really be *played*.

Nobody is stronger than Tom. For his final monologue, Tennessee brings down a scrim and hides the stage, while the actor talks directly to the audience, trying to make them understand: "I didn't go to the moon, I went much further—for time is the longest distance between two places . . ." It isn't something said inside a house or a room. Tennessee's language is fascinating. Tom is a man without an exit, but he is a wanderer, looking for a certain road. I once staged it in New York with a pack on his back, as if he were going through the world trying to find someplace to put the pack down and stay. He comes down front to tell the audience something about the truth of his life. He wants to reach them, to communicate with them.

You've got to come out with that action.* It would be better for you to walk around, not just step in and find a place to stand. I want you to know where you are going to do this monologue. From which point? Where exactly do you want to do it from? You have to do it center stage. Ask yourself, "What am I doing?" The answer is, "I've come to talk to the audience." You're Tennessee's mouthpiece.

People sometimes say something very poetic to the whole world: "I didn't go to the moon . . . " Tom is going to find his way. He may end up in a garret, or worse, but he is the artist Tennessee loves and puts into every play. He's the strongest man on earth. Nobody can measure up to the dynamic inner soulful strength of a poet. "I didn't go to the moon, I went much further . . ." Don't try to make common sense of words that don't have common sense. Get the rhythm of it. When you've got a really big poetic speech, don't drag it down. Up, *up,* UP! Not television size. There's no little man or little image on the stage! You have a monologue so full of meaning, so full of your life. Give it away with poetry and beauty. Don't try to communicate that there's a tablecloth here or napkin there—that's not what the play or the monologue is about. It's just like Shakespeare wrote in *Hamlet:* "To be or not to be . . . " It's the monologue form, which has very little to do with the rest of the play.

This is a poetic situation, and you are giving the audience your life: "Here I am, this is me." It's very Chekhovian. It's not just "I wanna tell you something," but "I'm going to reveal myself, my life, to you and to the world!" You seem to be adding a lot of emotion that you don't really feel. You're putting it on. If it comes from what you want to say, all right—let it come out. But don't lay on extra emotion if it doesn't come out of what's going on inside of you. Don't let it break the rhythm. Don't take your own rhythm, take the playwright's rhythm. Study it. After this monologue, you're going off on your road. "I'm at the end of my speech, we're at the end of the play, and I wish Laura would let me go." With that inner thought, you walk out.

When you speak of something like Laura's little fragments of colored glass, you have to *see* them yourself. If you don't see them, we don't

* The actor to whom Stella directs her comments in this section is Dan Bachner.

see them. Any image in the text that's spoken by the character—the actor has to have it in him. "I stopped on the street and saw pieces of colored glass, like bits of a shattered rainbow . . ." He doesn't want Laura's broken glass, or the past. He has to go away. It's in Miller, too, when the salesman's son says, "Let me go, Papa, let me go!" Breaking away from the family is a sacrilegious thing. In modern plays, you will find that many characters want to break away. They want to go, but they're still being drawn back. Those are the two powerful urges. A lot of Tennessee's characters have that.

Don't scratch your head, don't put your hands in your pockets—you can do that at home or with your girlfriend, but don't do it on the stage. On stage, people are watching you, and they don't want to see you do that. If you communicate with me, then you must use the same tone of voice that I use. If I talk in a big voice, you can't respond in a little voice. This is one of the most beautiful monologues we have in the American language. I'd like you to work on it, keep it—do it for an audition. Let them hear some poetry before they die.

You don't trust yourself as an actor. You're a splendid young man, and you should bring that on the stage with you in the character. Tom may be torn, but he has achieved manhood in order to break away. Don't bring on the boy. Males over eighteen here are men, not kids. You've carried around the image of "kid" too long. I don't want it. I want a full-grown man with full control. "I'll find my own way" is not something a baby says, and you're not a baby. One of the most attractive things in the world is to see a man on the stage. That's what an audience likes.

Your job is to understand what the author is saying. Tom's a wanderer, which every artist is. He never really settles down. Tennessee wrote that epic quality, that universality, into this character. It's a quality that has largely gone out of the American actor, who brings in a babyish quality instead. That's happened at the White House, too.* Nobody needs a baby for a president. It is a dismal moment. So reach up high when you have to, and higher still! Don't be little on the stage—it's boring. Life is boring. We're too little in life. That's why we come to the theater—because it's not boring here.

[*Students applaud.*]

---

* Adler, speaking here in June of 1988, was no fan of the declining president Ronald Reagan.

Thank you very much. I'm glad we have actors, I'm glad I'm one of them, I'm glad to be with you. Nothing in the world makes you as happy as when you find the character. When you do, the audience and the world know it. A student of mine once said as he was walking off, "Goddammit, Miss Adler, when you really get it, it's better than sex!"

SEVENTEEN

A STREETCAR NAMED DESIRE

(1947)

SYNOPSIS OF *A STREETCAR NAMED DESIRE:*
Blanche DuBois has fallen on hard times, having lost
Belle Reve, her ancestral home, as well as her teacher's
job in Laurel, Mississippi. She arrives in New Orleans
to visit her sister, Stella, who is married to Stanley
Kowalski, a hard-drinking ex-GI. Blanche is told to
take a streetcar called Desire to Elysian Fields—the
Kowalskis' neighborhood in the French Quarter.

Initial tensions increase. Stanley and Stella quarrel
about the houseguest's intrusions into their cramped
quarters: Stanley rails against Blanche's uppity airs,
her snide remarks, and the loss of Stella's inheritance.
He vows to check into Blanche's past—more sordid
than romantic, he suspects.

During a poker game that night, Blanche meets
Stanley's good-hearted pal Mitch, much devoted to his
mother, and flirts brazenly with him. Stanley, getting
drunker and angrier, breaks up the game and again
argues with Stella, this time striking her. Stella retreats
tearfully to a neighbor's apartment, but then returns
and—over Blanche's indignant objection—retires to
Stanley's bed.

Stella is all smiles the next morning. But Stanley's

Marlon Brando as Stanley and Jessica Tandy as Blanche in Tennessee Williams's *A Streetcar Named Desire* (1947): "This match-up is a battle to the death."

mood darkens ominously when he overhears Blanche urging her to leave her "ape" of a husband—especially now that Stella is pregnant.

When Stanley and Stella step out for an evening, Blanche tries to seduce a newspaper delivery boy who drops by to collect. Later, she has a date with Mitch, who unburdens his heart to her. Blanche, in turn, confides to him about her brief, tragic marriage to a homosexual boy, who killed himself. The act ends with the emotional recognition that they need each other.

Some weeks later, it is Blanche's birthday, but Mitch is late for the party. Stanley reveals what his detective friend discovered: Blanche's promiscuity was why she had to leave Laurel. He hands her a one-way bus ticket home, adding that Mitch knows all and won't be coming around again. Later that night, Stella goes into labor and Stanley rushes her to the hospital.

Soon after, a drunken Mitch shows up and bitterly reproaches Blanche, declaring her too tainted to marry. Stanley returns from the hospital and rapes Blanche. Her unhinging is now complete.

A few weeks later, Blanche prepares to leave to visit "an old admirer." Stella, unable to believe her accusations against Stanley, is in fact packing her sister's clothes for an imminent trip to an asylum. A doctor and nurse arrive. Henceforth, more than ever, Blanche will depend on the kindness of strangers.

—B.P.*

BLANCHE DuBOIS is taken by a streetcar to a place where the melody is not completely understood by her or by us. I am going to take you there, too—to the old French part of New Orleans.

Tennessee says she arrives there dressed very daintily, as if for a ladies' summer tea party. She has no idea where she's going. All she has is an address on a scrap of paper. She is lost, literally, and has to ask for directions. The answer sounds allegorical, or even satirical: "You take the streetcar called Desire, then Cemetery, then you end up in Elysian Fields." That is an itinerary from life to death to glory.

I would like you to deal with *A Streetcar Named Desire* not in terms of Blanche's weakness but in terms of the strength and madness of these people in the French Quarter of New Orleans. The streetcar

* *A Streetcar Named Desire* premiered on December 3, 1947, at the Ethel Barrymore Theatre in New York City under the direction of Elia Kazan, starring Marlon Brando (Stanley), Jessica Tandy (Blanche), Kim Hunter (Stella), and Karl Malden (Mitch).

deposits her in a poor but quaint part of town. We hear jazz music coming from some bar. We see her come around the corner with her suitcase and stop in front of a little run-down apartment house. She looks down at her slip of paper and then looks up at the building with "shocked disbelief."

A train is going by, a cat is screeching, a Negro woman is crying, a man in evening clothes is being beaten in the background, a vendor is yelling, people are running back and forth . . . Nobody knows exactly what's happening now, or what will happen next. She takes that streetcar called Desire and ends up in a place of dirt, decay, conflict, and violence.

You have to have a good idea of this kind of life. People in the French Quarter are drinking and gambling and fighting and fornicating. The movement, the anger, and the tone are all violent. When a person reaches what he wants in this city, it is insanity. It is a caricature of how people live. The needs of the people who live here are the needs of insane people. It is appetite without end. Even animals rest, but people don't rest here. Nothing rests here; it is always going. There is a craziness in their way of talking, acting, reacting. The rhythm is violent.

Blanche comes from the aristocracy of America and still has the fragrance of magnolia blossoms in her nostrils. She goes for the poem in life. But in this place, compulsiveness is the regular way of life. Everything seems to hinge on sex and violence. There is an orgy of emotions without control. Emotions out of control lead to hell. Nobody is inhibited here. Poker and bowling and screaming and screwing and hitting each other—that is their way. They are unashamed and contented with this life. They are driven by debased circumstances—the lack of money, the lack of education, the lack of mercy all around them. But those circumstances create a terrific vitality.

You must know about Stella's life with Stanley. You must see the opposition of two women—the realist Stella and the poetic lady Blanche—whose ways are deeply antagonistic to each other. Stella has entered this rough proletarian world and finds her happiness in the rough, sexual Kowalski. Blanche needs quiet and comfort but finds herself in a crude, noisy, working-class atmosphere, clinging to her aristocratic superiority. You can't help pitying her, because this life she despises seems so alive, while her life seems so fixed on the past and on some inner mix-up. To Stanley, her mix-up is funny and so is her refinement. But it is also offensive and threatening.

They are three of the most important characters ever created in the American theater. They are worth examining carefully—first separately, and then together.

Blanche has the mood of a life which has come down through the ages. She is weather-beaten. Blanche has weathered the storms of life that are found through the entire history of woman, and she has emerged from it with a weakened body and a weakened psyche. She symbolizes the woman—or man, for that matter—who is not so much sick physically as sick inside. She cannot take being alone, without being taken care of. Aloneness is not a way to live in the world. It creates sickness.

You must see and understand how Blanche has naturally evolved, in history and in the theater. *Camille* was a play about a prostitute much like Blanche. It was always played very romantically. She is poetic but worldly-wise. Men send her diamonds. She gives freely. She sacrifices. She coughs. She can't move. She has taken many blows in life. She cannot take another.

Stella, by comparison, is rather indefinite. It's hard to believe that she is Blanche's sister. What she has accepted in New Orleans has alienated her from Blanche completely. We see Stella sitting in the house, a broom is lying on the floor, she is eating candy from a paper bag. This is a pregnant woman, soon to be a mother, from a good family background, looking and moving almost like a George Grosz caricature.* When Stanley says, "We're going bowling," Stella says, "Can I come and watch?" It's the sort of thing a child would say, looking up from her candy. You see, without her saying very much, that she is without a growing self. She is reverting.

"Nothing's the matter," she keeps telling Blanche. "Leave it alone. I'm all right." But Blanche slowly awakens in her the realization that Stanley is dirty. He eats with his hands. He talks with his mouth full. For the first time, Stella begins to notice something in him that is not right for the table. A table needs a knife and fork. If you use the table

* George Grosz (1893–1959): German expressionist artist noted for his savage caricatures of emaciated lowlife types—beggars, prostitutes, thugs—amid urban chaos and decay.

without using the knife and fork, you are a killer. The knife and fork and table are a development that lets you not eat on the ground—lets you rise to your place as a man and differentiate yourself from animals.

But what if the thing Stella likes and is attracted to is precisely that animal quality, that animal power given back to the primitive man? It took many centuries for man to be tamed and become controlled. From that man came an English culture, a French culture, a German culture, and eventually an American culture. But it doesn't take long at all for him to become untamed.

One piece of Louisiana culture that Stanley retains and talks about is the Napoleonic Code. He knows very little, but what he knows he hangs on to. The Napoleonic Code is a set of state laws that says whatever belongs to the wife belongs to the husband, and vice versa. Stanley tells Stella she has been swindled—"and baby, when you get swindled, I get swindled, and I don't *like* to get swindled!" What he thinks he's been swindled out of is Belle Reve, the DuBoises' old Mississippi estate.

Belle Reve means "beautiful dream." A dream has no reality, but this one existed for Blanche and Stella and others of their time, and not just in the South. In the North, it was the Vanderbilts and the Rockefellers at Newport. The interior of those mansions had marble floors, curving staircases, tapestries, velvet curtains, painted ceilings, brocaded chairs, pipe organs, potted palms . . . The homes were on that kind of scale, and so was the life. On a typical day, a young girl would be out riding before nine a.m. She would return from her ride and change in time for tennis at the country club. Then a carriage might take her to a landing, where she'd be ferried out to the yacht for lunch. At about half past four, she would leave the yacht to watch a polo match. Then she'd go home to bathe and change for a dinner party, which would break up by nine-thirty p.m. After that, many girls had trouble keeping their eyes open, but if she could, she might go to a ball.

That's the kind of girlhood these DuBois sisters had. No slaves, but very much gone with the wind. In the terrific first scene between them, Blanche tries to explain how it was lost and tries to transfer her guilt to Stella: "You're the one who left, Stella. You left not only Belle Reve but two thousand years of culture and tradition that went with it. In exchange for all that, you came here and went to bed with Stanley, while I stayed behind at Belle Reve and tried to hold it together alone. The whole burden was on me."

Stella defends herself. "The best I could do was to make my own life, Blanche." Blanche says, "I know, but you're still the one that abandoned Belle Reve. I stayed and fought and bled and almost died for it." Stella says, "Stop your hysterics and tell me what happened!" Blanche says, "You're a fine one to stand there accusing me. I took the blows on my face, on my body. All of those deaths! The long parade to the graveyard! Father, Mother, Margaret . . . You just came home in time for the funerals. And funerals are pretty compared to death. Funerals are quiet, but death isn't. Sometimes their breathing rattles and they cry out, 'Don't let me go!'—as if you could stop them . . . How in hell did you think all that sickness and dying was paid for? Death is expensive, Stella. The Grim Reaper put up his tent on our doorstep! Belle Reve was his headquarters! You stand there, thinking that I let the place go. Where were you? In bed with your Polack!"

It's tremendous. This monologue is as big in size as any in Shakespeare. You cannot abandon it to just whining, "Oh, how I suffered . . ." You really have to howl! "I was the little girl who savored this tradition and knew its glory!" Blanche is saying. "I took the blows for it because I understood!"

You have to be a big actress not to bring it down. You mustn't be afraid of this monologue just because Stella says "Stop being hysterical." Blanche took the blows but was deeply injured. A little French actress got up in one of my classes once and said, "Miss Adler, I should be the one who plays Blanche in this scene because I, too, have been very hurt in my life." I said, "You don't say. Really?" Then I asked the class, "How many girls here have been badly hurt?" They all raised their hands, including me.

Pain in modern life, or life in any period, has been a major part of woman's existence from the ancient Greeks on down. Medea is so pained—so outraged that her beloved Jason could divorce her for a younger princess—that she kills his and her own children for revenge. Euripides did pretty well with a play about that. It's been running continuously since 400 B.C. From then until now, playwrights have been making plays about the tragedy of the hurt woman.

Blanche is saying tradition doesn't always leave you with anything securable. Security goes when the mortgage goes. Everything goes. Yet you are still responsible for everything. It's the worst of both worlds. She has a keen understanding of who she is in her long line, but she is not strong enough to uphold it. You have to be very strong to maintain a tradition, and even stronger to survive it once it's destroyed.

Blanche is at the point where she would need great tenderness to survive. Her pain might be alleviated by kindness and understanding—not by the primitive brutality of men like Stanley. That craziness in the way they act, the way they drink, the way they play cards, makes them wild. A case of beer brings out their savagery. Tennessee feels the common people are full of depravity and that even their normal sexual behavior takes on a brutish, degenerate air. Blanche arrives and must suddenly become the fighting force against this mob? It is too much for her. It is asking too much to bring these two classes together. From Strindberg on, the mixture of classes inevitably leads to disaster.

She is hysterical, weakened, half gone. She constantly needs hydrotherapy. She knows she is sick. She can't handle this. But she has two eyes and a brain that tell her she can't be silent. Blanche has something to say, and she says it first to Stella in her famous "apes" speech, the morning after Stanley's card-game explosion and belting of Stella.

It starts with Stella apologizing for him. "Stanley's always smashed things," she says. "You saw him at his worst last night."

"On the contrary, I saw him at his best!" says Blanche, getting more and more worked up. "Stella, I have a plan for us both to get us both out!"

Stella tells her to stop assuming she's in something she wants to get out of, adding, "There are things that happen between a man and a woman in the dark—that sort of make everything else seem—unimportant." Blanche says, "What you are talking about is brutal desire—just—Desire!—the name of that rattle-trap street-car that bangs through the Quarter." Stella says she loves him. "Then I *tremble* for you," says Blanche. Stella replies, "I can't help your trembling if you insist on trembling!"

Then Blanche lets her have it:

"He's *common!* . . . You can't have forgotten that much of our bringing up . . . that you just *suppose* that any part of a gentleman's in his nature! . . . Oh, if he was just *ordinary!* . . . But—No—There's something downright—*bestial*—about him! . . . He acts like an animal, has an animal's habits! Eats like one, moves like one, talks like one! There's even something—sub-human—something ape-like about him . . . Thousands and thousands of years have passed him right by, and there he is—Stanley Kowalski—Survivor of the Stone Age! Bearing the raw meat home from the kill in the jungle! And you—*you* here—*waiting* for him! Maybe he'll strike you, or maybe grunt and kiss you! . . . Maybe we are a long way from being made in God's image, but, Stella, there has been some progress since then! . . . *Don't hang back with the brutes!*"

Blanche thinks she is saying these devastating things confidentially to Stella. What she doesn't know is that she's also saying them to Stanley—who is eavesdropping, and who will be her mortal enemy from now on, if he wasn't before. If a woman tells an ignorant man "You are ignorant," he says, "What are you? A goddamn stinking whore!" That's his answer. You cannot say "You are ignorant." If you do, he will strike back at you from the animal side of him that doesn't reason. Stanley's unreasoning rage is what will be attacking Blanche from here on out.

The masses from Ibsen on are in deep, aggressive ignorance and anarchy, with no desire to get out. "Rules? I'll give YOU the rules!" Stanley is always doing something to show the anger and the exclusion. "Be like us, or begone! Who do you think you are with your fancy clothes, your diction, your poetry?" It's not an individual man saying it, it's the masses, who don't know why they elected Huey Long governor in Louisiana—but they did. Long was a demagogue who aroused people, made them frenzied like Hitler did. They felt their strength that way—a very fascist European way that became a part of the American way as well.

Tennessee is making a play of the overall vulgarity of the masses, represented by this man called Kowalski. These people always come out and multiply after wars. After the First World War, the decadence in Germany was incredible. You could get anything you wanted, any kind of human perversion, practically for free, because of the inflation and the starvation. At the end of the Second World War, the Russians raped every woman they could find in Berlin. Lust and brutality are the postwar standards. It takes a long time to get over wars.

Stanley represents the way many American men coming back from the war talked and thought. "What do you mean, college? Who the hell needs it? Cut the crap!" You get that in *Cat on a Hot Tin Roof* too, when Big Daddy says, "Forget Europe—it's a mess!" This Stanley and this Big Daddy have become the enemies of civilization.

Later, toward the end of the fifties, the Soviets would put the first man into space, a tremendous blow to the United States, and America would finally understand that devaluing education and the rest of the world—"Never mind Harvard, never mind Europe!"—wasn't such a great idea. It wasn't so smart to knock down and abandon the old culture in favor of money and fame. "Are you a success?" Nobody wants to know who you really are; they want to know *what* you are. "Oh, you are a movie star! What's your name? . . . I never heard of you." It's as if Hollywood had infected the whole world with its values. If your movie doesn't make money, it's a bust. Movies don't succeed as an art form. They succeed as vulgar entertainment. Should that surprise anybody? It isn't art here. It's just one of the great industries, and industry is always ruthless. It reflects the ruthlessness and vulgarity of the masses.

So does *Streetcar Named Desire.* The play is bigger than you dare to make it. It is not just *The Ballad of Stanley and Blanche.* Tennessee is giving you the two big forces in America and the impossibility of their coexisting peacefully. Stanley represents the seductive, destructive male force, born of primitive instincts. Blanche represents the aristocracy of mind, clinging to her strength in judgment. She at no point gives that up.

Tennessee pits them against each other. It is like the fight between the Soviet Union and America. If you go to Moscow, you hear Russian cab drivers talk about the filthy capitalists. American cabbies talk about the dirty Commies. "We're going to kill them, or they're going to kill us." It's an absolute battle-to-the-death of cosmic hatreds. The playwright is predicting this man will destroy centuries of civilized progress. He says the Dark Ages are returning with this match-up of Kowalski and Blanche and their two great passions: Stanley's need to battle for life and Blanche's need to understand it—with Stella caught in between.

It is not an even match. Why? Because Blanche is sick. She and her sensibilities and her tradition are constantly under attack by the vulgarity around her. Swimming in her stream of memory, she sees how it was destroyed and complains about it, but she is weakened. "You left it to me," she tells Stella, "and you see that I am sick."

She is like a Chekhov character in that sense of the downfall of the family plantation. Before coming to the Kowalskis, she might have stayed a teacher and saved herself. But she was too psychologically muddled to understand her situation. She is a victim of a sickness that came from her husband killing himself after she told him his homosexuality disgusted her. She might have adjusted to that reality, but his suicide didn't give her the chance. Tennessee suggests that the boy-husband's failure and her own failure have something to do with mortal sin. He gives her this extraordinary relationship to a homosexual as an added difficulty, in that she feels guilt.

How does Blanche manifest this sickness? It is clearly indicated by her mannerisms, and especially by the way she speaks. Her language is different from the rest of the world's. It creates absolute poetry. There is no way to escape the poetry of this language. Yet it makes Tennessee's play realistic in that it contains the truth. I have told you before, and I will tell you again, that realism is not reality. It is the truth. It is here in Tennessee's language, which is his biggest gift to the world—so hypnotic. He is a poet in prose, and you have to be careful with each word because the meaning is not just in the common definition of it.

You cannot play Blanche without the kind of lilt and melody that go with her language. It is the melody that goes with southern English, not the melody of the North. Her melody is very much what keeps the play up. Blanche has a refinement of language. She is well bred, with sufficient education to be a schoolteacher. Her greatest need is to constantly express her refinement in order to conceal and compensate for her inner state.

Blanche is so full of contradictions. She doesn't recognize certain truths in herself, such as the fact that she is an alcoholic. She doesn't face the truth that she could be called a whore. It's not in her understanding anymore to realize that if you go around having sex with boys, you can be called a whore. She can't face that. Tennessee has brought her to such a point of mental blockout that she no longer knows that. She doesn't have it in her memory. The blocking-out of that reality from her life is why she can pretend to be above anything impure. "I don't drink, no—not a drop!"

But the reality is, she is an alcoholic, and she is now becoming more and more ill. Tennessee dramatizes the shock of that with music. She hears the music of the past and says, "I think I'm going to faint." And then, suddenly, she somehow gets back. Blanche lives with memories and recreates them a lot. Tennessee says it is memory of the heart.

Those memories are unbearable, but if she gives them up, she will be lost. She also cannot bear her present circumstances, and since she cannot come over to the real world, she creates a dream world. She is engaged in a kind of crucifixion of herself.

This is psychological realism. Blanche, who psychologically could be institutionalized with her grandeur, says, "I don't want a vulgar word spoken." Her mask of gentility is a necessary defense against the outside world's opinions of her. Placed opposite this vulgar Stanley, she feels superior and looks down on him. She must feel "up to" the situation. It would be even more terrible if she felt as helpless as she really is.

That helplessness makes her put on airs. When you cannot keep it together anymore and start going over the edge, you begin to be very critical of everything. Nothing is good enough for you. You look at everything around you and say, "That is very vulgar." If someone wears cheap perfume, you look at her and say, "Oh, really . . . !" A woman is beneath contempt if she doesn't use the right perfume, and it has to be expensive. Blanche defends herself by denigrating Stella. "How can you live like this?" Blanche also has a tremendous fear of getting old. In fact, she's not really old—she still has plenty of time—but she flits back and forth like a moth, saying, "Oh, I'm just beside myself! I just can't survive another minute without my bath! Oh my, this and that . . . !"

Blanche puts two thousand years of culture into the performance she constantly lives. It is a way of sustaining herself and entertaining others, even at Stanley's house—an entertaining feminine way with all her things around her, and la-di-da-da! She never stops playing the role of the delicate one, even when her tongue is very sharp. She can't stop. If you are strictly trained a certain way, it doesn't leave you. My brother Luther played Hitler once for a movie in Vienna,* and he was out shooting a scene in an open car, and when people in the street saw him, they saluted! They couldn't get over their training.

Blanche is like that—the prisoner of her training. She was brought

---

* *The Magic Face* (1951), directed by Frank Tuttle in semidocumentary fashion, was an unusually inventive and underrated Third Reich tale, featuring historian William L. Shirer as himself.

up to entertain. Women were raised that way. Imagine a woman going into a Ninth Avenue Irish bar and saying, "May I be seated, please?" I used to do it. There is something insane, something abnormal about carrying it into that atmosphere. But Blanche does this, and she awakens the absolute curiosity and hostility of this mindless man Kowalski who wants to know, "What is she doing? What is this for? Why does she have to do this? What are all those things she wears? What is it with all the baths she takes? What's the matter with her?"

When Blanche's complexity comes through, it is incredible. Can you see why she creates such antagonism in Stanley—and why she's such a threat to his home?

* * *

Stanley's home is revealed in all its roughness, in its ugliness, in the breaking plates, the gambling, the fighting, the screaming. The vulgarity verges on obscenity. Something in the way things are said and done seems almost obscene. What we see here is family life that's on the verge of animal life. Tennessee doesn't give you a family, he gives you a grotesque cartoon of a family.

When a man says, "You're not a queen, I am a king! Every man is a king in his own home!" he is angry. If you have to say you're a king, you are not a king. Stanley is thrown off base and into a real battle. He is constantly battling Blanche one way or another—about her clothes, her legal papers, her baths, her trunk. Whatever it is, it's not really about the objects, it's about his anger. It's his battle against what she represents.

"Yeah, I'm a brute," he tells Stella, "the worst brute in the world. Remember Belle Reve with the white columns? I tore you away from there and brought you down to me, where you've been happy." He screams at her and then he begs her, "Don't leave me, I need you! I pulled you down from those white pillars, now you stay with me!"

Stanley is battling Blanche because she calls him an ape out to destroy decent people. If Blanche and her values are right, Stanley and his values are all wrong. She's making him feel like a pariah in his own home. "This beggar woman says I'm wrong? I say she's wrong. I'm the king here. I am the male force of this world."

That roughness—Brando could do it. Marlon's a liar, a crook, a playboy of the Western world. He was in Paris once when I was in

Paris, and the biggest director there* asked me, "Is Brando a good actor?" I said, "Yes, he's a very good actor." He said, "I heard he's the greatest actor in America—is it true?" I said, "He's a very, very good actor." He said, "I want him to do *Streetcar* in France. If I give him the part, it means my whole season."

Marlon said, "Of course, I'll play it in French." That's Marlon. So, I bring them together and the director says, "Could I see you do something?" Marlon says, "Sure." He gets an actress in Paris and they give him a theater and Marlon does the birthday-party scene in *Streetcar* where he throws all the dishes on the floor and says, "There! I've cleaned my place, now do you want me to clean yours?" He does that scene, and when he banged that table, he absolutely killed it. Everything and everybody went flying in all directions. The French director said, "I have never experienced anything like that in acting." Marlon had to go to the hospital because he hurt his wrist, practically broke it.

I don't know why I told you this story, except it tells you something about Marlon. Why he was such a great actor in this play is that he is not Marlon the first but Marlon the second—his father had the same name. His family is connected. His mother played the piano very well. His English is perfect. He got expelled from high school in Illinois for riding his motorcycle through the hallways. Then they sent him to a military academy to get straightened out. He worked as a ditch digger before he decided to be an actor, came to New York, and studied the Stanislavsky system with me. One day, I told the class to act like chickens that are going to have a bomb dropped on them. Everybody else ran around and clucked like crazy, but Marlon just sat there, very calmly and intently. I said, "What are you doing?" He said, "I'm laying an egg."

He did summer stock on Long Island for a while, and then he did a few parts on Broadway,† and then he heard about *Streetcar*. He drove

---

* Jean Cocteau was adapting and mounting the first French production of *Un Tramway nommé Désir* in 1949.
† Brando's pre-*Streetcar* Broadway roles consisted of a small part in *I Remember Mama* (1944), followed by the Messenger in a revival of *Antigone* and the leading role of an anguished veteran in Maxwell Anderson's *Truckline Café* (1946), co-starring Karl Malden. Directed by Harold Clurman and produced by Elia Kazan, *Café* ran just thirteen performances but gained Brando a critics' award as "Broadway's Most Promising Actor" of 1946. It was his first teaming with Kazan and Malden, with

Producer Irene Selznick, director Elia Kazan, and playwright
Tennessee Williams (December 17, 1947)

up to Provincetown, where Tennessee was spending the summer, because he wanted to play Stanley. I had a house there, too, and when he came, I took him to Tennessee, and Tennessee said, "You'll play it." I don't know how he knew Marlon could do it, but he did. He said later that the minute he opened the screen door, he knew instantly he had his Stanley.

Brando's performance in that was revolutionary. It set the model for an American form of Method acting. What Marlon created in Kowalski was an image that America adopted for itself afterwards—all the boys. What he did with Stanley was to break the man in half. There was never a whole man. He broke him from the neck down. It was absolutely new. Marlon creates new characters. There were other good actors, but they could not create a new type that was copied by other

---

whom he later did the stage and film versions of *Streetcar* (1947 and 1951) and the film *On the Waterfront* (1954). Also on stage in 1946, he played the young hero in *A Flag Is Born* and Marchbanks in the Katharine Cornell revival of Shaw's *Candida*. Brando once said, "If it hadn't been for Stella, maybe I wouldn't have gotten where I am. She taught me how to read, she taught me to look at art, she taught me to listen to music."

people then, and still is. Brando's Kowalski was the new "hero." It became part of what was happening around the world. It was a very impressive thing.

You must recognize the standard bearers. In England, actors of all ages say, "I'll do a small part." They never fail the theater. They understand that if you want to be a great actor, you have to do the great plays. If you are going to become a Henry Irving or a Gielgud or an Olivier, you should play every classic, every play. The English tradition is not to be as well known as a movie actor. It is to be well known because "his Richard" was the greatest Richard III, or "his Hamlet" is as great as Irving's. English actors don't dare die without playing Hamlet—they don't dare! They don't dare because it is England, and England has this tradition. That is the measure for the English. It should also be a measure for you. It is tough to keep to that measure in America, because right away you are sent out for auditions. Nobody says, "Why don't you do two or three years of Shakespeare first?" You are expected to be a ready-made actress the moment you stop studying or go to an agency.

The ability of an American actor to have succeeded in creating so many portraits in the moving-picture industry is remarkable. Brando didn't create the pictures, but he created the portraits. People in Russia, England, France, all over the world revere him as someone who can play all those parts. That is what they admire. It is not the films they remember so much as the portraits he created in them.

In thinking about acting a part, think of Marlon. You don't have to be a gangster to play a gangster. He could be Brando and play the gangster. He didn't have to go out and become one and kill somebody first. Someone else I admire very much for that reason is Al Pacino, who has succeeded and failed in the American theater but has come back again and again and is doing a great performance Off Broadway.* He can't get enough of it. He is down there in the Village, with an audience who doesn't understand the play because it is difficult. There's no air conditioning, they're sweating and eating popcorn, but

---

* Speaking on May 6, 1982, Stella is referring to Pacino's performance as Walter "Teach" Cole in the acclaimed Off Broadway revival of David Mamet's *American Buffalo* at the Circle in the Square, which ran 262 performances before moving to the Booth Theatre for 93 more. Pacino's Broadway debut in *Does a Tiger Wear a Necktie?* (1969) had won him a Tony Award, and he won a second for David Rabe's *The Basic Training of Pavlo Hummel* (1977).

they go to see him because he's there. He left and came back and has been at it for two years now, not leaving the part. That is a good actor. He risked his movie work, again and again, and found a way of playing a part as close to him as Kowalski is to Brando.

An actor shouldn't think, "I have to be fat and gain eighty pounds so I can be the part, because the fat will make my character." Brando could play Kowalski one night and a gentleman the next night and a poet the third night. I don't think you're an actor if you have to gain eighty pounds. I think you should be ready to wrap the fat pad around your waist and play Falstaff one night, and take it off and play Iago the next. That is what the English do. It's what Olivier does.

Olivier was known for Shakespeare, for the classics, for things like Heathcliff in *Wuthering Heights*. Then he played *The Entertainer*—and it was his greatest part, a terrific characterization.* I went up to Toronto to see it. He was absolutely great—so big and yet so little, in every way. The next night he played Strindberg's *The Father*. But he couldn't do the *Father* part. He is, psychologically, not that actor. He himself says, "Brando does those roles." He can't play from inside; he has to play from outside. He doesn't really reach for the inner parts like *Long Day's Journey into Night*. He tried but couldn't do those. But he still has such a range. The great ones all have such a range.

As actors, don't ever type yourself. You have the ability to play many kinds of parts. Play Blanche, play Stella, play the walk-on bit, play everything. Don't limit yourself. I want you to say to yourself, "I am aiming at something. I am in the world of theater, and I must do something about my place in it." Unless you aim high, you won't get anywhere. It will mean a lot of sacrifice, and I don't know whether you are ready for it. But I think it's more fun to talk to you about theater than to win an Oscar. I understand my tradition. It is very strong. You can't beat it.

I told you English actors feel responsible for the theater. They have that responsibility, and they don't abandon it. In America, that tradition is lost—but you are still responsible for it! Stella says she left Belle Reve because she had to make a living, and Blanche says, "I know, but

---

* British "Angry Young Man" playwright John Osborne wrote *The Entertainer* (1958) specifically at Olivier's request. He played Archie Rice, a seedy old alcoholic song-and-dance man unable to face his decline, on the stage in Toronto and New York, reprising the role in Tony Richardson's 1960 film version.

you abandoned the tradition—you owe it something." It is the same with you. The actor, more than anybody, has given up his tradition.

If you have to make a living, you can't wait to go up to Toronto and hold a spear and learn the Elizabethan theater. I had to make a living, so I couldn't do that. All of us, really, are being attacked for "I have to make a living." But you can't make a living if your diction isn't right and if you don't know the history of the theater and read the plays. My God, I congratulate you for being here. Practically nobody offers it, but here somebody is offering it to you, and you come. Actors can't do it for themselves. They can't be somewhere in the Midwest and just somehow know what to do.

The actor gets a public funeral in France. Olivier, Gielgud know they are going to be buried in Westminster. They know if they're good, they will be buried there. I wish we had something like that here, to know that we will be honored. But we don't. We are left alone, surrounded by all the Kowalskis. "What commercial are you doing? You need an agent. Let's go advertise." You lose your way.

Not just actors. Tennessee is talking about America losing its way and not knowing that it is turning into a Neanderthal culture. This is what Blanche sees happening with her own sister. Tennessee is saying that Stella's backward breakthrough to Neanderthalism is like a young ape who was raised in captivity and then suddenly is put back with the wild apes. "Oh, I belong to them, too? So I'll live and act like these apes from now on." This girl married a man who cracks her across the face and says, "I pulled you off your pedestal and threw you into bed, you bitch! I'll do it again, whenever I want. Got that?" And she takes it. She not only takes it, she likes it.

Blanche is begging Stella, "Why don't you wake up from this? Don't you see where you are?" And Stella says, "I don't think I'm anywhere bad. Why, if Stanley left me for a week, I'd go crazy." This is new and attractive to Stella, but not to Blanche. It is new when a culture says, "We'll make something that will destroy everything." Ruthlessness is attractive. Even nuclear war is attractive now. Look what you can do! You can destroy the whole world. People like Stanley think that is interesting, and so does everybody around him. I think it is insane, but most people don't. People are living happily with this attraction to war—like Stella is living happily with Stanley: "What's the matter with it? It's nothing bad." Blanche says, "You just don't *see* that it's bad!"

You never heard anybody speak more clearly about the age of the new ape man than Blanche does. And yet she can't recognize the primitive desire in herself. Tennessee does something brilliant to illustrate this. He puts in the newsboy scene.

* * *

> Blanche's "apes" speech in scene 4 ends the first act. Act II opens with her anticipating a date with Mitch. She's in a bright mood until Stanley grills her ominously about her past. He and Stella then step out, leaving Blanche alone. Unnerved by the threat of exposure, she takes a stiff drink, sinks into a chair, fans herself, and is just beginning to relax when the doorbell startles her. It is the young man, a newsboy, come to collect for the *Evening Star*. She invites him in flirtatiously and makes seductive advances. Below, Adler critiques several run-throughs of that scene, performed by Anjanette Comer as Blanche and Tony Zimbardi as The Young Man.
>
> —B.P.

Why are you wearing that dress, Anjanette? It's flowery, it's beautiful, but why did you choose it? The house is ugly. The furniture is vulgar and ugly. The dress is too beautiful. You clearly rehearsed this, which is good, and in the beginning, when you rehearse a scene, you can use your voice very quietly. But at the second or third rehearsal, you must be conscious of raising your voice. You'll bring rehearsal sound onto the stage unless at home, during rehearsals, you consciously begin to project. They can't hear you with rehearsal sounds. I don't want you to come on stage and have me say, "Make it loud!" I want it done while you're in the rehearsal process.

Now, a prop has its own life. If you need that palm-leaf fan as a stage prop, it won't help if you've taken its life away. The fan has its own life. You use it to cool yourself. Once you're cool, then stop. You don't keep fanning yourself all through the scene. Every actress does that all-over fanning business, instead of just fanning their bosom, which is sweaty, or the back of their neck, which is hot. You fan to cool a specific place, not all over the place. So where are you hot? You were faking it. That's a bad thing to do. I want you to be right. When I see that you're wrong, you have to admit it and swear to stop!

[*Comer: "Yes, you're absolutely right. I was doing it by rote."*]

Thank you very much.

Now, the scene is about Blanche and a newsboy—about being alone in the world, and being hot. Don't put in another act, there's no time for that. You take off your scarf, sit down, pick up your glass, and the bell rings. There's no time for this other stuff.

[*Adler says to Irene Gilbert: "The moment she picks up her glass, please ring the bell." Then to the class: "I have an assistant here. She's trying very hard to help me. There's something in her nature which is not helpful. But I thank her anyway."*]

Feel what you feel, Anjanette, but when the bell rings it's surprise and panic. The way you're doing it is too cued. You seem to know too much about him—it's cue on cue. Do it very private, to yourself. If you're over the top, you're not going to get better, you're going to get worse. Do it so that everything that comes to you has new meaning for you. You suddenly see him and say, "You look like the prince that came to life!" He says, "I'm just the newsboy." But you are mystically drawn to this beauty. Blanche is not you. She's not anybody you'll ever meet. She's a piece of chiffon, floating around without any purpose. Don't make her so logical. Make her more southern.

When you see him, get up. Why? Because he's an apparition and you want to stop him from leaving and catch him. When you really want to stop somebody, you go toward them. You don't say, "Hey, wait!"—you move to stop them from going. If you have nothing in life at all, sometimes you find a moment where you can touch life before it disappears. It doesn't last long, but this is it. Otherwise, she's dead. It's like a person in a coma who opens her eyes for a moment and says "That's my daughter!" and then, *boom,* she's back into the coma. It should be a moment of rapt attention between these two. Don't use the whole stage, just hold on to that moment. He's an imaginary knight. Don't think of him as so real. The magic is yours for a moment. Don't try to spread it or make it so heavy. It's a very touching scene. It makes me cry that she gets this moment. Most people live forever in desperation without finding it. She finds it.

It's a very special scene Tennessee gives her that reveals how much beauty she has in her soul and how she tries to grab it in the midst of all this dirt. Don't move so much when you speak the words. They're beautiful. Just say them. Suppose, for a minute, he's the dead fiancé. Keep the mood for yourself, don't milk it.

Tony, as she speaks to you, it should feel like you're looking at an Indian with feathers. She's that strange, and the more she talks, the more you get involved with her strangeness.

Blanche, you're not strange enough. You're sitting plunked down in the middle of your chair at the beginning. When the bell rings, you're frightened. You look through the window. "Who's here?" You're afraid. If you're as comfortable as you look, that is for middle-aged people. Use the back of the chair or the side of it. Your coyness has to make you talk to him from behind the chair or leaning over it, then going back and sitting again. He must keep seeing this strange, wonderful, floating creature. Why don't you contribute to what the author has given you? He has given you a chair, but if you could just get yourself off the chair—she's not a sitter. She's not someone who would keep sitting after the doorbell rings. Get up and then sit on the edge of it. Do it fast! Sit on the very edge of the chair, almost falling off. When he rings the bell and looks through the curtains, it makes you jump. Do something with that opportunity. Her whole body is nervous. Sit on the arm of the chair, facing me. It's not so uncomfortable, is it? Go to the back of it and lean over and talk. Then go to the other arm. Do it, darling. Hurry up.

I don't want to inhibit you, but I want you to know that what you're doing is not nervousness. Come to my house, I'll show you what nervousness is. She's nervous. She's upset. She's frightened. The thing that frightens her to death is that she has nowhere to go, no home in the world to go to. That's on your mind all the time. All the time there's something on your mind—you can't figure out what's going to happen. It's suicide time. You're awfully slow. Respond faster! Now, try it again.

[*Comer and Zimbardi do so.*]

That was a movie kiss. It's too heavy. But it's a beautiful scene, and a lot of it was very good. Each actress will interpret it differently. At one point later, when Mitch is talking to her, she walks away from him and the music comes to her as she thinks about her fiancé. If you could hear that music here—"that young man! that love of my life!"—and incorporate it into this scene, it would be even more beautiful. But you did it very well. You have a lot of quality, darling. Bravo.

[*Applause from the class.*]

Did you see that strange moth flying all over? She held his interest, and Tony was able to sustain it and help her put it all together without saying more than a word or two. The actor's instinct—seeing her for the first time—is to play it as a love scene. Actually, watching her can make you fall in love, you can be drawn to that quality, but you don't immediately feel "I'm in love." I think it doesn't matter so much how you feel as how you react to watching her. Did you catch the "lover" climate? Mesmerizing.

This Young Man with his black eyes and dirty clothes suddenly comes into something that is not catchable, not holdable, not reachable. When an actor can get that and say "That fills me," he has found the golden treasure. He has discovered the part.

The way she played it—you couldn't catch her for a moment because she was going so fast. Anjanette, what you did by not settling in the middle of that chair was to create what the author wants. Blanche can't settle in the middle, there is no middle for her, there's only the edge of things for her! These are the things an actress has to make work. Now you understand that the logic of what's onstage has to be logical to the character, not to your own life. It was very well done, darlings. Brilliant.

*　*　*

The minute Blanche pushes the Young Man out the door, Mitch shows up for their date. He is a very interesting and important character. Tennessee puts him in to offset Stanley. He does something very similar in *The Glass Menagerie,* with the character Jim, the Gentleman Caller. They are men who do have inherited values and positive qualities in them. Mitch lives with his sick mother and has a sense of behavior because of her, and because of caring for her.

At one point, Mitch even takes on Kowalski—he's ready to fight him, because Stanley offends his sense of honoring womanhood. The thing that Mitch understands in women is what Blanche finds attractive. His behavior with her is awkward but very respectful. He is drawn to her melody, like the newsboy—like a lot of men are drawn to actresses. Why are brokers drawn to that kind of floating girl? Because she is floating, she is fancy. She is not brokerish, not something they know. Brokers like them. They marry them. There has always been a melody about artists that attracts the better men.

So Tennessee has in the plays certain men who aren't Neanderthal, who are responding to a lost tune. It has been lost, but somehow they can still hear it. It isn't in the reality; it's a tune that is floating in the mind from centuries ago—a melody of beauty, of poetry, of loveliness.

But later, after Stanley exposes her past, Mitch comes stumbling in, drunk and angry, and he's an altogether different person. He wants to have his way with her and see her face in bright light. He says he wants her to be "realistic." When Blanche says she wants magic, not reality, Mitch laughs at her. He says she lied to him. She says she never lied in her heart. He says she's not "clean" enough to enter his mother's house.

How many women ever had a panic attack from some terrible disillusion, and just started drinking or running? Everyone, at some point. But you can't call a woman who says "I never lied to you" a whore. If a woman is able to say that, she should be understood. If she is in panic, if she's drinking—there isn't anybody worth a dime who hasn't gone through that. The point of this scene is "I didn't lie to you in my heart."

Blanche is not, in her heart, a liar, and she takes that with her wherever she goes. Stanley is what he is in the world. Stella is lost and is going to reproduce the ape. You have a triangle which very much reflects the society we live in.

The social playwrights, from Ibsen on, make it clear that society's ideals permeate people who strive in the outside world to survive and get ahead, but that the ideals don't work. Miller's salesman is destroyed not by the sons who deserted him but by the business world that deserted him. In Odets's *Country Girl,* the theater is taken over by industrialists and money people, who treat artists badly. The outside world has affected the artist, has made him drink, made him think he is a failure. Blanche fails to live up to society's morals and her own morals, or even Mitch's morals.

Society never says "You're a failure" to rich people. That's why the playwrights became political. They came out of the Depression and unemployment. The trauma of that Depression will never be fully healed. People were so destroyed, the desperation was so widespread, they began to understand the politics of it. They saw that while we were going to go to war, we were selling Japan scrap iron to make the arms they'd use to fight the boys we were going to send! It was the unions on the West Coast who said, "No, we will not ship it!" The working class finally took some control over the situation.

These social playwrights were fighting against that kind of lack of ethics in government, in industry, in the arts. The artists were terribly hurt, then and now, by the politics and militarism of capitalism: "We'll make lots of money selling armaments to anybody who wants them, but there's no money for artists or poor people." The more people suffer, the more they want to revolt. Tennessee understands that. It is implicit in his plays, but he doesn't push it.

In all of Miller and Odets, you have the social or political fight. Here, you don't. Williams doesn't dwell on the outside struggle in order for the battle to be understood. He gives it to you in the characters. Blanche's sister marries a Polish working-class man. Tennessee says Stanley fought in the war, which makes him as American as anybody. It doesn't matter where his parents came from. Tennessee was chastised by the left wing for portraying Stanley as such a bad reflection of the working class. Other playwrights were doing that, too—Brecht, especially—but not in the same poetic way.

The battle between Blanche DuBois and Kowalski is the battle of the breaking-down of the politeness and clarity of behavior that took a thousand years to create. In *Streetcar,* everything is broken down. It's the end of "Allow me to open the door for you" and "May I take your hand?" I lived abroad a lot and watched the behavior of the different classes, from the woman who sold tomatoes in Rome to the man who went to Maxim's in Paris. The Italians are especially fascinating—"O Signora Stella!" The middle class in Italy is fascist, still very much with Mussolini. But the upper class and lower class are marvelous. In Europe, class distinction is still present.

In America, it has completely broken down. Tennessee comes from the South and, more than any other writer, touched on what the South was. It was the part of the United States that held on to nineteenth-century formality and elegance and esteem for women the longest. The South started to go down when the plantations and the money went down. When the Civil War did away with slavery, people had to start paying labor down South. That was a political development, and so is war. Did you ever notice that southerners always volunteer to go to war and fight more than northerners?

Those historical facts are not in play, but they are understood—and you must understand. It is understood that the Kowalskis are coming in and the DuBoises are dying out. Tennessee is trying to make you understand that with his own unique kind of poetic realism. It is not what Mitch means when he says he wants Blanche to be "realistic." That's a deliberately misused word that Tennessee puts in Mitch's mouth.

Realism in the theater means the search for what is absolutely true in every situation. It means giving up the romantic or idealistic way of portraying things, no matter how romantic or idealistic certain characters might be. It is related to naturalism, but not the same thing. Certain scenes in *Streetcar* are very naturalistic, such as the gambling scenes. What is naturalism? It came out of late romanticism with Zola's book *Germinal* {1885}, about the working class. Zola said, "I have to show people what life actually is, not what they'd like it to be." He shows you the red goo dripping out of a package—what's coming from there? Oh, that's meat with the blood running out of it. That is naturalism. It is for you to see life as you'd see it in the emergency room at a hospital, with someone's mouth smashed open, gushing blood.

That was in novels, but the same is true in theater. The audience is forced to see life with no trimmings in this style. Tennessee uses it in the card scenes, and you have to play those scenes with all their roughness and anger—the fighting and the tables falling down and everything in shambles. When you get a scene like that, play it with that kind of naturalism. Don't play an ordinary card game. There is anger in this one. There is a winner and there are losers, and there's anger in all of them. "Dammit, are you in or out? Come on!" The tone and the scene get violent. It is not your kind of cards. It is a naturalistic card game with four people who have no education and are accustomed to being with each other in this rough way. It is very naked and harsh.

The atmosphere in this play is highly charged. There's not a moment when something isn't happening to create a mood or a threat of violence. They are like cats stalking each other in an alley and then suddenly turning and fighting. You don't know why this cat or that poker game might turn violent—but it will.

You get a lot of violence in the film version. Kazan and Brando did it very well there, because the masses want violent pictures, as we know. The audience is already violently inclined. They want cockfights. When Stanley cracks his pregnant wife in the face and she falls

Marlon Brando, Nick Dennis, Kim Hunter, Rudy Bond, and Jessica Tandy in *A Streetcar Named Desire* (1947). "Please don't get up—I'm only passing through."

over, or when he corners Blanche at the end—it's the equivalent of a cockfight. But Stella will get up again. Blanche won't.

Stella avoids being shipwrecked by compromising—by marrying Stanley. She has the ability to satisfy herself with him and with their common gratifications. In that respect, marriage is gratifying for ordinary people who share an inclination for the commonplace way of life. They are very fortunate. But Blanche isn't Stella. Blanche is alone, and her aloneness signifies something; her isolation will still have meaning.

So nobody wins, and the playwright succeeds, I think perhaps more than he wanted to. One erudite critic wrote, "After all, she intruded on a happy family situation." I was there on opening night, and behind me was a famous musician, who got up after the final curtain and said, "I don't know what she wanted. Why did she come in and make trouble?" A lot of people in the audience think that about Blanche. A lot of people think she deserves to be raped—"She was asking for it!"—as a punishment.

Blanche cannot give up her self-image as a rare and delicate individual. It's impossible for her to be on one side of the line and stray over to the other. She is therefore broken into two pieces—and abandoned by both sides. She cannot recognize this situation, let alone accept it, which creates trouble in Stanley's little paradise. From his viewpoint, she has brought hell into the home. His only recourse is to bring hell to her, which he does by revealing her past. Stanley has to get her out, or his home will be shattered. He would rather have her shattered.

Stanley is ruthlessly good at everything he does—bowling, playing poker, indulging his sexuality. He likes his radio but throws it down and breaks it and then fixes it again. He takes Stella, throws her around, and then he fixes her again, too. He is enthusiastic, passionate, wild—partly based on Tennessee's own abusive father. It is the beginning of the new killer quality in man in the society. Stanley is taking over and represents, for Tennessee, the upcoming male of America. He carries the American seed in him and sires the new American child. Stella is not "just pregnant." She comes from the aristocratic line, but she's going to have Stanley Kowalski's baby. He can rightfully say, "I'm the founding father, the Abraham of a new race!" He is the symbol of what will now be reproduced in America.

It's shocking when he's in the red pajamas yelling, "I'm a father!" Tennessee tells you he is an enormous symbolic penis, who will impregnate the world. From now on, there won't be a play in America that doesn't cry out that the apeman cometh.

Blanche knows she is dying out and that Stella is going to die out. Stella means "star," and her star is fading, too, along with Blanche. At the end of the play Stella sobs, "Oh, God, what have I done to my sister!" With that last cry, the play achieves the size of the destruction, of Stella as much as Blanche.

You are responsible for understanding the size of Belle Reve. It stood for the civilization that was brought from England, France, and the rest of Europe and developed into a country called America, with the culture of the South. Blanche understood that, but now she is alone, the way most people get, stranded on her way to the two thousandth year. You get stranded when you don't know where you are going.

Blanche says to Stella, "You went to this and left me with the tradition. I am smashed! I am smashed by life now." There are two ways of life, and Stella has chosen the new one. The play ends with Stella saying, "My sister, my sister!" People don't usually say something like that. It is biblical. The two sisters are severed forever.

The doctor at the end offers Blanche his arm and says, "Come and look at what it is outside." He is not saying or doing this out of cruelty, he is going to show her not to be so poetic—this is what the world is really like. The aloneness of this individual and the togetherness of that couple in this place of ignorance and vulgarity cannot coexist.

Blanche goes out of the Kowalskis' house alone in that last scene. Is she better or worse off than the people inside, playing cards? I think that you think she lost. She loses, but she loses *her* way.

EIGHTEEN

SUMMER AND SMOKE

(1948)

SYNOPSIS OF *SUMMER AND SMOKE:*
Part I, "A Summer," opens on the Fourth of July, 1916,
in the park of tiny Glorious Hill, Mississippi, where
prim Alma Winemiller, a minister's daughter, still
carries a torch for the boy next door, John Buchanan,
who is following his father's footsteps to become a doctor. They played together as children around the plaza's stone angel fountain called *Eternity.* Alma wishes
John would forsake his wild ways with women and
booze, while he urges her to give in to her sexual side.
When she demurs, he turns to the more accessible
Rosa Gonzales. He has gambling debts at the Moon
Lake Casino, owned by Rosa's father.

In Part II, "A Winter," Alma tells John's father that
John and Rosa are having sex in his house. When the
senior Dr. Buchanan tries to throw Rosa and her father
out, the girl's enraged father shoots him. John sub-
sequently takes over his father's practice and distin-
guishes himself. Alma, increasingly desperate, throws
herself at John. But he has changed his ways and is now
engaged to a "respectable girl"—one of Alma's own
music students. In despair, back at the angel fountain,

Margaret Phillips as Alma and Tod Andrews as Dr. John Buchanan Jr. in Williams's *Summer and Smoke* (1948). The angel fountain failed to guard her well.

she meets a young traveling salesman and follows him off to a rendezvous at Moon Lake Casino, where she had resisted John's advances the summer before.

—B.P.*

* *Summer and Smoke* (later rewritten as *Eccentricities of a Nightingale*) premiered October 6, 1948, at New York's Music Box Theatre, and ran 102 performances. Margaret Phillips and Tod Andrews played Alma and John. Geraldine Page played Alma in a 1952 revival directed by José Quintero at the new Circle in the Square Theatre, where her celebrated performance was credited with beginning the Off Broadway movement and vindicating the play itself. The 1961 film, directed by Peter Glenville, starred Page, Laurence Harvey, Rita Moreno, and Una Merkel. (Page and

ALL ACTING is imaginative. You cannot go on the stage without using your imagination. When you do that, you can break the logic of realism. If you're getting on a streetcar, the logical thing to say is "I'll give you a dollar and you'll give me back fifty cents. That's my fare." But if you use your imagination, you can say, "I don't have fifty cents—I'll give you a rose." The man will say, "Oh? Well, thank you . . . Where do you live?" And you'll say, "I live up there, in that star."

You can do that if you leave logic. That is what happens—and what you have to do—with a great many of Tennessee's characters.

Something very important in modern life and modern plays is that we are all troubled and we don't know why. If you're upset because you have no job, that's one thing—that's logical. But if you feel, in a general way, "I don't know what the hell is the matter with me—give me a drink. Give me some coke, I'll snort it!"—that's different.

That not-knowing is what Tennessee deals with, more than with somebody without a job. Like O'Neill and Strindberg, he says man's inner confusion is so dark, he doesn't know how to deal with it. If a mature doctor is troubled, he says, "I accept it. Just because I am troubled doesn't mean I'll give up my work." Most of us, when troubled, do something about it, or go to somebody for advice. Tennessee brings you characters who have things inside they don't know what to do with, but can't ask for help.

It's hard for you to attack Tennessee. He's not the easiest playwright. To explain the characters of Alma or John or their fathers, you must understand that Tennessee is as distant from us as Chekhov in Moscow. He's that far away. If you want to understand him, and this play,

Merkel both received Oscar nominations.) *Summer and Smoke* was the first Williams play turned into an opera (by composer Lee Hoiby and librettist Lanford Wilson) in 1971 at the St. Paul Opera Association.

you should know that he grew up much like Alma, in a parsonage. His grandfather Reverend Walter Dakin was an Episcopal minister like Reverend Winemiller, Alma's father. Tennessee's portraits of women are all studies of different aspects of the same woman, but under different circumstances.

Alma is a southern woman who has come down through time with a need for beauty and soulfulness. You'll say, offhand, that she is "neurotic." I don't like that word. She's not neurotic. She is not just "frustrated." I don't like that word, either. "She's suffering from a father complex or a mother complex." Society likes those cheap five-cent answers. Alma is not a "nut case." She is a woman who hears the southern breeze coming—more than you and I hear. She is aware of things that God is aware of. Most people are not, but Alma is. John is attracted to her but ends up with an inferior girl. It doesn't mean he's in love with the inferior girl; it means that he cannot reach Alma. It's a wonderful play. It is very southern.

The first thing you learn, if you live in the South, is that the most important thing is heritage. It's not about money. Money is okay if you have it. But the vulgarity of money is not acknowledged and respected there the way it is in the North. It's about tradition. There are different kinds of white people, from aristocratic on down. You must understand how that class system functions, how they could never get over the fact they were defeated in the Civil War. No southerner has ever given up the sense that they fought much better than the North but were outdone by this or that, by Lincoln or the blacks. The South's spirit is permeated by this tradition that we in the North don't know.

I was invited to Dallas a few years ago to do a critique for a university theater. The first day, from eight-thirty to eleven a.m., they did six one-act plays about the Civil War or the aftermath. The next morning, from nine to twelve, another six. In each and every one of them, the South won. I couldn't get over that mentality: "The curtain falls, and we win!" I said, "Okay, who am I to argue with them?" Once, walking up to the platform, I stumbled and said, "This is the southern revenge on the North." While I was there, this wealthy gentleman invited me to a dinner he was giving for his brother-in-law, a congressman, to support a proposal that Texas secede from the Union. He proposed it at this formal banquet, with hundreds of people, during the Carter administration. I said, "Jimmy wouldn't possibly hear of a thing like that!" Read Cash's *The Mind of the South.** It explains a kind of fairy-tale quality in them. It's fantastic. There's this living anger. They're ready to fight the North again. I felt very uncomfortable in Dallas. I was frightened. I wouldn't want to live there.

You get the idea. Southern tradition is not to be monkeyed with. It doesn't let money interfere with the kind of girl a man has to marry. Southerners marry each other's children so they can stay united and pure. The North destroyed them, and they had to start over again with a land erased into social and economic chaos, but the southern mind and will arising from that conquest remained unshaken.

With that unshaken mind and will, a minister like Alma's father was not touched by compromise—and neither was she. You must understand the woman's place in the southern mind: their great pride and sense of racial superiority centered on women, who would give birth to the next superior generation. It's an enormous tradition that the woman be kept high and pure to perpetuate their master race. It was evident, above all, in her remoteness from men—exactly as Williams writes it in the play. The southern woman is not intimate, not bending, not "here." She is always "there," away . . .

What impressions do you get from the title of this play? Summer is hot. So is smoke. It comes from fire, which is a powerful force. Smoke clouds the eyes, obscures the road. Alma is smoked in. She can't see clearly. That is the first image you can take for her. But how are you going to make it physical, make it work for her onstage? What does it mean to be clouded in? If you can't see, what road do you take? What road in the twentieth century has been clear to man? If you don't understand it that way, don't act. It won't help you to go to the logical with a text that is illogical. Alma doesn't see your reality, she sees her own reality. She seeks escape from society's reality, which is also what a lot of writers do—they get away from real circumstances as a way to deal with their problems.

Tennessee comes from Strindberg and O'Neill into psychological problems, but in *Summer and Smoke* those problems can't be blamed

* W. J. Cash's seminal article "The Mind of the South" was written for H. L. Mencken's *American Mercury* in 1929. Blanche and Alfred Knopf liked the piece and asked Cash to write a book-length version, which—after a decade's delay—was finally published by Knopf in 1941. Cash's intuitive, sociohistorical exploration of Southern culture received wide acclaim.

so much on society. Alma and John live well, they both have a good middle-class income. They function, they're not jobless. Yet still, they are very agitated and obsessed—each in different way. We'll explore those obsessions more deeply later, but let's take it the way Tennessee does so brilliantly. He gives you the main elements in the very first scene.

The characters in *Summer and Smoke* start out in a plaza where the band plays, where people walk, where there's a marble fountain and angel called *Eternity*. It is a place that will never be altered. They won't pull it down to build a forty-story building, because it is their tradition. The tradition is so strong, nothing moves it. This setting is very important. As an actor, you typically don't know where the hell you are. The author knows, the director knows, the set designer knows, even the stagehands know—but you don't. You say, "Just give me the lines." Get away from the words because they'll mislead you. Don't begin with lines. Begin with what the playwright says is there.

Tennessee gives you a park in a town called Glorious Hill. Do you find anything ironic or unrealistic in that name? That's where he wants you to be. He wants you to be in *that* park, not in the *Central* Park or the *Beacon* Hill that you know. It's a small southern town, where it is very hot in the summer. In 1916, there are no fans to cool you off, no weatherman on the radio to tell you anything. All that technology is not there.

It's the evening of the Fourth of July, before the First World War, when you don't have the problems you get after society's collapse in the thirties. There's no television, no radio, none of the things you know. There is carousel music. There's the church. There are people on the street, but they don't smoke pot, they don't speak easily about sex, and they don't wear jeans. You'll have to really understand the costumes.

There's a band concert in the square. That's something else you don't know. Every town in Europe still has a band concert and a square, where young men and women promenade and sit. It's beautiful and it fills an old-fashioned need, but we haven't got it anymore. There's a fireworks display. The author tells you the light is fading from sunlight to dusk—that time of day when you really don't know what is happening. Is it night? Is it day? It's past supper, but not yet bedtime. Sometimes it's called "the blue hour"—a kind of stranded hour when nowadays we might take a martini or two.

When the curtain goes up, Reverend Winemiller is standing on the ramp or upstage level of the set. There's a marble fountain with water flowing from the angel's hands, and Mrs. Winemiller is sitting at the base of it. You don't see anyone sprawling on the ground. It's not the moment for sprawling on the ground. That happened after 1933.

The reverend's wife is spoiled and selfish, used to being catered to and given everything she wants. She married the reverend and had a daughter. She doesn't drink, but her equivalent of alcohol is ice cream. "I want my ice cream!" It's like heroin—she has to have her fix! The mother is perverse. She torments Alma about being in love with John, saying she has seen Alma watching John through the curtains. She is infantile, with no understanding of a woman in her fifties. She couldn't take on responsibilities. It wasn't in her to be a minister's wife and receive people in a grown-up way. She couldn't do that, and she lost her marbles. She is known as "Reverend Winemiller's cross to bear."

Alma has to bear it, too. She has to preside over the rectory and entertain for her father, manage the home. When her mother went bananas, she had to take over. You can't create Alma unless you know who her parents are and what happened to her because of them. You have to grab this right away.

The other main character onstage is John Buchanan Jr. They've known each other all their lives. Tennessee describes him as "Promethean." What is that? It's Greek mythology. Prometheus was a very bad boy—very bold and powerful. He made man out of clay and then stole fire for him from the gods. Zeus excommunicated him for it. If you play a Promethean man like John or a woman like Alma, it takes a certain spiritual and physical size. They feel superior, they have to be. They are superior to gossip and to what most people talk about. They tend to exalt themselves. They need that. A lot of people do.

So at the outset, you have a lovely place with flowing water and steps and a bench or two for sitting and relaxing. It's a place Alma knows, where she can be. But she and her space are invaded. John starts down the steps behind her and sees a firecracker. He picks it up, lights it, and tosses it underneath her bench. When it goes off, she jumps up with a yell and drops her parasol. Talk about getting a rise out of somebody—literally. He runs up to her, pretending to be outraged, as if some naughty boy did it, and says, "Hey! Are you all right?"

Alma suddenly sees this man she grew up with and adores, but she's almost speechless—traumatized by the noise and smoke. "I can't seem to catch my breath! Who threw it? There ought to be a law in this town against firecrackers!"

She is weak. Women are capable of being shocked, of fainting, of being upset. John has been gone for a long time, and she didn't even know he was back in town. He is a naughty boy himself and takes advantage of her situation. He says, "I think you need a little restorative, don't you?" and offers her a drink from a flask. She asks what it is, and he says it's applejack brandy—"liquid dynamite."

Now, applejack is the roughest kind of booze. It's as if he offered her marijuana or cocaine today. John is the modern world. Alma is yesterday. She was brought up with him, but he has changed. He is not dressed properly in front of her—he's untidy, his tie is undone, he has dropped propriety. Instead of water, he offers her a slug of whiskey. It is not in Alma's nature to drink from a flask, and it should not be in the nature of a gentleman to offer a lady applejack. Women don't drink in public. She sees he's not the doctor or the doctor's son that she knows—he's somebody foreign. He's a bum. When a man openly says "Have a drink," it's as if he spits in her face. You just don't do that.

Once I gave a big party and I had just about everything in the bar: whiskey, brandy, vodka, champagne . . . Some lawyer arrived and asked for a beer. I said, "I'm sorry I invited you. Would you leave?" My home is Venetian. I created an ambience for myself which is very theatrical, very eighteenth century, because I can't live in the twentieth century. A man has no right to ask for beer in that kind of house, and he should have known better. I think I'm right. I'm on my side. It has to do with propriety.

So Alma is trying to compose herself after this inappropriate thing with the firecracker and the liquor. "You're home for the summer?" she says. "Summer is not the pleasantest time of year to renew an acquaintance with Glorious Hill—is it? The Gulf wind has failed us this year, disappointed us dreadfully . . . We used to be able to rely on the Gulf wind to cool the nights off for us, but this summer has been an exceptional season . . . "

Understand her from her language. She has the inherited sense of nineteenth-century graciousness. It is so fantastic how Tennessee lifts the language: "The Gulf wind has failed us this year . . . " It's poetry. You can't possibly get all the facts about it right away, but I'll tell you something: this speech cannot be spoken, it has to be *danced*. She is giving a performance—as always. Southern women were taught to talk that way. Alma is high with the Gulf wind, and he is high with his "liquid dynamite." John speaks simply; Alma does not. She has a fancy, traditional formality. See the difference. See the fight that's shaping up. This is Stanley and Blanche, thirty years earlier.

When Alma says, "We used to be able to rely on the Gulf wind to cool the nights off," it means she's up walking around all night these days, knowing he is there next door. It means she is not sleeping because of him. She is sweating and shaking. She is a wreck. This beloved man, grown up as a doctor, didn't come to see her. He throws a firecracker at her instead. It's pretty sad.

"That firecracker was a shock," she says, fretting and fussing with her handkerchief. John looks at her and sees this injured, hysterical woman, but switches to professional doctor's mode and says: "You should be over that shock by now." Alma says, "I don't get over shocks quickly."

What is she talking about? The shock that he went away and didn't write, the shock of her crazy mother, the shock of firecrackers and flasks, of nights when she couldn't sleep and went to John's father to get pills. Her nervous system is destroyed. Her heart is palpitating. She has never had sex. It is dense. You have to build in her the soul of a woman suffering in every way but trying to keep herself together.

"You're planning to stay here and take over some of your father's medical practice?" she asks. "I hope so, we all hope so. Your father's so proud of you . . . You should have heard him singing your praises. Telling me you'd graduated magna cum laude from Johns Hopkins. That's in Boston, isn't it?"

John says no, it's in Baltimore.

"Oh, Baltimore!" she says, "Baltimore, Maryland. Such a beautiful combination of names! I have been told Johns Hopkins is the finest medical college in the world . . . It must be a great satisfaction, a real thrill to you, to be standing on the threshold of a career in such a noble profession as medicine, to which some people are divinely appointed by God! There is so much suffering in the world it actually makes one sick to think about it, and most of us are so helpless to relieve it . . . But a physician! Oh, my! With his magnificent gifts and training what a joy it must be to know that he is equipped and appointed to bring relief to all of this fearful suffering . . . And with your father's example to inspire you!"

It is not easy to understand her. People hear her but don't understand. She speaks fancily, elaborately—she raises herself that way. When I used to travel by ship, I'd look out at the ocean and a nice man would come over and say, "So you're going to Europe?" I'd say, "Yes, I love architecture and Renaissance art . . . " The man would say, "Ah, yes . . . " I did this a lot. It was a way of trying to cover up being alienated: you talk about art, books, Sartre—things you don't really know. If you know something, you're calm and quiet about it. If you don't, you embroider. You say, "Oh, I saw a play last night by Wycherley—such a marvelous writer! I just adore him . . . " On and on. You don't remember the name of the play or anything else Wycherley wrote, but you've got to talk.

That's the rhythm of Alma—the rhythm of improvisation. "Oh, the palmetto leaves! Oh, what a beautiful word, 'Maryland'! Oh, a doctor—what a wonderful thing to be!"

So Alma is talking about something she doesn't know. She idealizes the medical profession and how much humanity can be helped by it. She believes in the goodness of man. John's view is that that attitude leads to sickness; that such traditional, handed-down ideas will make you sick. When she says it's been a big comfort having his father right next door, he zeroes in on her: "Why? Do you have fits?"

Alma doesn't like that word "fits." She says, "No, but I have attacks!—of nervous heart trouble. Which can be so alarming that I run straight to your father. . . . He always reassures me." John says, but only temporarily—adding that she's his father's patient, not his, and that it's really none of his business. But Alma presses him: "What were you going to say?"

What *can* he say? She is sexually repressed. He can't say it in so many words, knowing it's not in her nature to hear it. So he just says, "I suspect you need something more than a little temporary reassurance." But she keeps pressing, so he says, "You're swallowing air when you laugh or talk. It's a trick hysterical women get into. You swallow air, it presses on your heart and gives you palpitations, and—what I think you have is a doppelganger! And it's badly irritated."

What the hell is that? Alma has no idea. "Oh, my goodness! I have an irritated doppelganger!? How awful that sounds! What exactly is it?" Again she presses: "That's downright wicked of you! To tell me I have something awful-sounding as that, and then refuse to let me know what it is!" She wants to know, but she's frightened of his answer. She should be. A doppelganger is another self that you conceal, another soul that lives in you. Our world, and especially her world, forbids the expression of another self.

But this play doesn't blame society. That belongs to other plays. If you're a successful doctor or a respected minister's daughter and music teacher—you have money and religion, but you're still absolutely convulsed—it's not really society's fault. There's no real answer to inner turmoil. That's what Tennessee deals with in John and Alma. It is very difficult and requires very deep acting, because you're trying to express something and you don't know what it is. The characters *themselves* don't know what it is.

In plays of the twentieth century, loneliness and the quest for personal happiness are very strong. The focus was on the individual, and the individual was often eccentric. England produced a great many eccentrics: we've all heard about Lord So-and-So, who kept his dead grandmother inside a box and conversed with her. Eccentric characters have great power. They're fighting to be something else, to get away from this or that. Do you know the disapproval that brings? I acted all my professional life in theaters. I liked theaters, I liked pavement. Once a producer came to me and said, "We're going to do our next play in the country, surrounded by grass and trees." I said, "I don't like to act with trees. I can't act with nature. I want to be closed in. I don't want trees where I work." They said, "What's with her? She doesn't like trees when she acts? She's eccentric."

Male and female eccentrics are very different, of course, in general, but especially in the South during this period. Why? Because there is no equality between men and women. A man acts one way with a man and another way in front of a woman. A man gives a certain performance of chivalry for women. But a woman *always* gives a performance, no matter where she is, or with whom. When she's buying something in the drugstore, she gives a performance of gentleness. If she takes a walk and opens her parasol, it's a performance of elegance. If she's frightened, she gives a performance of weakness. You see Alma perform in the scene where she says, "The wind hasn't been very good to us this year"—her hot-and-bothered performance. This comes naturally to her. It is demanded of her always to be with this artificial quality. It's what gives her her femininity—and what gives him control of her.

In *Summer and Smoke,* you see the heritage they are bound to, this closed corporation into which those who don't belong can't penetrate—the gulf between them and the rest of America. This sentimental legend, this magnificent vision of the old South, was so elegant and powerful, and it was built on woman's untouchable image. She wasn't equal to man, but she was elevated by him and held so high, she had to be aloof and haughty. Left over from antebellum days when she was surrounded with slave children who had unidentified white fathers, there was a kind of frigidity and disgust with sex in higher-class southern women. Whatever passion they have, they keep down.

The life around Alma is clean, it is pure. If she goes to a lecture, it must be about something lofty. If she talks to a man, he must be on a certain level. She tries to raise everything. John can't just be a good doctor—he has to be "a *great* doctor," has to save people all over the world. Everything has to be so awfully high, it's difficult for her to come down from the angels—or the angel fountain—and just walk. Miss Alma's voice and manner have an airy quality. Nothing lands or falls to the ground. To be a "Miss" is to be girlish. It is natural to her, but she seems affected. That's what people say about her. People say it about me. This southern woman—her delicacy and frailty, the fan and the smelling salts, the sensitivity to noise—is something you have to pick up. Maybe the director will give it to you, but I doubt it. I don't think he has the time. You have to find it for yourself. She seems to belong to the eighteenth century in France. Go look at Fragonard, Boucher, Watteau in a museum—you'll see Alma's gestures in those canvases.* Tennessee tells you she comes from a more elegant age, when families still had servants and lived in great colonial houses. Alma comes out of that and has that inside her.

So does John.

*   *   *

Southern men saw the world as their fathers had seen it a hundred years before: self-contained and self-sufficient. The biggest difference between North and South was that strong basic paternalism of the old South: "If you are my slave, then I'll take care of you. If you need

---

* The works of French Rococo painters Jean-Honoré Fragonard (1732–1806), François Boucher (1703–1770), and Antoine Watteau (1684–1721) depict idyllic pastoral allegories featuring elaborately dressed women in theatrical modes.

something, you come to me." After slavery, it shifted to the labor struggle. The southern cotton barons and factory owners said, "Don't worry, we're still the boss. Come tell Big Daddy what y'all need." The trade-union movement in the North said, "Don't be my father. You represent your side and we'll represent ours. We don't want to rely on your paternal kindness."

There's a wonderful story about Robert Taylor at MGM. He wanted a raise, and his agent said, "You're a big star. Go talk to Louis Mayer and tell him you need a 50 percent salary increase." So Taylor went in, but before he could open his mouth, Mayer said, "Robert, I just want to tell you that I never had a son. But I knew the minute I met you that God had blessed me, that as of that sacred moment, I—Louis B. Mayer—finally have a son in this world! Therefore, I beg you: don't ask me for more money." Taylor went out and the agent said, "Well, did you get a raise?" He said, "No, but I got a father."

Paternal obedience runs deep in common people everywhere, but especially in the South, where the upper class was so admired: they didn't sell out before, during, or after the Civil War. They behaved in the grand manner. They created an ideal for the common man to emulate, and learned how to steer him so he wouldn't be angry about wealth. They manipulated him without arousing his jealousy or independence. It was very well done. True paternalism. Does it exist in your life? Of course it does. You have it on a small scale in your parents' home. You are looked after.

After the Civil War, all the southern classes were struggling, but the generals who led them into war were the men they most respected and wanted as leaders. That paternal military idea is very German, almost Hitlerian. It's something we don't understand in the North. They were starving, but they knew every leaf and limb of every tree in their land. The intensity of their love for it, the price they paid, the sense of comradeship were such that they still wanted to be led by an army.

In the North, we don't want the army to lead us. "What do you mean, army? Maybe I want my senator to say something now and then, but . . ." Our idea of patriotism is different. The Yankee victory festered in them. We tore away all their fine notions of chivalry—General Sherman, for example. I think he's great. The North tried to destroy all the things the South loved, but even in poverty and defeat the South stuck together. Southern paternalism remained the strongest power you've ever seen, and the women in these plays are going insane because that force is constantly on them.

John is the perfect "Promethean" example of that force. Tennessee calls him "brilliantly and restlessly alive in a stagnant society." Why is American society stagnant in 1916? Because its middle-class values—based on money and status—are useless. You get it in Europe as well. [Ibsen's] Master Builder wants to make a fortune building little houses and then make up for it by building monumental churches. He does it, but his own house has a terrible fire and his children get burned up. What's his conclusion? He says, "Well, I'm still the great Master Builder!" From Ibsen and Strindberg on, you get these powerful men with the wrong channel, or no channel at all.

I know one of those master builders—a great friend of mine, whose wife was one of my students. He's a very sweet, very big real-estate man who builds fifty-story office towers. One day he said, "You must come and hear me do something." So I went. He'd bought a pianola, and when he touched a button it automatically played "Twinkle, Twinkle, Little Star." He was beaming. "Did you hear that?" He thought he was making music. It was poignant. He got such huge satisfaction from that—not from building a skyscraper. It's a good example of the hunger of the powerful, looking for some channel.

Williams says John has not yet found a channel for his power—and if it's not channeled, it will burn him up. Man has to create for himself a situation where he does not burn up from drinking and whoring and going to pieces. John doesn't have this control over himself yet, even though he's a doctor. A doctor can't be guided by science alone. He needs something to awaken his soul. Science alone paralyzes the soul.

That is why he has always been attracted to Alma. Her name means soul, and the metaphor is pretty clear: she represents the restlessness he has and the soul he is missing. He has dedicated his life to medicine, but he feels, "I'm dead. I don't love children, I don't love flowers, I don't love anything. The hell with medicine, I'll be a bum." He is a good doctor, but he's a drinker and gambler and womanizer. He whores around so much that his father throws him out of the house. That's pretty far down for a doctor to go. He is like Tennessee himself: he has to touch bottom in order to touch top. That's true of people with religious callings, too, isn't it? Like *Night of the Iguana*? Man is in a bind. If he is too logical, his heart dies out; and if he's too soulful, he can't function in a useful way. You have the same problem today, looking for some balance of the two things. If you spend your whole life jitterbugging and watching television, you wither away.

John is the son of a doctor, in his father's tradition. He leaves that tradition for a while, but eventually he returns to it. You are dealing with a character who knows the rules and tends to be chivalrous, at least superficially, despite his actions or ulterior motives. You don't break those rules; you stick to them. That's how you get John. The playwright says he has "the fresh and shining look of an epic hero." Tennessee loves the people who are lost, but he admires the macho because he doesn't have it. It's a kind of jealousy. He wants it but he can't get it, so he creates characters who have it. It's mind-blowing. Understand the duality in Tennessee, and in John.

* * *

Eccentrics like Alma tend to be or become lost, but she is more grown-up than John, in her way. It happened because her mother never grew up. Somebody had to. If she had to take care of things and be her father's wife, it meant she didn't play with other children—or have children of her own. So she is alienated. She can't admit anything is wrong with her when she sweats and can't sleep and pops pills. But the doctor knows there are things she is suppressing—sexual instincts, the ability to identify with people.

Trace it in yourself.

I went away to a kind of boarding school when I was twelve, but I had to act. Nobody sent me back to New York. I just did it myself. Nobody knew I was doing it. Nobody followed me or took me back to the school. It was a theatrical family. I don't think I ever played with a girl in my life until later on when I noticed, "Other kids seem to have a lot of friends on this street." Growing up without those young friendships isolates a child.

Alma, at twenty-five, thinks, "I am better than other people. I dress conservatively, my hair must be a certain way . . . I'm special." She has isolated herself with her specialness. She is excessively proper and ill at ease. You see a lot of women like that, who keep checking their hair, looking in the mirror. "Where's my lipstick?" "What did you say?" "What time is it?" They fuss and smoke cigarettes. They're nervous, and they put people down or turn them off. "I speak four languages and I've read all French literature—what have you done?" Then they go on to something else. It's particularly embarrassing and annoying to men.

Once I had a poet up for the weekend and we were both nervous. I said, "Do you want to go to the movies?" He said, "No, I'm not terribly fond of movies. I have enough here to look at." I said, "Oh, yes, of course, so do I. That's great." If I'd said, "Let's just sit here and talk," he'd have said, "Well, there's a good movie on." We drove each other crazy. That's Alma. Tennessee tells you, "Out of nervousness and self-consciousness she has a habit of prefacing and concluding her remarks with a little breathless laugh." That gives you something you can use.

Remember, in your work, to externalize the inside. Find a way to make it external. You have to give her things she can do with her hands and clothes. Get things about her movement from that up-in-the-air quality she has. If she wears a skirt, it must have sway in it. If it's a blouse, there should be chiffon that can blow. If she has earrings, they jangle or move. Her hand would always have a hanky or bracelet attached to it.

The costume must help you show that Alma can't make the transition to modern life, which has nothing to do with gallantry. Modern life has to do with "Let's lie down, you need some sex." Today, a guy could say that. In Alma's era, no. Play with this moment and with the fact that when he touches her and her heart is palpitating and she's swallowing air, she has a certain serious nervous condition. If a doctor tries to tell her what she really needs, she can't face it, because she was raised to avoid such modern truths.

Southern women like Alma were trained to ingratiate, to make themselves available through their loveliness and weakness. It's interesting that Ibsen does just what Tennessee does. In *A Doll's House*, Torvald tells Nora, "Don't worry about being weak. It's better for me, because then you can lean on me and I can do whatever I want with you." He's telling her to be helpless. Her weakness is there to strengthen the man. That technique lasted until very recently. It is in your heritage, and in Alma's: she cannot live down-to-earth. Nothing makes her leave the sky and the trees and the breeze. She is bound to be a Nora. She doesn't know who she is. Tennessee says, "Her true nature is hidden even from herself." There's a lot of "I don't know who I am, I have to find out!" going on, then and now. But a great philosopher once said, "Do not try to find out who thou art. Thou art an unknowable entity. It is better to find out what you can do, and do it like Hercules."*

All your life you want answers and don't know where to get them. Marriage gives you some answers right away, but not the answers you wanted: the honeymoon's over and you find out the main event isn't at Niagara Falls. After that, the man is out by eight or nine a.m., working. Or if he isn't out, he is not with you—he's at the office, he's doing his writing—while she does the house, the pregnancy, the child care. I had maids and governesses to help look after my daughter. That makes a marriage healthier.

If you depend solely on love, the flame dies down and you're disappointed—even if he's wonderfully attentive. That's the other extreme. I don't like a man who sends flowers to his wife all the time, I don't believe it. There's a man in my building I get roses from every week. They're not really for me—they're for his wife on the eleventh floor. But the florist is so used to bringing me flowers that I get everybody else's, too. I open the card and it says, "For my beloved wife." Every week he does this! I don't mean to disparage the man, but—I don't quite trust him. Call me a cynic, but I keep thinking, "What's he doing that he has to make up for?"

Illness in modern man is not so much physical; it comes from his anxiety and spiritual stress. When he satisfies his material side, it kills his instinct for the spiritual side. He's in trouble, and he knows it. People with inner troubles used to be told to go read or paint or do carpentry, or go to a rabbi or priest and pray. In the Jewish faith, you weren't allowed just to study the Bible. You also had to use your hands. You had to weave, sew, do or make something useful, because it's not in a human being to be God-directed all the time. You had to balance it. That's smart. I've never been psychoanalyzed, but everybody I know has been. "What should I do?" they keep asking. Finally it hits them all that they have to go to work.

Actors have to go to work, too. You get the basic struggle between

* Adler's reference is to Thomas Carlyle's *Past and Present,* chapter II: "For there is a perennial nobleness . . . in Work . . . In Idleness there is perpetual despair . . . The latest Gospel in this world is, Know thy work and do it. [The old Gospel was] 'Know thyself:' long enough has that poor 'self' of thine tormented thee; thou wilt never get to 'know' it! . . . Think it not thy business, this of knowing thyself; thou art an unknowable individual: know what thou canst work at; and work at it, like a Hercules! That will be thy better plan."

Alma and John early on, from your impressions in the scene where she brings him coffee. The doctor's office and the church share a wall with a passageway—they're connected, just like Alma and John are connected. When she comes through the inner door, he hears the sound of praying and says, "What's that mumbo-jumbo your father is spouting in there?" She says, "A prayer." John says, "Tell him to quit. We don't need that worn-out magic . . . " You can do many things in a doctor's office. You can make the place serve you against what it is. You have to take care not to immediately marry the cliché. I don't understand the words or the plot yet, but I'm getting some great things from there. The office is about medicine. The prayer is coming from another room. I get medicine and Christianity. Medicine is science. Prayer is God and stone angels. The masses serve religion without knowing why. Science is a force that needs to be controlled—if not, it gets out of hand—but it's the best thing that happened to man. I begin to see a conflict of big ideas. From what I find here, I'd say it's a conflict between two forces that began with the origin of the species. That's how long religion and science have been at war.

Do you see how I am working? These impressions are essential. You can always change them. There's no rule that says they're all necessarily truthful or useful. But it is a way of working to get yourself alive to the thing, to the ideas, to get more aware of the place and the era. These plays are written for great actors. They are not written for would-be actors. Prepare yourself to get there.

Behave yourself and stop being would-be actors! You must create out of this vagueness. Let it reach you that religion and medicine are mixed up in a room which is scientific. You can bother your head a thousand times with the words, but they will not give you either the play or the style. Understand what you are doing, and experience what you understand. Never, never mouth the text until you've read it a hundred times and something penetrates you. Don't ever speak until you have the *need* to speak from inside. Don't just do lines. It's not Shakespeare. You can't get Williams that way.

Use images, use anything that helps you find the character. The different rhythms will give it to you. Compare the rhythm of bringing in coffee to the rhythm of people praying and the rhythm of a scientist who says, "Never mind that bunk!" You see that one rhythm is in control while the others are not. The rhythm of eternity is outside. Alma speaks of "the footprints of God," but John doesn't believe in that. You see that they and their traditions are out of sync. It's very important to know what he wants from her. He calls this woman he's been brought up with all his life "Miss Alma." If he calls her "Miss Alma," he is not going to say, "Can we do it tonight?" But that's what he *wants* to say.

John is a highly sexed man. Sex is pretty much the agenda all around, and it leads to disaster. When Rosa comes in, she's very real. She dresses for men—to be picked up. John sees her red skirt and low neckline; and he sees sex. What he sees in Alma is the Virgin Mary. It's fine for him, but it's an absolute disgrace for his father. This can't happen, any more than a Mexican girl could walk in and openly solicit on a white man's property. Yet here she is—and even worse, her father comes in, too. It's terrible if a man named Gonzales barges into a traditional house that for generations has said, "Nobody like you can get in here." A southern aristocrat is outraged by the intrusion. Dr. Buchanan is a gentleman; the Mexican is not. Intermarriage is his worst nightmare.

The doctor says, "What's going on in my house?" Rosa says, "John's giving a party because we're leaving tomorrow—together!" Dr. Buchanan says, "Get your swine out of my house!" and hits her father with his cane. Gonzales pulls out his revolver. Rosa says, "No, no, Papa!" When the doctor hits him again, Gonzales shoots him.

Alma is indirectly, or directly, responsible for this. She's the one who told Dr. Buchanan about John and Rosa and got him worked up about it. Her soul is so smoked in, she didn't know what else to do about all this sexuality in the present. She resisted John's advances when he showed her the anatomy chart and said "Here's a lesson"—to a woman who rejected sex. She needed it; she was sick for the lack of it. But she pushed it down so long, it made her sick. She was sick with no love, sick with nostalgia, sick with it all. When he told her what the problem was in the present, she said, "No, that's a lie." She is only secure in the past, where her creative imagination can raise it.

John is part of the changing world and knows how to make changes. Once his father is dead, he goes back to the senior Dr. Buchanan's medical tradition. But just when Alma finally makes her own big shift in the present, she finds out John has made an opposite shift, *away* from sensuality. It's almost like Romeo and Juliet—these "star-cross'd" lovers and the tragic reversal in their final scene: John says, "It's best not to ask for too much." Alma says, "I disagree. I say, ask for all, but be prepared to get nothing!"

She tells him she looked up "doppelganger" and discovered it meant another person or self inside. "I don't know whether to thank you or not for making me conscious of it!" she says. The interesting thing—the brilliant thing, in Tennessee's writing—is that John found out there was a doppelganger in himself, too. Together, he and Alma make a whole person: he's the body and she is the soul.

Alma has been denying her sickness up to now. "I haven't been well, I thought I was dying," she says. "But now the Gulf wind has blown that feeling away like a cloud of smoke . . . The wind is cooling things off a little. But my heart's on fire."

John doesn't know what to say or do now, so he reverts to professional doctor mode: "Anxious about your heart again?" He takes her pulse, picks up his stethoscope, loosens her jacket, bends down to listen to her heartbeat. She puts her hands on his head and then suddenly leans over and kisses him. He says nothing. For once, he is speechless. But for once, Alma is not: "The girl who said 'no' doesn't exist any more, she died last summer—suffocated in smoke from something on fire inside her."

He says she has won the argument about the chart—he's come around to her way of thinking, that the soul's there even though it can't be seen. Alma has won the argument, but lost John. She tries to be brave. She says, "I suppose I am sick, one of those weak and divided people who slip like shadows among you solid strong ones. But sometimes, out of necessity, we shadowy people take on a strength of our own."

John doesn't have that kind of strength at that point. He can't take her truth. It makes him feel ashamed to see that underneath her spirituality is a fire burning so hot, it is consuming her. "I thought it was just a puritanical ice that glittered like flame," he says. "But now I believe it *was* flame, mistaken for ice."

But it's too late. It's over. He's engaged to marry a nice white respectable virgin. Alma goes out in a dopey haze, addicted to pills, and becomes a whore because she can't fight anymore. She is left to her own Blanche-like devices.

Don't act the words, don't go to your temperament. Temperament and talent and beauty are cheap. There's enough "talent" here to drown the world. The point of speaking English out loud on stage is nonsense unless you are interpreting a world—the world within the play! You can't act in this play unless you understand that when John offers her a swig of liquor in the park or says, "How would you like to go up to a private room in the casino?" and she says, "No, no, excuse me, I'd like a taxi!"—it's almost like rape. It is a pretty bold thing, even now. I think I'd have killed him, then and there. When he says, "Don't you know that I am much more afraid of your soul than you are of my body?" they are talking about inner values. He says, "I would never have touched you." Maybe that's true, or maybe it isn't. He understands the rules—but he is tempted.

Are you tempted to betray your tradition? We have arrived at a point where the actor thinks he deserves a lot of money. Nobody in the world deserves six million dollars for ten minutes work as an actor.* But society has made you think, "Why should I want to do anything on Broadway when I can get ten times as much in the movies?"

John wants to say: "Look, I don't want to spend my life with sick people and blood and death. *You* do it. I have one life and I want to enjoy it. I want music, dancing! I want to lose myself. I don't want to be a martyr! I want to go out with that Mexican girl." But his tradition doesn't allow it, any more than my tradition would allow me to be in burlesque.

I'd like to, actually. I had a proposition once, when I was sitting with Clifford Odets and Harold Clurman after a performance in Philadelphia. A man came up to them and asked, "Do you mind if I speak to this lady?" They said, "Not at all." So he said to me, "I run a burlesque theater, and if you are interested I'd like to talk to you. Would you like to do burlesque?"

I was very much Alma at that time. I said, "Me, burlesque? Where's Chekhov?"

---

* With mathematical hyperbole, Adler is referencing the then-astonishing deal given her protégé Marlon Brando to play the cameo role of Jor-El in *Superman* (1978): a salary of $3.7 million plus 11.75 percent of the film's profits, eventually totaling about $19 million—for thirteen days work.

WILLIAM INGE

William Inge (c. 1952)

NINETEEN

OVERVIEW

W ILLIAM INGE'S SPECIALTY—what he's recognized for, among other things, as a major playwright—is that he wrote about a period in America that wasn't understood, wasn't touched by anyone else. Nobody knew how to write about it. His plays seem overly simple. And that's what they are. They're very simple. People live an everyday life, nothing terrible happens, nothing too shocking—a little problem here, a little there. But you can usually fix it.

Most great playwrights understand and incorporate the political situation at the time a play is written. Odets's *Awake and Sing!*, for instance, was written during the Depression, it was written on the East Coast of America. You know an awful lot about that, the characters, the language. But nobody knows about the Midwest. And when you hear about it, you realize that they didn't know anything about themselves, either. They're the simplest people in the world. For instance, they don't seem to remember in 1950 that there was a Depression. Nobody talks about it, or about any other time. I never heard of a play where you don't refer back—to Grandpa, to where you came from, where you swam, what school you went to. Inge leaves all that out. He just takes care of the everyday family life and its difficulties. He is not a social playwright and he's not a moralist like Miller or like Tennessee, who says, "Whose side are you on, Stanley Kowalski's or Blanche DuBois's?" You have to make a decision about the characters. Inge doesn't make you do that.

So you start with the fact that it takes place in the Midwest. He wrote his plays in the fifties and sixties. That was his time. He makes you understand that in the Midwest, the life and the lifestyle revolve around the family. There's this family and that family and the other family across the street. Sometimes there is a child, sometimes there isn't, sometimes there are two children, there's maybe an aunt . . . After a while, you say, "Ah, yes, here's the brother-in-law—let's see what Inge thinks about *him.*"

He tells you a lot about each character. He doesn't actually say much explicitly, but he makes you understand certain things that he wants you to know. When a playwright like Harold Pinter or Samuel Beckett wants to keep so many secrets, I as an actress say, "You want to keep secrets? You don't want to tell us? Go to hell, Mr. Beckett, with your secrets! Don't tell me to unravel my mind to find out what you want me to keep secret."

Beckett has a kind of pretentious audience. When *Waiting for Godot* opened in Florida, they had a lot of trouble because nobody understood it. So they brought it to New York, and the New York management very cleverly said, "This is a play by Samuel Beckett, whom you don't know, and it's only for intellectuals." The house was sold out because the management said, "You're not going to understand it." People still don't understand it. That's how you know it's a masterpiece.

I'm very much impressed by I. B. Singer, a writer, Nobel Prize winner, a Jewish intellectual and playwright—a master. He says if you want to read Proust, open it up and read two or three pages, and if they don't give you great stimulation, don't worry about it, put the book down. You're not supposed to read the whole thing. Everybody says, "Did you get to the fourth volume?" It's pretension. To get through Proust you have to have nothing else to do in life.

Inge makes no pretension about giving you situations that are hair-raising. The action is low-gear. The dramas are low-key. The one drama that is social, that is very big, is *Dark at the Top of the Stairs,* where he has a large problem in a single monologue. Otherwise, you just adopt a certain kind of simplicity and find out why the husband married, whom he did or didn't marry, what's the matter with the marriage. There's a crisis very often in the marriage. It can be straightened out. A man only really abandons a woman in Inge when he dies. He doesn't abandon her in life. Inge cares too much about women. Inge loves women for their helplessness, their tenderness, their ability to raise families, their goodness of heart to the people they're involved with. He's very much a woman-protective writer.

In terms of his women, there are those who are stricken, absolutely deadened by the fact that they can't have a child. There are those women who have to deal with their children to save the family situation, by knowing how to control them and keep them from becoming nuisances or bastards. He's on the woman's side. He reaches out to domestic life.

After having gone to the moon—there are no railroads anymore, there are just airplanes. But you would think in the Midwest there must be some information about what happens. There isn't. They're stuck. There's all this space, and nothing ever reaches Kansas. Nothing. Nothing from the Pacific or the Atlantic gets to Kansas. They are isolated in what they talk about, what they need. If a child needs a dress and the father says "Under no circumstances, no!" it's not a big, vast, universal problem—neither the dress, nor the father, nor the screaming about it. What Inge feels is important is that the father doesn't *want* her to have it. The cosmic problem is left out. He says, "Give it to the other writers. Give it to Tennessee, give it to Miller. Let them talk about the death of a salesman."

Inge doesn't. He talks about this man meeting that woman, he begins to flirt with her, and then this, that, and the other thing. His attitude toward women goes from being overprotective to having them in their forties and fifties with the husband calling her "baby." That kind of thing seems old-fashioned. You can say, "Once in a while I call my wife 'baby.'" But throughout forty years of marriage to still call the woman "baby"? That is the truth in this Midwest family. The relationship between husband and wife straightens itself out. It is for you to understand that there is a woman and a man, and the man wears cowboy boots and jeans and he's a nice fellow. But Mr. Inge says he is a sexual ornament in life. He doesn't really have a mind, he doesn't know where he's going.

His emphasis on the sexuality of life in the community is very big. The women secretly say, "My husband does it twice a night." Things that you wouldn't think of talking about, even to students. It's very enriched, intimate daily life about the sexual habits and feelings aroused between men and women.

The most important thing he says about the male-female relationship is that men think because they have the muscle that they're important. Muscle and power. "I'm the boss and I know what to do and don't tell me, I bring in the money. I forever will be the power, I, with my muscle and my job, I am the power."

Inge discovers in every play that men who want to be the boss, who want to be the head of the family, have in them a universal emotional sickness. They don't truly believe in themselves. They know they're weak, they know they're vulnerable, they know they have to save themselves. Every man in Inge's plays needs salvation. He comes across big, but he needs salvation. And salvation for him is the family. That's why he dwells on it. He takes this mug and gives him family life to play around with. This big strong muscular leader of men, in or near Kansas, has a lot of inner psychological problems.

Not for a minute does Inge care to make a statement about what is wrong with America. What Inge does is tell you there is a fatal weakness in man that pretends strength and is afraid of marriage, afraid of woman, because he fears she will take his sexual power away. In Inge, there is a great deal of mix-up. The woman understands, "You want to love me, marry me." Sometimes she sleeps with a man before marriage—that isn't considered so bad. But it's always leading to the marriage. She understands that once he gives in to the marriage, she is the boss. That the home is not for the leadership of the man, not for the father or uncle or husband. He is *useful* to the woman in the marriage. She loves him, it's all right in bed, but don't try to tell the kids anything—if you do, tell them in the right way, don't fool them, don't lie to them.

He concludes that what marriage does is take the man's power away. So you have a conflict. Does she really take the power away? Desexualize him by usurping his power? Or does she help solve his problem by being less fearful of failure? What gives him the strength to bear failure is that he has a family. That is the standard of America. If you've got a family, you're all right. *Family life is the feature presentation in America.* Her price for getting the husband is no cheating, no going away from home for six months on business—none of that. You've got to be married in the no-nonsense sense: togetherness, understanding, solving the problem of the children, solving the money problem—or, if not solving it, at least fighting about it. But the fights are small. They don't create another war.

This fear men have of their power being taken away by women is a big subject, a contemporary subject, and it always has been. In the Bible when Delilah cuts Samson's hair off, he loses his virility. It goes far back. Marriage is conceived by Inge as a domestic situation in which the struggle is "I don't want you to talk that way to me! I want you to know who's boss." The man tries those tricks. But they don't work.

You have in many Inge plays relationships on different levels where the woman begins to figure out how to treat this big gorilla. Inge doesn't give him a mind. The trouble in *Dark at the Top* is what to do now that there are no saddles. The saddle industry has gone down the drain. He gets at the deep problem of what really is masculinity. The plays concern sexuality. The man is the rebel until he's tamed, until he becomes part of the family. He never really takes over the family, because of what the woman becomes. She saves the children from disaster, leads them on the road they're going down, helps them go down that road. If a girl is shy, it's the mother who says, "Don't be shy, it's bad for you." If the girl is impertinent, the mother says, "Don't talk like that in front of older people, you must listen." Inge leaves out all intellectual aspects of life. Only in one play does he mention the unborn talent in one of the children—for writing. A boy of ten has artistic aspirations and is encouraged by the mother.

Inge has caught something in America that is the truth of domestic life. The language is simple, the ideas are uncomplicated. The problem of sex is dealt with rather than love because the business of love belongs to another class of people. There's a lot of feeling a woman's ass, touching her breasts, sleeping with her, wanting her, no, yes . . . It's the way sex is and the way it was and the way it always will be.

Fine. But I have to know if there's going to be a new president. It affects me. I may not do a lot about it, but I have to know. These people don't care if there's a new president. You must accept the characters in those terms, their ignorance, their inability to bring the world closer to them, their contentment with the most mundane aspects of life, never to reach out to anything heroic, never to really reach for the cosmic things. You will see that through these kinds of relationships, especially in the Midwest, America had a whole life that consisted only of kids and family problems—not the war, not Nazism, not the ghetto we made for the blacks. In *Dark at the Top,* he brings out anti-Semitism. That's the only really big problem he comes up with.

There's not much action on the street, there's not much action in the garden or on the porch. It all seems to be between the kitchen and the small living room. Or at a bus stop. The bus stop is on a corner nobody ever heard of, and the buses go by once or twice a day—it's small. The characters in *Bus Stop* include a lot of aunts that are old maids, sister-in-laws that have happy marriages . . . Again, it's family business. It's the Midwest.

When it gets to basics, Inge is the purest writer. Not one line is a lie. It may be simple, it may be "Have a cup of coffee"—but he means it.

TWENTY

COME BACK, LITTLE SHEBA

(1950)

SYNOPSIS OF *COME BACK, LITTLE SHEBA:*
Set in the cramped, cluttered Midwestern house of
middle-aged Lola and Doc Delaney, the plot centers on
how their life is disrupted by the presence of a boarder
named Marie, a college art student with a strong lust-
ful appetite.

Overweight and slovenly, the housebound Lola
engages in mild flirtations with the milkman and
mailman, still playing the role of the ingratiating
coquette she once was. She sees in Marie herself at that
age, and encourages her pursuit of wealthy Bruce as
well as athletic Turk.

Doc was forced to abandon a promising career in
medicine when he married the pregnant Lola. Now
a recovering alcoholic, he maintains his precarious
sobriety by avoiding the past, as well as his sexual
frustration of the present—heightened by such close
proximity to Marie. She is an aching reminder to him
of the youth and opportunity he sacrificed. His even-
tual realization that she is not as pure as he wanted to
believe sends him back to the bottle and a descent into
unbridled rage.

The title refers to Lola's missing dog, who remains

Shirley Booth as Lola in William Inge's *Come Back, Little Sheba* (1950). "Lola is very loving and childish, and Doc fell for her, which is what Torvald did with Nora in *Doll's House.* I was offered this part but turned it down. I wanted to be glamorous, right? I should've taken it."

lost at the final curtain. So, essentially, do Doc and Lola. Like most Inge characters, they undergo no major transformation, ending where they began—diminished but resilient.

—B.P.*

---

* *Come Back, Little Sheba,* written while Inge was a teacher at Washington University in St. Louis, premiered February 15, 1950, at the Booth Theatre in New York and ran 191 performances. It was directed by Daniel Mann; Shirley Booth (Lola) and Sidney Blackmer (Doc) both won Tony Awards for their performances. Booth also starred opposite Burt Lancaster in the 1952 film adaptation. An acclaimed 1977 television version starred Joanne Woodward (Lola), Laurence Olivier (Doc), and Carrie Fisher (Marie).

YOU GET A FEELING for the South from Tennessee, for New York from Odets, and for the Midwest from Inge. The author makes you conscious of the place. In *Come Back, Little Sheba,* the first impression you get is a lack of dimension: there is no broad horizon, no expansion here. You can't see anywhere, and it's not going anywhere; it's closed in. The text itself is small. On the surface, it revolves around a singular situation: is the Doctor going to lay the girl or not? Inge gets immediately to the emotions at work here. "If this is sex," he seems to be saying, "I don't want it."

But it's not that simple.

One thing you find all through American plays after the thirties is that the nature of each period is very distinct, and the playwrights are very aware of the moment when they're writing. Think about that moment historically. You must be aware of America in a particular time and place and set of social circumstances, from *their* point of view. You start with impressions of the cultural atmosphere that influence the characters and their aims. Later, you work on the ideas.

The Delaneys live in a provincial town without the sun, even though it's Kansas. It's the fifties, but their living room has the atmosphere of the twenties—no modern technology, no TV, no electrical gadgets. It is decorated with a "cheap pretense of niceness." It has a heaviness, a cramped feeling, an old-fashioned static quality that comes from leftover things. It's a chiropractor's home without taste, nothing individual about it. The mohair furniture was either handed down or bought on sale somewhere. There's nothing visible here that has a human hand in it—no antique desk fashioned by an artisan. It's all machine-made. This same overstuffed furniture is in every store, without refinement or choice.

Inge paints a corner of the American world that is cut off from ideas except the basic day-to-day ideas of eating, sleeping, and functioning. There is no taste for books or music, no quality that ignites the imagination. Nothing comes through except the daily regulated married life. Midwesterners lived with that regulation: you live a certain way, you eat a certain way, you talk a certain way, with no expansiveness. It is a deeply passive, middle-class home where you put things up on the wall that are from your mother or grandparents—pictures from twenty or forty years before. The atmosphere is dim, dingy. Create that atmosphere before you go any further!

The Delaneys are products of the fifties, and the fifties are a product of the postwar prosperity, when there was a tremendous expansion of the country economically. The Depression was finally, *really* over. America was at its peak in relation to the rest of the world. People were becoming richer than ever before; many were moving west; the old-fashioned "extended family" was breaking up. Kids moved away. The big gravitational force at the center was weakening. It's an enormous country with huge horizons.

But Inge is concerned only with a dismal section of it. The bigness of the country hasn't penetrated to the hearts of these people. If you go to the midwestern painting of this period, you see the plainness, the run-down quality. The people look faded. They are kind of gray—absolutely American. It's a part of America that belongs to you, but you don't want to be part of it. You must feel this, and the transition they're in.

Even the language is skimpy, narrow—also without horizon or vision. You can almost reach out and touch the words . . . A play is a skeletal form, and the soul of this play is not in those words themselves. You instinctively want to speak them as soon as you see them. But Meyerhold said, "Don't use the lines of the play until they are in your soul!"* Only when they are in your soul should you say them out loud. Don't go so fast to emoting the lines.

Those lines are in American English because the play takes place in America, where there is no longer any respect for the language. The

---

* Vsevolod Meyerhold's "biomechanics" acting system was at odds with the method acting concept of melding a character with the actor's own memories to create internal motivation. Meyerhold believed the actor's emotional and physical states were inextricably linked, and that one could call up emotions in performance by assuming certain practiced poses, gestures and movements. Among the revolutionary artists he inspired was Sergei Eisenstein, whose film actors employed his stylized techniques. When Stalin clamped down on all avant-garde art, Meyerhold's works were declared "formalist" and anti-Soviet. His theater was closed in 1938, he was arrested in 1939, forced to "confess" being a spy, and executed in 1940.

language is no longer important. Something else is. Why? We were a country known for public speaking. But it declined. Something in the culture faded out. Always compare your culture to the play's culture, and compare the play's culture with the culture that came just before.

Something has been lost, and not just in the language. There is a kind of mist over this whole play, which takes place in a middle-class home and deals with the struggle in middle-class family life. There are many kinds of struggles going on: hot and cold wars (the political struggle), strikes (the economic struggle), cultural upheavals (the social struggle). There is also the inner struggle of each man in his own life and family. There's nobody to help modern man in his struggle anymore; he is deserted. There's no more cohesive religious community that he was accustomed to formerly, back when heaven was his guaranteed compensation for the struggles of life—back when the family situation was idealized, and nobody's children took dope or turned out to be homosexuals! Those things are all changing now.

See, in each play, how the struggle takes place.

* * *

Take it easy before you decide how to work on a script. This moment is producing a Lola, who has to be opposite in character to the girl Marie. She has a past that you have to figure out. Don't add things unless they make sense and you can do them. Get rid of your habit of deciding what she is right away—"she's kind," "she's lovely," "she's strong"—don't do that. Wait and see how she balances out with the other characters.

In *Come Back, Little Sheba,* you find the loss of tradition. Morality is gone—the new language with its four-letter words, the increasing suicides, the different relationship between men and women, boys and girls—no hint of traditional behavior.

All through the Western world, the old ways were broken. Those who survived and could adapt were lucky. Many couldn't. They didn't know how to live without the values they were taught and which they respected. In every period, the one right before it always seems to be better, but in this particular period everything went: the way a woman dressed at home, the way she kept the house, the way religion was treated, the way of social and community life. Why go out to the movies, now that you had television at home for free? The social situation creates your character. You can't possibly play this play except in the fifties.

Here are some facts. The first is that she can't sleep late and is sleep-deprived. The second fact is that she doesn't know what's the matter with her. The third fact is that the man speaks to her in covered language—"People change, habits change." From those simple facts, you get a play.

He makes her breakfast, for example. Now, she knows she's the wife and that *she* should be making *his* breakfast. But he's the one who gets up early, while she gets up late and talks about her dreams. He knows about her dreams. They're very real for her. She asks him a lot of questions, and he answers. She keeps talking about the dreams and about her little lost puppy. This is the soulful situation of these two people: they have no kids and have substituted a dog for children.

Lola is a kind of American Nora. She's very loving and childish, and he fell for her. She's proud of the little things she does, the way Nora is: "I bought this toy for the dog and that doll for the girl!"—"Look what I got today!" She adores her puppy. She has that ecstasy about it. We don't see that he has any feelings for the puppy. We see he treats her like a baby. She has no vitality, she doesn't do anything, she's depressed, she doesn't keep up her appearance, and the house has a worn-out twenties quality.

He sees the situation, he faces it, he takes care of her. The first thing you notice is no big ego: there's no Do Not Disturb Me sign on him. You see for the first time an American man of culture taking care of a woman who has lost her way.

Break it down: The little things in life typically belong to the woman, not the man. But in this play it's reversed. He says, "Here's your fruit juice. Can I heat some coffee for you? Do you want an egg?" It's the role of a man who is no longer traditional. He is a doctor and he's married, but his way of life is now transitional. We don't know much about this man or what will happen to him, but for the first time we see a situation in married life that is turned around.

They don't have friends. They talk a great deal about religion. From an Ibsen point of view, that's very important. He married her because he loved her, especially sexually. He loved her all the way, but he married a woman with no capability of matching his mind—which is what Torvald did with Nora in *A Doll's House.* You meet it again and again, from Ibsen on. Men and women marry, but it's mentally lopsided. The tradition in middle-class European marriages was the woman is weak. She just has to be pretty, she just doesn't have to do anything. She's like a child.

So Inge's American equivalent of Nora, to a fair extent, is Lola, and you must build her character. She is very dreamy and impractical. She doesn't do anything, doesn't bother with anything. A good thing for you to do with every character is pick it up, don't pull it down. If there's a garden, make it the Garden of Eden. Lift it up and make it higher, because the playwright is not writing on that lowest level. It's hard to play these plays unless the dreamer is free to fly. It's not "She's a slob." That's not what the play is about. It's just "Habits change."

Inge is writing about marriage. In the play we see that in the middle class, a doctor is no longer an eminent man who drinks port, with a long, respected tradition. Something has gone out of American life in the middle class. You can say that the middle-class life of the doctor has very little poetry to hang his hat on. There's no poetry in the street. It isn't in the school, the pharmacy, or the movie theater. Life is run-down.

But through history, in all the different changes, man somewhere keeps a spiritual light. If you don't see that in this play, look a little deeper and you'll find that—despite everything—she keeps the dream alive. When an author writes about dreams, he is saying, don't worry about her worn-out slippers or the dirty dishes—she's a dreamer. Don't think the playwright is always saying what the words say. You have to understand realism. In this marriage there are two people: one is a doctor, and the other is a dreamer who depends 100 percent on what Tennessee says Blanche depends on: strangers. She doesn't really belong to anyone. That's Nora, too, in the beginning. She keeps it all her life. The husband lets her because he married her, he believed in marriage, he believed that if you vowed to be husband and wife, it meant you were going to create a life of oneness.

He has the virtues of a man who understands that sex and spirit are not about the Bible. He gave her everything sexual and spiritual that he could, but she still got lost. She got lost in the fifties, when everybody got lost. From the fifties on, in American Theater—theater of the capital T—it's always an analysis of what's happening in the country, and why: there's a lot of money everywhere, and in that sense it's a good moment, but the values have gone down. The doctor sees his patients' money piling up, but he says he is disappointed in them.

People who don't know history and discuss themselves in their moment in history will never understand that moment. And if you want to really discuss your moment in history, you have to have background. You can't just shoot your mouth off. You can't say that the doctor doesn't understand history; he understands he is caught in a moment where there's nothing left that he once believed in.

The other characters in the play show you this: the young man is brutal, the young girl is a born cheat. But Doc likes her. Make it sexy. His wife is childlike. She knows she is alone, without really understanding it, and she gets very depressed. Her intuition tells her, "I'm stranded. I'm alone on this big sea." She should have never been allowed to grow up. She was too much like Nora. The degree of suffering is the extent to which they've paid the price and been emptied. The men are emptied, too, but they don't suffer to the same degree, because they're not in a dream state. It's good for you to know a little about Ibsen to see how closely these two plays are related.

By the way, I was offered this part but turned it down, and it was given to a great friend of mine.* I sent her some flowers. I had just done two plays in which I was a character part, and I wanted to be "dressed" onstage. Glamorous, right? Irwin Shaw has a great short story about an actress and a playwright: he comes to read her his play, and she hits him and throws him out. That was me. I should've taken the part. I turned down maybe five of the greatest plays. I didn't need it. I like teaching. I really do.

Anyway, Inge's two main characters here are both in their forties. He married her when he was at school and she was the prettiest girl there. She is one of those women who can't do anything if she doesn't belong to a man. They both say to themselves, "I've stayed in this marriage now twenty years." She believes everyone is pure and that Doc knows everything and will tell her everything she needs to know. But he is of no use to himself anymore, let alone her. She didn't "need" in any real way until she lost him. But then she lost everything, because she didn't grow up to be a woman.

Now she lives in a little town a thousand miles from where she grew

* Shirley Booth (1907–1992)

up, she doesn't know anybody there, it's a typical scene of American isolation. People are trying to make it in a community without any contact. Yet they are still rather religious, even though the church isn't cohesive anymore. It's interesting for you to know that in his desperation, this educated American man looks to religion—something has to help him. You see that he clings to it. He's lost in Middle America. There's nobody for him to talk to. There is nobody with him. It's all money, more money, baseball, football, TV—the whole superficial American scene. It's in the first few lines: "I can't sleep late like I used to," Lola says. "Habits change," says Doc.

In every play, the first thing is the place. Where are you, what time is it, what season is it? If you know the time, you can play everything Chekhov wrote, because he always tells you it's spring or winter, so then everybody knows how to dress. If he says it's raining outside, everybody knows exactly what to do.

So here you're in Middle America, it's early in the morning, the school year is almost over, it's about May . . . She's drifting, she never really talks to anybody, she eavesdrops . . . Don't make her factual. You must do it yourself, instead of going to the "logic" of it. For someone who is sick, everything seems strange—"I'm here, but I didn't sleep." She can't analyze it, but you can. When does a person sleep well? When they're safe, when everything is quiet, when they're really in the nest and the nest is covered. Without knowing it, she has no nest. She doesn't know where to land. She would never know. Her whole action is to see no harbor. Let these thoughts come out, but don't expect anyone to hear them; don't want or look for an answer. She doesn't really need an answer. You have a piece of great poetry in a dilapidated house with a woman who has lost herself. She is nothing. She's like dust.

Now, what is Doc? His main action is "I'm committed"—it's to keep his commitment. Nothing could make him braver: he's a man in the tradition of civilization. Mr. Ibsen questions the man who stays with a woman out of duty. He doesn't say it's right or wrong, he doesn't ever give you an opinion, but he says you pay a tremendous price for duty. It doesn't really give you much back. He says people you are dutiful toward will resent you for it. But that's the man thing: to keep the commitment. That gives him patience and a higher degree of understanding. He wants to say "Have some coffee!" but he sees she is still in her sleepiness, that he has not really helped but deserted her, that in his heart he can't give himself to her anymore, that she is lost. When he says "Would you like some fruit juice?" it's weary, not cheerful. It's "Let's get it over with." He's trying to help, but she doesn't *want* him to give her juice. She knows it's wrong.

Understand that realism is not talking. Don't go to the words, go to the place and see what is causing you to say every line—what's making you open your mouth. You have here a rhythm of morning and birds are singing and the whole outside is an opposite to what is happening. The rhythm is there, and it's created by the actress. Shirley Booth brought something wonderful to it—she was always in two places at once. "Habits change," indeed! Language isn't the same, politeness isn't the same anymore, the things that meant a lot to people who inherited a way of life—little has remained of all that. Lola herself is an example of "Habits change." She used to be a doll, taken out for strolls in the morning; she was sent for, she went along, her father never spoke to her, she was a virgin . . . And now look—look how habits change. What he's saying is "Look how *she* has changed."

Raise it. You cannot ground anything in realism. There's too much poetry. You must not ground it. You have to keep up his commitment—your commitment—for the whole play. When he says "Habits change," he's talking about everything—the Bible, living by God, or if not by God, living by the ethic of man, the family structure. He feels it's not up to us to break these things.

Doc's way—his action—is to try to take care of it all, right there. He puts the coffee on, he draws the curtains, he gives her the fruit juice. It's about *caring.* She wants him to buy her some presents. What size? he asks. "I'm really getting so thin," she says, "I'm going to be so beautiful by next week . . . " To be taken care of is exactly what the place needs: the window needs a shade, so he'll do that because it's needed. She needs her fruit juice. It's all about finding out what she needs next, and then taking care of that. It's like having a one-year-old child, making sure he's breathing—that full attention to everything he needs. It's a very noble action. I've only seen it done in a hospital, when a nurse's whole attention was on her patient. This kind of action isn't easily understood unless you go into it. I go into it, so you're lucky. When I give you actions, it means they have some sense.

What is Lola's action? She says she had another dream about Little Sheba: "I dreamt I put her on a leash and we walked downtown to do some shopping, and everybody turned to admire her—but suddenly I looked around and she was gone." Lola can't go to that action in reality, and neither can you because you don't know where it is. But Inge is such a smart writer, he lets her go there in a dream or reminiscence, because that feeds her. It's not actual, but she has it. Nobody can take it away from her.

She's like all the women who can't take care of themselves in so many of the Ibsen plays. They depend on love. Inge knew this about them, and he's on their side, and he gave it over to later authors who also liked women. There's a certain author who doesn't like the women in her plays, only the men—and in life, too. That's Lillian Hellman. But that's not Inge. When Lola goes to reminiscence, Doc hears it as poetry from his charmer girl. He sees this baby standing by the window, listening to the birds and giving him the only poetry that's left in the Western Hemisphere.

Please don't think this is easy.

*   *   *

Inge gives you an aspect of young people and their problems then. So go to their historical moment. America in the fifties had reached its most affluent period. The culture was all about consumption, and the target was youth. Mitchell Wilson, a great physical scientist, said that modern man has had ten years added to his life span, but not to his maturity—in America, they've been added to his adolescence. You became an adult at twenty-eight, not eighteen any more.*

Youth of the fifties were looked at as being different human beings. It was important to be young, stay young, go along with the young, dress like the young. To be old was to be obsolete. It was glamorous to be young, and the value of being young kept rising. That new affluence brought about all kinds of luxury businesses and new markets catering to young people—clothes, cars, records, motorcycles, etc.—multi-million-dollar industries. The "teenager" with "disposable tastes" was created, and adults to a large extent mimicked them. From now, you buy a new car every year—or you want to.

* Mitchell Wilson (1913–1973), physicist and novelist, was Adler's third husband. They were married from 1967 until his death. Among his novels are *Meeting at a Far Meridian* and *My Brother, My Enemy*. His most important nonfiction works are *American Science and Invention* and *Passion to Know*.

At one time immaturity was something to criticize. Now, it was accepted, if not encouraged. Freudian philosophy and Dr. Spock's permissiveness in child rearing hit their stride. "Don't criticize the child, he has to be unique!" Progressive education placed an inflated worth on adolescents and novelty. It was a confused moment—confused between "You have to grow up" and "You have to be indulged." The message was contradictory, and the kids came to rebel against it. Their affluent, white, privileged life was guaranteed for alienation and rebellion.

Look at the way they dressed. Listen to the music. That discontent was taken up by record firms, and the music reinforced what to complain about and rebel against. It antagonized older people, but otherwise it was a pretty quiet moment with no political upheaval. It was an age where society was ruled by its children—a child-centered anarchy, dependent on parental indulgence. The child became a part of the parents' spending habits. There was always money for "the kids." They didn't have to work, just study a little, date and lounge around. Teenage buying power became such a crucial force that the economy would have suffered if the parents had tried to stop it.

What were the schools doing all this time? They were becoming less and less a place to train the mind, and more and more a place to train the consumer. What Turk's brain missed out on in college was largely the university's fault. They were making big efforts to steer students into fields like "hotel management" and "public relations" and "packaging." Conformity was crucial: "Don't associate with the wrong people," "Don't be seen with anybody wearing an outdated blue serge suit," "Don't be an egghead and spend your life writing essays on D. H. Lawrence," "Don't rock the boat!" Did you know that the university was the major American institution to be reshaped by the corporations? Colleges got business-oriented and started admitting more students based on their sports activities and earning potential than on academics. Commercialism on the faculty did a lot to "reform" rebellious teenagers by turning them into cautious, materialistic status seekers, who defined the future by what they would buy and own.

Like any other generation, of course, this one wanted security. For the girls, security meant "the right man" and marriage. For boys, it meant a family and a nice corporate job. But having been "protected" as teenagers from any deeper or more philosophical concerns, they became largely unproductive adults, except as consumers. Kids in

Turk's and Marie's day were apathetic, cynical, and politically naïve. They took McCarthyism and the bomb as givens. They were vaguely anti-Communist, aware of the Korean War and willing to go if drafted. But, like their parents, they repressed all the problems of poverty, racism, juvenile delinquency. In Europe, the young Hungarians were revolting against the Soviets and getting crushed by Russian tanks. In America, they were having panty raids and rioting at football games.

When *Life* magazine did a midwestern opinion survey in the fifties, it showed that the biggest fear of young people in Oklahoma was not being able to find a parking place.

* * *

So you can make certain generalizations, but you must also understand Turk and Marie as peculiar individuals—don't treat them as dead stereotypes.

Marie is a boarder in the Delaneys' home. See the economic situation: for a small-town chiropractor, business isn't that great, they need the extra income. So Marie pays rent and has her breakfast there. She is a college girl from a relatively refined family. How do we know that? Because she calls Doc and Lola "Dr. and Mrs. Delaney," which is a little old-fashioned. Nowadays, people don't call women "Mrs." Everybody's on a chummy first-name basis. I'm "Stella." The president's wife is "Rosalynn." If I insisted on being called "Miss Adler," I would feel estranged from you. But we are dealing with the fifties, and a woman over forty is called "Mrs. Delaney" because she's married. It gives her a certain status or position, especially in a society with no horizon. There's a marriage, there's a Mrs. Delaney and there's a Dr. Delaney. In this society, there is both tradition and transition.

Pay attention to names. "Turk" is not a real name. It's a kind of abbreviation; it's sharp, and he's sharp. Years ago, to say somebody was "a young Turk" meant he was a kind of revolutionary, a kid who didn't quite fit in. In the East, maybe he could. But not in the Midwest. In this society, he's a stranger. He and Marie are both in college. Somebody is paying for both of them to go to school and make something better of themselves. But they think differently. What is the difference between them?

Turk is "studying at a university"—not really studying, but being there. He gets support. He is not criticized for his lack of marks or his behavior, because people come to see him win at sports. College is supposed to give you values, but what kind of college boy is he? He behaves like a bum. He is impetuous, doesn't like discipline. When Doc leaves, Turk says, "He hates my guts!" He slams the door shut and pulls Marie away from it. He is a man of action. If you're a man of action, you *do* a thing, you don't *say* it.

Marie says "Don't be silly!"—meaning, don't be out of control. In any domestic situation there must be control. You have fights, but you control them. The rhythm of life goes on without being completely upset all the time. Middle-class society is fashioned on rules, but fifties life is getting more out of control. The young people are fighting for some kind of individualism in this regulated society.

Doc is a man who knows how to control himself. He's from another era, born about 1910. He is a civilized person who can live in dinginess and still be "nice." In school he behaved, wore a tie, made good marks. He married, he didn't make passes, didn't break with tradition. He takes care of what he has, takes responsibility for the people around him. He opens the door for a guest, looks after the boarder. Inge was that kind of a man himself: very polite and soft-spoken. The doctor is much like him. It's the portrait of a gentle American, who doesn't hate Turk or anyone else, but Turk thinks he does. Turk thinks Doc is jealous of him. (Hate and jealousy go together.) He is a little worn out, but he has an inherited gentleness, and he does nice things in the home. He makes coffee, brings flowers, runs his fingers through the girl's hair affectionately . . .

Turk interprets those things as making advances. You see his crudeness by the way he speaks. He uses the word "crush," which is dated—today it would be "He has the hots for you!" To Turk, being nice is being a jerk. If you're in college, you don't need to be nice. He says Doc should make a pass at his own wife instead of Marie. The words "wife" and "pass" don't go together. You don't talk that way about a married woman of forty and a man who has supported her and believed the marriage vow "till death do us part." They should be respected for that, if nothing else. It's outrageous from a kid with no background. But everything with Turk is one-dimensional immediacy. He improvises life—which is a tendency of people who are mindless. He always comes in without knocking. He doesn't listen, he has no language, he's rough in his judgments and movements, without control. He acts in the living room as if he were in the woods. It doesn't occur to him that laying a girl should be private.

There is a big threat in this small household: Turk. He says, "I am a powerful bull and nobody can touch me." He is taking over, tainting and destroying this home by what he brings in—nothing but sex. Lacking anything else, he emphasizes the only thing he has: "I'm a sexy guy, I can do whatever I want!" He's not going to give that up easily. The hero of his day is the athlete. That reverence for the body and muscle is what Turk can hang on to. He has this macho bulk, size, sex. He should be out in Hollywood making Tarzan movies.

Marie is caught between that and the civilized niceties—between Turk and Doc, the one-dimensional bull vs. the one who has kept the amenities. Turk is an intruder without manners in a house that is politeness without ideas. Dr. Delaney's life is not brilliant, but it has a regular, civilized rhythm. Turk comes in and acts uncivilized. There are two views of Doc here: Marie thinks he is nice; Turk thinks he's lecherous. Marie can't believe a married man would act that way. Her background tells her that older men are not fresh with young girls. She knows that certain rules of morality are handed down, and certain things aren't talked about. You don't air your dirty linen in public. You don't discuss other people's sexual business. It is not polite.

But Turk breaks every rule in the book. He'd call his own mother "a good lay" if he felt like it. Previously, if your father beat you, you would never say "Go to hell!" or beat him back. But Turk's revolt doesn't respect parents, family, education, class—doesn't separate the older generation from the younger, or one profession from another. He makes no distinctions. What is Marie doing with him? How did they get mixed up with each other? Their realities are in conflict. Turk's only reality is "You're a girl and here's a couch!"

Know the difference between them and how they use the stage. Turk would drink the Delaneys' liquor when they weren't looking. Marie would never do that. They're in a small town where nobody is interested in twelve-tone music or Picasso, just in keeping the home fires burning. Doc and Lola are "nice" people—polite, kind, helpful. In America, money gave the middle class the privilege of culture. People could exchange money for cultivation. But after World War II, the middle-class need for anything more than daily living and good manners decreased. There was no drive to build opera houses in the fifties.

People became Mr. and Mrs., settled in, were satisfied with the house, kids, and pets. What did they give up? The drive that made man aspire higher, the intensity that propelled science, culture, ethics—the big advances. Aiming just to be nice is not a masculine drive; it's a feminine, indoor drive. A man doesn't walk with a parasol by a lake. He fishes, drains the lake, builds a house on it. When he settles for the walk, he emasculates himself from the big effort. It takes a lot of training and taming to be a nice man in this society—to keep that idealistic civility. Doc achieves it at a big price. He is not a driving force. Where did his drive go?

And on the other hand, why did Turk stop being nice?

You have to examine what a character *isn't* to find out what he *is*. See where the opposites are, to find out how the characters arrived there. Get the solitary situation of everyone here: Each is on his own. Modern man no longer feels part of the community; he is dissatisfied and adrift. Either you conform to the old values or you create new ones. The shift is difficult to make—and not to make. If you go against the conventions of the middle class, how do you survive? Where do you go? What are your choices?

The new set of rules and realities hasn't quite come around yet. It's hard to make that transition. Willy Loman couldn't do it; he was a victim of the changing rules in society. He couldn't make the break or take welfare, either. Neither can Doc. This is what playwrights like Inge and Miller are writing about. These are social plays. The American progression is from Torvald to Biff to Turk.

But Turk is not you. He doesn't have the freedom he wants, that complete freedom of the sixties and seventies. "Freedom" is the symbolic word for every new generation wanting to get away from the old one. Women today, for instance, demand to be called "Ms." and to have equal pay, equal rights, everything a man has—and they want it *right now*. This is what Turk wants, twenty years earlier. He wants everything *now*. The breakaway here is with Turk—his treatment of women is totally unlike men's treatment of women in any earlier period.

The fifties produced Turk, who is dynamic. Doc is not dynamic. They are opposites. Turk is the new, breakaway "beatnik" type. He doesn't give a damn about Doc, but here he is in Dr. Delaney's home—this untrustworthy Turk, with a young girl entrusted to Doc. Marie is a nice girl exposed to this dynamic, masculine force. It's the new macho rule breaker vs. tradition. Marie is in trouble. This place makes it difficult to lay her, but Turk is uncontrollable—he owns everything around him, including her. If he doesn't like something, he tears it up. He has no sense of what belongs to anybody else, no nuances, just a primitive masculinity. His mind is uncontrolled; he has not picked up a vocabulary to say what he wants articulately. A young Englishman or Frenchman is taught to express himself on both sides of an issue, but the American school system emphasizes sports, not intellect. What Turk wants, he takes. He is ruthless. He gives Marie no overture or traditional rhythms of lovemaking. He is animalistic, with no sense of her. There is a certain bravura in it. Don't take the attractiveness out of it. That fast rhythm is attractive to people.

A girl of that period didn't sleep around. Turk treats her not as a girl he might marry but as a girl to have sex with. He has no sense of what it really is to be a male in the society. He just wants her to cut the crap and give in to him. Marie has to pull herself together and do something. She is a passive girl, but she has a strong inherited sense of what is acceptable in lovemaking. She knows conversation in the living room is different from in the bedroom. In the living room, it's traditional for a man to get up when a woman walks in. Turk not only doesn't get up—he wants to lay her right there. She tells him to stop. She stops him from being the force—for a while, at least. He quits quickly when he doesn't get his way. Marie would like to have it both ways: she doesn't want to marry him, but doesn't want to lose out on the sex, either.

There's a disparity between a man and a girl in this permissive society. The girl maintains certain values. Even if she does sleep with him, Marie is "conditioned." It's not easy for her to go the other way. She is a girl who likes kindness and gentleness and has a real vocabulary, but at this moment of her life she sees no alternative—except maybe Doc. But Turk is too strong; he comes across as much stronger than Doc. Turk puts down the Delaneys' values and, with his nasty sense of humor, laughs at Lola's way of talking.

This talk about talking is important. Nora says to Torvald that in fifteen years of marriage, they never sat down and talked. Marie talks about politics, psychology, religion—mature subjects. Turk is resistant to any subject except his body. She has sex with him, but she still wants to be able to talk to the guy! They are on two sides of the social moment. In all plays you find the discussive element, and this is theirs.

The one thing Turk brings to this discussion is the Kinsey Report, which revealed how rigid America's sex roles were in the fifties. The male was aggressive; the female was expected to be passive and a virgin on her wedding night. The wife had a sense of propriety. She could enjoy sex but only if she catered to the man. It was about role playing in bed, and it was all very embarrassing to the middle class.

Now, Turk didn't read the Kinsey Report for educational value. He read it to get some kicks and to give himself some cachet for being graphic and shocking to her. The taboos were very strong then, and they still are now in America. Inge puts it in for shock value. It's another example of how Turk's way of talking seems to pull down the whole family structure—asking her, "Did you ever have sex with your grandfather?" Her grandfather the minister, who brought her up with religious values!

If you're the actor, Turk has to be attractive as this new macho creature. It can't be "Marie is good" and "Turk is bad." You have to play him as appealing. Women want him, people applaud him on the field. The audience must make up its own mind as to whether he is morally attractive. If you just say he's no good, you have no play.

Even though she eventually gives in to Turk's sexuality, Marie is still going to be a wife and mother. There is no effort by Inge to push for women's liberation. Kinsey said the married woman during sex was expected to act passively no matter how she felt, but once Turk gets her in bed, Marie no longer has to be so passive. Going to bed with him reveals the other side of her nature. Once that happens, he knows her in her deepest emotional, sexual aspect—better than she knows herself. After that, he's the boss.

What Inge is talking about, in a larger sense, is modern man's silent agreement in marriage to give up that I'm-the-boss thing in exchange for the woman's caring and loving. It is a problem in Ibsen and Inge alike: the man doesn't want to give that up in marriage, doesn't want to sit down and talk with his wife about their sexuality. The Inge man resists that; he doesn't really think that should be part of marriage. But in reality, the price of marriage is to have the man domesticated.

Turk's revolt is against that whole middle-class system—but it's aimless. With fascism, you kill people to put your dictator-leader in charge. With communism, you kill rich people to share their wealth with poor people. With anarchy, you kill people to put nobody in charge. Turk's kind of nihilism has no purpose, no aim. It just wants to break with what's there, and the need is so strong that nothing can hold it back—not the church, the government, the family, or the cultural tradition.

The image of Turk posing with his javelin is not subtle. "You hold it like this, erect!" he says. This is Turk's signature. It is what's going to get this young American male by. Everybody loves the erect sports hero. Turk is the new voice in America. He is saying, you are old-fashioned. You are trying to do something with my masculinity, but I'm going to beat you at it.

The historical moment is useful to an actor. If you get the playwright's theme, don't push yourself ahead of it. The ideas come more slowly in Inge than in *Death of a Salesman,* because the style is different. The author, through his language, is revealing the *breakdown* of the language. It is extremely realistic, never flowery. Since Ibsen, everybody takes the middle class apart and analyzes it. Miller is more concerned with the social situation of that class. *Come Back, Little Sheba* is more psychological, and more concerned with these psychologically complex people.

Inge is a fascinating playwright, on a small scale that is emotionally touching. You see people struggle through the day. Inge gives you a portrait of a fair-minded, open-hearted American man who greets everyone with fullness of spirit and hasn't fallen into judging people. It's not about big ideas, but about civilized man in his smallness. Modern characters are unresolved. They are not going to win or straighten themselves out. Every modern character pronounces himself from the inside.

The style is realism. Realism has nothing necessarily to do with reality. It is the revealing of truth in each character and situation.

ARTHUR MILLER

Arthur Miller (c. 1960)

TWENTY-ONE

DEATH OF A SALESMAN

(1949)

SYNOPSIS OF *DEATH OF A SALESMAN:*
Willy Loman is a sixtyish traveling salesman past
his prime—and his prime wasn't all that remarkable. Coming home early from an aborted trip to New
England, he tells his wife, Linda, he can't keep his
mind on driving anymore. He seems to be drifting
back and forth between reality and memory.

His sons, Biff and Happy, have come home for their
first visit in years. Willy and Biff were close when Biff
was a high-school football star full of promise, but
they've long been at odds—and are quarreling again
now—over Biff's failure to live up to Willy's expecta-
tions.

Now in their thirties, Willy's sons bemoan their disappointments but also worry about their dad: Willy is
carrying on conversations with people in his past, from
the glory days when he drummed into the boys that
the key to success was not being studious or honest
but being well liked: "It's not what you know, it's who
you know."

Biff knows more than he wants to know, but when
he tries to open his family's eyes to Willy's delusions
and deceptions, they rebuke him. The quarreling con-

tinues until Hap gets a brainstorm: Biff should ask an old boss for a loan so the brothers can start their own business.

Act II opens the next morning with Willy savoring his sons' idea and resolving to ask his own boss for reassignment from the road to the city. The three plan to celebrate at a restaurant, but that celebration of lies (complete with call girls) turns into a revelation of ugly truths: Biff's ex-boss didn't even remember him, and Willy's boss didn't reassign but fired him. The father-son recriminations escalate into violence.

Back at the house, Biff prepares to leave the Loman homestead forever but tries one last time to make his father face reality. Their final furious confrontation ends with Biff sobbing, which Willy interprets as evidence of Biff's love.

Willy settles on a spectacular exit to prove himself heroic to his sons: he will leave them his $20,000 insurance policy to start their business. His importance as a salesman will be confirmed by the grand funeral he imagines, attended by buyers from the whole East Coast.

A brief "Requiem" reveals that the policy didn't cover suicide. Only Willy's family and a neighbor show up at the funeral. That morning, Linda made the last payment on the house. "We're finally free and clear," she says. "We're free . . . "

—B.P.*

* *Death of a Salesman* opened February 10, 1949, at the Morosco Theatre in New York and ran 742 performances, winning both the Tony Award and the Pulitzer Prize for drama. The production was directed by Elia Kazan, with Lee J. Cobb (Willy), Mildred Dunnock (Linda), Arthur Kennedy (Biff), and Cameron Mitchell (Happy).

O N O P E N I N G N I G H T O F *Death of a Salesman,* the audience was crying, men and women alike, because everybody in the audience had somebody in the family—their uncle or their brother-in-law—who was a salesman. This country was built by salesmen, and the play reached them because of that. I was the only one that wasn't crying. I was sitting with Harold Clurman.* He said, "Doesn't this affect you?" I said, "No. Nobody in my family was ever a salesman." They were actors or writers or dancers or boxers, but nobody ever tried to sell anything. It never occurred to me that Willy was tragic. That didn't reach me until later. It should reach you a little sooner.

To understand Willy Loman and this play, however, you can't think, "My father was a salesman, so I know all about salesmen." It's not about any salesman you know. It's about this salesman's particular kind of denial and way of thinking. Miller is saying there are millions of men across the country that think like this salesman thinks and symbolize what is going on in their world. But this character is going to open up a much larger social situation that is not just about salesmen and the work world. It's about a break in the home and family as well.

In Miller, the size of this break was biblical—the father letting go, the son having to go his own way. It was an enormous historical breakaway from the previous tradition of father and son. Miller is going to

---

* Harold Clurman (1901–1980), visionary American director and theater critic, was Adler's second husband (1940–1960). With Lee Strasberg and Cheryl Crawford, he was one of the founders of the Group Theatre in 1931; he directed its premiere of *Awake and Sing!* (1935), which starred Adler, and many other Odets plays. *The Fervent Years,* his book about the Group and its richly creative era, was much acclaimed. He earned a Tony nomination for directing Inge's *Bus Stop* (1955). Clurman was drama critic for *The New Republic* (1948–1952) and *The Nation* (1953–1980). He and Adler remained fond friends until his death.

reveal it to you through the last days of a man who is desperately trying to find out just where and how he went wrong.

Miller introduces the salesman's boys in the second scene. Their names are Biff and Happy. Your first impression is that there's no tradition in those names. They're not George and Jacob. Their names are shortcuts. It's the American way—a way of saying, "We'll leave out tradition; let's call him Happy." Right away that tells you something you'll see throughout the entire play: they are cut off from custom. You wouldn't think of calling a doctor or a professor Bobby. There is something unserious about that, about the way we're treating each other these days. That is what Mr. Miller is saying. You expect a full response from half a name? Forget it. That's not a "good old" American tradition—that's ours today. It's not old and it's not good for us. It's a fact in our lives, but there's something wrong with it. It doesn't let us grow up. It is comfortable, but it is not right. There is something childish in it that we like to keep up for too long. It's a playfulness that thinks it's natural, but it's unhealthy.

Young people don't say "Father" or "Your Honor" anymore. They say "Hey, man!" or "Hi, guy!" That's not the way people in other countries talk to their parents or elders. It's just very peculiarly American. It starts with "Pop" and "Mom" and other diminutives and goes all the way up to the White House: "Ike" Eisenhower, "Jack" Kennedy, "Dick" Nixon, "Jimmy" Carter, "Gerry" Ford, "Ronnie" Reagan.

Now, Arthur Miller is a social-moralist playwright. His aim is to tell the truth, to say you don't have to be Oedipus Rex—you don't have to be a king or a president—to have a tragedy. You can be a "low man" like Willy Loman. The way he does this is through symbolic realism. The intimate circumstance when the curtain goes up is an upstairs bedroom in a house in the suburbs outside of New York, which is owned by the father and mother.

The historical moment is America in 1949. You have to know when and where you are in the play's present time, but also the background. They moved into this place about thirty years earlier. So it started with Willy moving his family in the 1920s to the suburbs of New York, which was a good thing to do considering what the suburbs were in the 1920s. But when you look at something you did in the twenties later in the fifties—let alone the 1980s—you can't help seeing that it has changed.

The growth of those residential neighborhoods outside Manhattan meant lawns and picket fences and shade trees and lots of little cracker-box houses. It still has some fragrance of an earlier America, when Willy bought it. He scraped and scrimped to pay the mortgage from the beginning. It was really fragrant back then. It was lovely. I want you to be able to smell it and to see there was something in Willy that needed that. If you play Willy, you must know he really needed that picket fence and that space around him with grass and trees—that's Willy Loman.

Arthur Miller gives you the "East Coast" of America. It is good for you to know the East Coast then was not all high-rise prisons—those little hole-in-the-wall boxes everybody lives in now. Such an undistinguished way to live. The high-rise does something sinister to man. It takes away his instincts to relate to nature. There is no way to pronounce yourself an individual if you are boxed up and crowded together with everyone else, without trees, without the sunlight coming in.

The play is about a man who wanted to live in the country, or as close to it as he could get. He took his wife and two children and went to the suburbs. This means the salesman, in his character, wanted something that had nothing to do with selling. It had to do with planting. He still carries seeds around in his pocket. Right to the end. These circumstances give you a beginning. You see a father who is aware of his family to such a degree that, though he started out fairly poor, he was determined enough to buy and pay off his own little house, with land on each side, for his wife and kids.

But when the curtain goes up, we find that the land around the house he bought is gone. He had to sell it, and now there are only bricks and other houses to look at, jammed closer together. So that, as the play opens, Willy is imprisoned—there's nothing but stone and concrete in sight. The apartment buildings all around have hundreds of tenants in them. Those new high-rises mean that the dream he spent decades fulfilling has been blotted out and blocked up by the new "culture" of the American scene, which says people don't really need all that space. It says you should live just like everybody else. Buy a cubicle on the thirty-seventh floor. Live there without any sun or fresh air. You don't really need it. You can buy air conditioning and a tanning lamp.

Willy is going back and forth in his mind with this, back and forth in time, trying to grasp what has happened to him and his sons.

Where did all that time go? What happened to that young man, their father, who went to the country with his family to build a life that had fresh air and trees? What happened to the ability of that father to plant seeds and make things grow? What happened to a respect for sunshine, to a love of the ground and of nature?

From the social circumstances we go to the larger historical circumstances. What is the country at large thinking and doing then? You must know this in order to understand the play. You have to go to the time period in America just before and during the time of the play. The Second World War occupied and obsessed everyone, either fighting it or building armaments for it. But the war has been over for a while. In 1946, the men started to return at the rate of 650 an hour, twenty-four hours a day, every day. By 1947, 350,000 men were discharged. In '48 and '49, thousands more came home and flooded the job markets.

The country was used to full employment in the factories that produced all those guns and munitions—not just for us, for the whole world. But then in New York and everywhere else in America, most of those factories had to stop making armaments and be converted. Billions of dollars of old war contracts were canceled, and two-and-a-half million men and women were released from production.

This is the larger circumstance Miller deals with for 1949 and 1950: millions of people dismissed from the war effort are looking for jobs. Which is why, in the play, Willy's boys can't find work. Some people their age, like Biff, went west looking for farm work, but they didn't find much, and there wasn't much work in the suburbs, either. Most of them were crowding into the cities while the military industry of America was switching over to other kinds of manufacturing. Industrialism was spreading and changing to a degree never dreamed of in this country, but a lot of people got left behind.

These are some of the things you must understand when the curtain goes up, and the things you must make the audience understand—that when Willy comes home and looks around nowadays, he sees people everywhere, in the streets, in subways, on buses, moving around fast in what used to be such a calm, quiet place, because of the disruption. The unemployment problem had to be fixed, but it couldn't possibly be fixed in a hurry. When arms building stopped, there was nothing on hand to replace it. That would take many years and tears. A lot of people would be redundant.

Traveling salesmen in New England aren't needed anymore. Inflation is bad, people are exhausted, the society is unsteady. That's a key word to remember. Willy says, "I can't take the road anymore, I'm unsteady." He's not the only one. People all over America—on and off the road somewhere—are becoming unsteady.

There was no AFL-CIO yet to unite the working class. There were just dollar-a-day men striking all over the country, trying to get increased wages—and five million unemployed! America is retooling, making cars and railroads but firing people at the same time. There is tremendous impermanence, and to be impermanent is not to be at all. Impermanence is the whole subtext of America. If you know that, it will open up the characters, the play, and why Mr. Miller wrote it.

Crowding is familiar to you now—masses of people on the streets, rushing, commuting, shopping, sleeping on the sidewalks, filling up the stores, the restaurants, the office buildings and the high-rises. But it was unfamiliar and disturbing then. Where were all these people coming from? Some were soldiers returning home from the war; some were part of an exodus from the rural areas; some were the new refugees from Europe—people whose homes and lives were destroyed in the war, forced to leave the "old country" to get away from dictators and religious persecution, drawn here to look for jobs and a chance to get into the new "industrial act." They were all jammed into city life that was already overcrowded and overenergized with a shortage of housing and space and jobs.

That is the industrial scene behind Miller's salesman—the scene in New York, in Chicago, in all the big overpopulated cities. You have to know this because you have to know why, the moment Willy Loman comes in, he is *lost,* and why the life around him is lost. It's the beginning of a whole new way of American life, which is why Willy feels so "dismissed" from the play's outset.

The disruption is not just economic. There's also a big disruption in behavior in this brave new world. Willy talks a great deal about the "old way of life"—about courtesy, about friendship, about honesty. He misses the way a waiter gave you coffee, the way a taxi driver took your tip. Life has became classless and hysterical.

Family life is more disrupted than anything. From the late 1940s on, there's no control by the parents of the children. That was the biggest change in postwar America. The moral system inherited from the Puritans and the other Europeans (whose rules are still very strong over there) was broken. You get this in virtually all the plays from Odets to Inge to Miller, because they lived through it. What they saw was tradition and traditional behavior—the way people dressed, the way they talked to each other, the way they behaved socially and morally—all breaking down.

Conversations became, "You makin' any dough? Will you gimme a slice?" That substituted for social interaction—and you are the children of this behavior. You are the products of that post–World War II moral disorder. What's interesting is that Miller doesn't give it to you through the street life. He gives it to you through the family life—the lack of respect inside the home, the lack of job security, the lack of rules you could trust.

Prior to this time, you never heard of "juvenile delinquency" or foul language everywhere or muggings and murders in the street. There were rigid rules in the schools, rigid moral instruction by the synagogues and churches, rigid standards at work. Things were "under control." There was always prostitution and dirty hotels and bars and clubs and places to get drugs, but only in certain parts of town that you either went to or that you avoided. It wasn't all around you, where your grandma could see it, out in the open.

You think that's normal, because that's what you've always seen and you're used to it. You don't see what it has done to the country, because you're too young and too close to it. But Miller saw it. There are many books written about alienation, and it would not be a bad idea for you to read one or two of them. If you do, you will begin to realize the size of that alienation between children and parents, not to mention people of different classes and races in the street. You will see the enormous gap between older and younger generations in this period; that a certain toughness took over in American life, where from now on you have to live with the daily threat of the atom bomb.

That defines the moment of this play and gives you an idea of the pain that exists between these parents and children, the pain of separation and cutting off from the family—"I can't get through to you, I can no longer reach you." I'm sure you have experienced it and might still be experiencing it yourself.

The playwright wants you to know why this is happening in our society, then and now. He wants you to see it not just in Willy's situation and character flaws but in the alienation and moral corruption of his boys. The further you go into the play beneath the text, the more

Lee J. Cobb and Mildred Dunnock as Willy and Linda Loman in Arthur Miller's *Death of a Salesman* (1949). "The key to success is being well liked, but Willy says, 'I can't take the road any more, I'm unsteady.' He's not the only one."

clearly you see that Biff learned his low moral standards from Willy as a boy and is now trying to come to grips with that. But the younger son, Hap, who maybe didn't steal things as a kid, is on an even lower moral plane—the absolute lowest, most immature one now.

You have your first clue to that permanent adolescent mentality the first time the lights come up on the boys' upstairs bedroom. They grew up in this room, which still has a childish look to it. It still has the same two skinny single beds where they slept as kids. Their old pennants are still up on the wall. There's a punching bag in one corner, a football somewhere, pairs of shoes with their names written on them. It's a Smithsonian museum of their boyhood. There's no poetry in this room. No sign of books. No framed photo of their mother. It tells me, as an actor-interpreter, something about the bareness of American boys' life. The only things you see there relate to games and fighting. From the fact that this room is so "undressed," that there's no warmth or natural light, just a little dormer window, no pictures of anyone—we get the barren environment of where they grew up, which symbolizes the barren nature of how they're still living.

Many times in the play, you see the boys fighting. You see that the whole atmosphere of their youth is a battle, with each other and the next-door-neighbor kid. In the flashbacks, one boy takes another boy down, the other one starts punching. The need to hit—to be violent—has become an accepted part of the society. It still is now, and you see it on the streets. Miller says it came out of all that iron and steel making. "When you make so much steel," he says, "the steel gets into the heart, too."

Now, when these two brothers get together for the first time in years, they're so totally distanced from each other, they have nothing to talk about, except their father's decline. After that, Hap goes straight to sex: "We screwed about five hundred girls in this room and got away with it!" He says it with pride, like an adolescent, not with any sort of regret or reflection, like an adult. That's how this modern American man talks about women and sex. I think it probably still is. "You remember that Betsy somebody-or-other we slept with? Boy, was she a pig!"

That's the vocabulary of the younger generation after World War II. Miller uses it to make clear that their sense of a woman is not of a mother or a sister or a companion or a sweetheart but just of one of five hundred girls to be screwed. Hap hasn't seen Biff for years, and the first thing he does is get girls for them to lay. He does that so often, he says, it's like bowling—"I just keep knockin' 'em down, and it doesn't mean a thing." It's just another game he enjoys. He especially likes to lay his co-workers' fiancées, and then go to their weddings!

The Loman boys are typical of these new young men and their new attitude toward women. If you play them, as always in preparation, your own life should intrude on the character's life only in ways that honestly relate. In this case, the play should make you see where your own lack of morality or decency matches theirs. The play will help you find that, and when you find it, you can use it.

If you play Willy, you must do the same. You have to see what HE sees and doesn't see. You have to see his family the way HE sees them, the way HE sees everything around him, in the present and the past. In the flashbacks, he sees his kids as good fighters, good at games—good at punching and winning. He encourages that atmosphere of competitive violence inside his family, which was in the outside, too. He's trying to prepare his boys for that "in the business world."

What Willy doesn't see is the social breakdown right around the corner, where he lives. He doesn't see that if you don't teach your kids to respect the old rules of behavior that held the American culture together—if kids don't respect and obey their parents—then they also won't respect or obey their teachers or their preachers or their boss or the policeman on the sidewalk. Willy sees this in his own children. He's the one who taught them it's okay to lie and steal to get ahead. He liked that idea in the past. He doesn't like it now, in the present. That's a big part of the irony and the tragedy.

The other irony in *Death of a Salesman* is that the salesman lives in New York but sells in New England. Why there? Miller chooses New England because it represents the best cultural beginnings of America, the enlightened sense of equality and learning, the new non-European way of life. Willy says, "I am not a New York man, I am a New England man." He likes it and feels he is needed there. If you play this character, you must know he doesn't associate himself with the suburbs or the noise and the dirt of New York. New York has become a hellhole. If Willy can't live in it, then the older son can't live in it, either. The younger son can, because he has basically become a pimp.

The truth is, Willy is a man who never really made any money, who kept borrowing and lying about it to his family, who kept a mistress hidden from a faithful wife and got caught by his son. Those things are gradually revealed in flashback, which, by the way, is the wrong word. People say "flashbacks" to describe those scenes, but that's a movie term. Miller called them "concurrences." Movie flashbacks are used to fill in some history or objective information from the past. Miller's concurrences give us Willy's totally subjective memories in searching for where his life went wrong. His mental state is crumbling, and so is the difference between past and present. The two time zones have started to exist in parallel for him.

Mr. Miller gives us the benefit of both time zones, with the gradual revelation of a man whose life has been undermined, a man who ends up lost and lonely. Almost everybody ends up lonely. What's needed on the stage for Willy, if you play him, is your ability to make the audience know how and why you're lonely. They can only get that from what you do and the way you speak his thoughts.

Is he talking about important things? Soul-shattering thoughts? Damn right, he is. If you're playing him, you can be alone with those thoughts. You don't always have to pitch them to some other character. They're better when they're alone. Miller learned that from Williams, who learned it from Chekhov. Tennessee has a marvelous one-act play called *The Last of My Solid Gold Watches* [1946], in which the main character is a great traveling salesman. He was so great, his company gave him fifteen gold watches—one for each year he outsold everybody else. But he ends up alone in some dump of a hotel, talking about how great he used to be to some younger salesman who couldn't care less.

Since *Death of a Salesman* came later, we assume Arthur stole from Tennessee—or "borrowed" would be a politer word—and not the other way around. Anyway, *Salesman* is awfully close to *Solid Gold Watches* in the idea that being a great salesman was like being a king. But Willy's kids know better: "You're not a king, you're just a two-bit salesman! You're a phony!" No matter how many gold watches or gilded memories you have, you wind up utterly lonely with nothing to show for it.

He's alone, whether somebody else is on the stage or not. That's why you can take your time and why you don't necessarily have to address all these dark inner thoughts to a partner: nobody else on stage is actually personally listening to the salesman. He is making a personal statement that is really a social statement. He—and we, the audience—wind up with a problem, not an answer. These playwrights have no answers. As an actor playing such a character, it's better for you to have that in mind—that you're stating the problem, not that you're trying to persuade the other character or lead the audience to some solution of it.

The problem in *Death of a Salesman* is that Willy pretended to be important in order to get the respect of his family, and his own self-respect. But he couldn't live up to the image and the lies are finally catching up with him. He's finally starting to realize that he taught his sons the wrong things and that that's why their lives are so barren. The disillusionment is huge.

It's not just the loneliness and disillusion that are unbearable. It's not just the past failings but the present insecurities that are killing him. Hap tells Biff, "He's going to get his license taken away if he keeps driving like that. I'm getting nervous about him."

They are talking about a man who is just sixty years old! Here in the United States, they take away your license if they don't like the way you drive. It's a real threat. They talk about it—and talk to him—the way you'd talk to a child. "If you don't do what I say, I'll take your toy away!" This is how you intimidate people, how we are all intimidated. If you don't pay the rent on time, or don't do something else right, you're out!

Everybody feels threatened. Either there'll be a fire in the subway or a power blackout or you'll have your driver's license taken away. The play has this enormous tension and pressure in it, and so do the characters. "Something bad is going to happen, I can feel it. I'm constantly nervous about it." That's the nature of this postwar society. You can't take a walk on the street without worrying about getting mugged. A man doesn't know whether the taxi driver is going to kill him, or whether he's going to kill the taxi driver. With the breakdown of all the old rules, people are extremely anxious.

It's *A Streetcar Named Anxiety*—about losing your license or your job, about not making the mortgage payment, about the boys not doing what they should. Miller makes you see they are living under all sorts of conscious and unconscious tension. The play comes out of an atmosphere where people aren't sure how to live anymore. "Will I get a job interview? . . . If I get the interview, will I get the job? Will they like me?" "Will the play actually be produced? . . . If it gets produced, how long will it run?"

There is no relaxation. "There's no rest for the wicked," my mother used to say. There's no space or blade of grass for Willy to come back to and sit down, open up the paper, smoke a cigarette, watch the sun go down. That kind of life just doesn't exist anymore.

This alienation, this anxiety that you see in *Death of a Salesman*, planted itself and took root so strongly that by the time it got to your generation, the whole fabric of American family and social life was eaten away by it.

There's nothing left to do but turn on the television.

TWENTY-TWO

AFTER THE FALL

(1964)

SYNOPSIS OF *AFTER THE FALL:* The time as well as the subject is the 1950s. The three levels of the set are dominated by the stone tower of a Nazi concentration camp in the background. Quentin, a middle-aged lawyer, emerges from a dim light, sits on a chair at the edge of the stage, and speaks to an unseen Listener (the audience) as if confiding to a friend—or on trial, addressing the jury in his own defense.

Trying to make sense of his life, Quentin probes his unhappy childhood, his mother's abandonment of him and her fury with his father, who lost the family business. But he is most obsessed by his destructive relationships with women—for failing them as well as his closest friends. As those key figures move in and out of Quentin's mind (and on and off stage), his monologues become dialogues with them.

Act I focuses on the waning days of his marriage to his first wife, Louise, who wants to be "a separate person." Quentin says he doesn't want to be separate but to support those he loves, including his gentle old mentor, Lou. The McCarthy-era witch hunts are under way, and leftist friends like Lou and Mickey are being forced to inform on others. Mickey makes self-serving accommodations. Lou will commit suicide.

But Quentin is most haunted by his second and even more disastrous marriage, to Maggie, the sexy blond switchboard operator and aspiring singer (a thinly disguised Marilyn Monroe) he met in a park. He also converses with his prospective third love, Holga, who was raised near a concentration camp, and whose arrival he now awaits at an airport—even as needy Maggie calls out for him at the end of Act I.

Act II opens with Holga's plane landing from Frankfurt but soon dovetails back into Quentin's and Maggie's intense battles, as she becomes increasingly unmanageable and dependent on booze and pills. Betrayal and guilt are the symbiotic issues all around. Quentin struggles with his equivocations about Maggie. Rather than watch her kill herself, he abandons her. He and Holga suffer different forms of survivor guilt. The relentless exploration of his past motives and compromises forces Quentin to move forward and finally feel capable of loving the admirable Holga. In the end, hope replaces despair.

—B.P.*

* *After the Fall* premiered on January 23, 1964, at the ANTA–Washington Square Theatre in New York City as the first offering of the Lincoln Center Repertory Company, under the direction of Elia Kazan, with Jason Robards Jr. (Quentin), Barbara Loden (Maggie), and Salome Jens (Holga).

AFTER THE FALL is a strange play. If you want to play Quentin or Maggie, I think it's very brave of you. They are not really playable. In many ways, it is not really a very actable play. It is Miller transitioning into symbolism without scenery. He has a right to do it—and you have a right to play it any way you want.

But it's easier if you understand what each scene and character is about, and if you don't just blindly stumble into the words of it. The words are like a kind of jungle you can easily get lured into and lost in. You'd like to have a guide to lead you through it, but you're not going to get one. There isn't one here. You have to be your own guide and find your own way through it.

The man Miller continues to write about is the one who got so mixed up in the American way of life—of business, of making a living, of existing—that he forgot to replenish his soul. Especially in the realm of love and family life, he failed to nourish himself enough. In a lot of Miller's plays you will find this man who overestimated or underestimated his value and ended up paying too much attention to keeping up with the neighbors, getting his career going, going to work—just getting along. Then at the end—as with the two boys in *Death of a Salesman*—he says, "I got the house, I got the car, but now I don't feel anything." There is an aspect of all Miller's plays in which the man is devalued and eventually devastated by buying too much into the American way: "Make good, make money, and never mind everything else—the spiritual things, the emotional things—going on within you." In doing that, he ends up bereft, with no history, no past, no present, and no future—just lots of mistakes.

But this man Quentin in *After the Fall* is not Willy Loman. Willy couldn't and didn't change. In Quentin, there's a certain change, or at least a desire for change. Something that didn't happen to, or inside, Willy is happening to him. Something has happened to make him start reexamining and reconsidering, even if it's too late.

Quentin is much more intellectual and self-analytical than Willy

Loman. Mr. Miller goes much further inside this protagonist's head than Willy's because Quentin *is* Miller, and this is his confession—not to God or a priest or a rabbi or a psychiatrist, but to us. He tells us what we're in for in the opening directions: "the surging, flitting, instantaneousness of a mind questing over its own surfaces and into its depths."

You think it's about Marilyn Monroe. But it's about his mind, even in the second act, with all the confrontation and torture leading up to her suicide. In a way, her whole decline and fall is just another staging ground for his introspection. There's a coldness to him, even in his passions. All his women feel it and eventually call him on it.

There is also a political element to him that Willy Loman didn't have at all. Do you know or understand that in the 1930s and 1940s there was a big left-wing movement, when America tasted a sense of liberalism and universal goodness? That whole left-wing view was shared by almost everybody, or at least the majority, until McCarthy came along in the 1950s and destroyed it. Miller is writing about *that* time, and after it, when the liberal movement was choked off. And you haven't had it since.

Speaking of politics, I suppose most people will be watching Dukakis tonight on television.* Maybe that explains why a number of people aren't here. But the way I feel about it, the only excuse for not coming to a class or a performance is death. That's an old slogan in the theater. If you say "I was sick" or "I had to do this or that," there's no forgiveness! The definition of an actor is total dedication—nothing else.

Well, the hell with anybody who's not here. You're here. And you know that there are many characters in a play like *Death of a Salesman* that you can't understand at first, because it's so big underneath, and because Miller is so deceptive in the lines. But you also know that what makes it a great play is how it works together, how it gels, and that is even more true with *After the Fall*.

Early on, we get first wife Louise† in a fury at Quentin. It's a con-

---

* Adler is speaking on the afternoon of July 21, 1988, at the time of the 1988 Democratic National Convention in Atlanta. Governor Michael Dukakis of Massachusetts and Senator Lloyd Bentsen of Texas had been nominated for president and vice president the day before. Dukakis's acceptance speech would take place this night.

† Based on Mary Slattery, Miller's college sweetheart and first wife, whom he married in 1940 and divorced in 1956.

frontation over their marriage. They are not playing on the same key. She's on a high key because she's been kicked around for a long time, but she's talking to a man who can't be reached. Therefore, Sandy, you can *go*!* We don't have a scene if you have no sense of saying, "Look, I am really truly a woman, and if you don't really look at me and raise your voice more than your usual professorial, condescending level when I talk to you, I'm going to kill you. Goddammit, don't you think a woman needs more than that?"

Get the difference in tone between her and Quentin. You've got to stay up, Sandra! I don't mind if you have temperament, but you're not feeling the part, darling. It's just a lot of screaming. Anybody can scream. Do you know what it means in a country to have the men deadened? The women were going *crazy* with that lack of energy in the male, with his deadness. It was the end of American men—they were becoming mice. She's saying, "It has to stop, don't you hear me?!"

She's going crazy with his aloofness, his intellectuality. Even Quentin has to admit it. He says, "I saw that we are killing each other with abstractions." But he didn't see it until he met Maggie. There's nothing abstract about *her*.

She doesn't even enter until page 60 of the script, about two-thirds into the first act. But when she does, it's a huge transition. Quentin is in the park, sitting on a bench, minding his own business. The playwright tells you, "Maggie appears, looking about for someone." But it's not really some *person* that she's looking for.

I'd like you to read it.† [*The actors do so.*]

> MAGGIE: 'Scuse me, did you see a man with a big dog?
>
> QUENTIN: No. But I saw a woman with a little bird.
>
> MAGGIE: No, that's not him. Is this the bus stop? . . . I was standing over there and a man came with this big dog and just put the leash in my hand and walked away . . . And then

---

* Adler is speaking to Sandra Tucker and Dan Keough, playing Louise and Quentin.
† Stella is speaking to Charles Boswell and Beverly Leach, playing Quentin and Maggie.

this other man came and took the leash and went away. But I
don't think it's really his dog. I think it's the first man's dog.

QUENTIN: But he obviously doesn't want it.

MAGGIE: But maybe he wanted for me to have it . . .

QUENTIN: Well, you want the dog?

MAGGIE: How could I keep a dog? I don't even think they
allow dogs where I live . . . He probably figured I would like
a dog. Whereas I would if I had a way to keep it, but I don't
even have a refrigerator.

QUENTIN: Yes. That must be it. I guess he thought you
had a refrigerator.

All right, stop there. Now, this is the closest Miller gets to comedy. It's
full of nonsequiturs. It almost reminds you of what they used to call
the screwball comedies of the thirties, or the kind of ditzy dialogue
that Anita Loos wrote and Marilyn Monroe had in *Gentlemen Prefer
Blondes* or *Bus Stop.* Did you get the Inge in-joke about the bus stop?
It's not the Marx Brothers, but it's funny. Miller and the play don't get
any funnier than this!

Anyway, Beverly, let's start with the fact that you are overdressed,
and overgirlish. You give us the impression that she's already some
kind of actress or performer, which Maggie isn't at this point. What
you're wearing is very beautiful, but it's very much what a theatrical
actress would wear, not a secretary—certainly not in the fifties.

[*"Well, she caught the eye of a judge," says Leach.*]

Sweetheart, to catch a judge's eye you could have pop-bottle-thick
glasses and be sneezing and wiping your nose—you don't need much
to get to a judge. This woman has had a *loss*—she lost her dog. I'd like
you to have lost your dog. There's a very quiet, sober tone about anybody in the world that's lost her dog. "I'm desperate to find him! Can
this man help me, maybe?" Recognize him as *she* recognizes him: he
has a bigger place in life than you. She's a lousy secretary. What you're
playing is a vampire. It's too theatrical. It's not coming psychologically from an author who wants a real person on the stage. He doesn't

want an actress to imitate an actress imitating a secretary. He wants a *secretary* on the stage. It should be much softer, quieter. She just wants to reach out to this gentleman and discuss this thing with him—"Do you think the dog will come back?"

The way you choose your clothes for a part makes it live or die. A secretary shouldn't wear things that raise her bosoms. That's not the best choice for this. Do it another night. This is a secretary who went for a walk and lost her dog. If she wore what you're wearing, men would treat her as a joke. Don't be a joke. You're beautiful and you'll get men, personally. But I want a girl looking for a dog, and I don't get the feeling you really care about this dog. You're not doing what the play says.

It's not a very realistic play, so I don't want you to play it in the style of realism. I would like you to see if you can use this almost totally empty space to sit down on a bench next to a complete stranger, so that we see two strangers sitting separately together. Or sitting together separately. Whichever of those makes sense to you. What we're seeing now from you is 100 percent too much acting—old-fashioned acting that was thrown away a hundred years ago! What we see is a kind of female Hollywood bum. We are not seeing a real person, a secretary, somebody who leads a boring life and got stuck taking care of somebody else's dog.

This is a girl that sits down, maybe shaking her head in confusion, and says, "I just can't figure it, a guy comes over and hands me a leash and then runs off and . . ." It's not so personal or direct to Quentin. It is not "Listen, I'm going to tell you the story of my dog!" It's just two people accidentally in a park. Whenever you play a park scene, remember that it's a symbol of a place where the characters can say things that can't be said in a kitchen or some other room with doors and windows, where people know each other. Don't be responsible for the whole play, just be responsible for your character.

What I would do, Beverly, if I had the chance to play the part, and if I had your hair, I would have dyed it dark brown or rinsed it. You must take the trouble to dress her to such a degree, because that's who the character *is*. You are so close to this blondness and this attractiveness of yours, you've lost the fact that Maggie has no self. She's a receptionist. She has no real personal identity, she just does what other people tell her to do. She only exists, or thinks she only exists, to fill other people's needs, when in fact *she* is the neediest person in the world. You can't bring in anything belonging to yourself, not your shoes, not your stockings—nothing. You have to say, "She wears dark stockings because she doesn't have enough money to buy sheer ones." If you came in with black shoes and dark stockings in a thin little tailored thing, you'd look more like her. You see a lot of girls like that, fidgeting in the subway or the bus stop, looking at their watch: "Dammit, it's late again . . . Where the hell are my . . . I forgot my goddam cigarettes . . . " You must be physically as well as psychologically true to that character.

Maybe you should have a wig that would disguise your real self and your real beauty. Otherwise, the reaction in the audience and in your partner is "Look at her!" If you could keep that out of the scene, if you could get rid of being like you are on the street and wearing your hair like you do on the street, if you could go back and darken a few circles around your eyes, you would be a person that doesn't mean very much—and then you would be in the part. As it is, we're so busy with your looks and your body—and so is he. You're distracting him because of it.

[*"I could be back in half an hour," says Leach—to sympathetic laughter.*]

That's all right, just take it easy. Everybody here in Hollywood is hitting you to go fast with everything—your life, your career, your lines . . .

Just give us the meaning of the loneliness that you encounter in him, the loneliness in your own life, the loss of the dog, the waiting for a bus. There's nothing meaner, uglier, more pulled down to the bottom of the earth than waiting for a bus. There's not a drop of beauty left in you after you've been waiting an hour for a bus.

The irony is, she doesn't know where she or the bus is going, anyway. She finally takes his five-dollar bill to get a taxi, but she doesn't know where to go. Mr. Miller uses the word "separated" a lot, referring to alienation over the whole country. If you can play that alienation—that inability to feel the humanity in the other person—then you will get to what he means. If actors know the playwright, they will play what he wants to say about two people in the park who are alienated from life.

Charles, in the same way she doesn't really need you, you don't really "need" her. Keep the idea that nothing interests you. Don't puff up to her and be so gay. Keep the character as just "I have nowhere to go, I've done it all wrong, I'm a failure." Don't play such a happy failure. Why do you look at her that way? You've had two or three wives. You know girls.

[*"I'm still trying to figure them out," says Boswell.*]

Yes, and so is Quentin. He says he can't stand to wake up every day and feel so numb. He wants to figure out how to be a boy again . . . but he can't.

I don't want *you,* I want somebody else, somebody far from you, on the stage. Unless a part hits you in *here,* don't do it. There isn't money enough, unless you can say, "I know it, I have it." What both of you are doing now is trying to play it, but you don't know what you're trying to play. All your talent is useless if you don't know what you want to do. When you speak, you seem to want an answer. There are no answers for any feeling. You think that by talking softly, it's the truth, but it's not. It's an imitation. It's comfortable, but it's not the truth. Not for the stage. Be as large as the stage is. Don't be afraid of size. You need it as actors—we need it in America.

* * *

What does "after the fall" mean? Among other things, it means everything was falling apart, not just personally but politically. I would like you to know something about what the political life was like during and after this fall.

Quentin is Mr. Miller's mouthpiece for the end of a period of American life when liberalism was dismissed and a fascist element entered the scene with McCarthy and the House Un-American Activities Committee. Every intellectual, every man of mind, had his head cut off by the red baiters. Americans were left with no compass to guide them, because they had given themselves over to the liberal movement and were part of it, but it let them down. Miller is talking about that moment when you no longer believed in liberalism, you no longer believed the Soviet Union was going to share the world—they wanted it all. And suddenly people were being accused and put on trial and put in prison for even *talking* about Russia, about progressivism, about socialism or communism.

What devastates Quentin's friend Lou is that he was so truly and honestly committed. He went to Russia to study Soviet law, came back and wrote a book about it. But he left out certain things "for a good cause"—which turned out to be a lie. And now he's paying a terrible price, hauled up by HUAC and forced to defend his own lies.

You'll never know the terror of those words "I've been subpoenaed!" Many of Miller's friends—and mine—were victims of HUAC. The Mickey character here is his representation of Elia Kazan, a great director of many great plays of the period,* who named members of a Communist cell out of fear and the need to work. Mickey says, "I think we were swindled—I'm going to name names." He testifies against Quentin's old friend Lou, who kills himself.

Nothing could stop the HUAC trials. It was a witch hunt, which is why Miller wrote *The Crucible* [1953]. In this play, Mickey is the accommodator, who decides it's better to protect yourself—to hell with the others. Quentin doesn't want to separate from either of them, but he also doesn't want to be known as "a red lawyer." He wants to be loyal, but he is being told to withdraw his support from them by Louise, the first wife, and other people. He says, "I don't want to separate from my friend just because he's in trouble." Louise says, "What the hell do you care?"

There's something you should know about all Jews in trouble: they could kill themselves if they wanted to, or they could kill somebody else, or to save their lives they could convert to Christians—all those, and other things, are morally excusable. The only thing that is not excusable is being an informer. If you inform, you are guilty of the ultimate crime. That is punishable by exclusion or death. *You must not inform!*

This is the pivotal moment Quentin is coming out of—the political side of *After the Fall.* Miller is creating Quentin as a symbol of how these developments deadened the spirit of man. He can't be a decent husband; he doesn't care about his business or his art anymore. It's all gone. He is floundering in the wreckage of the democratic idea.

The power of the enlightened liberal movement in America has been smashed and given to McCarthy. That deterioration of the political man was a debacle. It produced a lot of tremendously painful soul searching, including a deeper sense of awareness and education about Auschwitz and the concentration camps, and who was responsible for

---

* Including *A Streetcar Named Desire, Death of a Salesman* and—amazingly enough—*After the Fall.*

it. In *After the Fall,* Quentin says it wasn't just the maniacs. It wasn't just Hitler's and the Nazis' "crazy aberration of human nature." It was all the "perfectly normal contractors . . . carpenters, plumbers, sitting at their ease over lunch pails . . . laying the pipes . . . good fathers, devoted sons, grateful that someone else will die, not they." He sees the walls and the barbed wire and the ovens and says, "Believers built this."

All the children who were killed in the Holocaust had names, and many of their names are known. The New York theater community has raised millions of dollars, and each year they give poor American children enough to live and study on for the future, in the name of one of those dead Jewish children in Europe. They were in the millions, and they will not be forgotten. I think it's an extraordinary way to remember them.

The one who speaks for them in the play is Holga, the German archaeologist that Quentin is meeting at the airport—his last chance for a real relationship after the disastrous marriages to Louise and Maggie.* Miller gives her a monologue where she talks about the unfathomable experience of growing up outside a concentration camp where two hundred thousand Dutch, Russian, Polish, and French prisoners were killed. She is showing Quentin the camp, and she stops to read a plaque on one of the walls. It is beyond horrifying, but she feels she has to translate it for him. She wants him to hear it, and the playwright wants you to hear it: " 'The door to the left leads into the chamber where their teeth were extracted for gold; the drain in the floor carried off the blood. At times, instead of shooting, they were individually strangled to death. The barracks on the right were the bordello where women—' "

At that point, Quentin makes her stop.

To reveal your life without shame, you have to take what it is and acknowledge it. That's what Miller is doing in *After the Fall* with this

---

* Holga is based on Austrian photographer Inge Morath (1923–2002), Miller's third wife. They met in 1960 when Morath was working with John Huston on the set of *The Misfits* (starring Marilyn Monroe and Clark Gable), for which Miller had written the screenplay. Morath and Miller were married on February 17, 1962. Their daughter, Rebecca, was born that September. Their son, Daniel, born with Down syndrome in 1966, was institutionalized and largely excluded from the playwright's personal life. Miller's son-in-law, actor Daniel Day-Lewis, is said to have visited Daniel Miller frequently and to have persuaded Arthur Miller to reunite with him.

Holocaust monologue. An actress named Ilse Taurins did it here once. She understood it doubly because she was an immigrant—she understood that country and this one. She did it with such nobility and such clarity and such control. It was brilliant.

If you play Holga, I want to see something great on the stage—a woman who knows what grief is. I don't want *your* grief, I want the grief of the world, through her, which we have inherited. Go to that woman. Use the platform! Go to it. Don't make it small. It's big.

*   *   *

It's no accident that the only concrete scenery the playwright gives you in this play is the concentration-camp tower in the background. It is *literally* concrete. Otherwise, the scenery and scenes exist only in Quentin's mind, inside his psyche, as he goes from place to place, back and forth from political to psychological, in what Miller calls his "endless argument with himself."

Quentin's biggest argument is with Maggie. He is trying to save her . . . or trying to convince himself that he is. She desperately needs to be loved, but she is so full of insecurities and she is destroying herself with booze and pills. It escalates in Act II, after she has become a star, when they reunite and get married.

You think she is Marilyn Monroe. A lot of people think so, and a lot of people think Miller was exploiting his relationship with her. I know Simone Signoret thought so.* You think, "Quentin is busy with Maggie, and Maggie sounds like Marilyn." But I don't think that's what *After the Fall* is all about. There was that episode in his life, to be sure, but it's not all about Marilyn and Arthur. He said he actually started writing the play more than a year before she died.†

---

* Actress Simone Signoret was married to Yves Montand, Monroe's co-star in *Let's Make Love* (1959). Monroe disliked the original script and Miller rewrote it to beef up her part, whereupon her original co-star, Gregory Peck, bowed out. The role was then offered to Cary Grant, James Stewart, Charlton Heston, Yul Brynner, and Rock Hudson—all of whom declined—before Montand finally accepted it. Shooting progressed well enough until Miller left California on a business trip and Signoret returned to Europe to make a film, whereupon Monroe and Montand began an affair. Signoret later expressed contempt for Miller and Elia Kazan resuming their artistic collaboration in *After the Fall* "over a casket."

† On August 5, 1962, at age thirty-six, of a barbituate overdose in Los Angeles.

It's interesting but irrelevant, unless you're a gossip columnist. Most characters in most plays have aspects of their playwrights and people in the playwrights' lives, to a greater or lesser extent. All writers' creations contain facets of themselves. It's fascinating, but if I were you, I wouldn't be distracted by any fame or celebrity business unless it somehow opens up for you how these particular characters behave.

For instance, when Quentin compliments her "Little Girl Blue" record and says the way Maggie does it is so moving: with her terrible neurosis and inferiority complex, she's so thrilled by that. What's her line? [*Someone reads it:*] "Really? 'Cause, see, it's not I say to myself, 'I'm going to sound sexy,' I just try to come *through*—like in love . . . " From that, he gets to understanding something about her strange innocence.

Or her idea of how to help him face the HUAC committee: to offer him good sex the night before. He says, "There's one word written on your forehead . . . 'Now.' " And she says, "But what else is there?" He says, well, there's the future—which he's been carrying around all his life like some expensive Chinese vase he's afraid he might drop. But then it hits him. "You're all love, aren't you?" And she says yes, "That's all I am! A person could die any minute, you know . . . "

It's a lovely scene. If it sheds some light for you on Marilyn Monroe, that's fine. But that is not its purpose, or your purpose. It must shed light on Maggie and Quentin. What she liked about him in the beginning was that he took her seriously, while all the other men in her life treated her as a joke. She saw how smart and how serious he was, and she felt respected by the fact that he didn't try to go to bed

---

Miller was coy on the subject, contending the play "seemed neither more nor less autobiographical than anything else I had written for the stage . . . the link between the private and the public life is what is involved in the big dramas of our civilization. Hamlet is not just a fellow; he's also the heir to the Danish throne." Miller and Monroe first met in Hollywood in 1950, but not again for five years. Monroe married Joe DiMaggio in January 1954 and divorced him nine months later. In May 1955, she and Miller started dating again. The press was calling them "the Egghead and the Hourglass" by 1956, when Miller was subpoenaed by HUAC, refused to identify the Communists he knew, and was charged with contempt of Congress. Various studio officials urged Monroe to abandon him rather than put her career at risk, but she was steadfast in her support. They were married June 29, 1956, and divorced on January 24, 1961.

with her. "She took it for a tribute to her 'value,' " Quentin says, but then he adds: "I was only afraid! God, the hypocrisy!"

He is telling the truth to his Listener—to *us,* now, not to Maggie, then. At the time, he's still giving her backhanded compliments. There's a moment early in Act II, when he stumbles around, trying to express what first drew him to her. I think it's their most important exchange in the play—read it, please. [*Two students do so:*]

> MAGGIE, (*in pain*): . . . I'm a joke to most people.

> QUENTIN: No, it's that you say what you mean . . . you're not—ashamed of what you are.

> MAGGIE: W-what do you mean, of what I am? . . .

> QUENTIN, *suddenly aware he has touched a nerve:* Well . . . that you love life, and . . . It's hard to define, I . . .

She is smart enough to catch it. She lets it go for now, but it keeps coming up and escalating later, when she says: "I . . . don't really sleep around with everybody, Quentin! . . . I was with a lot of men but I never got anything for it. It was like charity, see. My analyst said I gave to those in need. Whereas, I'm not an institution . . . "

If anybody was pretending to be a charitable institution, it's Quentin. He admits it to his Listener and calls himself a fraud: "I should have agreed she *was* a joke, a beautiful piece, trying to take herself seriously! Why did I lie to her, play this cheap benefactor . . . ?" He admits again later that it's fear—not nobility or shame—that's behind his disapproval of her sexuality with other men: "I wasn't sure if any of them . . . had had you." He's no different or better than all the rest of them, who thought she was a slut and abandoned her for the same age-old male jealousy.

Their conflict cannot be resolved. You've heard the term "irreconcilable differences." It's a legal cliché for divorces, but in this case it's true on half a dozen levels. On top of class differences, there are all the sexual and intellectual and personality and behavior differences—her passionate nature and chronic insecurity and pills and booze vs. his chronic soberness and coldness. He says he's been spending 40 percent of his precious lawyer's time on her problems—he knows, because "I keep a log!" That's not something a man should say to a woman like Maggie, especially when she's drunk. She's mortally wounded by it. Her response is that they "should never have gotten married—every man I ever knew they hate their wives."

At that point, it's over between them. All that remains is to see who walks out on whom . . . who survives, who ends up with the survivor guilt. They wrestle over the pills, but it's hopeless. Finally he says, "You want to die, Maggie, and I don't know how to prevent it." He says she's been setting him up for a murder. "A suicide kills two people, Maggie, that's what it's for! So I'm removing myself, and perhaps it will lose its point."

He's giving her a rational argument why his leaving should make her NOT kill herself. He says that's his reason for leaving her. It may or may not be true. He, of all people, should know the impossibility of taking any kind of logic from his own mind and giving it to her. She is not logical. It is just as likely, or more likely, that he's leaving because he doesn't want to be around and be responsible when she does it.

Either way, the result is going to be the same: her death and his tremendous guilt.

Quentin has a pattern, a long history, of detachment and regret. Early on, in a flashback, his mother is talking to him as a boy and she says, "Darling, when you grow up, I hope you learn how to disappoint people. Especially women." Both his wives accuse him of being so emotionally distant that he makes them feel they don't exist. The first one, Louise, says, "I think now that you don't really see any woman. Except in some ways your mother." That's pretty Oedipal. It probably wouldn't be there if there weren't some truth to it. What's most agonizing to him, he says, is that "I could have brought two women so different to the same accusation—that I could not love."

It's tough to make Quentin—or Miller—more sympathetic than sanctimonious. The portrait of Maggie is the thing that really brings the play to life. In the end, she may or may not be Marilyn, or Miller's therapy for Marilyn.* But that's what intrigues people about *After the*

---

* *Finishing the Picture,* Miller's final play came closer to that. It opened at the Goodman Theatre in Chicago (with Matthew Modine, Stacy Keach, and Linda Lavin) on October 5, 2004, just four months before his death on February 10, 2005. It is a thinly veiled autobiographical dramatization of *The Misfits* shoot in summer and

Fall. Someone called it "Miller's *Long Day's Journey into Night*—with a glimpse of dawn."

The glimpse of dawn is Holga.

* * *

It's interesting. Despite the fact that Quentin sees mothers and girl-friends and wives as disasters, he still looks for redemption—or at least the hope of redemption—in a woman. Holga reaches him in a way none of the others ever could or did. She's wiser and deeper. She says, "I think it's a mistake to ever look for hope outside oneself," and she brings out something deeper in him. There's a nice exchange between them where he says, "I noticed your pillow was wet this morning." She answers, "It really isn't anything important," and he says, "There are no unimportant tears."

Remember your mother's old warning to stop doing something "or then there'll be tears"? Lamentations is a whole book of the Bible. Miller was like Milton, lamenting man's Paradise Lost. Banishment from Eden was a big theme in American literature, from Hawthorne and Melville on down. Mr. Miller is saying that fallen man must accept his complicity in the Holocaust, in all the personal betrayals, in a wife's suicide.

Quentin is in agony. "God, why is betrayal the only truth that sticks?" he says. "I am bewildered by the death of love. And my responsibility for it."

"Fall" doesn't mean autumn. It means that the whole country fell, lost its moral strength. After the fall, there's very little left. Just the dream—America was a dream in the eyes of the world, and still is—and the hope that he and Holga could meet "not in some garden of wax fruit and painted trees, that lie of Eden, but after, after the Fall, after many, many deaths."

---

fall of 1960, when the Miller-Monroe marriage was unraveling. The characters are based unmistakably on director John Huston, Monroe's acting coaches Lee and Paula Strasberg, and Miller and Monroe themselves: "Kitty," the Marilyn figure, is to star in a major new film, but her acting is increasingly hampered by mental illness and a drug-induced haze. The producer must decide whether to abort the over-budget picture or let her finish it. Kitty's kind young secretary is said to have been modeled on painter Agnes Barley, Miller's then-girlfriend, who was fifty-five years his junior.

To know this play, you have to know its past—what it was like in the fifties and sixties, when Maggie was still floating in his mind. Modern writing has nothing to do with realistic writing. Miller went this far. The 1970s and eighties produced other playwrights who went further. But I don't think those hyperstylized forms of writing have been very beneficial to actors. If you think you understand it, you can try and play it. But if you're mixed up about it, the performance won't work. No great acting style has evolved from Beckett or the others who've gone as far as he and Ionesco did. If you do plays like *Waiting for Godot* or *Rhinoceros,* you take a risk—I personally don't want to tangle with them. I'd rather tangle with a playwright whose message is clear to the actor—the one in between the playwright and the audience—so that his emotions are freed, his part is freed, and he can use all of himself to pull it out of the text. I am all text, I don't know anything else. I don't know how to cook, I don't sew. I have completely violated my life with this profession and with these precious few authors who know and write about the world. There aren't enough writers like Odets and Miller today who can give audiences a real sense of time and place, instead of just a sense of jokes. They understand that the last hundred years have not been a joke.

Some of them have a sense of humor, some don't. With Wilder, there was so much love and laughter and camaraderie in his characters because of his upbeat philosophy—and in his life. I knew Thornton. He was the most educated man that ever lived but also the biggest clown. I never saw a man make such a fool of himself. Jokes and laughter and imitations. It was really something to be with him. So much fun . . . Arthur Miller once walked into the house, to a party I was giving when I was much younger. Arthur came in, so serious—it was like Death walking in. I wanted it to be a party. I looked around for the maid and said, "For godsakes, ask him to leave!"

EDWARD ALBEE

Edward Albee (c. 1980)

TWENTY-THREE

THE ZOO STORY

(1959)

SYNOPSIS OF *THE ZOO STORY:* This one-act, two-character play is set in New York City's Central Park, where Jerry, in his late thirties, finds Peter, in his early forties, peacefully reading a book on his favorite bench. Jerry, an unkempt, aggressive loner, announces he has been to the zoo and says Peter will learn all about it in tomorrow's papers. Peter, a complacent upper-middle-class executive, would rather be left alone but is dragged into conversation. With intrusive questions, Jerry learns that Peter lives on the trendy East Side with his wife, two cats, and two parakeets—and then makes Peter listen to stories of his own life.

Jerry's vivid description of his rooming house and its sordid occupants on the Upper West Side embarrasses Peter. Jerry says he owns little except a deck of pornographic playing cards, some empty picture frames, and an old Western Union typewriter that prints only capital letters. Peter wonders why the picture frames are empty. Jerry says he has nobody to put in them: his promiscuous mother deserted him and died. His relations with women have been limited to prostitutes.

His only love affair was at age fifteen with a Greek boy.

He then launches into "The Story of Jerry and the Dog," a long monologue about his alcoholic landlady and her vicious dog—with red, bloodshot eyes and a constant red erection—that terrorized him whenever he came home. He tried to pacify it with hamburger meat, but when that failed, he poisoned the meat. Kindness and cruelty are inseparable, he concludes.

Peter, now figuring Jerry for a lunatic, says he really must be getting home to the wife and parakeets. But as he tries to leave, Jerry starts to tickle him mercilessly, first reducing him to hysterical laughter, then poking and insulting and forcing him to move down—and almost fall off—the bench.

Peter, goaded to anger, fights for the bench. He was there first, after all. Jerry pulls a knife, then drops it. Peter grabs it and holds it out defensively. Jerry charges him and impales himself. He says the world is a zoo, and thanks Peter for ending his anguish, urging him to hurry away. His dying words are "Oh . . . my . . . God."

—B.P.*

* *The Zoo Story,* Albee's first play, was originally rejected by New York producers and premiered in Berlin at the Schiller Theater Werkstatt on September 28, 1959. The first American production was by the Provincetown Playhouse in 1960. In 2008, he added a "prequel" called *Homelife,* depicting Peter at home with his wife just before his visit to the park. The two-act version, first called *Peter and Jerry* and later *At Home at the Zoo,* raised controversy because Albee would no longer allow theater companies to mount the old version; but Albee defended the change, saying that *Zoo Story* was his to do with as he wished.

THE POET IS the only one who can make you aware, emotionally and psychologically, of the depth of a play. No play is understood by reading it. You can read it twenty times and you will not get it. You will only get it if you write it or act it.

In *Zoo Story,* Albee is writing about New York in the late fifties and sixties. I don't know whether you remember anything about the sixties. If you don't, make some inquiries.

Albee tells you a lot. His main character tells you a million and a half people were killed in Spain. Is he talking about the sixties? No. He is referring to the thirties—the Spanish Civil War.

Jerry's historical knowledge is on the level of what happens in the world at large. What you need to know about Jerry is a certain size he has, no matter what wild things he says, that is bigger and more important than the other man's big intellectual qualities.

You have to draw from the text whatever the text opens up, wherever it opens. Is the character saying something usual or unusual? Is he living usually or unusually? Does he talk like a man who is living in a rooming house on the West Side? What does he know, and what do *we* know, about that rooming house?

Pull out the attitude of the character. What is Jerry's attitude to poverty? To war? To sex? To money? To loneliness? To New York? To the dog? To the zoo? You don't really know what his class is about, and you need to.

It is not enough for Stella to tell you Jerry is a man who has size. It is for you to see through the words and find out where this size comes from. I don't know where you come from and I don't know where you are going, but you cannot come into a stage workplace and do a play with passivity. Your passivity belongs in a flat—and in *Zoo Story,* it belongs to Peter. That notion of, "Oh, I think I'll go to the park and read a book." Do you have that kind of miserable, un-lived-through attitude?

The play is giving you a life. A genius, Mr. Albee, is telling you that there is a colored queen who does exactly what you and I do, but you don't know her. She's a person who constantly cries. What does that awaken in you?

There is a lot of desperation in people. You go down to the Bowery and you watch them and see them sleeping. They're in the corners of the houses or the doorways, sleeping on the ground. It's cold and they have nothing to cover them up. I want you to awaken yourself to something that reaches you. If you are not reached by a play, you mustn't act in it. I don't want the facts. The facts are for the business people. They like facts. Actors like experiences, and they like to experience what they read about and what they're trying to act. I'm telling you that you are too automatic in your reactions to things.

We had a Civil War in order for black people to have equality. They didn't get it. Instead, we created a servant class and a homosexual class and a working class—underpaid and not allowed into white clubs.

I feel they've been given a dirty deal by America. How do you feel? When I say to you "Tell me about that colored queen," I don't mean how tall or short or fat or skinny she is. I want the facts about her. I want to know how she became a colored queen. The queen's home was broken. What other black homes are broken? I want to know more. If you tell me what you see in the Bronx, that's your experience. What I'm wanting comes from history, it comes from my imagination. It comes from the Bowery. I see grown-up men lying there.

How can that happen to men in a country like this? I need to see and feel and understand Jerry more. I need to understand that he will either kill or be killed because of what's going on, and it's going on and on and on.

People are hungry. It's a lousy moment—it has been since the Civil War. I feel a whole history in me. I'm paying a price for Jerry, paying a price for the colored queen—a big price. I say to myself either "I'm guilty" or "I didn't do anything bad, did I?" But did I do anything *good* to help black people? Haven't I used them as servants all my life? Haven't you?

You have to *experience* your play. You can't just *understand* it. Your understanding is not what is featured about you. You are not an intellectually constructed mind. I can't just cite a moment in history and you can tell me exactly what happened or who was the minister to Louis XVI. You are not structured like an intellectual. You are another kind of person. You are the kind of person who is coming to awaken in yourself—in your guts, your inner self—your ability to laugh higher, louder, bigger; to understand another person historically. You can't sit in a class as important as this with a play as important as this and think that somebody can give it to you. You have to learn how to give it to yourself.

Who is that person who never comes out, who never stops crying? Who is she? I want you to ask what a lonely person does—not what lonely "is." What does a lonely person do? I'll tell you what she does: she sleeps and then she wakes up. She can't go out in the street because it's lonely there. She is treated as a stranger, a freak. She is insulted. If she is poor, she is even more insulted. She has no way out. She is trapped in a room without an exit because she is alone and she is a girl. You surely know girls who are trapped like that.

Have you ever been to an institution for girls that have breakdowns? Do you know about that? Do you understand what a breakdown is? There is no way out. No place to go. She can't go to the park. She can't go to the zoo. She can't go out to meet other people. There is nothing for her to do but cry. Albee says she never stops crying. There is a scream in her, leading to tears all the time. All the time, weeping. There is something in her that is never quieted down, day or night. Jerry has lived there for years, and he knows that kind of person. He hears her. He doesn't just go to the zoo. He hears that thing happening with her, and understands it.

The reason you don't is that you don't think it is your business. You think you're too young, you're waiting to grow up, maybe you want to wait to have somebody lead you. But I want you to lead yourself. *I want you to know that if you don't react to what is there from the depth of your goddamn-son-of-a-bitch selves, I'm not going to do the next classes!*

So bring me back a breakdown of every character. Don't try to fool me. I know an awful lot about acting and an awful lot about plays, and I didn't get it the easy way like you. I didn't wait for somebody to tell me. I had to find it myself.

You have to understand about black people in this country. Jerry feels responsible for the black people, for the girl who is crying, for the fat landlady who is ugly and defecates and still has sexual desire. He is responsible for the madness of the dog. A dog is man's best friend—until it becomes a beast and attacks you.

Zoo Story is a big play. It is about your guilt and my guilt and the guilt of Peter, sitting there on his ass with his lousy house and his income and his parakeets and not knowing he is a part of a world that he has no awareness of. That's all of us. We are all middle-class. Jerry calls him a "blockhead." That is what you are and what I am. Blockheads. Satisfied. Complacent. Smug. Self-contented blockheads. You didn't have to go on picket lines. You didn't have to be thrown out of school because you were accused of being a Communist. You didn't really have anything to fight for.

Well, now you have something: You've got this play and this character. Jerry is a complete thing. He has a place where he lives. It's New York. Mixed-up New York, with a Puerto Rican family he never sees, with a black queen, with a landlady, with a girl who cries . . .

These plays aren't easy. Nobody knows the answers to them. A man like Albee writes them in this style, takes away the scenery. There are two benches. On those two benches, he gives you the world. He gives you the upper- and lower-middle class, these two classes of people. They have to kill each other—one or the other has to die. They cannot live together any longer.

Jerry's point of view is that Peter is wasting his time sitting there on the bench, reading his book on Proust. He has a wife and two kids and two parakeets and he wants his bench. What is the metaphor of the bench? It's what life owes him. Life owes him this. It's coming to him. He has earned it.

Jerry doesn't think it's coming to him. He says, "Fight for your bench, for your parakeet—fight, you son of a bitch! Fight for it! Don't think it's coming to you! With three-quarters of the world dying, it's not coming to you! It is not your privilege to sit here. If you want it, fight for it. Die for it. Take part in it. Stop sitting on the bench, it's not yours. Get off!"

Jerry is willing to die for that point of view. He is willing to die because he has achieved himself, reached himself. When you reach yourself as an actor or a writer, you understand. You don't just listen or hear. You understand.

What does Peter's or Jerry's class want? Security. Comfort. How are they going to get it? Any way they can. They are going to steal if they have to. The lower class wants the money the upper class has. If there's a chance to steal, of course they'll steal. They steal because there is no morality, no ethic.

Jerry tells Peter he can't have a son because his particular moment in civilization is finished. You don't have a continuity. You cannot

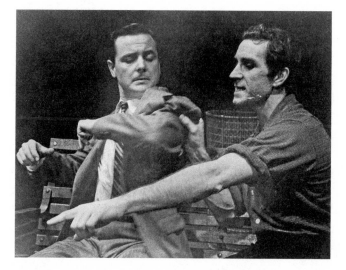

William Daniels as Peter and Mark Richman as Jerry
in an early 1960s production of Edward Albee's *The Zoo
Story*. "Fight for your bench, for your parakeet—fight, you
son-of-a-bitch! If you want it, fight for it!"

produce a man to fight for your country, to fight against communism,
to really go out and fight against poverty. You cannot produce that
because you are defunct.

What is "poor"? Poor is a man who digs into garbage cans. That's
poor. It only helps you if you can imagine it. When you say it, the imagination has to work. Words alone mean nothing. Words don't belong to
an actor; they belong to a man who wants to *chat* about acting.

There is a moment in Albee's *Death of Bessie Smith* when a man comes
in and says, "We've had a crash. The woman is bleeding. Half of her
body is in, half is out." The nurse says, "Sit down." He says, "But she is
dying—it's Bessie Smith!" She says, "I told you to sit down." Another
Negro comes in and she says, "Do what I say because you're a nigger."

Mr. Albee is describing conditions in this country. He is describing
the loneliness, the inability of these two races to be together. They have
separate hospitals for whites and blacks. Jewish hospitals and gentile
hospitals. Black hospitals and white hospitals. All this is going on and
you are sitting here thinking, "What's so bad about that?" Let me tell
you, it's the end of two thousand years of trying to become civilized.

I'm interested in the characters and in the depth and size and power
of an author who is able to put into fifty pages the whole history of
America, with all its vulgarity, its cruelty, its degeneracy—an author

who is able to represent that. There is no difference, really, between the lower-middle upper class and the upper-middle lower class. Whatever the hell you call Peter's class, it's a class that has defeated the culture of this country and defeated itself. Each individual who represents that class is a bust, a failure, a worm. Jerry says, "You want to continue owning this? Move over! Find another bench! I'm not going to let you have this anymore."

You can say that's revolution, but if you know Albee you know he is not really a revolutionary. He is a humanist. He just says, "Move over! You don't have to have the whole goddamn bench. You don't have to have it all and leave everybody else on the West Side, millions of people all over America, with no place to sit. You have to be responsible. If you are not going to be responsible, then fight for your parakeets! I'll help you because you're not my size. I am bigger than you. Here's the knife. Here it is! Now, fight for it!"

For the first time, Peter understands he is a killer, like the dog—that he will kill. He will take the knife and kill. He didn't know this before because he was too busy reading Proust.

What Mr. Albee says about intellectuals is: "You have to change the vocabulary in this country. Just because you read a book or go to Harvard doesn't mean you're not a son of a bitch or a killer—even if you're the president."

Jerry is trying to communicate with Peter, trying to make contact with another fellow human being. He succeeds only at the moment of death. He says, "I'm sorry. You're not a vegetable. I was wrong. You're an animal. You better hurry, Peter, or you'll get caught." He cleans the knife for him. Peter has found out the truth about himself—that he is an animal. Jerry, too, has reached a solution for the rotten way things are. Death frees him from it.

Both these men have found themselves through death. This is one of Mr. Albee's ideas: through death you find yourself, not through life. Jerry says before he dies, "Wait, Peter—take your book. You have killed. Take your book. It will console you."

But it won't, of course. Nothing consoles the girl in the room who cries all the time, either. Is Jerry being sincere or ironic, giving him something to console him in his state of savagery? You decide. "Take the book, Peter . . . Good. Now . . . Hurry away, your parakeets are making the dinner . . . the cats . . . are setting the table . . . " He is in supplication, which has something to do with prayer. He says,

"Oh . . . my . . . God . . . I have found myself. I know who I am. I am not this intellectual. The book, the parakeets . . . " He remains in supplication, thanking God that he is free of all the torture in a world he finally understands.

Peter is finally free, too. He says, "I am free of Jerry. I am free of the black homosexual girl-boy. I am a killer, but I am free!"

The audience does not usually understand this play. It understands a little play, but not this one. This is the Big Time. It's important. With the story of the dog, with the house that he lives in, the reaching out for something bigger that releases man from his torture . . . *Zoo Story* is a metaphor. A zoo is where animals are. *We* are in a zoo story. The clash of the classes is a desperate one because it doesn't stay on the level of human relationships. It goes to the animal in us. It goes from "I'd like to talk to you" to "Are you married?" to "You can't have children?" to "Is it your fault or your wife's?" to "You'll never have a son."

What Jerry is saying is: "You and your upper-lower-middle-class won't have sons anymore. You will become impotent and go down because you live impotently. You live without faith in yourself, and you don't participate in anything in the world except your parakeets."

He is not very nice. He is a very angry young man. He has an animal quality himself. He is saying something to the world. He is not really talking to Peter. He keeps calling him a vegetable. He pushes him, insults him, from which he gets to understand Peter's life. Peter lives on the East Side, has a wife, makes thirty-eight thousand dollars. Every time he gets Peter to reveal something, Jerry laughs at him. Why does he laugh? He is not taken in by Peter's life or Peter's revelations or Peter's nonsense. Jerry has passed all that. He understands the problem from the Civil War on: that, as Tennessee says, we have used the black man. We have made him eternally a servant, never stopped asking him to wash and clean for us. Nobody should expect another person to do that for him.

Playwrights like Albee have a greater moral mind than most. Tennessee has it. Thornton Wilder has it. We produced Eugene O'Neill in 1918, but after that, nobody until the thirties. Then, one after the other down to Albee. They are good at putting two benches on stage and cutting all the crap. Putting houses there without houses, putting an automobile there without an automobile. They want to say something. They don't want you to be distracted.

We'd like to escape, but we can't. The artist doesn't escape, because he has to experience what life is, up to the death. If you want to know what death is, watch a great actor die onstage.

If you want to know what a character is, you don't have to see Olivier. Just go abroad anywhere, and watch the size of the acting. You'll see their understanding of the human situation, and of their own. They don't mingle. Do you mingle very much? No. You hang out with other actors? Yes. As a group, you don't go out much with people who make cars, or even people who *own* cars. You might go out with them if you had a chance, but they are not really your brothers. You wouldn't join the Young Executive Umbrella Carriers Society. You'd observe them, but you wouldn't go out to dinner with them, you wouldn't marry their sisters. How many of you would marry into the Umbrella family?

The artist—when I say "the artist," I mean the actor—escapes. But he doesn't go to religion. He goes to the play to understand life. The play gives him enough. If he studies Shakespeare, he knows a lot. If he does Tennessee, he learns an awful lot.

If you go to Albee, he tells you a lot about yourself and your world. *Zoo Story*'s plot is very simple: Peter defends himself against Jerry. He doesn't give in, doesn't admit his life is a lie. He doesn't say for one moment "You're right." Albee makes Peter constantly upset because Peter doesn't know how to tell the truth. He is so constantly flustered by Jerry's questions and viewpoint. At Jerry's death, there is a quote from the Bible: "I came unto you and you have comforted me, dear Peter." He reveals the truth about himself. Jerry now knows Peter, and Peter knows himself.

At one point Jerry says, "It's just . . . it's just that if you can't deal with people, you have to make a start somewhere. WITH ANIMALS!" He's saying we have not dealt with people in all these hundreds of years. "Man is a dog's best friend," and vice versa. If you read the history of man, you will know that the dog is the only animal that fully entered the family of man. Maybe the cat, too. But only the dog protected man against the other beasts and followed him around. So the man started to trust the dog.

"But animals don't take to me like Saint Francis had birds hanging off him all the time," Jerry says. It's a nice religious reference. He mixes things up. First, he says, "I'll kill the dog with kindness." He made his first contact with the dog from the point of view of love. He brought him food and the dog ate the food but still snarled at him.

"This dog had an antipathy toward me." So then he poisons him. "And it came to pass that the beast was deathly ill . . . " He says all this in a kind of grand, biblical language. The richness of Albee's language, with its psychological nuances, is remarkable.

Peter isn't used to that kind of talk. Neither was the audience. The play was a tremendous success. Somehow, the audience understood something that made Mr. Albee the most important writer in the country at that time.

Peter says, "I'm sorry, haven't you enough room on the bench?"

Jerry says, "I'm crazy, you bastard! Don't you know that a man who lives with a colored queen and a vicious dog in a rooming house and goes to the zoo is crazy?"

I wouldn't want to put up with Jerry, either. He's too strong. What makes a person that strong—anger or truth? Both. Truth makes you angry because you know the other man is lying.

It is a play about two ideologies, two spiritual ways of living. Jerry says, "Don't you have any idea, not even the slightest, what other people need? . . . Now you pick up that knife and you fight with me. You fight for your self-respect, you fight for that goddamned bench."

I think that is one of the greatest lines I have ever read. You want freedom? You're going to have to fight for it. Most countries know they have to fight and die for freedom. We never have, on our own territory. He is saying, "You will all soon have to fight for your freedom."

Jerry wants to die. It gives Peter a chance to kill. Jerry has made his contact. They have met, for the first time, at the point of death. Jerry is not playing your game or mine. He is playing a bigger game. The game is, "Here's what you want, you American son of a bitch!" One of them has to be killed, and they both know it.

I'd like you to prepare for the next war. If you're handed the bomb, I'd like you to get involved and say, "I won't kill you. Take the bomb away. Now, we're evenly matched."

Zoo Story is about isolation and loneliness and disintegration. It is about the largeness that has gone out of man. Chekhov said that man shrank within his lifetime, which was just forty-seven years. Both Peter and Jerry, through the author, reach out to God. One of them says, "I have come to you and you have released me." The other one flees.

Chekhov also said that he only got away with one play where he didn't have somebody die.

TWENTY-FOUR

THE DEATH OF BESSIE SMITH

(1959)

SYNOPSIS OF *THE DEATH OF BESSIE SMITH:*
It is 1937 in Memphis, Tennessee. In their shabby
home, the Nurse and her decrepit Father argue about
her loud phonograph music, his pills, and her need for
a ride to work. The action then shifts for the bulk of
the play to the admissions area of a hospital, where this
daughter of the crumbling racist aristocracy resent-
fully works.

She taunts and abuses the polite young Negro
Orderly for his high aspirations. She is equally condescending to the white Intern, who has waged a long,
fruitless battle for her affections—or at least for sex.
When he finally hits her with the truth of her sleazy
character and situation, she vows to retaliate by wreck-
ing his career.

Into this ugly lovers' quarrel bursts a blood-spattered
black man named Jack, desperately pleading for help
for his lady friend outside in their wrecked car. They
had a terrible accident but were turned away from a
white hospital. The Nurse now orders them away from
this one, too, but the Intern defies her and goes out to
attend to the injured woman. He returns to announce

Rae Allen as the Nurse and Harold Scott as the
Orderly in Edward Albee's *The Death of Bessie Smith*
(1961). "She has nothing to turn to except her hate:
'You try to stay on everybody's good side, you nod
your kinky head and say yes to everything,' she says."

that she is dead, and that she seems to have been an
important blues singer.

In that intense revelation, the nurse's murderous
racism is defeated—for all the good it will do Bessie
Smith.

—B.P.*

* *The Death of Bessie Smith* was first performed on April 21, 1960, at the Schlosspark
Theater in West Berlin, Germany. It premiered in New York at the York Playhouse
on March 1, 1961, in a double bill with Albee's *The American Dream,* directed by
Larry Arrick, with Rae Allen as the Nurse.

ARE YOU AWARE that many important American play-wrights were first produced in Europe? Germany is a good place to open a play, if you've got something to say. They're more apt to accept it. They had already broken through to theatricalism. It wasn't so strange to them. They were used to it. We were not. We prefer motion-picture stories: there's a girl and a boy next door, and they meet each other, and there's a little trouble, and her father says "You can't marry him because he doesn't go to church," and she says "Oh, yes, I can!" and they end up having a big church wedding, and every-body's happy.

The audience goes out and says, "What a great film!"

When I was working as associate producer at Metro, I went through it all, every twist and turn. Once I was called in by the head producer, who said, "Miss Adler, we want to know your opinion about the Pierre and Marie Curie film we're doing. We want to know why you think it's important." I said, "Well, it's important because Madame Curie had, beyond any other woman, the patience, the talent, the foresight, the survival instinct, the massive amount of pain and effort to become a great scientist." He said, "I don't feel that. I think it's a love story."

You think life is truthful, but it is not. It is logical, but not truthful. From the sixties on, the plays are confusing. They're not like movie or television scripts. There isn't a play I know of in the last twenty years that has the logic of, say, Sidney Kingsley's *Dead End.** Albee was very much the acclaimed new playwright when he wrote *Bessie Smith,* but the establishment was still saying "He's way out"—like Sam Shepard today—and like Wilder and Saroyan and a great many other playwrights, he had trouble getting an opening here. Why? Because our producers didn't want to take a chance with an untried play in

---

* The grim 1935 stage play of slum life in New York tenements was turned into a 1937 film with Humphrey Bogart and Sylvia Sidney. Both versions starred the Dead End Kids—Huntz Hall, Leo Gorcey, and gang.

an untried form; Americans didn't understand them. So he went to Europe for his opening, and they did it in German, and I don't think he understood a word of his own premiere.

But he understood English. One of the great writers of the English language is Edward Albee. Saroyan was poetic and Wilder was a genius, but thirty years later, a new master of the language emerged. Albee wrote some very beautiful one-act plays. He is a master of dialogue. Don't just think, "Oh, yes, he was the first one to use dirty words." His mastery lies in his selection. Albee shows you the use of proper language as well as rough language. Just don't get so caught up in the words that you miss the play. That's a habit actors have. It's better to catch on to other things.

The Death of Bessie Smith takes place near Memphis, in a hospital receiving room. The playwright gives you only a desk and a few chairs on stage, and a raised platform in the back. The set is your key to the style: you never believe that any scenes on the platform are taking place in a real room. It is theatricalized—theatrical realism—in which you take a lot of physical liberties. But the acting is not different from realistic acting. America hasn't yet found the way to do commedia dell'arte. We don't know how to do that, so we mix it up. It was already mixed up with Wilder's Adam and Eve, when Sabina was dusting chairs and saying, "I don't know what the hell I'm doing in this play." From then on, you don't get a nice clear three acts and realistic scenery.

Bessie Smith is simpler than *Zoo Story* in the sense that it is much less psychological. It starts out, in the hospital, with a black Orderly and a white Nurse. One is in the servant class, or close to it. The other is in a higher political and professional class. But the servant class has manners, whereas the higher class is full of open prejudice. The white class has descended; the black class has kept tradition.

The larger social situation is the South, which formerly was the center of culture, with its colonial architecture and its traditional English respect for good manners and the family. The strong father there was like the king in England: he protected his southern girl against everything—but especially the black race. She was kept innocent. She was not allowed to speak to anybody unlike herself. The absolute rule was *do not mingle.* A poor white man didn't talk to a rich white girl, any more than a black man did. There is complete segregation, based on wealth.

Wealth goes to wealth. Did you notice that Prince Philip didn't marry a sweet girl from the street or somebody he met at a dance? They don't do that in England. They do things traditionally. That girl has to become the queen. She has to belong to a certain family, the father of her children has to be a duke or at least the Earl of Something-or-Other, and you can forget all that nonsense about love.

The same kind of thing exists in America. A young man at Harvard can marry a girl he meets at Vassar, but if there are millions of dollars involved, he won't control the money. He will only control what they give him. The big money stays in the hands of the lawyers. Big money doesn't fool around. If a Rockefeller marries a servant and then divorces her, she gets a couple thousand and then—finished, goodbye. Big money is not democratic.

The South used to be like that, times a thousand. But then something happened. All of a sudden, the southern girl was working. All of a sudden, a black man is talking to a white girl on the job—not just serving her, but talking to her. That's the downfall of the white society. The Civil War took away the cotton business, they've lost the estate and the slaves, and now white girls are out looking for a job just like black girls.

It created a great deal of conflict. Read Harold Clurman's *The Fervent Years*—the best book on the American theater. He describes organizing a company of actors called the Group Theatre, and there was a lady named Stella Adler in it. He says Stella never could or should have been in an ensemble anywhere. It wasn't in her to do it. She suffered hell. I was like the Nurse, this upper-class white girl, going out to work in the South. You could not put me into an ensemble. I was a princess. My father was a king, my mother was a queen. You couldn't do that to me. I hated it. I hated everybody. It was part of my tradition. I had been treated royally by people who bowed to my father. If they bowed to him, they bowed to me, too. All of a sudden, now, they're my equals?

The young Nurse in *Death of Bessie Smith* has the same problem. She cannot speak civilly to the white doctor—to somebody who makes forty-six dollars a month. It is not in her capability to understand him. To her, he's lower than a bug. Even though she doesn't have any money herself, she is conditioned to putting on those same airs I put on. Once a producer called me and said, "I want you to go to Chicago. It's a wonderful play, and there's a great part in it for you." I had done about seventy-five plays on Broadway by then, and I said, "Why don't you send your wife to Chicago to play the part instead?" That's the kind of snobbishness I had.

This terrible Nurse is very close to me. I understand her perfectly. To become a nurse means training. She was subjected to cleaning up whenever people defecated or vomited, to a kind of stoic professionalism she wasn't suited for. What it did was create hatred in her for the patients. Everything that has happened to her has made her hate.

The American father is getting weaker and weaker. The Nurse's Father, who is supposed to be big, is small—a failure. She calls him a bum and a son of a bitch, and he calls her a whore. The woman in this society is always supposed to be subservient to the man, who gives her the seed of the child. She's the conveyor for him. When that all changes, as it does in this play, she is arrogant to all men—black and white alike. You see the failure: the South decayed because family life decayed, which was because of money. Unless the Nurse is with money, she feels cheated, lowered, belittled. Unless she rides in an expensive car, she feels the person driving it is shit. If you see that capitalism provokes a respect for power but a disrespect for democracy—a great disrespect for financial failure—you will get a better sense of your own country.

How many of you had parents who were shop clerks or servants and worked their way up? Most of you—at least half of you. How many of you came from money? Anybody here whose father was a professor at Harvard? No. Lower middle class. That's what you came from. You know who you are.

The Orderly is a type of servant, trying to work his way up. Do you know who else in our society does that? Every president's son. Most sons from money are required to work their way up to get to their father's higher class. The Roosevelts' and Kennedys' sons worked as waiters. Do you know that Joe Kennedy was a bootlegger—basically, a gangster? You live in a society that makes it possible for you to mix.

What's the difference between the Nurse and the Intern? He's a white man willing to take care of black people as well as white people. She is a liar, putting on airs. He says, "You never had an estate or a mansion. Your father was never anything but an ass licker to the mayor." She says, "I hate what I do. I hate myself. I hate everybody else." What will happen to her if she doesn't nurse?

The doctor says there's not a white man in two counties that she hasn't slept with. Can she sleep with an upper-class man? She either has to sleep with lower white men or with black men. She is so bitter and angry because she is trapped. She has nothing to turn to except her hate. That's what happens when you're trapped. Why doesn't she like the doctor? Millions of girls all over the world say, "I'll sleep with whoever will push me up. I'll whore around in the hospital if I need to." So why doesn't she sleep with him?

Because she doesn't respect medicine, and she doesn't respect herself. This is in all of us! We don't respect our work or the people we work for. We don't respect where we come from. We don't understand why mugging is going on in the street. We say, "Something in society must be making that particular kid mug people." But the author does not really deal with that particular individual. He deals with what's going on in the whole Western world. You cannot just play the local situation. It's not the important thing in a universal play.

What makes a man called Albee write about a situation that is really universal? In this southern moment, it was going towards a police state. The doctor knows it, the Orderly knows it, Bessie's black boyfriend knows it. Don't make it into a rotten melodrama. It's not some lousy television play. Don't pull it down.

The Nurse tells the Orderly, "You try to stay on everybody's good side, don't you? You nod your kinky head and say yes to everything, but I'll tell you right now, you better watch out, you're going to get yourself into trouble." Do you know what that means?

Try to understand what the author is doing with the character, line by line, so you get a sense of his progress—where he's failing, where he is afraid. Why is a black man frightened when a white woman says "Watch out"? Do you know about the lynchings in the South? Does every black man have that in his blood? How many white people have it in their blood? Raise your hands. Nobody. You see he has a right to be frightened, because the blood memory is there, which is bigger than anything.

If she can't lynch him, she's at least going to blackmail or blacklist him. You have no experience of that. I experienced it once. My passport was taken away, I had no freedom, I was not allowed to travel or work. How could I pay my rent, send my child to school, take care of myself? Did you know that people lived under such a blackmail system here? That's what Mr. Albee is writing about, and he's no schmuck. He's writing about the strain in America that is fascist. Was that what was promised, what people expected when they came here for refuge? He's saying the whole country has this sickness in it, and that you are part of it. You'll go along with it; you will not fight it. If you fought it, you'd have to risk your life. He says you wouldn't risk your life because you are lower-middle-class.

The Nurse is threatening to get the Orderly fired or put in jail. Do you know how many people killed themselves when their jobs were taken away and they couldn't work or travel? Albee is painting a woman who keeps blacks out of the hospital, calls them niggers, and even treats the intern doctors like bums. This is the one tool she is left with in her life. You've seen people like her, when they have to serve you in Alexander's or wherever you shop. "Would you wrap my parcel?" What is her attitude if you ask her to do that? She hates you. Most of us are in a position that develops our hate. There's nothing in working for another person that develops your love. If you work for me, you're lower than I am. Have you ever ridden in a taxi in New York? Does the driver treat you as if it's his job, or as if he's doing you a favor?

Does the Nurse have any understanding that she's working in a hospital for sick people? She says to the orderly, "You are a genuine little ass-licker if I ever saw one." What is she doing to him? She is stripping him of his manhood. What happens when a man is stripped of his manhood? Do you feel the fact that he is being destroyed?

How are you going to act a man who is talked to like that? He says, "There's no need—" for her to destroy him. You'll never learn to act unless you understand words. A person who needs an operation will die if he doesn't have it. A person who needs respect will die without it. Don't say the word "need" without elevating it. Don't just say it as if you just need more sugar for your tea. It's epic!

She is degrading him. I have a maid at home who says "Yes, ma'am" fifty times a day. Do you know what that does to a woman like me? My father, my mother, my family came to this country to escape being killed. By saying "Yes, ma'am," she has taken me for someone high, whereas I'm here by accident, by fate, rescued by my parents, who came here to save their lives like all the other Russians and Jews. But she has been trained to be a servant, and it's going to take another thousand years to get that out of her. It's tragic. There are dreadful situations that can't be helped. One of them is "yes, sir," "yes, ma'am." It can't be helped. But as long as I live, I need to remember that I am not big enough, not rich enough, to think of myself as "ma'am."

I'm getting this from *The Death of Bessie Smith,* and it's killing me.

* * *

The play is a great educator of the actor. If you know this play, you know that Mr. Albee has a pretty good sense of where America is heading in the sixties. He is painting a kind of fascism in the white race that existed in Germany, Italy, Spain—a fascist streak in us that says, "I am bigger and more powerful than you are." That's not *all* of America, but it's part of America. In *Bessie Smith,* Albee sees it very clearly. I saw it very clearly in the South, when they invited me down to the university there. I saw that there were white toilets and black toilets, and that a white person couldn't enter a Negro cab. I saw that there were no black actors on the stage.

How much do you have to see, to see? Mr. Albee, like every great writer, reveals the social and political situation. The Orderly wants to better himself, maybe become a doctor. He comes from a traditional family, probably Baptist, and he respects women. No matter what the Nurse says, he doesn't answer aggressively. If somebody spoke to me the way she speaks to him, I'd take the desk and throw it at her. But he doesn't. He has control. It's not that he doesn't feel the insult, but he has been handed control over it. You get a sense that one way or another, he's going to get to the university and somehow benefit America.

With the mayor, on the other hand, you get the political along with the human decline. The author uses large strokes to paint him. He says he's a big man, chewing on a big cigar, and he's got big hemorrhoids. We don't see him, but we know him by how he talks to the black Orderly: "Get the hell out of here, my ass hurts!" The Orderly says, "He's lying right there on his belly . . . " The Nurse says, "He's got his ass in a sling . . . " The black man does not use language that is not respectable. So the mayor is lying there, chewing on a great big unlit cigar—a prop fit for "His Honor." The other people smoke cigarettes. A man with a cigar has a certain status, even if he's just chewing on it like a bum. The mayor can belch, he can vomit, he can spit, he can say "shit" if he likes. He still has the title of mayor, even though he doesn't have the language or the soul of one.

The mayor is in deep decadence. He's very much like Big Daddy in *Cat on a Hot Tin Roof.* It's the decay of southern tradition. From the 1660s till the 1930s, the man who ruled the manor was respected—so much so that during the Civil War some of the slaves did not want their freedom because they felt the northerners were low-class. Sherman walked around in a dirty uniform. Lee looked like a king. Southerners don't really like this democratic thing. The mayor doesn't acknowledge the fact that the black man speaks to him honorably. Instead, he insults him. We know the mayor will try to stop blacks from voting, will sabotage them when he gets the chance. In the mayor, the education is gone, the respect is gone, the language is gone, and the prejudice is big. In the black man, the language is good, the respect is there, and there's no prejudice.

But he makes the mistake of telling the Nurse he wants to do more than empty bedpans, which enrages her. "Listen, you should count yourself lucky, boy," she says. "Just what do you think is going to happen to you? Is the mayor going to rise up out of his sickbed and take a personal interest in you? Write a letter to the President, maybe? And is Mr. Roosevelt going to send his wife, Lady Eleanor, down here after you? Or do you plan to be handed a big fat scholarship somewhere to the north of Johns Hopkins?"

They'll let blacks in Harvard? It happens now. It didn't happen much then. Martin Luther King had to be killed first.

She gets even more vicious and says, "Would you like to hear a little poem? Here it is: 'You kiss the niggers and I'll kiss the Jews, and we'll stay in the White House as long as we choose.' That's what Mr. and Mrs. Roosevelt sit at the breakfast table and sing to each other over their orange juice!"

She's talking about Mr. and Mrs. Roosevelt with contempt, making fun of them. This woman is talking about the one president who really did something for poor people, following Hoover, who promised a chicken in every pot when people were starving. What the Roosevelts did in America was put people to work, build roads and bridges, create the WPA so painters could paint and writers could write all over America. If there was eventually something in every pot, it was because FDR set up Social Security and let people organize. Unskilled workers had no unions then, and Roosevelt understood they have to have them. So the CIO was formed, not without his knowledge, not without his political approval. He said, "Go ahead, kids—if you can do it, do it!" And they did.

If you don't know all that, you can't interpret the play. The Nurse is mocking them. You have to know more about Lady and Mr. Roosevelt. What did they do? They reopened the banks, they put through the FDIC so banks wouldn't fail again and people could have faith in their savings accounts. But the South was still bitter, about money and about race. This southern hate of President Roosevelt still exists.

Mr. Albee takes note of that. When he refers to the political tradition, he is taking you back to Lincoln and reminding you that certain promises were made. What was our promised land supposed to be? You must realize that America did something immoral when it broke those promises. "*Lincoln?*" she says. "That's a lot of shit."

In every play, refer to how biblical is it. You know damn well that if you said "Honor thy mother and father" and I said "Screw that!" you'd be shocked. How many thousands of years has the instinct to honor our parents been in us? If I said "The Ten Commandments are toilet paper," you'd say, "Don't talk like that, Stella." The Ten Commandments, no matter how low you are, you must respect. You know by instinct "Thou shalt not kill" is correct. If someone says the Ten Commandments are toilet paper, you'd object—not because you go to church but because something inside you says you can't go that far. You can't be low in one area without it affecting your attitude toward everything else. This Nurse has no respect for her father or a doctor or a dying woman who isn't white enough to get into the hospital. She is on the lowest possible level.

The Intern's attitude, on the other hand, is "I would rather treat somebody with a wound that's bleeding than the mayor or anybody else, because I am a doctor." He wants to go to Spain and treat the people who are wounded fighting against fascism. He is a man who respects the black woman that the nurse is trying to turn away.

If a writer in the fifties is writing about the thirties, he will have a point of view of the fifties in it. Before you become a playwright or an actor, you must become a person. Do you have a political point of view? Do you know anything about the Spanish Civil War? Do you care? You better care. It matters that you look up the thirties and fifties and find out that the Socialists and Communists and anarchists and all sorts of other American idealists went to fight the fascists in Spain, who were supported by Hitler, and that everybody who went there was later persecuted and blacklisted for it by Senator McCarthy. Do you know or care that Senator McCarthy was wholeheartedly endorsed by Mr. Nixon? Did you ever think Nixon would be impeached? What an incredible spectacle—those congressmen, each one trembling when they had to say yes or no!

Mr. Albee wants you to think about these things. He has a right to talk about these things, and you have a right to hear them. It's a right that goes back to ancient Greece, with Aeschylus, Sophocles and Euripides. They wrote about things like cohabiting with your mother, saying it wasn't such a great idea—not because they were so interested in sex, but because it was a problem then. I've heard a lot about sex, but I've never heard anybody say, "Oh yes, I have a friend who sleeps with his mother." Have you? It's something rotten and miserable, as sex relationships go. We don't do it anymore. But it was pretty important back then, and they finally got—through their playwrights' understanding of human psychology and history—that it would spell their downfall if they kept it up. Civilization would become extinct if they broke that rule.

I once did a play called *Success Story* by John Howard Lawson, in which an opportunistic boy was doing everything to advance himself, but he was losing his heritage. His father and mother came over from Europe for freedom, because in Poland they didn't allow a man the one thing he wants most—freedom. A man without freedom will make a revolution or do anything else to get it. Lift the word "freedom" to its eternal value. If you don't do that, you're in television. They don't need to have eternal value in television. But you can't afford *not* to have it.

The Death of Bessie Smith isn't now. It's in the middle thirties, like the boy in *Success Story*.* He didn't care about freedom, just about get-

---

* *Success Story* opened September 26, 1932 at Maxine Elliott's Theatre and ran 121 performances. A Group Theatre production directed by Lee Strasberg, it starred Luther and Stella Adler, Morris Carnovsky, and Franchot Tone. Playwright John Howard Lawson (1894–1977) was an organizer and first president of the Writers Guild of America and head of the Hollywood division of the Communist Party USA. Called before the House Un-American Activities Committee in 1947, he refused to answer questions and became (with Dalton Trumbo, Edward Dmytryk, Ring Lardner Jr., et al.) one of the Hollywood Ten, convicted of contempt of Congress and sentenced to a year in prison. Blacklisted thereafter, he wrote the

ting ahead. I had no lines to say—not one word. I was at the window in the back, and when they went offstage, I just went to the door and gave the most hysterical cry you ever heard in your life. Why? Because I was looking out the window and seeing all those emigrants coming here, ship after ship, hoping and praying for freedom. They were deceived, or they deceived themselves. She saw it was an American lie that they were going for: America was just out for the money. Bang! That's how the curtain came down. It nearly killed me, as an actress, to do that every night. But that's the way we acted it, and it was a big success. People appreciated it. What was cosmic was the question it raised about the American Dream: do we take care of our poor, or is it just all about me? It was about the failure to fulfill what was promised. I think it was a pretty important subject.

Mr. Albee is writing about a pretty important subject, too: prejudice—the poison in man that eventually destroys him. He says man today is more prejudiced than ever, and it's going to destroy the civilization by instilling more and more hatred. You will produce children that are degenerate, you will beat them and scream at them, you will get a divorce, you will drink, you will go to jail, you will be on the lowest level.

The author puts it down. The actor has to pick it up and give it size—has to raise the play and the words, wherever they go. Look for the size in each character, for how he relates to money, morality, sex, everything. If you don't know how he thinks about the world he lives in, you can't play him.

In *Six Characters in Search of an Author,* the imaginary characters want to be put on the stage because Pirandello created them and brought them to life. They say, "We're alive now, put us on stage!" The producer says, "No, you're not. You're alive today, but what will you be tomorrow?" One character says, "Were *you* the same yesterday?" The producer says, "No, I was entirely different—but Hamlet doesn't change. Once he's down on paper, he is not subject to your personal ups and downs. He's only subject to the ups and downs of the play."

I can play a Communist today and a fascist tomorrow. But if I play Hitler, I'm not going to turn Communist in that play. You have to

---

screenplay for the great anti-apartheid film *Cry, the Beloved Country* (1951) under a pseudonym.

trace the character through what he does in the play, not compare him to you and how you feel. You feel one way today and next year you're going to feel another way. That's the nature of life. How many of your tastes have changed in food, men, women, games? What you are and what you believe today has nothing to do with what the character does or doesn't believe in. The actor must be able to play both Othello and Iago. If he can only play Othello, he's not an actor. If he has to only believe in God, he can't take the part of a character who is an atheist.

I can believe in God and I can *not* believe in God. I can believe in Hitler and I can also *not* believe in Hitler. The actor, through his craft, must have a range that's different from his own opinion.

Let me ask you something: Do you think Elizabeth Taylor deserves a standing ovation? Would you say the Senate would treat you, as an actor, with respect if they dragged you in to testify? Will they recognize the actor as one of the most important elements in the society, as they do in every other country? That he should get respect—what they didn't give Tennessee Williams? The English gave it to Olivier. But do you understand that Tennessee's worst play was better than all Olivier's performances? Do you understand why America did not give Tennessee a state funeral? All the important producers and political people were very, very sorry about Tennessee's death until they put their hand in their pockets. There are a dozen theaters permanently playing Tennessee Williams in Moscow. But nobody is doing him here. It's crazy. He'll be considered the greatest playwright of the twentieth century, even over O'Neill. But nothing happened when he died.

Well, never mind.

Back to the play. The doctor has a tradition. His oath is to save, to heal. He has taken an oath that's bigger than Jesus's oath. Can you seduce him with money or sex to break that? He is not someone that's been seduced and lowered, like actors . . . But she talks to the doctor as if he were black, because he's poor, and because she has a certain power. She says, "I'm the boss, and you are the hired help. You have your place, and I can put you there. I've done it before, and I'll do it again. If I want to drown you, I can drown you. You want out? I'll send you out in a leaky boat, the way they did to the Jews, and you'll drown. I have the power, and you can't do anything about it."

He says, "Never mind all that. Did you see the sunset?" He suddenly takes the hundreds of years of dominance of this power-hungry little louse and puts it up against the sunset. The sunset has *real* power. She doesn't. This is what's wonderful.

Marlon shows you what happens to power in *The Godfather.* His producer said to me, "Stella, I don't understand what he's doing—tell me." I said, "He's playing a Roman emperor who has gone down." It was a genius of a performance. Brando said, "I'm not going to play some mafioso pisher out in Brooklyn, I'm going to play a Roman emperor who is losing his power. I'll still sit and hold out my hand to be kissed, but my power is shrinking." I know this bastard, and he doesn't play little. Every role is cosmic for him. He will play it big or he wouldn't be Marlon.

Don't let your measure be too small for the theater. If you raise the idea in yourself, you will act differently.

The Intern says, "The west is burning. Fire has enveloped fully half the continent and the fingers of the flames stretch towards the stars." Listen to Albee's language, which is absolute poetry. "There is a monstrous, burning circumference on the edge of the world." He's saying fascism is spreading and embracing the entire West. He is aware, in poetic terms, of the world situation. This is how he's talking to the lowest woman in the world: "The sunset is beautiful, go have a look at it." She says, "Oh, Doctor, I'm chained to my desk of pain. Talk the sunset to me, you monstrous big burning intern, hanging on the edge of my circumference, ha ha . . . ! No sunsets for me. Don't give me your bigness. You're just like a nigger. All you want from me is some sex from my circumference, which is very small. It's not the edge of the world."

It's a playfulness between two people who both know about sex and circumferences and penises. She knows damn well that he wants to lay her, this big white doctor who speaks poetry . . . "I can ultimately crush you. One of us is going to win . . . Come look at the sunset and stop it with your vulgarity." The doctor knows the difference between talking to a whore and seeing a sunset. Big people know it. People like doctors and scientists understand the size of the sea and the sky. This doctor has that view of the world, but he's closed in in this hospital. She talks of her "circumference" and flirts. He says, "Well, when can we do it? Here I am, tangential, when I could serve more nobly as a radiant, not outward from but reversed, plunging straight into your lovely vortex." He's a man and says, "Come on, let's go! There's not much else around town." He's able to go from the big sunset to the small woman, and she likes it. Women of a certain kind like it when men talk to them that way. "I'd like to screw you": men don't talk like that to their sisters, but they talk like that to some women, don't they?

She brings it out in him. Everything she says is with a "ha ha ha." "Never mind the sunset, why don't you plunge into my vortex?" It's a game some women play, and he plays it from the start. He says there's nothing like the kick of the heel of a southern girl, the thing they do that's like an invitation to men. Southern girls were both no and yes. "And while you're here with your hot breath on me, hand me a cigarette. I sent the nigger for a pack. And hand me a match." He throws her one. If a man ever threw a match at me, I would kill him. It shows that he doesn't respect her. He says, "Light it on the sunset." Then he says, "You owe the boy for three packs of cigarettes, you stinking little crook. You are stealing the little money he has." He's aware of her cheap tricks.

She throws her cigarette at him. She's a rough girl. He says, "Have you told your father that I'm hopelessly in love with you? Have you told him that at night, when I go to bed, the sheets of my bed are pointed up like a tent?" He's saying in no uncertain language, "I've got a hard-on for you."

A game is being played . . . this game, this mood of the thing, between them. She says, "I'll tell my father what you said and he'll send the police down here after you for talking to me like that." He says, "I forgot myself, O cloistered maiden . . . I thought I was talking to a certain young nurse with a collection of anatomical jokes for all occasions." She giggles and says, "Oh, be still. Just because I play around . . ." He says, "I'm always in tumescence for you." She says, "Now stop that." He says, "Then marry me, woman."

Do you see what's going on between them? She leads him on, and stops him when she wants to. He knows it but doesn't stop the game. He says, "O gentle nineteenth-century lady out of place in this vulgar time . . . maiden versed in petit point and murmured talk of the weather . . . " He is being sarcastic. She says, "Cut it out!" He says she's the type his ancestors died for in the Civil War, to keep women pure. "My great-grandfather fought and died for forty-six dollars a month, and the best I can afford is lust. Jesus, woman!"

Do you see that Mr. Albee has written poetically, has given us the decadence of the South and the need for power, whether it's the power of an animal over another animal or of one man over another man?

Albee is not easy. There's a certain amount of despair in his characters. I'm opening it up for you because I don't want you to just suffer. I thought I'd die when I saw it. Albee is one of the most important playwrights we produced in the fifties and sixties. I know you have a great respect for *Sophie's Choice*. Nothing warms your heart more. *Sophie's Choice* is going to get some kind of a prize. But Saroyan and Wilder and Albee got the Pulitzer. This class of playwrights is going to remain.

The logic is gone, and so is the scenery. Anything can happen. From the sixties on, with Albee and Lanford Wilson and Sam Shepard, you have a profound change in the American play form. There's no comfortable room for the characters to inhabit. Now it's an empty set that nobody knows how to act in. The characters in *Bessie Smith* are very realistic. It just so happens that the set isn't. The abstractness comes from that, so the "realism" of the characters must become bigger. This kind of theater is going to make actors and audiences think. You give them too much set, they don't think.

Without furniture, they've got to think.

> The premise of *The Death of Bessie Smith* is based on an account of the singer's death that was undisputed for thirty-five years until testimony and research to the contrary appeared in Chris Albertson's definitive biography, *Bessie* (1972). As reconstructed by Albertson, the events of her fatal car accident are as follows:
>
> At 3 a.m. on September 26, 1937, the singer was barreling down Mississippi's dark and winding U.S. Highway 61 in an old Packard driven by her lover, Richard Morgan. Too late, Morgan saw a truck on the shoulder with its lights out; he swerved hard but crashed into it at high speed. Smith, in the passenger seat, evidently with her right arm out the window, took the full brunt of the impact.
>
> Memphis surgeon Hugh Smith and his fishing partner, Henry Broughton, were the first to stop at the scene. Bessie had lost much blood, her arm almost completely severed at the elbow. Dr. Smith dressed the injury while Broughton walked to a nearby house to call an ambulance. When he returned twenty-five

minutes later, she was in shock. With no sign of the ambulance, they decided to take her to Clarksdale, Mississippi, in the doctor's car, but just then another vehicle plowed into Dr. Smith's car and ricocheted into a ditch. Two ambulances now arrived, one from Clarksdale's black hospital (summoned by Broughton), the other from the white hospital (acting on the trucker's report). Bessie was taken to G. T. Thomas Hospital for Blacks, about a mile away, where her right arm was amputated. Hospital records say she did not arrive there until 11:30 a.m., more than eight hours after the accident. She died later that morning of severe internal crush injuries.

One report maintains that a slightly injured white woman in the second car was rushed to the hospital first in the ambulance that had come for Smith. Another account—by jazz writer John Hammond in the November 1937 issue of *Down Beat* magazine—held that Bessie was taken to the white hospital but turned away because she was black. That version, heralding her as a martyr to Southern racism, was the widely accepted one immortalized in Albee's play.

Albertson quotes Dr. Smith as saying, "The Bessie ambulance would not have gone to a white hospital. In the Deep South cotton country, no ambulance driver would even have thought of putting a colored person off in a hospital for white folks." No one has fully clarified the discrepancies or explained the inordinate length of time between the accident and the singer's arrival at the hospital.

Whether the argument of Albee's play is validated or invalidated by the still-murky hospital facts continues to be debated by critics and historians but, predictably enough, was of no interest to Stella Adler.

—B.P.

A NOTE ON THE TYPE

The text of this book was set in Garamond No. 3.
It is not a true copy of any of the designs of Claude Garamond
(ca. 1480–1561), but an adaptation of his types, which set the
European standard for two centuries. It probably owes as much
to the designs of Jean Jannon, a Protestant printer working in
Sedan in the early seventeenth century, who had worked with
Garamond's romans earlier, in Paris, but who was denied their
use because of Catholic censorship. This particular version
is based on an adaptation by Morris Fuller Benton.

Composed by North Market Street Graphics,
Lancaster, Pennsylvania

Printed and bound by Berryville Graphics,
Berryville, Virginia

Designed by Iris Weinstein